Resource Sharing and Library & Information Science Networks

Resource Sharing and Library & Information Science Networks

Anil Kumar Dhiman
&
Smt. Yashoda Rani

Ess Ess Publications

4837/24, Ansari Road, Darya Ganj,
New Delhi-110 002
Tel: 011-23260807, 41563444
Fax: 011-41563334
E-mail: info@essessreference.com
www.essessreference.com

First Published **2007**

ISBN: 81-7000-461-6

Rs.995/-

Published by:
Ess Ess Publications
4837/24, Ansari Road, Darya Ganj, New Delhi-110 002
Tel: 011-23260807, 41563444 Fax: 011-41563334
E-mail: info@essessreference.com
url: www.essessreference.com

Printed in India at:
Printline, New Delhi

Preface

The concept of Resource Sharing is a need-based concept founded on sound principle of *give and take.* History reveals that the first evidence of resource sharing met back to 200 BC when Alexandria Library shared its resources with Pergamum Library. There are also examples of Library Cooperation among monastery libraries in the 13th century also. H.C. Bolton compiled first major Union List 'Catalogue of Scientific and Technical Periodicals' in 1885. The formal cooperative efforts of the 1950s and 1960s known as resource sharing were born out of a union between necessity and possibility. This was the time when government agencies, professional organizations and individual institutions begun to set standards and organize information networks. It took the speed during the last quarter of 20th century and now days, we cannot think to be in library and information centers without sharing our resources. At the time information era ushered the proliferation of publications and this phenomenon has transformed the collection development policies, collection, processing and dissemination techniques of information and service patterns in libraries. Collection development policies had to be introduced in order to select the most important and core documents and share the remaining with other libraries or networks because of rising costs of publications and their phenomenal growth in each subjects. To make resource sharing more fruitful among libraries at different geographical locations such as city, region, country or globally and to cover all types of documents, various library networks came into being. Further the advancement in information and communication technology gave the birth of Library Consortium to share the resources online. So the concept of resource sharing is now well developed, which provide a platform to share the resources of one library with the others.

The present book on '*Resource Sharing and Library & Information Networks*' provide an opportunity to its readers to be well acquainted with the concept of resource sharing, its functioning, advancement and the technology used in this field. This book is divided into ten chapters. Introduction is the first chapter that explains the concept of resource sharing and its history. Second chapter is dealt with the Conceptual Framework of resource sharing. In this chapter, resource sharing categories, process of resource sharing, its forms, and web-based resource sharing are explained. Next chapter forms the Tools of Resource Sharing, where with the traditional tools, modern tools like e-books and e-journals are also discussed. Today the advancement in information and communication technology has leaded the formation of library networks, which are providing the facility to its users of online access of information. Fourth chapter tells us about the Library Networks including wireless networks and their uses in resource sharing. It also explains the concept of consortia formation on the international as well as national basis and some of the important library consortia are also discussed in this chapter. In spite of various developments and advancements, there are some barriers, which hamper the process of resource sharing. These are discussed under fifth chapter that is on Barriers of Resource Sharing. User expectations and needs play important role in developing and fruitfulness of resource sharing because these are the users who lead us to improve our present resources and services. This is because of users suggestions that the particular library be able in the race of existence in modern environment of information and communication technology. Todays, the libraries are bound to train or educate its users in handling modern tools of information gathering. All these, User Expectations, Needs and User Education are discussed under its sixth chapter. Its seventh chapter 'Management of Resource Sharing' tells us how effectively we can manage the resource sharing among libraries. The future prospects of resource sharing are discussed in its next chapter. In the last chapter 'Important Library & Information Networks', some important Indian Library & Information Networks are discussed.

The book is appended with some appendices on Important Library Consortia, Subject Gateways, Modern Inter-Library Loan Code, Policy on Confidentiality of Library Records, Model Policy on Photocopying and IT Act 2000.'

In compiling this book, the works of various authors have

been consulted. The authors are thankful to these authors, whose work is used in developing the concept. In person, Dr. Dhiman is indebted to his parents *Shri Ramlal Dhiman* and *Shrimati Kamla Devi* for their blessings. We are also thankful to *Ms. Alka Rani, M.A., M.Lib. Sc,* Lecturer at Dr. Nagendra Institute of Vocational Studies, Roorkee (Uttaranchal) for her valuable suggestions in developing the concept into reality. *Aman,* our son deserves appreciation because to him like our other works, we could not pay much attention, which he deserved while writing the book. In the last but not least, we are also thankful to Shri Sumit Sethi, the owner of Ess Ess Publications, New Delhi for taking interest in publishing this book in time.

In the era of information technology, any work cannot be said complete in all aspect but we have tried to make it complete as much as we could do. The suggestions are welcome on the topic, if any and we will try to accommodate them in next edition of the work. We hope this book will be useful not only as a supplement to enhance the knowledge of the persons already engaged in the field of resource sharing but also to the students of library science.

Dr. Anil Kumar Dhiman
Information Scientist
Gurukul Kangri University
Haridwar - 249 404 (UA)

And

Smt. Yashoda Rani
197, Maktool Puri
Roorkee -247 667 (UA)

September 2006

Dedicated to

Coming Generation of Library Community

CONTENTS

1
Introduction

1. Introduction

Libraries are the centres of learning where knowledge and information is preserved in the form of documents. Since the inception of the library movement, librarians have been interested in co-operative librarianship and fascinated with the comparative aspects of the profession. Early sharing of experience took a variety of now familiar forms – professional education and training, short-term advisory service to further effective planning and managing, borrowing and lending librarians to handle operating responsibilities, contributions of books, even demonstrations of modern library method. Moreover today, in an environment of information and publication explosion, it has become practically impossible for any library the remain self reliant. In a situation of growing demands of the readers and depleting levels of financial resources, no library is able to obtain all the material on demand.

Resource sharing is a method of overcoming these and other limitations of the individual libraries in respect of their resources by way of co-operation and co-ordination among the participating libraries.

The term "resource" applies to any thing, person, or action to which one turns for aid in time of need. When the term is used alone, it is not necessarily seen as implying reciprocity. The word "sharing" connotes apportioning, allotting, or contributing something that is owned, to benefit others. "Resource sharing" in its most positive aspects entails reciprocity, implying a partnership in which each member has something useful to contribute to others and which each is willing and able to make available when needed.

Resource sharing is nothing but sharing of library resources by certain participating libraries among themselves on the basis of the principle of co-operation. It denotes a mode of operation whereby library functions are shared in common by a number of libraries. The goals are to provide a positive net effect : (a) on the library user in terms of access to more materials or services, and / or (b) on the library budget in terms of providing level service at less cost, increased service at level cost, or much more service at less cost than if undertaken individually. These goals should be realized without harm to the missions of participating libraries, although their methods of operation invariably must be adjusted. Similarly, the goals are realizable only with some changes in the habits of users.

Generally, it has been said that inflation and budget reductions are the primary forces that lead to resource sharing in libraries, but these are not the forces that make resource sharing work. They are only pressures that force consideration of problems and opportunities. The only approach that permits resource sharing to work is that which entails having resources to share, having a willingness to share them, and having a plan for accomplishing resource sharing.

Thus, through resource sharing, libraries can improve the total collection of reading material, consolidate their technological capabilities, improve their information dissemination tools and extend their library and information services to a larger user community. On demand, each participating library voluntarily come forward to share its existing resources with the other participating libraries. So, in this system, each library is both a giver and a receiver. Thus, resource sharing is an imperative need to develop a spirit of co-operation among the librarians, information scientists and documentalists. This spirit of sharing the resources would entail the participant libraries in a system to benefit for advancing their individual goals and objectives.

2. Definitions of Terms

The term 'Resource' applies to any thing, person or action to which one turns for aid in time of need. The word 'Sharing' connotes apportioning, allotting or contributing something that is owned, to benefit others. As stated earlier, 'Resource Sharing' in its most positive aspects, entails reciprocity, implying a partnership in which, each member has something useful to contribute to others and which, each is willing and able to make available when needed.

'Library Resources' however, have been defined in several ways.

To John Fetterman, it denotes "...any and all of the materials, functions and services which constitute a modern library system... It is ...amalgamation of people (manpower), processes, ideas, materials and money which form the substance of a library and can be described as its resources." These resources are very expensive (in terms of monetary costs) and scarce. It is essential that such resources should be put to optimal use. This is more relevant to the situation obtaining in poor countries, which not only face scarcity of resources but also severe competition for allocation of resources. It is in this context, resource sharing among libraries becomes inescapable and inevitable.

The American Library Association (ALA) Seminar, on Network and Multi-type Library Co-operation defines it as follows:

"The co-operative structures, which cross jurisdictional, institutional, and often political boundaries to join in a common enterprise, several types of libraries - academic, special and public."

According to Miller, it is a co-operative system established by libraries and information centres which are brought together by common subject, geographic proximity to share informational resources, human resources and all other elements essential for providing effective information service.

In the library world, institutions form network primarily to achieve better sharing of resources - resources consisting of bibliographic information and of collections and better service to patrons.

Library resource sharing, library co-operation, library consortium, library network are various terms given to the same activity which means that a group of libraries have come together and entered into some kind of formal understanding for the purpose of sharing the resources of each other's materials, functions, services, and the staff to their mutual benefit, realising that only through resource sharing the greatest amount of the best information can be provided to most of the users at the most reasonable cost.

A network according to Alphonse F. Trezza is defined as "A formal organisation among libraries for co-operation and sharing of resources, in which the group as a whole is organised into sub-groups with the exception that most of the needs of a library will be satisfied within the sub-groups of which it is a member."

Raynard C. Swank defines library networks as a "Concept that includes the development of co-operative systems of libraries on geographical, subject, or other lines, each with some kind of centre that not only co-ordinates the internal activities of the system but also serves as the systems outlet to and inlet from the centres of other systems."

Library Network may also be defined as "A distribution system composed of two or more libraries and/or other organizations engaged in a common pattern of information exchange, through communications, for some functional purpose." The National Commission on Libraries and Information Science (NCLIS) in its National Program Document (1975) has defined a network as:

"Two or more libraries and/or other organizations engaged in a common pattern of information exchange, through communications, for some functional purpose. It is usually consists of a formal arrangement whereby materials, information and services provided by a variety of libraries and other organizations are available to all potential users. Libraries may be under different jurisdictions but agree to serve one another on the same basis as each serves its own constituents. Computers and telecommunications may be among the tools used for facilitating communication among them."

According to United Nations Information System for Science and Technology (UNISIST), "Networking is a set of inter-related information systems associated with communication facilities, which are co-operating through more or less formal agreements and institutional agreements in order to jointly implement information-handling operations with a view to pooling their resources and better serving the users."

So, it is clear that a network is a cooperative system of sharing resources among two or more libraries through a formal institutional agreement, Common pattern of exchange of information among libraries in a network is through communications system. The networks are often called information networks, electronic information network, library networks, etc.

According to Brett Butlet, a library resource sharing network should have the following characteristics:

(a) A dependent system, which is operated multi-laterally in response to the common desires of a group of member libraries;

(b) A duplex element, which enables two way communication which separates a network from a publication or information service which is one-way;

(c) Digital, which involves some use of computers or digitalization;

(d) The distribution of information, which may take many forms such as catalogue card, print-out, etc.; and

(e) An independent organisation, separate from the administrative, political and fiscal bounds of its members.

The concepts of resource sharing and networking have become an important aspect of present day practical librarianship throughout the world and they can be used as synonyms to each other. Explosion of literature and large scale duplication of documents even among the nearby libraries of a place, and on the other hand, shrinking budgetary provisions force library authorities towards sharing of available resources. Some envisage networking as a means of access to the resources available even at distant places. The advent of the computer and state-of-the-art telecommunication technologies, has come to play a major role in support of resource sharing and networking.

3. Historical Representation

Though, the time immemorial, Indian saints, seers and indeed the lay public have been sharing knowledge for the common good but the term 'Resource Sharing' has been used in the library profession since 1960s. However, the practice is as old as librarianship itself. In the olden days, it was called library co-operation and was mainly existed in the form of inter-library loan. Some evidence of inter-library loan was found in the period around 200 B.C., with material borrowed by the library of Pergamum from the great Alexandria Library of that time. In the words of Kraus, "Well before the beginning of the 20th century, the basic methods of library co-operation had been suggested and in some cases, attempted with some success." Joe W. Kraus, states that library co-operation can be traced to the monastic libraries in the first half of the thirteenth century.

Specifically, *The Registrum Librorum Angeliae* indicated the location of manuscripts in 138 English and Scottish monasteries. Later, in 1410, the monk John Boston deBury, in his *Catalog Scriptorum Ecclesiae,* attempted a Union Catalogue.

A number of years later, in 1627, a form of library co-operation was mentioned by Gabriel Naude in his *Advice on Establishing a Library,* when he stated that catalogues might well serve to "please a friend, when one cannot provide him the book he requires, by directing him to a place where he may find a copy as may be easily done with the assistance of these catalogues."

Nicolas Claude de Peirese, a Frenchman, attempted to begin an Inter-Library Loan System in the year 1634. The Royal Library in Paris, the Vatican and Barberini Libraries in Rome were involved in this venture. Though de Peiresc was a very resourceful individual, his plan never materialized. There were also exchanges of agreements among the universities of Lund, Abo and Greifswald as early as in 1740.

Around the year 1770, Germany saw the beginnings of a planned library co-operation activity. G.H.Lessing, librarian in Wolfenbuttel from 1770 to 1781, formulated a plan for the exchange of duplicate materials between libraries. He also suggested the development of a plan for joint acquisitions between Wolfenbuttel and Gottingen.

The first major union list entitled *A catalogue of scientific and technical periodicals was* compiled by Henry C. Bolton in 1885. The American Library Association was organized in Philadelphia, in the year 1876. The first *Inter-Library Loan Code* became operative from 1917.

The World War II and the immediately following period saw the emergence of a concern among library professionals, to embark on co-operation and resource sharing activities.

As far as India is concerned, Motibhai N. Amin was the first person, who shared 50,000 rupees to supply books, periodicals and other articles to Gujarati libraries. He also accepted funds and deposits from libraries. This was the first venture in the field of Library Cooperation.

More recently, within a period of two decades, the *Library*

Trends devoted two issues to library co-operation/resource sharing. This fact shows how the subject has gained importance in recent times. It is true that library co-operation had its beginnings during the 1950's and 60's but the interest in resource sharing rose in the 1970's and 80's and more so, in the 90's.

Therefore it is noticed that the efforts made for cooperation in the 20th century began with the compilation of union catalogues, for no cooperation could be effective without the knowledge of the resources of other libraries. The scope of cooperation took a big leap. It became diversified and incorporated in it the various activities of the libraries such as abstracting and indexing, acquisition, bibliographic access, cataloguing, circulation, collection development, continuing education (for staff and users), literature searching, management and accounting, microfilming, photocopying, processing, referral services, storage and union lists.

Resource Sharing through the Ages

Year	*Country*	*Main Features*
200 BC	USA	Alexandria library shared its resources with Pergamum Library.
13th Century	England	Library cooperation among monastery libraries. Specifically *The Registrum Librorum Angeliae* indicated the location of manuscripts in 138 English and Scottish monasteries.
1410	USA	John Boston deBury prepared a Union Catalogue, *Catlog Scriptorum Ecclesiae.*
1627		Gabriel Naude .mentioned the library cooperation in *Advice on Establishing a Library.*

1634	France	Nicolas Claude de Peirese, attempted to began an inter-library loan system. Royal Library in Paris, the Vatican and Barberini libraries were involved in this venture.
1740		Exchanges of agreements among universities of Lund, Abo and Creifswald. Projected Union Catalogue of the libraries of Weimar and Jean.
1770-1781	Germany	G.E. Lessing, the Librarian in Wolfenbuttel, formulated a plan for exchange of duplicate materials between libraries. He also suggested the plan for joint acquisition between Wolfenbutel and Gottingen.
1885		Catalogue of Scientific and Technical Periodicals compiled by Henry C. Bolten.
1901	USA	Library of Congress begin card distribution service and work on the national union catalogue.
1909	U.S.A.	Union card catalogue of public library holdings developed in California.
1916	UK	Cooperative lending begins with the establishment of the Central Library of Students (CLS).
1917	USA	American Library Association (ALA) publishes the first inter-library loan code.
1924	India	Motibhai N. Amin organises a

		cooperative venture — Pusthakalaya Sahayak Sahakari Mandal Limited with a share capital of Rs 50,000 to supply books, periodicals, and articles to Gujarat libraries and also to accept trust funds and deposits from libraries.
1927	USA	*Union list of serials in libraries of the United States and Canada* published.
1930	UK	Inter-lending of books promoted as Central Library of Students (CLS) was converted into National Central Library.
1932	USA	Library of Congress Cooperative Cataloguing established.
1934	USA	Bibliographical Centre for Research established in Denver.
1940	USA	Pacific North West Bibliographic Centre established in Seattle.
1944	UK	*British union catalogue of periodicals* published.
1948	UK	Royal Society Scientific Information Conference recommends greater cooperation among libraries to reduce undesirable duplication and to extend access to a greater portion of the world's literature.
1948-72	USA	Farmington Plan goes into operation form, January 1, 1948 and starts receiving material from Sweden, Switzerland and

		France. It results in cooperative acquisition of foreign materials by 60 American libraries with allocation of broad subjects to each library.
1948	UK	British National Book Centre opened.
1948	USA	The United States Book Exchange programme begins.
1949	USA	Mid-West Library Centre begins operation for cooperative central storage of less used materials held by the libraries of the Mid-West region. It becames the national Centre later and started acquisition programme.
1951	India	S R Ranganathan says that "Library service, bibliographic organisation and library classification recognise no national or political boundaries, they are international. The library profession is international. Bibliographers and documentalists are international."
1961	UK	National Lending Library for Science and Technology starts to promote centralised document lending system.
1962	USA	Library of Congress begins acquisition of foreign books programme using funds from Public Law 480 accounts.
1963	USA	Ohio College Library Centre,

		now, Online Computer Library Centre (OCLC) begins as the first successful library network.
1965	USA	Mid-West Inter library Centre in Chicago changes its name to Centre for Research Libraries, and expands its membership and acquisitions programme.
1966	International	UNESCO starts UNISIST to promote exchange of bibliographic data. It also develops ISBN, ISDS and Broad System of Ordering.
1969	US	Orin F. Notting of the University of Chicago introduces the concept of multitype library cooperation.
1970s	US	Adjustments occur between networks and participating libraries in regard to financial commitments for online cataloguing and various tiers' of cooperative programmes.
1971	US	Pre-natal classification and cataloguing to avoid repetition of the cataloguing process in each library introduced.
1979	Southeast Asia	The Congress of Southeast Asian Libraries (CONSAL) supports establishment of a Consortium of the National Documentation Centre of Indonesia and the National Libraries and Documentation Centres —

		Southeast Asia (NLDC-SEA), the consortium of the national libraries of Malaysia, the Philippines and Singapore.
1981	UK	ADONIS system established by six publishers in cooperation with the British Library Document Supply Centre (BLDSC) and the Centre de Documentation Scientifique et Technologie. During 1987 and 1988, 50,000 documents were printed and supplied to institutions and scientists in seven countries in Europe, USA, Mexico, Australia and Japan.
1982-86	US	Simple type library cooperatives increase by 12 per cent; multitype library cooperatives increase by 164 per cent and 30 multi-state networks go into operation.
1985	Europe	European Economic Commission presents a plan of action at the community level aimed at library cooperation based on the application of new information technologies.
1987	Europe	European Commission launches a major new initiative in the form of a *Policy and plan of priority actions for the development of information services* marked to cover the years 1989 and 1990.

1989	UK	Library and Information Cooperation Council established for furthering library and information cooperation.
1989	US	The Committee on Institutional Cooperation (CIC) is created to encourage interaction among major universities of the Mid-West and to promote preservation of research collections.
1989-94	US	British Library as per its strategic plan for 1989-1994: *Gateway to knowledge,* offers a range of cooperative relationship with other libraries in the UK and elsewhere.
1991-92	India	DELNET saves Rs 50 lakh through rationalisation of foreign periodicals in Delhi libraries out of subscriptions for 1991 and 1992 under a scheme initiated by NISSAT. Savings are also made in the other cities in India under this scheme.
1991	India	INFLIBNET (Information and Library Network) came into existence, which is providing assistance and developing comprehensive online databases of various holdings of more than 140 universities on cooperative basis.
1994	US	World Wide Web Consortium

		(W3C) International Consortium formed by Tim Berners-Lee, the coiner of world wide web.
2004	India	UGC-INFONET Consortium, an ambitious programme of University Grants Commission is launched for sharing e-journals throughout the country to about 150 universities through INFLIBNET.

4. Usefulness of Resource Sharing

Maurice B Line finds that cooperation in libraries or resource sharing in modern times is helpful in the following four main activities:

1. "Acquiring books - selection, ordering and purchase etc.
2. "Recording books- cataloguing and classification.
3. "Making them available - their own books by consultation and lending books not held by them by borrowing from elsewhere.
4. "Storing books - for present and future use."

The reasons for cooperation in the above four areas as given by Maurice Line are summed up as follows;

4.1. Acquisition

1. Each library has to acquire books before they can be borrowed.
2. Local user needs must be ascertained and information on such works ascertained from publishers, booksellers or from a central source or sources of bibliographic information.
3. The main *argument* for cooperation is surely not financial at all. It is simply that no library can be self-sufficient.

4. For acquisition of library materials there are several possible alternatives ranging from voluntary cooperation between a large number of libraries, through nationally funded support of a limited number of specialised libraries, to a national collection dedicated to the purpose of supplying loans and photocopies to other libraries.

4.2. Recording

1. A high proportion of staff expenditure is absorbed by cataloguing and classification. The librarians have begun to consider that if they can obtain, reasonably good quality cataloguing and classification of documents done by outside cooperative agencies in the form of conventional catalogue cards, or by the use of computer, off-line or on-line, they would like to use such services.
2. Detailed subject and bibliographic access can be provided to national and other bibliographies.
3. Networks and bibliographic databases to which participating libraries contribute records are cooperative in nature. Such schemes may be cooperatively owned or managed by a particular centre. The extent of cooperation varies but the common feature is that the records can be bought from an efficient centre.

4.3. Availability

1. Some means must be found of knowing what is in other libraries.
2. Union catalogues have their place, but the more limited it is the better it would be.
3. Local interlending services could provide 24-hour access to a limited range of material, but regional interlending systems could make little contribution to availability.
4. Automation enables union catalogues to be held and accessed online, or printed on COM. Updating is easier with online systems and so is input.

4.4. Storage

1. Shortage of space in libraries has been a perennial problem. The problem of storage of large quantities of books has become a matter of universal concern.
2. If a store cannot be built, bought or rented, books should be donated to a national repository.
3. A national store can save a lot of space, but if not linked to an efficient lending service it becomes a sort of national refuse collection. It should be linked with a central lending service and with a national loan collection to achieve space saving and fast supply of material.

5. Need for Resource Sharing

There has been a voluminous growth of published documents in the recent past. As a result, no library is able to procure, process or store all documents that its users demand. Todays no library can afford to acquire even half of all published material, both *in* terms of cost, and the investment in space and personnel time required to process and provide access to a burgeoning quantity of information. An average size library at a college or university may subscribe to 3,000 to 10,000 journal titles, a fraction of nearly 260,000 possible acquisitions. The reasons for this unprecedented growth are several. Interdisciplinary literary pursuits necessitates dependence on other libraries. The limitations of funds and space besides the lack of proper distribution channels for publications, and lack of proper book selection tools handicap the procurement of published materials in the libraries. It is also noticed that most libraries have been duplicating efforts and material, which has led to inadequate utilisation of the overall resources of materials and finances. There has been a great increase in the number of users as also their demands. The information being sought has become extremely diverse. In the circumstances, the libraries are left groping for ways and means of providing a wider range of services and collections. Resource sharing offers practical solutions to these problems.

Resource sharing is considered as an essential pre-requisite for effective library and information services. No library can have all the reading materials which may be in demand by its readers at any point of time. It may not be possible for any library to meet such demands by buying all the material. Resource sharing in every direction of library work will be conducive to provide proper books, serials and to provide the allied service of supplying information. It may not be possible for the librarians to meet the information appetite of all the readers with their own resources only. Hence, resource sharing is the only effective medium through which the primary and foremost objectives of any information system can be achieved.

Resource sharing may be considered necessary due to the following reasons:

(i) Recorded information and knowledge should be treated as a human resource to be shared by all - an ideal that can be met only through resource sharing of library system/ networks that link "collection in the region, state, nation, and the world".

(ii) Even the large communities are not sufficiently large and wealthy to support fully adequate library services by themselves. Now-a-days, no library can stand alone in this age of networking and co-existence.

(iii) There has been seen an explosion of information and the increase in number of publications enormously. This has posed serious problems. The information requirements of the users are becoming more and more diverse and complex. The dormant or depleting budget also threatens the libraries. Time delay is also one of the factors. Allen Kent points out the three impossibilities caused by information explosion:

(a) The physical impossibility, that no individual scientist or scholar in any field can read and remember all the literature that has a reasonable probability of being useful or interesting at an unspecified later time;

(b) The economic impossibility, that no individual or his

organisation can process for later exploitation, a major part of the literature that exhibits probable pertinent interest; and

(c) The mechanised impossibility, that the traditional library tools cannot cope efficiently with the detailed requirement of research workers, for information of specified relevance.

Resource sharing plays an important role in removing these impossibilities.

(iv) Information technology is complex, specialised, and costly; and the rising cost of conventional library operations requires that information activities develop co-operative arrangements.

(v) It is only through library co-operation and resource sharing, that we can ensure rapid, effective improvement/extension of library resources to more people on a more fair/direct basis.

(vi) The unsystematic and unintegrated library development often leads to wastage duplication, and the inefficient use of the total knowledge resource.

(vii) Many libraries have long been wastefully duplicating effort, performing repetitive processing, storing similar materials beyond those required to meet local everyday demands, and giving incomplete or limited information/ materials to the public because of lack of centralized services, for example, shared cataloguing, co-operative purchasing, and reference referral. The co-operative, time-shared, multi-institutional approach to computer usage would be the most efficient, cost-effective solution for computer installations in the nation-wide network, which would carry out such vital functions.

(viii) Increase of students, scholars and teaching staff in universities have led the increase in user population of the academic libraries. Due to the increase in users' demand for diversified information, the libraries are prompted to investigate ways and means for wider range of services and collections. Resource sharing offers practical solutions to these problems.

(ix) Users in the libraries have become more and more information-conscious and demanding more effective, quality library services. The very concept of library has undergone a great transformation. Free flow and availability of information is the user's need. The Current Awareness of Information and Selective Dissemination of Information repackaging would not be possible unless libraries share resources. Besides, disciplinary inter-dependence also calls for diverse collections of the variety of disciplines which is not within the capacities and competence of a single library.

(x) Increase in publishing output necessitates large intake in libraries to update their collection. This needs a large space to house the collections. Obsolescence of knowledge also calls for weeding of collection, co-operative acquisition, storage and services can eliminate the problems of space, balanced collection building, efficient services, etc.

(xi) Research institutions, universities, industrial and commercial organisations and other academic institutions are responsible for knowledge generation. These can be accessed only using cooperativeness.

To overcome all the above problems, resource sharing offers a practical solution.

Thus, the developments in library and information science warrant the need for resource sharing. The fast expansion of human knowledge due to knowledge explosion contributes a lot to the cause of resource sharing. The practical impossibility of the scholars, researchers and others to have access to a variety of literature owing to the geographical and financial constraints make resource sharing most relevant.

2
Conceptual Framework

Resources sharing is a way of library cooperation. Cooperation means, working together with some efforts to achieve the objectives i.e., common work for a common goal. Consortium, network, and cooperative-these are the terms used to label the organizational arrangements for achieving a variety of resource-sharing objectives.

The various facets of cooperation are:

(i) Growing of individuals having a common interest.

(ii) Action by a group for pursuing certain aims and target.

(iii) Setting up of a permanent organization as an operational unit.

Resource sharing is a sort of indirect agreement among the participant libraries. The member's libraries spare and exchange their resources when required. The main activities of sharing resources are:

(i) to avoid the duplication of costly materials co-operative acquisition is very essential for the libraries.

(ii) Availability of materials and services is possible at the minimum expenses.

(iii) Extending the resources and services to vast category of users.

1. Categories

The categorisation outlined below was used by Wilson and Marsterson and subsequently utilised by Edmonds. This approach offers the opportunity for cooperation to be viewed through three major forms of activity: firstly in terms of 'exchange'; secondly by 'coalition' or working together; and thirdly 'entrepreneurial and one-way marketing'. The last category has been disputed by those who claim it is not a true cooperative activity, but in recent times it has begun to gain more credibility as a concept.

Traditionally these three major forms have been discussed in the context of interlibrary cooperation, but now emphasis is being placed on cooperation with other information providers in the business, commercial and voluntary sectors. Furthermore, these boundaries are no longer parochial in character and have been expanded to embrace cooperation at various levels, including local and regional, national and international dimensions through informal as well as formal mechanisms.

1.1. Exchange

Resource sharing can be viewed first as a form of exchange. This can be subdivided and may be considered under such headings as:

- exchange of materials of all kinds
- information for staff
- information for reader enquiries
- users
- bibliographical
- staff

These headings cover a multitude of activities; of them some are initiated for reasons of altruism. At the other end of the spectrum the motivation is pure self interest. Some examples includes exchange of catalogues, catalogue information, serial title holdings lists, accessions lists, development of access policies, exchange of minutes of staff meetings and working parties. In the last example, this can be effected with the minimum of effort and expense but perhaps produce valuable cross fertilisation of ideas to assist in the process of decision making.

1.2. Coalition

The second form of resource sharing may be termed coalition. This can be defined as 'working together' in the broadest sense although Brewer, in his book, alludes to the campaigning nature of the activity. The concept of coalition has been gaining ground over recent years, encouraged and promoted partly by government initiatives, and characterised by the phrases 'partnership' and joint venture'.

There are many ways of working together, both within the library sectors and with other information agencies. Some of the main subheadings within the broad heading of coalition would include:

- development of service tools
- development of resources
- research
- training and
- publishing

Under the heading of development resources one could consider software developments, networking or general development and understanding of IT, organisation of events, acquisition and/or disposal of material. This might include conspectus, joint appointment of staff, and allocation of financial matters, building or use of shared accommodation, or dual use of transport and equipment. Under the heading of research, organisations might consider cooperative research for their common good, or to take it one step further, it could even be extended to the level of cooperative research about cooperation and sponsorship of research.

The heading of training includes the various ways of providing an effective, viable and systematic range of training organised from a cooperative view point. The cooperative publishing heading offers the opportunity of information providers to consider the production of catalogues of library holdings and joint publication of books and journals.

1.3. Entrepreneurial and one-way marketing

Although resource sharing is normally perceived as exchange and coalition, it has recently been extended to include entrepreneurial and one-way marketing in its own right. The activity under this heading could however also be included under coalition. A service undertaken by one party for another and for payment includes services such as British Library Document Supply Centre and Regional Library Systems, where it might be argued that unless there is close cooperation between parties, both are liable to lose. Equally, entrepreneurial and one-way marketing can be applied to those information organisations offering services for direct monetary gain.

2. Resource-Sharing Process

A fundamental step toward resource sharing in libraries is to understand a basic resource that a library has to share—materials. Before considering what can be shared, however, it may be instructive to consider what cannot be shared: a book owned by a library that is needed frequently by users of that library is not fair game for sharing, since it would not be available locally when it is needed. It is only those materials that are not needed frequently that can be considered for sharing. This raises two questions: How frequently needed and Why acquire those materials locally which are not likely to be needed frequently?

The answer to the first question needs to be negotiated, starting with some limiting parameters. It is probable that most librarians, clients, and administrators would agree that a book used locally, say, daily, *should not* be shared; likewise, a book that is used only once in 5 years *could* be shared, especially if the mechanisms are assured for retrieving the book from elsewhere when it is needed locally. The negotiation comes into the picture when considering the largest number of materials, those that may be used locally within the very wide range of use examples cited above.

The second question is more difficult to answer, especially

for research libraries which in the past were said to aim to acquire local holdings, typically, regardless of frequency of need or use. Given this type of acquisitions policy, it becomes possible to share holdings if some advantages of sharing can be perceived by the library which holds the wanted materials. These advantages can be payment in kind or payment in fact, which helps to provide the financial wherewithal for the library to continue pursuing its acquisitions policy.

Another important aspect of resource sharing is the involvement of bibliographic access to local holdings. In this case we are dealing mostly with services and processes, and physical materials need not necessarily be moved from the local environment. So, sharing in this sense entails providing other than local clientele the right to utilize the bibliographic tools for e.g., the catalogues, thus permitting them to locate that which is held locally. Reciprocity— that is, bidirectional movement—is again needed if resource sharing is to be meaningful.

Still another aspect of sharing, also relating to bibliographic access, has become increasingly interesting as the labour of cataloguing books which are acquired in many libraries, but are not necessarily available for sharing, is distributed rather than replicated, through shared cataloguing.

Once material of interest has been located elsewhere, it becomes necessary to determine whether it is indeed available, or is in use by others. Resource sharing requires access to circulation information to avoid disappointment and to accelerate the process of locating the required material at still another library. A next, basic step entails transfer of the desired physical material to the point of need. Resource sharing therefore involves establishing positive procedures for delivering materials, and for ensuring their return in a timely manner.

If resource sharing is to be deemed successful, all procedures must occur with sufficient speed so that the client has the desired material in hand well before the need has evaporated. It is here that the cooperative use of technology may become interesting.

The first step would be to identify all the libraries subscribing to the programme. Then, an authority to control the programme is to be formed. Normally, this body is composed of members nominated by the member libraries. To make a resource sharing programme effective and realistic ample funds are needed. These are normally provided by the State Government and the University Grants Commission and to some extent by the participating libraries.

There are other aspects of sharing to be considered, including agreements for implementing cooperation and the establishment of facilities for storing little-used materials. Given the maintenance of adequate use records, it becomes possible to arrange for cooperative decision making regarding selection of and storage location for those materials which, for example, may have "aged" to the point where further use is considered unlikely.

2.1. Basic Agreements

There are several basic agreements among libraries that must be developed if a resource-sharing system is to be achieved. Important ones are :

(i) First, obviously, is the agreement to share currently owned materials that is, to permit access to the holdings among partners, with protocols, limitations, and priorities carefully spelled out. The agreement should provide for an independent administration of resource sharing, but one which does not emasculate the goals and missions of the cooperating libraries. Funding should be based on an obligation for long-term support to permit the benefits to develop. The financial agreement should permit individual libraries to withdraw, but be sufficiently constraining to avoid disturbance of the system.

(ii) Second, there should be agreement on acquisitions policies, both to ensure consistent development of holdings and to avoid redundancy when this is judged jointly to be unproductive.

(iii) Third, there should be agreement on bibliographic control. Best is standardization, so that users of each cooperating library have a consistent means of accessing the catalogues of others. If standardization is not feasible, then the second best is the provision of adequate training for users and/or access to the local reference staff to provide aid in locating materials.

(iv) Other necessary agreements include definition of loan periods and renewals, procedures for earlier return of materials if needed, payment for lost materials, and other "housekeeping" or bookkeeping chores.

2.2. Basic Records

Record keeping is at least as important in resource-sharing systems as it is in individual libraries acting alone. Sharing of materials entails sharing, in a formal and consistent manner, the records without which the system cannot operate.

First is the acquisitions policy, which must be reduced to writing in as much detail as possible. This is needed in order that others in the system can make effective and efficient predictions of whether other libraries will or will not acquire a given item. The experience in preparing desiderata and parameters for approval programs may serve as a workable model in this regard. Convenient access, in real time, to on-order/in-process records of resource-sharing partners and to union catalogs of their holdings can then help in the application of policy to individual selection decisions.

Once a positive acquisition decision has been made, the local on-order and in-process files must be accessible to others who may be making an acquisition decision to purchase the same materials. The same goes for access to holdings as represented by the catalogues of the cooperating libraries. It is useful to consider the feasibility of establishing a union catalogue for the libraries and of keeping it up to date in order to make access more convenient for both users and library staff. The catalogues, whether individual or union, must have indications of library location and also any restrictions on use.

The client who has located material of interest must now know whether it is indeed available or whether it is circulating. In the latter case, the expected time of return must be known so that a decision can be reached as to whether the delay is acceptable or whether the holdings of other cooperating libraries should be addressed. The basic circulation files therefore need to be accessible; but it is typically not considered feasible to develop a union circulation file, since the cost-effectiveness of such a dynamic file is questionable.

Once a loan transaction has been completed, it is necessary to establish files, and also procedures for recall of materials and for dunning. If protocols are established for fines or other punitive methods for late return, or nonreturn, then appropriate files and procedures must likewise be established.

The files and procedures enumerated above provide the opportunity for analysis of usage and for making joint decisions on retirement of materials to a common storage facility. If such a facility is developed, then appropriate files and procedures must, of course, be developed.

2.3. Technology

Resource sharing makes more dramatic the need for maintaining careful records; but it makes more visible the added costs of increased traffic and transactions, if the system operates in such a way as to stimulate increased usage of collections.

For example, given the need to share data about acquisitions, holdings, inter-library loan requests, and completed transactions—and to share these data over distances—the technology of computers and communications becomes dominant in the design and operation of resource-sharing systems. The primary records containing such data can be recorded in machine-sensible form to permit cost-effective transactions to be concluded; to permit ready analysis; and to support, with consistent and up-to-date data, decision processes that must be made in various geographic locations.

There is a whole spectrum of computers which can be considered for resource-sharing systems. Small, inexpensive computers lie at one end of the spectrum, with much more expensive, large-scale computer facilities at the other end. Frequently, libraries participating in a resource-sharing system may wish to consider introducing a low-cost computer to support local library automation requirements. On the other hand, a larger computer or server may be attractive for the support of consortium requirements, with costs shared among the members. Careful analysis is needed to ensure that equipment choices for local and/or consortium requirements are reviewed carefully to assure compatibility. The variables involved in exploration of alternatives frequently are so involved that it becomes advisable to develop simulations of the resource-sharing activity before firm systems decisions are reached. Todays, much cheaper computers are in the market because of cheaper technology advancement.

2.4. System Alternatives

As pointed out earlier, there are several requirements that must be accepted as "given" if a full-service resource-sharing system is to be developed. These requirements include:

(i) Multilateral decision making;

(ii) Multi-directionality of service.

These requirements lead inevitably to a decrease in local autonomy—with the consequent threat, in the minds of many. This threat can be decreased or eliminated only by formal and firm agreements by participants in a resource-sharing system.

Once these requirements are met, system alternatives present themselves which need to be understood and negotiated. One such alternative relates to choice of partners: Should they have similar or dissimilar clienteles? Other choices concern size of clienteles, size of budgets, and size of holdings: Should they be similar, dissimilar, or mixed? Also there is the question of budget assumptions to be made for each of the partners: anticipation of more? same? or less?

There are, of course, other alternatives to be considered: full service or limited function. In the latter case, one or more functions or operations may be chosen; e.g., shared cataloguing, lending. Even for a full-service system the mix of partners may require consideration of a "star" system (one library with most of the resources) versus a "distributed" system (each library with equal, but different resources).

3. Resource Sharing Partners

The decision for consideration of resource-sharing partners can now be derived, once a given library has decided that it no longer can "go it alone". These are:

1. Collections useful to several institutions.
2. Bibliographic apparatus (now available or a willingness to develop them) which will be:
   (a) accessible and addressable by several clienteles.
   (b) able to instigate delivery efficiently.

In the 'ideal' case, one may wish to use as the basic criteria for joining forces: 'Equal' distribution of unique resources willingness to engage on 'enforceable' agreements.

The most necessary citation, however, is a library staff and a clientele willing to adapt to change. The ideal resource-sharing system requires that convenient access to bibliographic tools and materials be provided to patrons. The means by which such access is provided may well be other than customary ones. Accordingly, even in the ideal system, the librarian and the user will be obliged to unlearn old procedures and to learn new ones. This will require an understanding of the societal forces that make it necessary to be served in new ways, and participation in the consideration of trade-offs as libraries move into resource-sharing environments. Since these new environments will not, and cannot, be accomplished in a single dramatic happening, the librarians and the clientele will need to be willing to have changes occur over a period of time.

Given the increasing realisation that self-sufficiency is unattainable, certainly for a research library, there is consequent demand for the development of realistic, particable, and acceptable goals which are in consonance with the current environment. At any given budget level, the library must assign resources to each of the following three areas:

(i) Acquisition of materials.

(ii) The bibliographic apparatus to permit accessing the local holdings.

(iii) The apparatus to access the holdings of others.

The bilateral exchange model, the pooling model the dual service model and the service-centre model are the four types of resource sharing models in vogue today.

In the bilateral exchange model, materials are exchanged between two participating libraries. In practice, where such an exchange is found, the exchange rate is usually calculated upon a proportional basis, according to some agreed-upon value (e.g., one for one, two for one).

The second model is a multilateral development of the first, and can be called, for convenience, the pooling model. In this model, more than two libraries contribute to and draw from, a pool of materials.

The third model is called dual-service model. It is one in which two or more participating libraries take advantage of the facilities of one of the participants to produce a common output-for instance, a union list. The term "dual-service" is proposed both to distinguish this model from the next, and to emphasize the fact that all participants, including the facilitator, contribute to the common output.

The last model is known as the service centre. In this model, a number of libraries employ the services of a facilitating participant to input and process materials for individual purposes rather than to the end of a common output. Hence, it is called the service-centre model.

While the facilitator may be merely a service bureau, and not otherwise employ its own facilities, the model holds under the pricing conditions which will be stipulated for this type of cooperative.

The cost effectiveness of resource sharing is diminished at the present because it has to run in parallel with systems working toward self-sufficiency. As more integrated system of resource sharing develops, more benefits will be realized from redistributed responsibilities and resources.

The effectiveness of resource sharing depends on the availability of appropriate communication, technology and delivery systems. It has become a truism to say that the problems associated with resource sharing have more to do with behaviour modification than with technology. The computer has been an extremely effective device for processing and locating materials quickly and conveniently, regardless of distance.

4. Methods of Resource Sharing

The time has arrived, when the concept of resource sharing would envelope all basic library functions. Right from acquisition to storage and issue of material, co-operative action is feasible and has a useful role to play. Joint action should be practised in acquisition and utilisation of information resources. Ownership and use should be on a joint basis. Subscription to journals and other serials can be co-ordinated, so that duplication may be avoided as far as possible. Duplicate holdings should be freely exchanged between the libraries.

Catalogues can be prepared co-operatively, so as to produce union catalogues of books, serials, etc. Co-operation is necessary in the realms of abstracting, Current Awareness Service and

Selective Dissemination of Information Services also.

Inter library loan should be a regular exercise between the participating libraries. There should be an information highway between the member libraries. Reference and referral services should be part of a resource sharing programme. Document delivery and full text delivery through electronic media and other means would form part of a resource sharing programme.

Though there are various types of resource sharing system, a simple schema of a resource-sharing system is depicted in Fig. 1. In this drawing, limited for simplicity to two libraries, each has two "terminals", one each for users and for librarians. The user (1a, 1b) is able to access a "union data base" (2), which provides the catalog of the holdings of libraries A and B (with locations given for each item). If the desired material is not located in the union catalog, the on-order/in-process file (3) may then be accessed. If the desired item is located in a given library, the circulation file is consulted (6a, 6b) to determine whether it is indeed available immediately.

If it is available, a transaction is initiated to move the item to the point of need from the holdings of the other library (5a, 5b), with a record of the transaction maintained by the system (7).

An acquisitions librarian (8a, 8b) wishing to make a "buy/no-buy" decision would likewise consult the union data base (2) and the on-order/in-process file (3) to determine the decisions of other libraries in the system. A "buy" decision would then lead to entering the transaction in the on-order/in-process file (3), to cataloging the item when it arrived, and to entering the cataloging (and location) information in the local catalog (4a, 4b) and in the union data base (2). The material itself would then become part of the local holdings (5a, 5b), ready for access.

Use statistics (7) would lead to weeding decisions (9) and consideration for remote storage (10).

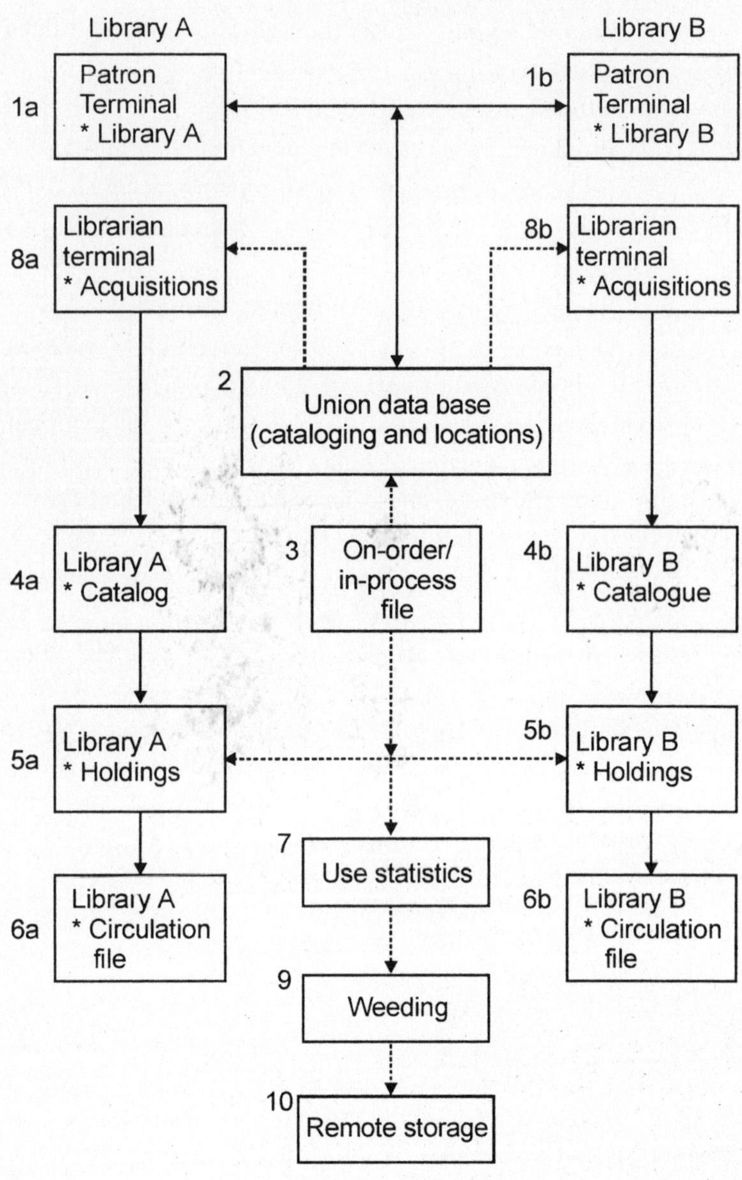

Fig. 1. Resource-sharing System

5. Forms of Resource Sharing

Resource sharing can take various forms. It can be found in the form of Inter-Library Loan, Co-operative Acquisition, Co-operative Storage, Co-operative Processing, Union Catalogue, Co-operative Delivery of Services, Exchange of Personnel and Training Facilities, Clearing House Functions, Technical Process, Translation Services, and web-based sharing etc.

5.1. Inter-library Loan

Reynolds defined Inter-Library Loan System as follows:

"It is a technique by which, one library lends its materials to any individual reader through another library".

Generally, a library and its borrowers are directly related. Through an Inter-Library Loan, a library is related to its reader indirectly, through another library. By this indirect method, a library broadens its readership. At the same time, a reader increases his bibliographic reach.

Inter-Library Loan Service is the most important concept to be considered in a successful resource sharing venture. The success of a sharing venture depends largely on the efficiency, efficacy and speed of one participating librarian in lending to another participating librarian. Coming to physical entities, each participating library should possess atleast one copying machine. However, the computers and scanners can also be used todays.

Though the participating libraries agree in principle, to share whatever material they have this is not always possible in practice. Any restrictions and hindrances should be identified and ways and means be found, to over-come the same. Such overcoming of restrictions would result in a successful resource sharing/network through Inter-Library Loan.

There has been a steep increase in the cost of books and rates of subscription of serials. So, it is high time that the libraries think in terms of a concrete plan by which, if one library purchases a very costly serial set, the other libraries may be allowed to use them for a certain period of time. Inter-Library Loan among libraries is considered to be a very important step in the field of resource sharing.

Many considered the whole process of Inter-Library Loan transactions as an ordinary clerk's job but, an accomplished librarian is also involved in this in two important ways:

1. to negotiate the request with the individual to ensure that the specifically requested document is necessary to fulfil his information requirement; and
2. to verify the bibliographic citation to be sure that the document is indeed not available in the borrowing library and to forestall the necessity of professional help at the lending library having to iron out bibliographic problems.

The information explosion and the advances made in the technological arena have changed and broadened the concept and scope of Inter-Library Loan. At present, Inter-Library Loan includes computerised, tele-type and even fascimile equipment; data or reference networks; bibliographic networks; subject networks, etc. It is apparent that the future of a library lies in Inter-Library Loan co-operation involving computerised library routines. Libraries represent information. In the near future, databases with bibliographic information will be common on the Inter-Library Loan circuit.

The need of the user under a Inter-Library Loan should be met without inconvenience to the regular readers on its own campus. Obviously, books in fragile condition should not be issued on Inter-Library Loan. If there is a great necessity for the reading material from fragile books, the best way is to resort to photo copying. Bulky volumes should also not be lent on Inter-Library Loan. The relevant portions may be photocopied and despatched to the borrower or it can be sent by e-mail after scanning as attachment. Likewise, rare collections and irreplaceable documents should be taken out of the purview of an Inter-Library Loan arrangement.

Some learned scholars advocate that the borrowing library should pay the postal and reprographic charges. But, this is not practical and entails some accounting and clerical job. It must be remembered that every library is both a lender and a borrower. So, the lending library should pay the postal and reprographic charges.

There could be some reasonable restrictions on the number of books in issue at a time to the same borrowing library. Period of loan can also be fixed reasonably. Sub-Lending is to be avoided; so, it may be prohibited. The borrowing library will be solely responsible for the safety of the documents on loan.

After identifying and locating material of interest, an attempt to obtain a copy of the same comes next. Basically, there is clear difference between the Inter Library Loan of print and non-print material like films, slides and video cassettes. This is not only in the price but in the durability also. Films and video cassettes are expensive compared to normal book material. So, generally, there is a fee for the loan of such non-book material.

An Inter-Library Loan request for book material is usually for use by an individual scholar, researcher or teacher. But, the audio -visual equipment are requested on loan, for the purpose of projection in the class or group-discussion. Much more care is necessary in handling and returning non-book material than in the case of book material.

5.2. Co-operative Acquisition

Most of the libraries spend their valuable time, money and efforts on acquisition of materials. It is here that a great deal of co-operation is possible. This is because, the procurement procedures are uniformly similar among all the libraries. So, when a Co-operative acquisition programme is put in action, the individual university libraries save a lot of precious time and money. Consequently, duplicate acquisitions can be automatically avoided. Decisions can be taken on which library will specialise in which subject. Then, each library will endeavour to build its collection so as to be strong in the selected subject. Normally in the university library, the subject is chosen according to the academic curriculum of the University. Though only one library acquires material on one subject, the identification of the material will be done by all the libraries in the programme, according to their requirements.

The Farmington Plan and the Midwestern Inter-Library Centre (MILC) in the USA, as well as the Deutsche Forschungewierschaft in Germany are the most well-known examples of useful and effective programmes of Co-operative acquisition. The Farmington Plan is a successful co-operative venture in acquisition and is limited to acquiring books and publications from overseas. The MILC in U.S.A. is a co-operative exercise in not only acquisition but also in storage. The German programme involves the co-operative acquisition among about 40 university and special libraries.

5.3. Co-operative Storage

The publications have been increasing in number, far beyond practical limits of easy storage. This has been happening with respect to publications on every subject and in every discipline.

Storage costs money. Co-operative storage would result in economy of space and money. It would also keep track of catalogue entries and help avoid duplication. The concept of co-operative storage can be put into practice atleast in respect of less frequently used material like certain books and back volumes of serials.

The photo copies of extracts of these stored material can be made available at various individual libraries to meet the more urgent needs of the readers. Needless to mention, the cost of such a storage system may be shared by all the participating libraries.

In 1949, ten university libraries in the United States of America got together and organised the Mid-Western Inter -

Library Centre (MILC) with the purpose of increasing library resources of the member institutions.

The first storage library in India was established in 1974 at the Inter-Library Resources Centre in New Delhi, under the patronage of the Indian Council of Social Science Research (ICSSR). Back issues of periodicals make up the bulk of the collection at the repository. However, the concept has not yet caught up with the imagination of the library professionals in India.

5.4. Co-operative Processing

Next to the acquisition of material, another phase of library operation, which involves time and expenditure, is the processing of material. It mainly includes classification and cataloguing of the books and other reading materials. Computers and other automated processes can be used to meet their cataloguing needs of the books and other reading materials.

5.5. Union Catalogues

For a satisfactory resource sharing programme, it is most essential that each participating librarian should know the resources available with the other libraries. In short, the Union Catalogue should be readily available with each participant library. A Union Catalogue is the most useful location tool with a librarian participating in a Inter-Library Loan programme.

Such Union Catalogues could be prepared and updated periodically, say once every quarter. It is also important to note that a Union Catalogue is different from a collective catalogue. A Collective Catalogue is simply a collection of the catalogues of all the libraries, one after another. It may include duplicate entry for the same book, if it is available with more than one library. However, in a Union Catalogue, all the titles held by all the libraries, are listed in an alphabetical order, showing the location of the same.

A well prepared Union Catalogue serves many useful purposes as listed here-under:

(i) It shows at a glance, the total document resources of the libraries participating in a lending programme.

(ii) It serves as a major bibliography in its own right.

(iii) It helps in identifying the material to be discarded because of less or no use.

Regularly updated catalogues and supplements should be circulated to all the participating libraries to enable the most effective exploitation of the common resources. With the compilation of a Union Catalogue, compilation of bibliography and location of materials will be easier.

Certainly, the use of a computerised environment would be most ideal for such activity, as regular revisions could be made cheaply. In this context, the efforts made by Indian National Scientific Documentation Centre (INSDOC) to produce several regional and local union catalogues of scientific and technical periodicals and serials may be mentioned. In fact, these catalogues will eventually form the basis of the proposed National Union Catalogue. The Social Science Documentation Centre (SSDC), New Delhi, under the Indian Council of Social Science Research (ICSSR), has also published a series of union catalogues in the field of Social Sciences, covering many major libraries in India.

It is essential that there is a uniform practice in compilation of union catalogues. The various factors to be considered while compiling a union catalogue, are as follows:

(i) The scope and coverage.

(ii) Which libraries are participating?

(iii) Which libraries have lending out policies and what type of documents are covered in that arrangement?

(iv) Whether libraries are linked with computing system and do they have computer readable catalogue and tapes or discs to be supplied for inclusion?

(v) Do they have sufficient stationery, staff, building, computing, publications, etc.

(vi) The rates of expenditure to be borne by the participating libraries;

(vii) The catalogue.

(viii) Form of union catalogue.

(ix) Circulation at cost/complimentary to participants/charges to others.

It is important that the participating libraries should ensure the updation of both additions and deletions to their collections in the union catalogue.

5.6. Co-operative Delivery of Services

In a regular Inter-Library Loan exercise, the required book moves from one library to another library. It is at this second library that the user receives the book from the librarian. This involves time and expenditure to the library establishments.

However, in a system of co-operative delivery of services, expenditure to the establishment is dispensed with; though it may mean expenditure to the user. The user directly goes to the library actually having the volume sought by him and takes it on loan. This form of co-operation is not in vogue in the libraries in India.

5.7. Exchange of Personnel & Training Facilities

Exchange of personnel implies sharing of expertise. Most of the time, recruitment of an expert on permanent basis may be unnecessary. Such expertise may be required only for a short period.

Borrowing the services of an expert from another library would automatically enable the training of in-house staff. The exercise, such as a new concept in cataloguing, started by the expert can be easily carried on by the in house staff.

5.8. Clearing House Functions

Like in a banking system, clearing house functions would form a part of a successful Inter-Library Loan arrangement.

For example, Delhi University Library may be chosen as

the clearing house for university libraries in and around Delhi. That would cover the other university libraries in Delhi and the library at CCS University in Meerut. On the same lines, the Maharishi Dayanand University Library at Rohtak could be selected as the clearing house for the libraries in and around Haryana.

5.9. Technical Process

Till recently, centralised cataloguing and processing work was thought of as not feasible in the university libraries. But now, the situation has changed with the advent of computers and copying machines. But, preparation of union catalogues and reference and bibliographic tools is now possible and must be taken up.

5.10. Translation Services

It is very useful to start a translation centre at atleast in one university library in the state. For example, the library at Sri Venkateswara University may receive a request for the loan of a book on a certain rare and historical aspect from a scholar in English. Let us hypothetically suppose that no book on that subject exists in Sri Venkatesware University Library, in English; but, the same subject is covered well in a Tamil book. It would be very useful in an English translation could be passed on to the scholar seeking the information.

Similarly, a Telugu scholar may be seeking the loan of a book on a certain aspect which is available with another library, but in English. It would be most useful if a Telugu translation of the same could be provided.

5.11. Web-based Resource Sharing

Computer and telecommunication technology are playing a vital role in the design and operation of resource sharing systems network. A library network means as a group of libraries are Inter-related through different areas. Now resource sharing among libraries has been accepted as a necessity. These are required for working of large systems on national and international levels also.

Resource sharing through library networks helps the member libraries in avoiding duplication of document procurement and in inter-library ending.

Web based resource sharing includes the sharing of resources hosted on the net. It is very important for bibliographic control of the explosion of literature and knowledge. It also avoids duplication in purchase of costly documents. It facilitates the adoption of new areas in every field of knowledge and improves the mobility of data. Library web resource sharing is a helpful way to development the flow of information among the special information centres / libraries and other types of libraries.

The main objectives of Web based resource sharing are to:

(i) improve the sharing of resources among the member libraries;

(ii) centralize the information processing system; and

(iii) reduce the communication gap among the libraries.

(iv) Improved ILL productivity with fewer blind requests, automated creation and tracking of requests, and faster turnaround.

(v) *Controlled ILL costs* : For one low transaction charge, you can route each request to as many as five libraries.

(vi) *Cooperative collection development* : Plan your acquisitions to avoid duplication of other group members' holdings and still ensure a group collection responsive to your users' needs.

(vii) Increased use of collections with instant local access.

(viii) A way for all group members to contribute, maintain and access information in the group's database.

3
Resource Sharing Tools

1. Introduction

Resource sharing can only be done effectively if appropriate resource sharing tools are available. The growth of such tools began with the preparation of catalogues of libraries, bibliographies on subjects, union lists of periodicals, union catalogues of books and of periodicals, etc. changing from card catalogue and printed catalogue forms to database, CD and online database forms. In India in the 1960s and 1970s, the librarians worked hard to create manually bibliographies and documentation lists while at the same time in the United States efforts to create such tools in machine readable forms had already begun. So had the creation of databases of union catalogues and union lists. A union list of scientific and technical journals was prepared by the Smithsonian in 1885 in the U.S. In India it was in 1868 when the catalogue of manuscripts in various parts of India was compiled by Whitney Stokes. In 1873 in India two catalogues, one pertaining to the Sanskrit manuscripts in private libraries in the North West Provinces and another in the Central Provinces was edited by F. Klelhorn. In the 20th century reference may be made to the union card catalogue of public library holdings developed in California in 1909. Thereafter the creation of union lists and union catalogues has been going on all over the world first in the printed forms and then in the machine readable database forms.

The rapid advances made in the information technology have ushered in a number of advanced information products, technologies and services that can be conveniently harnessed by the librarian community for achieving the objective of resource sharing.

In fact the modern concept of resource sharing overflows the boundaries as defined above and encompasses other spheres of activities like cooperative acquisitioning, cataloguing and classification; cooperation in the training and development of the professional workers in public libraries and cooperative acquisitioning of equipment and machines which are extensively employed in the activity of information dissemination and which are too expensive for individual libraries to acquire on their own.

2. Types of Tools

Various resource sharing tools in networked environment or information technologies era may include the following :

2.1. Databases

Exchange of information through electronic mail, online facility or a terminal is possible if a database is created. A database is an organised, integrated and often interrelated collection of computer-based data, records, files or information. The databases are collections of records in machine-readable form that are made available for searching from remote computer terminals.

There are available different types of databases, which are exceedingly useful: for example. Carl Uncover is a database that contains table of contents of over 17000 multidisciplinary journals published since 1988. The uncover database search is free for periodicals.

Besides, the above sources on Internet, it provides access to software achieves, directory of electronic serials, Frequently Asked Questions (FAQ) documents, workshops etc.

In bibliographic databases the data stored, comprises of inputs of bibliographic details of a document for identification, storage and retrieval purposes. Bibliographic databases can be divided into two categories:

(i) Internal databases and associated services;

(ii) External databases and associated services.

The internal bibliographic databases are those created by libraries and information centres of their published holdings, such as:

- Books including monographs, technical reports, conference proceedings etc.
- Periodicals publications.
- Manuscripts or rare documents.
- Information / documentation services like abstracting and indexing services.
- Computer based databases on CDs, DVDs, cartage etc.

External database comprising of bibliographic or textual data of one or more libraries is a major resource sharing tool if it is available online to the users. While union lists or catalogues give information about the resources of participating libraries, the online database of a single library if accessible online or off-line can become a useful resource sharing tool. The catalogues of a large number of institutions and universities the world over are available online for remote searching.

The online searching of external databases began in the mid 1960s. The first online retrieval system was developed by the Systems Development Corporation (SDC) in the USA. MEDLINE, prepared by the National Library of Medicine, USA began its operation from 1969 as one of the first bibliographic databases. There are, of course, several types of such databases such as online directories, library catalogues and full text databases now available all over the world. The following are examples

1. Abstracting and citation databases like PSYCINFO, the machine readable counterpart of *Psychological Abstracts.* And, SCISEARCH, the machine readable counterpart of *Science Citation Index,* and *Current Contents,* the

publications of the Institutions for Scientific Information. USA

2. Local, metropolitan, regional, national and international bibliographic networks. The following are examples:

   Local : A network in a campus or an institution such as IIT, Mumbai or IIT, Roorkee.

   Metropolitan: A growing city network like DELNET.

   Regional : A proposed network like NELIBNET for North- East India.

   National : A network like INFLIBNET.

   International : A network like OCLC that has outgrown its local, regional and national character and is used the world over.

3. Databases of indexes to newspapers, e.g. *New York Times, Information Index* or *National Newspapers Index* published in the USA and the *Hindu Index* published monthly and cumulated annually.

4. Databases of union catalogues, e.g. *National Union Catalogue of Scientific Serials in India* (INSDOC; now NISCAIR).

5. Databases of references sources like *Ulrich's Periodical Directory.*

6. Full text databases which provide the relevant information directly and give complete texts of documents. For example. *Harvard Business Review* (HBR) offers both bibliographic and text details. Full text newspapers available online through INTERNET may also be cited. *Hindu Online* (http://www. hinduonline.com) is just one example.

Many of the online databases were first made accessible to the users by vendors-computer-based agencies that arrange access to various world databases for a fee. For instance, vendors such as DIALOG, STN and Silver Platter offer access to a large number of databases with hyperlinks and cross references. DIALOG Information Services Inc. Palo Alto, California offers access to more than 400 databases. But now, the online mode of service is increasing the world over through WWW.

2.2. Cooperative Collection Development

Collection development is essential for developing efficient resource sharing tools. The acquisition is an important activity. A survey of science and technology libraries and notes reveals that the libraries are looking at the networks for help in order to reduce expenditure on materials cost. Such, libraries prefer to participate in cooperative collection development, prefer to coordinate acquisitions, receive volume discounts for database services and get speedier access to materials. Resource sharing networks have to provide better service to such libraries because they serve scientists and technical personnel. It is considered that since researchers are in need of specialised materials and technical reports, development of such collections becomes necessary.

Resource sharing can play an effective role in acquisitions provided the acquisition librarians takes effective measures in this regard. Resource sharing work in relation to acquisitions and notices show that two issues, viz. technological and economic need to be considered while making an analysis. Among the technological issues it needs to be noted that:

(a) Moving from printed text to machine readable text brought about fundamental changes in library activities;

(b) Integration of data unique to particular procedures such as borrowing records, payment records, etc. should become available at one place in an integrated form;

(c) Local holdings information in the catalogue in the form of a union catalogue helps in ILL at several levels — local, regional and national.

The economic issues are very important as resource sharing

takes birth because of them. When document delivery increases and document acquisition decreases one begins to notice the relationship between the two. Sheila S. Inter reveals "three circumstantial impacts" the resource sharing activity can have on acquisitions and the "three potential impacts" that depend upon the nature of the library organisation and the state of its computing systems. The three inevitable impacts are:

1. Changes in the mix of subjects and formats that will be acquired;
2. Changes in the rate at which requests flow to the acquisition department; and
3. Changes in the relative balance of power between the library, i.e., the acquisition department and each of its material vendors.

The three impacts that might be encountered, depending on circumstances are:

1. Changes in the nature, character, and range of acquisitive activities;
2. Changes in the decision making powers delegated to the acquisition department;
3. Changes in acquisition departments abilities to affect budget and allocations, quite the reverse of the expected cause-and-effect.

It has been noticed that the acquisitions departments in the libraries that need to share resources should be reorganised and revitalised. It does not help to entirely depend upon electronic databases for resource sharing purposes but the librarians have to make conscious decisions for rejecting or selecting titles for acquisition purposes.

2.3. Pre-order Verification

One of the important functions of a library network is to help the participating libraries to compare their lists of books to be ordered with the union catalogue of the participating network so that duplication is avoided in the acquisition, especially when the books are available in the neighbouring libraries. Also, for shared cataloguing purposes, comparison of books ordered with the union catalogue becomes essential. In order to ascertain the ideal role of a library network in pre-order citation verification, a comparison was made of the ILLINET online and OCLC. It was desired to determine the sizeable percentage of titles that were being verified on OCLC prior to ordering at Western Illinois University Library if they could be verified also at ILLINET Online database. It was noticed that:

1. The pre-order verification procedure at Western Illinois University Library needed to be changed.
2. ILLINET online was found easier compared with OCLC because the local call number could be obtained fast from ILLINET online.
3. The response from ILLINET was quicker as full words could also be searched from the text/notes, title and subtitle.
4. ILLINET searches are more precise, while OCLC hits could be in dozens.
5. On OCLC Author/title combinations or limitations of searches by format or date of publication could narrow search results but it was not possible on ILLINET.
6. ILLINET was not a detailed database for older records, especially before 1975 and therefore could not be extensive.

However, there had been a hit rate of 80 per cent on ILLINET and there had been a saving of $13 per record viewed. And so ILLINET was considered as the preferred online system for pre-order verification.

2.4. Union Lists

Union lists are important resource sharing tools for current materials in libraries such as periodicals. For instance, DELNET created the union list of periodicals available in 135 libraries and the database is regularly in use and is being updated. The lists can take various forms such as the union lists of library resources or lists of current acquisitions, etc.

In small libraries professional isolation can and does retard proficiency of library and information science professionals. The activities that encourage professional interaction between the library staff are important. The resource sharing programmes do enable professional staff to exchange ideas and keep themselves up-to-date. It provides a basis for the sharing of less tangible resources such as special subject knowledge, searching skills and ideas.

It has been noticed that the union lists of journals of regional cooperatives are a bit more reliable than those of the British Library Document Supply Centre (BLDSC). It is also noticed that the regional cooperatives are somewhat faster.

2.5. Union Catalogues

The union catalogues are the basic resource sharing tools that can be used for actual location and faster delivery of documents. The history of union catalogues dates back to over a century now but their utility as resource sharing tools is undoubtedly established. There are various aspects associated with the preparation and use of union catalogues.

In order to assess the issues concerning with the quality of union catalogues which are important resource sharing tools, the report of the Evaluation Committee of CD-ROM Union Catalogue of Associated College Libraries of Central Pennsylvania (ACLCP) may be referred. It found that :

1. The union catalogue database was capable of identifying materials held in member-libraries;
2. The linked-and-merged design was found to be a very effective means of creating union catalogue as it did not include the cost involved on a fully de-duped database,
3. All such records were merged with de-duped process which did not contain the Library of Congress card or OCLC control number;

4. The number of records in the other catalogue form were reduced by 35 per cent with the linked-and-merged design;
5. Whenever wrong LCCN or OCLC control numbers were entered the occurrence of false merges was considered insignificant;
6. Some minor bibliographic problems, in case of location stamps or variation in call numbers was noticed;
7. Several sorting problems were noticed with the title fields;
8. The vendor did not follow the finalised order for including databases of member-libraries, which resulted in less comprehensive bibliographic records serving as a master record;
9. It was noticed that the database organisation was inadequate for handling articles in foreign languages;
10. It was also noticed that if the catalogues provided indicators for articles in foreign languages, the vendor should be able to read and ignore them for filing purposes; and
11. The union catalogue enables the member-libraries to identify and resolve the problem with the hex code used for diacritical marks in foreign language material which was inadvertently and wrongly set by the regional provider of data from the National Bibliographic-Database.

The union catalogue of books created by DELNET has the following features:

1. It identifies books through various CCF tags held in the main database and through MARC tags held in newly developed MARC database;
2. It is based on the linked and merged design of DELSIS but all operations are not kept automatic because it was considered necessary to check the quality of two or more records before merging of the location codes and retaining of one entry that was more suitable;

3. The number of records in the union catalogue reduced by 3.2 per cent after merging;
4. All libraries did not give ISBN numbers and therefore the ISBN could not be the field for identifying duplicate entries. In DELSIS, the identifying fields were: Title, author and year of publication;
5. In some entries bibliographic problems were noticed in case of author, publisher and subject headings;
6. Sorting problems were not noticed in the software;
7. Though each library is following the DELNET standards but the variations were noticed in case of some libraries;
8. DELSIS provides facilities for handling data in other languages, except those in Perso Arabic script. However, most of the data are in English and much experience has not been gained in handling data in other languages;
9. GIST provides diacritical marks and these need to be compared with the international diacritical schemes used the world over;
10. Union lists and catalogues of serials form important tools for resource sharing.

2.6. Online Public Access Catalogues or OPAC

Historically, library catalogues have been rather insular, often based on specialised hardware and/or operating systems lacking industry-standard networking capabilities. Network access was not a major consideration in the design or selection of these specialised systems. Over the past decade, a number of online databases have become available for public use on the INTERNET. As a result, the competition and standardisation has resulted in the creation of online public access catalogues.

OPAC is online public access catalog. In traditional library it provides information about what is available in the library. Present day OPACs mostly reflect now a day's print as well as electronic collections. Research library catalogs serve as authoritative sources of access. The phrase, "if you can't track it, you don't own it," is quite real for the library that is trying to monitor thousands or millions of items. From the last few years, libraries have started retrospective conversion projects, bringing metadata about all their monographs and other collections into one place this has helped librarians and users to know about what is available in the library. But relatively few libraries track some of the newest, and most popular, resources they provide; the electronic journals available through database aggregators and online publishers.

The OPACs or Online Public Access Catalogues are playing an important role in information retrieval. These can be broadly divided as (i) OPACs, which are used in a particular library using either a multi-user system or a local area network and (ii) those, which can be accessed by other libraries through emergence of Internet. These are very easily and quickly accessible on the Internet from any part of the world The availability of these catalogues on web allows any one to see the contents of various library collections at their home There are some of web OPAC's, for e.g., Soul Web OPAC, Libsys Web OPAC, Slim Web OPAC and so on.

The reasons for changing the style of presentation and the scope of OPACs are several. By 1990 the following were considered to be the reasons:

1. OPACs have been used to access a greater variety of materials:
2. OPACs provide entrances to a large number of the libraries without walls;
3. The evolving technology has changed the accessing of OPACs from cathode ray tubes, or dumb terminals to the microcomputers capable of handling sound and image besides the text;
4. The microcomputer makes it possible for the OPAC to evolve from a static source of information to a powerful

and dynamic tool that can be controlled and manipulated by individual users.

The OPACs over the INTERNET have now become more user-friendly especially with the use of hyperlinks that enable the users to get related information from other INTERNET databases to supplement issues and ideas that need more explanation and references.

2.7. National Bibliographic Database

A National Bibliographic Database is an essential resource sharing tool at a national level besides being the bibliographic repository of a nation's holdings. The growth of such a tool has to be based on a vision and a set of national policies that cumulatively give rise to a national bibliographic database. The Library of Congress Network Advisory Committee which studied the network developments in the United States considered that the environment needed to be created to provide each individual with equal opportunity of access to the nation's information resources. The basic policy for a national bibliographic database was that authoritative information about the combined bibliographic resources of the nation would reside principally at the national level, stored and maintained by the bibliographic utilities and the national libraries.

British Library and the Bibliotheque Nationale of France produced their national bibliographies in CD-ROM form. Such efforts are also being made in some developing countries. In Israel, for instance, a national catalogue of books and periodicals in university libraries has been produced. INFLIBNET in India, is working towards this goal. This is preparing National Catalogues of various types of document available in University libraries of the country.

National Bibliographic Database in Australia was developed on the following principles of a national collection.

(a) aggregation of all library collections in Australia whether in the public or private sector;

(b) Comprehensive in relation to Australia;

(c) selective in relation to the rest of the world as present and future needs require; and

(d) adequately recorded and readily accessible.

As the concept of a distributed national collection was adopted in Australia for the purposes of the National Bibliographic Database (NBD), the following five aspects were rigorously considered and adopted.

1. Collection Development : The quality of NBD depend upon the relevance of available collections to a country's needs. In this regard it was important to note :

(a) the existing weaknesses and strengths of collections and the collecting patterns and policies;

(b) what the libraries in a country were doing in terms of collection development, avoiding of duplication and maximizing of relevant individual titles in the libraries; and

(c) how national collecting responsibilities could be pinpointed and appropriate libraries selected for the purpose.

If all these activities are to involve government, private and public libraries on an equal footing there is a need for a full financial backing by a government.

2. Bibliographic Control : NBD becomes an important and basic tools of bibliographic control. The more comprehensive it is the more effective it becomes for resource sharing. The libraries can borrow books after referring to it. In Australia, the Australian bibliographic Network (ABN) has developed a National Bibliographic Database.

3. Preservation : The policies of preservation leave an impact on what to preserve and catalogue and what to avoid in order to save finances. There has to be a nationally coordinated approach to this issue so that whatever is retained is not retained at several sites.

4. Access : The relevance of NBD becomes more meaningful in a distributed national collection scanario when ILL facilities are prompt and the delivery is fast.

5. National Coordination : Keeping the national interests in mind, some libraries need to specialize in certain subject and build up the collections with a national scenario in mind. This work needs to be looked after by a national agency or an agency sponsored to take up the national role.

Resource sharing becomes more functional if the National Bibliographic Database in a country is existing and operational or if there is an alternate database available to supplement the need.

2.8. CD-ROMs

The CD-ROM technology influenced since the 1980s, its wider applications in libraries as a major resource of information which can be used for:

(a) creating catalogues, bibliographies, union catalogues, full text databases, etc;

(b) distributing catalogues among libraries of a network for resource sharing;

(c) cooperative collection development;

(d) promoting cooperation among libraries of a network;

(e) increasing access to resources by users who are at a distance, within or without a country;

(f) making access user-friendly;

(g) reducing costs of accessing and disseminating information;

(h) building a technology base for research in IT; and

(i) storing large databases at several locations simultaneously for research and reference, etc.

A CD-ROM union catalogue can offer an off-line access to the resources of a library network which is both convenient and inexpensive.

The application of CD-ROM by commercial agencies and by the national governments progressed in the 1980s and the 1990s for the storage and dissemination of information. The Commission of the European Community since the early 1980s encouraged the use of CD-ROM technology in the European countries. Some of the important projects that received support include the ADONIS project of the British Library which supplied articles from biomedical journals; MARKUSH-DARC. generic chemical patent information system; MULTIMEDIA MEDITERRANEAN ATLAS; DISNET, an intelligent interface to electronic information; etc. Similar projects were undertaken in the U.S. and some developed and developing countries.

CD-ROM resource sharing was undertaken by the Southwestern Connecticut Library Council (Region 4) using Fax and CD-ROM databases. With an expenditure of about $200,000 for developing the CD-ROM databases and another $ 100,000 for providing fax machines to regional offices and public institutions the resource sharing facility was developed. Such a finance might not be easily possible to arrange in a developing country like India if similar facilities had to be developed.

Another interesting example of resource sharing through CD-ROM technology could be the New England Law Library Consortium (NELLCO) which launched the creation of the union catalogue on CD in 1987. The catalogue which became operational in 1990 could be used as an individual catalogue of a participating library. This union catalogue has several features which include browsing of shelves, map location which gives the details about the actual location of the book, etc. When an online system fails in a participating library, the rise of NELLCO-CD-ROM has proved very useful. It is a bibliographic tool which can be used in collection development research or for retro-conversion.

Some of the other examples of interest are :

1. Belgian University Union catalogue on two discs holding

2,300,000 titles. One can access through title, title words and author.

2. Access Pennsylvania Project: A statewide union catalogue. It has PAC (Public Access Catalogue) facilities. An increase of 300 per cent in circulation was observed due to this catalogue.
3. A pilot project between the British Library and the Bibliotheque Nationale of France to store on CD-ROM the National Bibliographies of these two countries.
4. National Library of Canada Voluntary Cooperative Resource Sharing Network with the use of CD-ROM.

2.9. Internet

It is also known by the name Information Super Highway. It is the network of many networks spreading over the world.

The roots of INTERNET go back to 1968 when the US Department of Defence established Advanced Research Projects Agency Network (ARPANET) to link supercomputers and highly specialised equipment. The purpose was to share large scientific databases and reduce expensive investments wherever possible. The first use of ARPANET was in electronic communication. This resulted in greater interest in the networks. In 1991, President George Bush signed into law the National High Performance Computing Act of 1991 which authorised the creation of the National Research and Education Network (NREN). NREN, became later known as INTERNET. It has been proved to be a highly reliable network. By January 1992 it was estimated that more than 800,000 individual computers were connected to the INTERNET.

Now-a-days, WWW has become a major tool for resource sharing. However, we have to evaluate the right kind of resources on WWW, but eventually they will get standardised and access may become pinpointed with the help of library and information professionals who have begun to handle the Web resources.

2.10. Virtual Libraries

Virtual libraries have no physical existence owing to the enormous growth of WWW become a major source of information in the 21st century. They will be scattered, accessed full text from any location or a workstation and used whenever the user wishes to use information. Already virtual library projects have been established. Reference may be made to the following two projects as an example :

(i) National Institute of Standards and Technology (NIST), USA has developed a virtual library on an intranet. INTERNET is a LAN with TCP/IP protocol which facilitates accessing of INTERNET databases from the terminal or a LAN or from a remote site the information is made available on the LAN.

(ii) Tilburg University in 1995 had started providing access to 120 journals of Elsevier in the economic and social sciences. By 1997, the university was offering full text information to 2450 terminals in the campus.

2.11. Mailing Lists

The latest information is becoming available through the mailing lists that are available in different disciplines. Also, discussion groups and list servs form part of handling the latest information which can be of great interest to the users. Reference may be made, as an example, to the following list in the field of library science which is being compiled by Wei Wu at the University of Houston Libraries:

http://info.lib.uh.edu/liblists/guides/alphalst.htm

2.12. Human Resources

Access to human resources is important in this time and age. At present, specialisations are growing in large numbers. Reference may be made to the following two sources:

1. DELNETs Specialists Database which maintains a growing WHO's WHO of about 2000 specialists.

2. Universitair Centrum Antwerpen (RUCA) Library of the University of Antwerp, Belgium. http://www.ruca.ua.ac.be/

2.13. Grey Literature Including Reports of Workshops and Conference Proceedings

Online/off-line access to grey literature, has become possible lately and it is likely to grow as a specialised databases on the Web. Reference may be made to the following as samples:

(i) Library of Congress Cataloguing Newsline (LCCN): Online newsletter of the Cataloguing Directorate, Library of Congress.

http://lcweb.loc.gov/catdir/lccn/lccn.html

(ii) European Library Automation Group (ELAG). Progress reports of libraries under the European Commission.

http://www.bg.univ.gda.pl/library/elag/progress.html

2.14. Patents Information

Access to patent documents is growing the world over, especially through the Web. This information on the Web is provided by the government offices and private agencies. In India, the National Informatics Centre has in its Patents database 28 million records from 1968 to 1997. It is available to the users on:

http://pk2id.delhi.nic.in

2.15. Multimedia Databases

Multimedia databases are going to grow as major resource sharing tools. Already databases have been created at important centres in the world using hyperlinks. Multimedia technology is growing very fast to cover book and non-book materials. Such databases are also becoming available on the INTERNET. Multimedia databases are being created in India by several agencies including the Indira Gandhi National Centre for the Arts. The use of interactive multimedia applications on the Web is going to give birth to a variety of resource sharing tools.

2.16. Digital Libraries

Various terms are used by authors to denote the concept of digital libraries such as Electronic library, Online library, Polyglot library, Desktop Library, Library without walls, Virtual library, etc. Among the entire terms digital library is popular among authors. Digital library is heterogeneous in nature and covers work related to information and how to digitize, link, store, visualise, find, use, and management of sharing information. With the help of information technology digital library provides instant access to digitalized information. Electronic library based on digitalized data is text replacing the paper based records and that is why with the help of networking, one can have access to resources round the clock. The advantages include resource sharing, document delivery services and data transmission in a minimal duration.

American Digital Library Federation has given the following working definition of Digital library: Digital libraries are organizations that provide the resources, including the specialised staff, to select, structure, offer intellectual access to, interpret, distribute, preserve the integrity of, and ensure the persistence over time of collections of digital works so that they are readily and economically available for use by a defined community or set of communities.

For computer professionals, a digital library may be simply a distributed text based information system, a collection of distributed space or interlinked information or a networked multimedia information system.

For researchers and people working on education technology, the digital library is a support tool of learning in both manners formal and informal. For high technology users of World Wide Web (WWW) the digital library provides the enhancement in performance, organization, usability and functionality.

Digital libraries are a set of electronic resources and

associated technical capabilities for creating, searching and using information. In this sense they are an extension and enhancement of information storage & retrieval systems that manipulate digital data in any medium (text, images, sounds, static or dynamic images) and exist in distributed networks. The introduction to the April 1995 Communications of the ACM special issue on digital libraries describes them grandly as the "opportunity ... to fulfil the age old dream of every human being : gaining ready access to humanity's store of information. The content of digital libraries include data, metadata that describe various aspects of data (e.g. representation, creator, owner, reproduction rights), and metadata that consist of link or relationships to other data or metadata whether internal or external to digital library".

(i) Need for Digital Libraries : Digitization includes conversion of any fixed or analogue media like books, journal articles, microforms, photos, painting into electronic form through scanning, sampling, re-keying, etc. It provides a solution to traditional library problems such as conservation, preservation, multimedia documents and remote access to information collection and storage space. The first and most vital reason being that the stored materials and documents start deteriorating after a certain period of time at a rapid rate. In spite of our best efforts it is not possible to preserve them in their natural and original form. Here IT can only help us; in fact storing the library resources in digital formats is a promising solution to this problem.

The other reason being the vast amount of information created every day and to store it physically is time consuming and retrieval of this information later on is equally difficult. With the help of IT the storage and retrieval of information can become easier and can produce the optimum benefits.

Digital library has minimised the gap that exists between "library and user". Any information pertaining to any topic can be accessed without any difficulty. It provides access for the teaching and learning equipment to enrich their existing knowledge and focus is laid to provide access to it whether it is of local or distant source.

(ii) Factors that Necessitate the Digital Library : There are various factors that created the need for digital library.

(a) *Rapid growth of scientific information* : Let us take an example to see the growth of scientific information. Chemical Abstract took 31 years (1907-1937) to publish its first one million abstracts, the second million took 18 years and the most recent one took only 1.75 years. Thus the articles published on chemistry during the last two years are more than articles published throughout the history before 1900. Most branches of sciences show an exponential growth of about 4-8 per cent annually with a doubling period of 10-15 years. This high growth of information demands for the developed techniques in processing and distribution of information.

(b) *Trend of specialisations in all spheres of universe of knowledge* : The direct result of specialisation of knowledge is growth of research scholars. But this growth poses certain economical and organizational problems. Economically it is not possible to offer a large number of documents to a large number of scholars. Specialized scholars lack the knowledge about the other colleagues working on either the same or related topics at their campus and other scholars who share similar interests are scattered at different places. Electronic communication forms a new electronic scholarly community and thus requirement of the physical proximity of scholars is no more an essential factor.

(c) *Transmission of information* : Conventional method of lecture system will not survive. Only specialised research and video servers with stored lectures by outstanding scholars are today's requirement. Hypertext books, computer conferencing, electronic distance education will become available through broadcast, cable online and satellite technologies. Such a form of instruction will satisfy the needs of even those who are engaged in full time jobs, family obligations, limited mobility and isolated location.

(d) *Storage of information* : Libraries are gradually shifting from investment in the physical presence of information to the creation of electronic access such as Internet and E-mail. The reason is that a comprehensive library collection is becoming unforgettable, electronic alternatives have become powerful in their storage capacity. Thus the role of libraries as the repository centre of information will be phased out in course of time.

Besides, Users' expectations, Information thrust, Comprehensive coverage, Future challenges strongly advocate the case of digital libraries.

(iii) Implementation Methodology : Converting collections into digital images begins with the planning followed by linear progression task which includes selection of library materials for digitization/scanning/indexing/storage/retrieval. The work flow is given below :

(a) *Collection development & preparation* : It includes :

- Determination of scope or extant of digitization (entire or subset)
- Access of the best format, e.g. fulltext conversion, scanned page image.
- Selection of the collection.

The four steps are involved in the process of digitization scanning, indexing, storage and retrieval. Software, variably called document image processing (DIP), electronic filing system (EFS) and document management systems (DMS) provides all or more of these functions.

(b) *Scanning* : The process involves acquisition of an electronic image through its original that may be a photograph, text, manuscript etc. into the computer using an electronic image scanner. An image is read or scanned at a predefined resolution and dynamic range. The resulting file called 'bit-map page image' is formatted and tagged for storage and subsequent retrieval by the software package used for scanning. Fax card, electronic camera or other imaging devices may also be employed for acquisition of an image, however, image, scanners are most important and most commonly used component of an imaging system for transfer of normal paper-based documents into an image.

(c) *Indexing* : Indexing of a document converted into an image or text file is the second step in the process of document imaging. The process of indexing scanned image involves linking of data base of scanned images to a text database. Scanned images are just like a set of pictures that need to be related to a text database describing them and their contents.

An imaging system typically stores a large amount of unstructured data in a two file system for storing and retrieving scanned images. The first is traditional file that has a text description of the image alongwith a key to a second file. The second file contains the document location. The user selects a record from the first file using a search algorithm. Once the user selects a record, the application keys into the location index, finds the document and displays it.

Most of the document imaging software packages, through their manu driven or command driven interface, facilitate elaborate indexing of documents. While some DMS facilitate selection of indexing terms from the image file, others allow only manual keying in of indexing terms. Further, many DMS packages provide OCR capabilities for transforming the images into standard ASCII files. OCRed text then serves as a database for full text search of the stored images.

(d) *Storage* : The most tenacious problem of a document image relates to its file size and, therefore, to its storage. Every part of an eletronic page image is saved regardless of present or absence of ink. The file size varies directly with scanning resolution, the size of the area being digitized, compression ratio, content and the style of graphic file format use to save the image. The scanned images, therefore, need to be transformed to the hard disc of scanning work station to an external large capacity storage devices such as an optical disc, CD-ROM/ DVD ROM disc, cartridge tape. etc. While the smaller document imaging system use offline media, which need to be reloaded when required, or fixed hard disc drives allocated for image storage. Larger DMS use auto changers such as optical jukeboxes and tape library systems. The image storage device may be either remote or local to the retrieval work station depending upon the imaging systems and DMS used.

(e) *Retrieval* : Once scanned images and OCRed text documents have been saved as a file, a data base is needed for selective retrieval of data contained in one or more fields within each record in the database. Typically, a document imaging system uses atleast two files to store and retrieve documents. The first is traditional file that has a text description of the image alongwith a key to the second file. The second file contains the document location. The user selects a record from the first file using a search algorithm. Once the user selects a record, the application keys into the location index, finds the document and displays it. Most of the DMS provide elaborate search possibilities including use of Boolean and proximity operators (and, or, not) and wild cards. Users are also allowed to refile their search strategy. Once the required images have been identified, their associated document image can quickly be retrieved from the image storage device for display or printed output.

(iv) Impact of Digital Libraries in Products and Services : A digital library enhances the quality of services offered by a library and information centre of any type. Some of these services and products are mentioned below.

(a) *Impact on Cataloguing Services* : As the library grew due to print technology, a mechanism was required to locate the book and thus cataloguing of books started. From time to time cataloguing rules were revised to reduce the complicities in cataloguing. Over the years the library permitted other local libraries to have their holdings catalogued to make them available to the readers. Now online access over the Internet is available. Thus the use of digital technology shows how communication has changed the trend from local work and authority to a service provider.

(b) *Impact on Indexing Services* : Indexes enhance the precision and completeness of subsequent retrieval from the bibliographic materials. Few libraries of the world use very high quality and comprehensive indexing, for example, US National Library of Medicine. But most fields of science do not have such high quality indexing services. Digital library solved the problem of redundant or near redundant terms and will give a good example of high quality and comprehensive indexing.

(c) *Impact on Editing Works* : Editing a manuscript demands high level knowledge that may not be available locally. Since many editors are freelancers, they provide their services remotely. Direct communication between author and editor is not so important as for a publisher to be able to access and market his work and digitization will be a great helping tool for him.

(d) *Impact on Reviews/Critical Works* : In future it is possible that a work will remain visible from the moment an author releases it and comments by reviewers and critics will be accessible through links. In this approach a critic who signs his opinion becomes a participant in the information process. Due to an open electronic environment anyone can send his comments to the paper, the quality of comments has to be assured with special services by referees whose main task is to consider the worth in terms of quality and originality of the papers.

(e) *Impact on Results' Processing* : The processing of retrieved documents, though validation abstraction, integration and presentation are also an agenda of specialists. Most end-users need more than rapid access to documents. Decision makers today depend on their staff to analyse, abstract and rank alternatives according to their world view. Today these tasks are performed by librarians. To be successful in all these, digital services will be online, accessible through networks and responsive to the customers.

(f) *Impact on Image Search* : Pictures, graphics and photographs are important presentations of information. Images collected in libraries are now located by specifying some external parameters; for instance, satellite images can be located by naming the spacecraft, the observing instrument, the orbit number and the longitude. This type of information says little about the image content itself. Locating images instead by their content requires much knowledge and the supporting programs are likely to be the agenda for improvement for many years to come. Image based retrieval services can deliver substantial added value for users that access image data.

(v) Library Projects: A Few Examples : Digital library concept is not very old. It is since the last couple of decades that the idea of digital library has become the topic of discussion and research. Several projects are correctly underway in USA, Australia, Europe, New Zealand and Singapore. These libraries are : the British Library, the Library of Congress, Stanford Digital Library and some of the libraries such as University of Sydney Library. The state Library of New South Wales, the national Library of Australia and Monash University Library have taken up the collaborative projects for digital libraries.

In India, however, the concept of digital library is new. Initial steps towards building a true digital library have been initiated at some places like IITs, the IIM's, JRD Tata Memorial Library, Hindustan Lever Research Centre, National Institute of Mental Health & Neurosciences, Indira Gandhi Memorial Library etc. The major problem with these systems in India are that these are developed in isolation and no integration of these systems are being thought of.

The benefits of digital libraries are :

(a) Digitization actually fulfils the need for preservation and conservation.

(b) Value addition through new or improved searching aids, text retrieval and links to other items, through appropriate use of metadata.

(c) Improved customer service through virtually instant search and retrieval of documents.

(d) More efficient collaboration with other institutions.

(e) Sharing the information internally within the organization or over World Wide Web.

(f) Fast execution of document delivery and inter library loans.

There are number of organizations such as SUN, IBM, HP, WIPRO, which provide total solution for digitization of library resources therefore our main thrust is on the selection of Library Resources for the digitization keeping in view of the targeted users.

2.17. Electronic Journals

Electronic journals are a fast developing feature of electronic publishing. In the 1960s, many scientists believed that journal articles were written largely to satisfy tenure requirements and that publications were overpriced, too slow, unread, proliferating explosively and a huge waste of paper. Meanwhile, hundreds of studies on the channels of scientific communication found that authors write for many reasons, that growth in the literature is strongly correlated with the number of scientists, and that articles are generally well read depending on the size of the audience, and considered extremely valuable inside and outside the academic community.

Many thought that electronic journals would resolve the flaws in the system. All the main components for an electronic-journal system existed by 1970 — authors could input digital text through magnetic tapes or cards; publishers used computerised photocomposition or computer-driven typesetting; libraries were beginning to automate; bibliographical databases were being searched online; scientists had computers and modems; and the foundations of the Internet had been established.

Yet a 1978 analysis by King Research forecast that it would be 20 years before electronic journals became commonplace, because acceptance of the necessary electronic processes would develop unevenly and slowly, as would their capabilities. In particular, standard codes for text input and better means of processing mathematical equations, chemical compounds and graphics were needed. The analysis predicted that the potential of electronic publishing would not be realized until all the components were fully in place and standardized.

These components continued to develop in the 1980s, and by the early 1990s, electronic journals finally emerged. Today, almost two-thirds of scientific journals are available both electronically and in print.

Electronic serials or journals may be defined very broadly as any journal, magazine, e'zine, webzine, newsletter or type of electronic serial publication which is available over the Internet. Within this broad definition, the titles can be electronically accessed using different technologies such as the World Wide

Web (WWW), gopher, ftp, telnet, E-mail or listserv. However, virtually all modern electronic journals are mostly available via the web. Several of the E-journals are also embedded within aggregators, such as Northern Light, EBSCO, Bell & Howell ProQuest, Information Access Company and others. There are web pages that provide a series of indexes, for e.g., title and Library of Congress Subject Heading, for facilitating easy access to different electronic serials.

The Library at the University of Glasgow provides its readers with the following definition:

Any journal that is available over the Internet can be called an 'electronic journal'. In some cases, print equivalents exist; in some cases, not. Some electronic journals or e-journals are freely available; others have charging mechanisms of different types. Some are issued by established publishers; others are produced from an individual academic's office. As with print journals, the quality and relevance of e-journals can vary considerably (University of Glasgow Library, www.lib.gla.ac.uk/Enquiries/faqwhat.html # E-Journal).

An electronic journal is also defined as a periodical — regular or irregular — and moderated unit made available in an electronic format, either on a static medium or via computer networks (K.rustard. http://www.rosa.nbr.no/ etids/e-tids.html). The same theme is expressed by Butler, who identified three essential characteristics of an electronic journal:

- It must publish original, scholarly research-based writings: the journal may publish other items, such as reviews, opinions and general information, but it is the original research component that sets it apart from other publications.
- Submissions to the electronic journal must be reviewed: UK-issue of peer review is central to the acceptance of electronic journals by the academic community.
- It must utilize electronic networks as the primary

distribution channel: at present, many electronic journals are either electronic versions of current print journals or offer a print version of their electronic publication. Todays, many journals are available only in electronic form only.

A more realistic definition of the present state of electronic dissemination of information in journal form is to describe an electronic journal as 'the concept of storing articles on, and enabling user access over, a computer network, or of distribution of articles over a network to subscribers'. While there will be structural changes to what we recognize today as a journal as a result of the electronic process, discussion lists and electronic conferences cannot yet be considered electronic journals if one considers the need to be referred.

(i) Advantages of E-Journals : The Internet has become a bonafide medium for academic information exchange and publishing. For example, in connection with its research assessment exercises, the Higher Education Funding Council for England (http://www.hefce.ac.uk) has agreed to treat referred journal articles published through electronic means on the same basis as those appearing in print journals. E-journals offer many advantages, the most obvious ones being:

- speed of access to the latest information, particularly relevant in the business and science sectors.
- ability to implement multimedia elements.
- quick searching.
- linking from and to other resources.
- security, i.e., e-journals can't be 'lost'.
- single user or location restrictions don't apply.
- availability of novel material.
- features such as virtual filing cabinets, eTOCs, etc.
- access to non-subscribed material.
- proactive response to issues raised in research papers - asynchronous/synchronous communication.

- ease of downloading an article to a personal computer for later use or printing which is easier than photocopying or scanning.

As opposed to the reader's perspective, the many advantages include :

- online submission.
- speedier reviewing process.
- wider dissemination of material increasing the visibility of the research.

Many groups publish E-Journals, from small organizations with a single publication to large publishing houses offering many titles. Some of the larger E- Journal publishers are: Academic Press, Blackwell Science, CRC Press, Elsevier, HighWire JSTOR Project. Muse, OCLC Electronic Journals Online and Springer Verlag. Many electronic journals are found in aggregations (e.g. EBSCOhost, Gale InfoTrac). These may be found by using Gold Rush (http://goldrush.coalliance.org), a system produced by the Colorado Alliance of Research Libraries that lists serials embedded within other aggregations or databases.

To get a sense of the truly breath taking number and range of subjects covered by electronic publications, one might wish to browse the "New Jour" site on the World Wide Web (http:// gort.ucsd.edu/ newjour/NcwJourWel.html). Besides, there is another site for Online Electronic Free Journals, (http:// www.geocities.com/ghosh_tbd/jnl.html). Here near about 624 online electronic journals are identified and linked in the above mentioned URL. Out of 624 journals 351 journals are available in full text.

(ii) Free Journal Resources on the Web : The web is a host to loads of free journals. A few of these links are given here;

Scholarly Electronic Journals

[http://www.library.msu.ac.th/arec/e-journal/nid.html)

This is a list of scholarly electronic journals available FREE on the Internet selected as per subjects, The Academic Resource Center Mahasarakham University, Thailand has compiled this list. Journals can be selected, subject wise or by alphabetically.

University of Houston Library: Scholarly E-journals

(http://info.lib.uh.edu/wj/webjour.htm)

The University of Houston Library maintains a directory with links to online scholarly journals available free on the net. An alphabetical list is available of all journals included in this directory.

Free Medical Journals Site

(http://www.freemedicaljournals.com/)

The Free Medical Journals Site is dedicated to the promotion of free access to medical journals over the Internet. It is created basically to promote the popularity of free journals on the web. The site also includes links to Medical Journals, whose archives are available free, trail period journals. It mentions that within the next coming few years, the most important medical journals will be available online, free and in full-text, else they will loose their popularity.

SocioSite: Electronic Journals and Magazines

(http://www.psew.uva.nl/sociosite/Journals.html)

It is an annotated collection of electronic journals and magazines in social science from around the world. Electronic journals are listed country-wise, thematically and contains lots of reference links also.

Serials in Cyberspace: Collections, Resources & Services

(http://www.uvm.edu/~bmaclenn/)

It is a good reference source for E-journals and related topics.

World Wide Web Resources in Economics

(http://www.helsinki.ti/WebEc/journals.html/)

WebEc is an effort to categorize free information in economics on the World Wide Web. It contains a list of journals available in Economics.

All Academic

(http://www.allacademic.com/)

All Academic is an academic index, which is designed to provide scholar's and researchers with useful on-line source information about scholarly works. All Academic catalogues free publications only. Links to commercial and fee based scholarly publications are not included in this database. Users can browse journals and magazines alphabetically by title within specified academic disciplines.

Scholarly Electronic Journals

(http://netjunk.com/users/sej/maiy.htm)

It gives an alphabetical list of scholarly electronic journals arranged alphabetically and also subject wise. This list also includes journals, which don't fall under the free journals category.

Psychology Journals

(http://www.clas.ufl.edu/users/gthursby/psi/journals.htm)

It is a virtual library of all Psychology journals, both print and electronic.

Health Science E-journals

(http://www.ispub.com/ejournals.htm)

Internet Scientific Publications LLC is an international medical publishing house on the web. It publishes about forty (40), e-journals, which are available free on the web.

(iii) How do you use e-journals? : Pedley outlined a series of scenarios where an e-journal might be encountered:

1. The publisher sends out a PDF file for use with Adobe's Acrobat reader, containing the complete issue.

2. The publisher sends out an e-mail stating that a new issue is available on their website.
3. The publisher announces by e-mail that a new article or section has been added to the website
4. The website is only a supplement to the hard copy as it contains merely a selection of articles, or ones from previous issues.
5. Articles are made available via an intermediary agent such as Sweats or Ingenta.

To add to the above we also have the landscape of linking, where the user follows a link from an abstracting and indexing database, or perhaps a chapter bibliography in an e-book, to the full text of an article. The changes in scholarly communication are beginning to have an impact on all aspects of the information chain, resulting in new 'locations' for e-journals. There is an increasing interest in both subject and institutional repositories, as well as the growth of open access journal titles. More and more the e-journal article is being embedded into the learning and teaching process and delivered directly at the point of need to the user. Direct links from VLEs (Virtual Learning Environments) and resource lists to the full text is, in a way, disengaging the article from the auspices of the journal envelope. Once again, several points of interest arise from this brief list. Although PDF is by no means the only way e-journals are published it is becoming the norm, and the effects might have on the local institution's resources. The second and third points indicate something that is very apparent in e-journals, namely the idea that a journal can now be bought or viewed article by article, whereas in the print world the purchaser had to buy and retrieve the entire issue. Another point in the list is of interest as it highlights the role of third-party agents arising in the electronic world as the data are often separated from the supplier.

Yet we should not lose sight of the fact that in the vast majority of cases people will access the e-journal via a standard web browser, which may or may not launch the Acrobat reader. At present, in contrast to e-books, there are no such things as e-journal-specific readers, or any utilization of the hand-held device for distributing articles. That is not to say that it will never happen, and there are signs that magazines and newspapers are interested in taking their experiments with WAP technology, i.e., the Wireless Application Protocol aimed at the mobile phone market, further by looking to deliver to the individual (via a PDA, for example).

(iv) Impact of Electronic Journals on Library Functions

(a) *Advantages* : These are –

- Economy in storage (shelf space).
- Economy in maintenance (replacement, wear; and tear).
- Reduced circulation activity.
- Reduced photocopying activity.
- Practically we can do away with all the traditional library activities.
- Progress towards creation of a virtual library.

(b) *Implications* : Electronic journals create both legal and economic problems for libraries and publishers. The legal issues relate to copyright, ownership of information and regulations about availability and use. The economic issues relate to the financing of access to information, as opposed to acquisition of material.

(c) *Threats* : Researchers can potentially access information resources from anywhere in the world without even entering the library. This could be devastating for the library in its role as an information provider unless it actively takes part in the changing reality. Scientific communication can take place in networks outside the library and the increased offerings of databases can make the library a small and marginal part of the whole network.

Perryman gives some guidelines on how libraries can work to prevent this from happening:

- Strengthen and expand the traditional library values of cooperation and resource sharing.
- Offer flexible, multifacted services.
- Provide access to new and developing formats.
- Foster new approaches to information access.
- Tap into the developing telecommunications infrastructure.
- Pursue and develop new funding sources.
- Develop a common vision of the future of information technology.

Print versions of scientific journals will soon be history at Denmark's National Technical Knowledge Centre and Library in Lyngby. It has decided to phase out print altogether, and deliver journals direct to staff desktops via the World Wide Web.

In itself this move, expected to be increasingly followed by universities in the developed world, is a revolution. But it is only one of the profound changes in scholarly publishing that are just around the corner. The very existence of research libraries as we know them is in doubt. Their traditional roles are being eroded on every front. Publishers and new electronic services are bypassing libraries and delivering sophisticated information products direct to users. Libraries increasingly act merely as brokers to squeeze better deals from publishers.

2.18. E-Books

An electronic book is the electronic content that is transmitted and or displayed on a device or system to be read by the viewer similar in experience to reading a physical book. An e-book is written in machine-readable form down loaded to a PC or digital assistant or place on a reader design for that purpose. It may be referred to a document of written record or electronic text. It can be delivered by down loading or as e-mail file attachment.

Generally, though, e-books refer to products that appear as single titles, and in terms of subject matter these are usually as fiction or textbooks. The new *Concise Oxford English Dictionary* defines an e-book as: 'an electronic version of a printed book which can be read on a personal computer or handheld device designed specifically for this purpose'. According to Ormes: 'the term e-book is used specifically to describe a text which requires the use of e-book software or hardware to read'.

In "its simplest level, an e-book is a book just like any other book," says Phyllis Rossiter Modeland, former editor of the e-book reader electronic magazine, *The Running River Reader*. It has 'cover' art, a title page, an ISBN, a copyright notice, an editor and publisher for whom it was a labour of love—and an author who wrote it because she or he had to.

At present the use of e-books is relatively low, yet it is often predicted that this will change. However, in recent years industry forecasts have varied widely, some forecasters predicted that one third of college textbooks will be sold electronically in 2004. E-books have become far more established in the US than in the UK but this is probably due to the fact that early players were US-based and thus targeting their products and services to the North American market.

The market for e-books is still new, but at the same time seems to be in constant change. In August 2000 Microsoft released their version of an e-book reader, and in the same month we witnessed one of the many corporate takeovers when Adobe acquired Glassbook. Only a few weeks later Barnes and Noble bought out Fatbrain and Mighty Words which shut down in January 2002, and then in November RCA bought up Rocketbook. To get an idea of the complexity of this one need only take a look at the e-book industry map (www.ebookmap.net) with an astonishing list of publishers, suppliers, intermediaries, production agencies, and so on. We should not always restrict ourselves to commercially available e-books. It is notable that one of the early adopters of the electronic resource was the textual community, who started to establish, quite early on, free e-text archives and repositories. Therefore it is not surprising that there is a wealth of free e-texts and e-books available on the internet.

(i) Benefits of E-books : The following benefits of e-books may be observed :

- E-Books can store multiple books for the weight and space of one print book. Storing e-books on computer drives or diskettes and CD-ROMs takes up much less shelf space than print books.
- Dedicated handheld reading devices weigh in starting at 17 ounces and can store up to twenty books—more if the memory is upgraded.
- E-Books can update and download documents immediately. E-Books can contain the latest, most current information.
- E-Books can be enhanced with live hyperlinks, sound, animation and simulation capabilities.
- A simple font size change will turn e-book into a large print edition.
- With e-book reading software allows bookmarks, annotations and search through the e-book.
- Desktop computer users can read an e-book anytime when they're at the computer.
- E-Books can be moved anywhere using portable computer, PDA (personal digital assistant) or e-book reading device.
- Business and recreational travelers can load e-books on their portable computers without adding weight or taking up space in their luggage.
- Storage capabilities and the ability to update and download documents immediately make e-book reading devices appealing to businesses, government personnel, colleges, universities and schools. Many professionals such as

doctors, lawyers and pharmacists are already using e-books and e-book reading devices.

- Schools, colleges and universities hope to use e-books to get students the most current textbooks. Schools and libraries are piloting programs using e-book reading devices and portable and desktop computers, so that students can access e-textbooks and digital libraries.
- For physically challenged or sight-impaired, e-books can fill special reading needs. A simple font size change will turn e-book into a large print edition, and e-books are less tiring on the hands. Some file formats are compatible with screen reading technology. People with special reading needs have more books and magazines available to them than ever before with e-books.
- Improved on-screen reading quality, portability, storage capabilities, more current content and speedy deliveries are just a few benefits of the e-books.

We can read the following on e-books :

- Full length novels and texts
- Annotated editions
- Short fiction and nonfiction
- Magazines
- Articles
- News and current events
- Old favourites and current releases from best-selling and well-known authors. Fresh, innovative fiction and nonfiction from up coming authors, Classics by authors and popular series of books such as:

Jane Austen	The Survivalist Series
Louisa May Alcott	Agile Manager Series
Mark Twain	Star Trek Series

(ii) Limitations of E-book : Though the e-book has great potential and bright future to attract the users, it also have some limitations.

(a) To read an e-book is not comfortable in comparison with printed book. It cannot be read in leisure time lying on bed or sofa. It can't be read in open air. Continuous reading of an e-book sitting in front of computer system affects the eyes and nerves.

(b) Reading an e-book while traveling in train or bus is not so easy and cheaper in comparison with printed books. Laptop or Palm top with battery system is urgently necessary to read an e-book, which is more costly than a book.

(c) In addition to cost, the user has to carry the machine which is difficult and a matter of risk like break / damage or theft.

(d) Students, faculties and research scholars those are staying in campus may avail the computer facility during working hours but if any student stays out side campus has to purchase computer and Internet connectivity for reading online e-books. Common students cannot afford such financial burden. Only in campus students, faculties and research scholars of IIT's, IISc and NIT's / REC's can avail this facilities. In India there are plenty of private Technical & Engineering Colleges who can't afford even in campus facilities.

(e) E-book is costlier than printed book. The expenditure of an e-book is sum total cost of e-book plus access charges plus internet connectivity and usage charges which is costier than that of a printed book.

(f) In addition to Indian Scenario the survey of Task Force of the University of California 2001 found that most institutions are still in trial stage with e-books and e-book market viable are not quite in pace.

(iii) How do you use an e-book? : One of the main considerations for the person charged with building a collection of electronic resources is how the user will access any purchased resource, and with e-books this is more complicated than usual. Most commonly there are five ways that people use e-books:

- online via the web;
- by downloading to a standard PC (or Mac) and reading them via their operating systems;
- by downloading them and reading them on generic PDAs (personal digital assistants, or handheld computers);
- by downloading them and reading them on specific devices used for e-books;
- by printing them to paper, i.e., utilizing POD (print on demand).

(a) *Via the web* : At present the reading of e-books via a standard web browser seems to be in keeping with the general moves for online delivery. Web interface allows the user to read the text, of course, but it also opens up possibilities of linking to other resources, cross-text searching, utilization of dictionaries and so on. NetLibrary, which was acquired by OCLC, and Books 24 x 7 are two examples of companies that offer web access to e-books.

(b) *Downloading to a PC (or Mac)* : This involves the reader downloading the e-book from an internet e-book service (e.g. Amazon), and interacting with it via a dedicated piece of software. Examples of such applications are the 'readers' produced by Microsoft and Adobe. The latter's was formerly known as Glassbook. Market research indicates that this method of accessing e-books is potentially as large as using the web, with estimated figures placing current ownership of PCs in the US alone at 200 million, with 80% of those already using Adobe's Acrobat reader. At present in India, Acrobat reader is generally used to read e-books.

(c) *Downloading to hand-held readers* : Palm Pilots and PDAs provide another means of accessing e-books. Here we can see utilization of an established piece of hardware originally intended for note-taking and calendars. These hand-held machines allow users to read e-books as long as they have a specific piece of software installed, for e.g., Microsoft's Reader. The distinction between these devices and e-book readers, however, is not always so clear cut. The Franklin eBookMan started life as an e-book reader, but had functions that would usually be associated with a generic PDA. Overall this is a promising area, though nowhere near as large as the potential offered by web access. However, a report on the use of PDAs in the UK academic market noted that it was unlikely that UK students would utilize them for study purposes. It was mooted, though, that developments in mobile phone technology could expedite the take up of e-books in the learning process.

(d) *Downloading to e-book-specific devices* : On the market at present are specific pieces of hardware that arc designed solely for reading e-books. The largest company involved in this was Gemstar, which bought up the ground-breaking Rocketbook reader series. However in July 2003 GemStar announced that they would no longer be selling devices or operating in the e-book market (www.gemstar-ebook. com/ cgi-bin/WebObjects/eBookstore.woa/wo/3.0.5.0.23.1.0.5). The fate of Gemstar does emphasize the question of why anyone would choose to go down this singular hardware route when the options above allow for much wider use. The answer may lie in the advantages offered by e-book-specific devices:

- they have larger screens and better interfaces
- they are light and portable
- they provide good storage; for e.g., up to 350 titles at a time, with an extensive battery life approaching 40 hours before they need recharging.
- they provide additional functions not offered by the desktop readers noted above.

However, it has to be said that many observers remain to be convinced by these arguments and much of the above applies to the new range of tablet PCs. The long-term future for such devices is very much in question. However, products such as the *e-book* reader which also allows the user the additional functionality of playing MP3 files and reading XML e-books; and the goReader, which is a larger, tablet-sized device aimed at the textbook market, showed promising signs for future developments.

(e) *Print on demand* : Although the e-book is a digital resource, some readers will still want print copies. Therefore many services also offer the user the option of selecting an e-book but having a paper copy sent to them, hence the term print on demand. Companies that specialize in this include InstBooks, ODMS, Sprout, and netLibrary.

(f) *Standards* : The file format for e-books varies, and the standards that are being adopted by publishers and how easy it is for these to be used, and migrated to or from, are of concern. Different types of file formats are available for reading the e-book. These different file formats require suitable software, which are as follow:

- *.DOC* files are read with Microsoft Word or WordPad.
- *.HTML* files are read with Internet Browser software, which is pre-installed on most computers and available as a free download.
- *.LIT* files are read with Microsoft Reader.
- *.OEB* is the Open eBook Standard format.
- *.PDF* files are read with Adobe's Acrobat Reader or the Glassbook Reader, both available as a free download.
- *.PRC* is Palm OS compatible format.
- *.RTF* is considered the "universal" file format because it works with any word processing program, PCs and

Macs. To read RTF files, we need Word Pad or a word processing software package.

- *.TXT* files are called "Plain" ASCII text. You need Windows or DOS to read them.
- *WinCE* files are for portable computers. It is used with Windows CE-based PDAs and Palm PCs.
- *.WPD* files are read with Corel's Word Perfect.

But the common one is the OeB ('Open e-book' — www.openebook.org/) which is based on XML, the Extensible Mark-Up Language, the next generation of SGML, or Standard Generalized Mark-Up Language; an attractive option to those worried about long-term use. This is the standard being used by Microsoft for their reader and .lit files, and netLibrary has recently adopted it.

(iv) E-Book Sellers :

Adobe eBook Store

(http: //bookstore.glassbook.com/store/default.asp)

It carries a large selection of PDF-based e-books delivered by download.

Amazon.com (http://www.amazon.com)

It carries downloadable e-books in their E-Book section and e-books on CD-ROM and diskette in the general book section.

BarnesandNoble.com (http://www.bn.com)

It carries downloadable e-books in their E-Book section, CD-ROM and diskette e-books available in the general book section.

Booklocker. com (http://www.booklocker.com)

Nonfiction and fiction e-books are available by download, e-mail attachment or on CD-ROM.

The BookShelf (http://www.txbookshelf.com)

CD-ROMs and diskettes are sold in their physical bookstore and from their web site.

CyberRead (http://www. cyberread. com)

Offers customers an easy to use bookstore with instant download digital books, forums, e-book club, public domain classics, and links for information on e-book news and technology,

e-Book-Studio (https://www.e-book-studio.com/index, shtml)

Readers will find an assortment e-books from Mystic-Ink authors, self-published authors, and authors associated with publishing partners of the Mystic-Ink Community. Available through digital delivery and a secure payment system.

M-Pro Bookstore (http://www.m-pro.demon.co.uk/)

Fiction and nonfiction e-books are available.

Palm Digital Media (http://www.peanutpress.com)

It is featuring a large number of Palm OS and Windows CE e-books from traditional and independent publishers.

Powells.com (http://www.powells. com)

This largest new and used bookstore, carries a large selection of Rocket Editions.

Word Wrangler (http://www. wordwrangler. com)

Fiction and nonfiction e-books are available.

(v) Free Online Information Sources for E-Books : Online information sources are referred to be free when access to the sources are not dependent on a subscription or membership in an organization or a publisher. Among the freely available online information sources, following are the important ones.

Electronic Books
(http://www.geocities.com/ghosh_tbd/inf3.html)

This section provides link of some organizations and universities who have taken initiatives to provide free access to thousands of online e-books free of charges.

Gutenberg Project on electronic books online
(http://www.promo.net/pg)

Thousands of e-books are available in this site free of charge. The site is having browsing facility by Author and by Title. It also provides advanced search facility by Author or by Title words. Author wise list of e-books is available at *http://www.promo.net/pg/ authors.zip* and Title wise list of e-books is available at *http://www.promo.net/pg/titles.zip* and current list of e-books is available as *GUTINDEXALL* at the FTP site at the University of North Carolina *ftp://ibiblio.org/pub/docs/books/gutenberg/GUTINDEXALL.*

The Online Books Page

(http://digital.library.upenn.edu/books/)

The Online Books Page is a website that facilitates access to books which are freely readable over the Internet. This site include the different sections like Books Online, News, Features, Archives. The Online Books Page was founded and is edited, by John Mark Ockerbloom, who is a digital library planner and researcher at the University of Pennsylvania. The online books listed on this page have been authored, placed online, and hosted by a wide variety of individuals and groups throughout the world. The local index of this page includes more than 15,000 English works in various formats. All are free for personal, noncommercial use. Users can search:

- Listing by Author and Title
- Browse new listings
- Browse by Author
- Browse by Title
- Browse by Subject
- Browse Serial Archives

Banned Books Online

(http://digital.upenn.edu/books/banned-books.html)

This special exhibit of books have been the objects of censorship or censorship attempts. The books featured here ranging from *Ulysses* to *Little Red Riding Hood,* have been selected from the index of The Online Books Page.

University of Virginia's E-Book Library

(http://etext.lib.virginia.edu/ebooks/ebooklist.html)

In this site 1,600 e-books are publicly available online. It includes British and American fiction, major authors, children's literature, the Bible, Shakespeare, American history, African-American documents and much more.

2.19. Search Engines

A search engine is a collection of software programs that collect information from the Web, index it and put it in a database so it can be searched. Search Engine is automated keyword searching tools, which use piece of software, usually known as a 'spider' or 'crawler' to gather the information from web and other servers and generate indexes. Search engine crawl the networks continuously to update their databases. It usually indexes the full-text of web page, meta data and holds lot of information in the databases. They are quite comprehensive and freely available but not complete. The key difference between subject gateways and the popular automated large-scale Web indexing systems such as AltaVista is the quality of the results, which the end-user receives. This is dependent on the nature of the cataloguing process.

Web search leader Google Inc. unveiled Google Scholar, a new search product aimed at helping users search scholarly literature such as technical reports, theses and abstracts. Google Scholar, at http:// scholar.google.com, searches a specific subset of Google's index and covers a wide range of fields, from medicine and physics to economics and computer science. Yahoo is another popular search engine.

2.20. Gateways

Moffat describes the establishment of the gateways as "a process of identification, filtering description, classification and indexing before they are added to databases which is freely available via World Wide Web (WWW). It has

- an online service that provides links to numerous other sites or documents on the Internet.
- selection of resources in an intellectual process according to published quality and scope criteria, which excludes e.g. selection according to automatically measured popularity.
- intellectually produced content descriptions, in the spectrum between short annotation and review. This excludes automatically extracted so-called summaries. A good but not necessary criterion is the existence of intellectually assigned keywords or controlled terms.
- intellectually constructed browsing structure/classification. This excludes completely unstructured lists of links.
- at least partly, manually generated bibliographic metadata for the individual resources.

So these are the internet search tools to help people to find resources on the internet, e.g electronic journals, software, data sets, e-books, mailing lists or discussion groups, articles or papers or reports, bibliographies, bibliographical databases, organizational home pages, educational materials, news, resource guides and more.

Gateways offer linked collection of internet resources via a database of resource description. This can be:

- Browsed - according to broad classification
- Searched - through index
- Quality controlled - due to selection

Gateways are useful because of :

- Innovative ways of providing information and services such as electronic resources, course specific, and library help pages and document delivery.
- Complex library searches due to the cross functions and links between the online catalogue, journal aggregated

databases, electronic resources etc.

- The need to identify and present high quality free information resources on the web and distinguish those from library licensed material.
- The increasing expectations of users for interfaces to lead directly, without undue hunting, to the information or service they need.

Many library web sites get congested with ample content, general objectives and duplication of services. It is no longer simple and clears how to do research or projects with a tool that provides gateways for getting information. There are number of steps that a library researcher must perform to successfully get information. Thus Gateways are needed to improve the effectiveness of Internet searching and serve as a source of information in specific areas and saves the time of the users.

2.21. Subject Gateway

The subject gateways emerged in response to the challenge of resource discovery in a fast developing internet environment in the early and mid 1990's. Due to the emergence of the network information retrieval systems (Gopher, WWW, Archive, netfirst, etc.) and access protocols (ftp, gopher, telnet, http, etc.) innovative information technologies and services emerge.

A subject gateway, in the context of network-based resource access, can be defined as some facility that allows easier access to network-based resources in a defined subject area. The simplest types of subject gateways are sets of web pages containing lists of links to resources. Subject gateways are online services and sites that provide searchable and browseable catalogues of Internal based resources. Subject gateways will typically focus on a related set of academic subject areas viz. SOSIG, EEVL, etc.

According to Dompsey L and others the "Subject gateways are internet services which supports systematic resource discovery. They provide links to resources (documents, objects, sites or services) predominantly accessible via the internet. The service is based on resource description. Browsing access to the resource via subject structure is an important feature."

Subject gateways are also known as : Subject-based information gateways (SBIGs); Subject based gateways; Subject index gateways; Virtual libraries; Clearinghouse; Subject trees; Pathfinders; Quality : controlled subject gateways etc.

Most subject gateways allow the end-user to either search or browse the database of resource descriptions. For example, the SOSIG gateway consists of a browsable multi-level menu of sub-areas and resources, as well as a WAIS-based search mechanism. In addition, most gateways allow the user the options of case sensitive searching and stemming, where resource descriptions containing variations of a term are located. SOSIG incorporates a thesaurus containing social science terminology. This gives users the option of generating alternative terms/ keywords with which to search the resource catalogue SOSIG also allows users to search on resources that are located in distinct geographic areas, such as in the whole world, just in Europe or in the UK.

(i) Different between Search Engines and Subject Gateways

Search Engines	*Subject Gateways*
General resource is available.	It is a gathering place of discipline specific resources.
It totally depends on the powerfulness of the elected search-engines algorithms.	High level of human input is there as the e-resources must meet a number, of criteria applied by a librarian or academic, who ensures that only high quality, relevant resources are included in the database.
The results can be overwhelming, unmanageable. and full of irrelevant references and are often too prolific to meet user needs.	The results are specific, precise and linked to relevant documents.

Records are created by an automatic process and typically consist of mixture of metadata offered by the author of the page (if this is available) and text picked up from the page itself.	Records are created by a cataloguer, which is designed to highlight the main feature of resource in an easily readable, concise manner.
Entries are displayed more as "raw-data".	Entries are described in a more "human- readable fashion"

(ii) Why Libraries should go for Subject Gateways ? Libraries are the most suitable institution to undertaken this work due to the following reasons :

- The natural metaphor;
- Browsing, reference desk;
- Expertise in relevant area;
- Classification, acquisition, keyword;
- Information, seeking behaviour;
- Guiding and helping users;

The benefits of Gateways for Libraries and Users are :

- Leading the way into the information age.
- Communicating with non-nerds.
- Access to huge-high quality collection.
- Integrate into existing structures on the Internet.
- Diverse resource brought together.
- Research, learning, leisure, enrichment - all brought together.
- Someone to ask - what's where?
- What's good?

(iii) Key Initiatives for building tools and standards in Subject Gateways:

(a) *ROADS (Resource Organisation and Discovery in subject-based Services)* : It is being funded by the JISC (Joint Information System Committee) through e-lib programme. It is an open source set of software toolkit, which enable the set up and maintenance of web-based subject gateways. A ROAD based information gateways is based on a database that contains information about internet resources. The records in the database contain information such as description and keywords. The user is given access to this information while either browsing or searching the database. This is particularly important for geographically distant resources that might require some time and effort to access. The software includes the database technology, required to set up a gateways. For downloading the, free online software visit its site URL: http://www.ilrt.bris.ac.uk/road

(b) *DESIRE (Development of European Service for Information on Research and Education)* : This is one of the largest projects funded by the Telematics for Research Sector of the Fourth Framework Programme funded by the European Union. In particular, DESIRE intends to provide:

- Tools for indexing and cataloguing information servers.
- Tools for management and maintenance of information servers.
- Demonstration and evaluation of tools and techniques for information catching and secure access to information servers.
- Background information for developers of networked information systems.
- Training materials.

Some of the important subject gateways are as follows:

- LibrarySpot.com: (http://www.libraryspot.com/)
- Librarians' Index to the Internet (LII) (http://lii.org/)
- Argus Clearing House (http://www.clearinghouse.net/)
- Galaxy (http://galaxy.einet.net/)

- Direct Search (http://gwis2.circ.gwu.edu/~gprice/direct.htm)
- Vlib: The Virtual Library (http://www.vlib.org/)
- Academic Info (http://www.academicinfo.com/)
- BUBL (http://bubl.ac.uk/)
- BIOME (http://biome.ac.uk/)
- The Scout Report (http://scout.cs.wisc.edu/report/sr/current/)
- Livinglnternet.com (http://www.livinginternet.com/)
- Edinburgh Engineering Virtual Library (EEVL) (http://www.eevl.ac.uk)
- Social Science Information Gateway (SOSIG) (http://sosig.ac.uk/)
- Digital Librarian (http://www.digital-librarian.com/)
- QUEST.net (http://www.re-quest.net/)
- Internet Public Library (http://www.ipl.org/)
- BioMedNet (http;//www.bmn.com/).

2.22. Portal

A portal is "A network service that brings together content from diverse distributed resources using technologies such as cross searching, harvesting, and alerting and collates this into an amalgamated form for presentation via a web browser to the user. For users, a portal is a, possibly personalised, single point of access where searching can be carried out across one or more than one resource and the amalgamated results viewed. Information may also be presented via other means, for example, alerting services and conference listings or links to e-prints and learning materials.

2.23. Aggregators

The aggregators may be a company who specializes in selling content from multiple sources-via the Web. Generally the aggregator's site is focused on a particular subject matter.

Although aggregators are most common in the Scientific, Technical and Medical (STM) world, many are now popping up in other fields such as Libraries, Technology Management, Education and other areas. These are companies, which have come into being as part of the electronic services environment to offer libraries a range of bibliographic and full-text services through a common search interface. Libraries have placed great faith in aggregators such as Ebsco, Ovid Technologies, Ingenta etc. because of their proven ability to package and present services in a reasonably transparent fashion to end users. The role of such aggregators, however, has been challenged over the past couple of years by the large commercial publishers who, for the time being, deny the aggregators access to valuable information content. This has resulted in libraries to have caution before they get on to access the journals through aggregator products.

There are, however, significant opportunities for content providers and aggregators to make strategic alliances, where both parties can benefit without eroding each other's market. From the customer viewpoint such strategic alliances are highly desirable as it works out economical. The interfaces and access which aggregators provide to libraries over a range of bibliographic and abstracting services which are highly valued by customers. The value - added component from the publisher viewpoint is that the customer can be directed in a transparent way to the content service whenever a citation to a journal in that content service is picked up through the bibliographic search on the aggregator platform. Such 'arms-length' arrangements are already a developing feature in the evolution of the market place.

The larger subscription agents developed services to address these issues, offering a broad range of functions and benefits, including:

- Single interfaces and search engines for accessing a range of titles from multiple publishers;
- Keyword searching across all the titles offered in the

service, usually searching within the tables of contents and abstracts;

- Browsing the contents of selected or favourite journals, as new electronic issues become available;
- Simplified password administration, usually on the basis that one password, or a small number of passwords, allows access by all members of an institution to all titles in the agent's service;
- Library management functions, including the facility to input information on holdings of print titles;
- Regular data for libraries on the usage of the electronic journals;
- Services to alert end users to new tables of contents as well as more comprehensive SDI services.

To reiterate, resource sharing denotes a mode of library operation whereby all or part of the library functions are shared in common among several libraries. The basic functions may be classified as acquisitions, processing, storage, and delivery of service. There is no single system currently in operation in which all of these functions are shared, although networks which might become "full service", i.e., all functions to be shared, are coalescing in connection with several developing national systems. And the effectiveness of resource sharing depends on the availability of appropriate communications, technology, and delivery systems. It has become a truism to say that the problems associated with resource sharing have more to do with behaviour modification than with technology.

4

Library Networks : Effective Means of Resource Sharing

1. Introduction

Human networking for sharing of resources has been in operation since the ages when man understood the limitations of survival as an independent entity. The compulsions of interdependence have given birth to the norms for cooperation in different scenarios . So have they done in the case of libraries which had to fulfil the growing demands of their users and to satisfy the legitimate use of their resources. Human networking in libraries had to pave ways for automated networking as day after day controlling and disseminating information was becoming humanly impossible.

Over the last two decades the libraries have witnessed impact of information technology that has been effecting the structure of the services to a great extent. Moreover, the problems of space, standardization, professional development of the staff, challenges posed by new technologies, drastic cuts in the library budgets have aggravated problem of the present day librarianship. However, the solution to the problems of information explosion, ever changing needs of users, increasing amount required for subscription to same number of periodicals, shrinking library budget, and devaluation of rupee and its impact on the library acquisitions can best overcome upon certain level by the (a) Use of computer and communication networks for resource sharing

(b) Use of national and international databases through communications networks.

A library network usually consists of a formal agreement/ arrangement whereby materials, information and services provided by a variety of libraries and/or other organisations are made available to all potential users. Libraries may be at different places but agree to serve one another on the same basis as each serves its own clientele.

To Alphonse F. Trezza, a library network is "a formal organization among libraries for cooperation and sharing of resources, in which the group as a whole is organized into subgroups with the exception that most of the needs of a library will be satisfied within the subgroups of which it is a member."

Raynard C. Swank defines library networks as a "concept that includes the development of cooperative systems of libraries on geographical, subject, or other lines, each with some kind of centre that not only coordinates the internal activities of the system but also serves as the system's outlet to and inlet from the centres of other systems.

Susan Martin defines the library network as "a group of individuals or organizations that are interconnected. The linking must include a communications mechanism, and many networks exist for the express purpose of facilitating certain types of communication among their members. In the library world, institutions form networks primarily to achieve better sharing of resources - resources consisting of bibliographic information and of collections - and better service to patrons."

2. Essentials of Library Networking

It may be necessary to refer to some of the following basic essentials of resource sharing library network:

(i) Library networking is meant to promote and facilitate sharing of the resources available within a group of libraries in order to provide maximum information to users, to lower operational costs and also to make optimum use of resources.

(ii) In order to do so it is necessary to create bibliographic tools like union catalogues and union lists based on the resources available in the participating libraries and these tools have to be in turn used for resource sharing and reference purposes.

(iii) Rationalization of acquisitions needs to be undertaken.

(iv) Interlibrary loan services should grow and may be interlinked with the search of the union catalogues. Delivery of documents should be fast, either electronically, through fax or through courier or mail.

(v) The libraries selected to join a network should be willing partners, ready to buy hardware, etc. and should be willing to send professional staff for training. They should be willing to pool bibliographic records to the central host of the network besides adhering to other network obligations.

(vi) In-house functions like acquisition, cataloguing, classification, serials control, circulation, SDI, current awareness service, etc. should be undertaken by the individual libraries. The network software may or may not support these operations of the libraries in the beginning but eventually the network software should not only be able to create union catalogues or full text databases, etc. but also get integrated with the in-house operations.

(vii) The network should be able to recommend to participating libraries the type of hardware they need for their in-house functions and for networking purposes. Hardware should be selected considering the number of comes the participating libraries can generate within the next 3-5 years. The hardware at the central host will have to be upgraded regularly depending upon the speed with which participating libraries generate records and the network pools them into the central host.

(viii) All libraries should follow a standard MARC format, AACR-II, a standard thesaurus like Library of Congress Subject Headings (LCSH) etc. uniformly.

(ix) Electronic mail and INTERNET facilities should be available with the libraries and they should be able to access international databases, preferably individually or through the network host to begin with.

(x) Although efforts, should be made to have one classification scheme in all participating libraries but use of different class numbers should not become a hurdle as search requests are mostly by authors, titles, editors and subject descriptors.

3. Aims and Objectives

The earliest aim of networks was resource sharing - that is, the use of distant computing resources by means of the network, but the aims and objectives of a successful library network vary according to the changing scenario and varying priorities. The following objectives of resource sharing and networking of library systems may be observed generally :

(i) It increases the availability and accessibility of resources. For the purpose, clientele of each participating library should have access to resources available in all the libraries. Resources can be moved from one library to another manually or through modern means. This provides an easy access to and free flow of information. Resource sharing should result in an increase in the range and depth of services offered by the member libraries.

(ii) Resource sharing helps in building specialised collection and all participating libraries need not duplicate the procurement of similar material. This facilitates availability of larger collection and even the basic material required by the users can be obtained without much delay.

(iii) Resource sharing advocates that the reading material of one library should be made available to the clients of other libraries, thus exposing the reading materials to a wider group of users. Similarly, the services of a library can be exploited by the users of other libraries.

(iv) To promote co-operative activities like acquisition, exchange, storage, binding, training, reference and documentation services, inter-library loans, etc.

(v) To eliminate record duplication.

(vi) To prepare union catalogue.

(vii) To rationalise the collection development.

(viii) To obtain improved bibliographic control.

(ix) To enhance the efficacy of exchange agreements.

(x) To achieve a regular Document Delivery System.

(xi) To promote the exchange of information with other cooperative networks.

(xii) To create authority files.

(xiii) To extend service to a wider user community and to promote programme for increased use of library resources.

(xiv) To assist member libraries in selection, purchase, catalogue and processing of library materials.

(xv) To stimulate the improvement of library facilities and services.

(xvi) To co-operate in the development of library personnel.

(xvii) To provide, resources beyond the reach of individual libraries.

(xviii)To achieve economies in the use of resources, human and material.

(xix) To facilitate sharing of material among members of the group.

(xx) To provide cost effective information storage and maintenance.

(xxi) To enable the optimum utilization of existing library information system.

(xxii) To provide current awareness services with minimum delay.

(xxiii) To give access to information resources within the state and other states.

(xxiv) To evolve a state standard for information handling.

(xxv) Promotion of research, development and innovation in information technology.

(xxvi) Provision of document transmission facility.

These objectives should be achieved without harm to the missions of participating libraries, although their methods of operation invariably must be adjusted. Similarly, the goals are realisable only with some changes in the habits of users.

Using computer networking, a library network support all forms of communication between libraries, between libraries and their users, and between libraries and their suppliers. This includes:

(i) providing remote access to one's own Online Public Access Catalogue (OPAC) and enabling access to other remote OPACs;

(ii) access to commercial bibliographic record databases and interconnection between bibliographic record creation utilities;

(iii) support for inter-library loan services;

(iv) providing access to users to external information sources such as databases, electronic journals, news, etc;

(v) linking library issue systems for support of reciprocal borrowing arrangements between institutions;

(vi) use of electronic mail, news and mailing lists for informal or formal professional communication;

(vii) provision of local networked information services.

Information networking is concerned with end-user communication and access to networked information services not in any way mediated by the library. It is this information disseminating and gathering activity enabled solely by the presence of the network that is seen as a possible threat by some librarians and publishers. These activities may include:

(i) use of e-mail and other services such as news for interuser communication in the support of research or education;

(ii) access to information in the form of public databases, electronic journals, bulletin boards and mailing lists.

4. Different types of Networks

The networks can be of following types :

1. Private : Such networks are usually owned by some corporation or other entity that confines access and use of network services to its staff.

2. Cooperative : This refers to networks that are supported and managed by their users. BITNET is an example of this type.

3. Integrated Services Digital Network (ISDN) : The development of public data networks for digital communications led to the existence of different networks for different purposes. This resulted in the duplication of networks. To avoid this, interconnection of two or more compatible or incompatible networks to form an Internet is attempted. The main aim of ISDN is to build to a public network providing end-to-end digital connectivity which is capable of supporting a range of digital devices and service, both voice and non-voice, on the same basis. This allows users to send and receive data text and image from computer systems as well as offering an enhanced telephone service. This is achieved over a single ISDN connection, so that one network can be used for all applications, providing higher speeds of transmission.

But generally depending upon the distance covered in a network, the networks fall into following types:

- Local Area Network (LAN)
- Metropolitan Area Network (MAN)
- Wide Area Network (WAN)

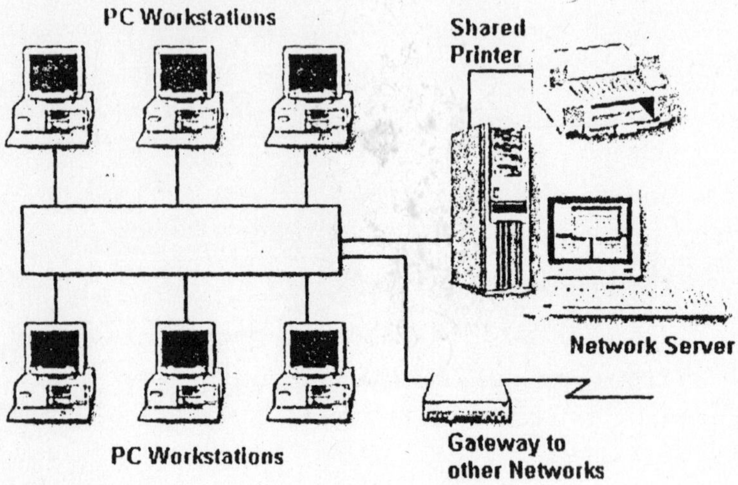

Local area Network (LAN)

(i) Local area Networks (LANs)

A Local Area Network connects a large number of different types of equipment, including computer terminals, fax, telex, CD-ROM players, etc. on a single site. The majority of LANs use packet switching technology and offer very high transmission speeds up to one hundred times faster than those available on public networks at present. Most of these are baseband that is they carry only digital computer data, but broadband LANs can carry video and voice signals as well data. The topology of LANs can vary greatly (i.e., linear, star, ring etc.) affecting efficiency, reliability and costs.

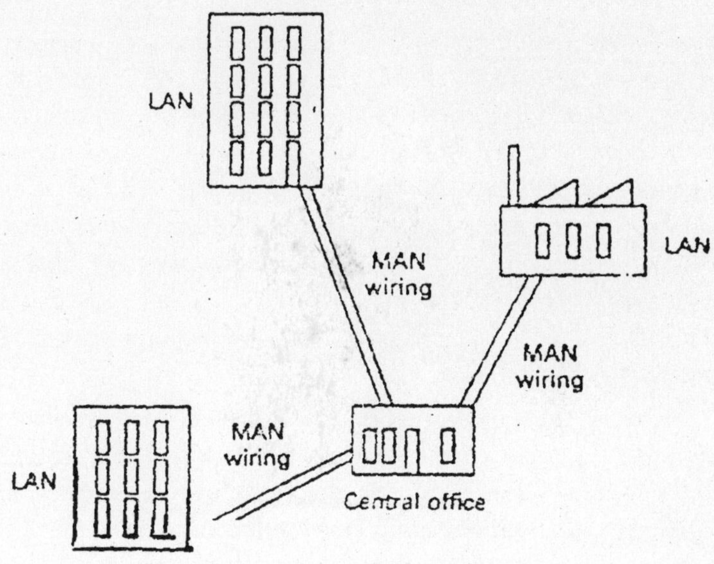

Relationship of LAN and MAN

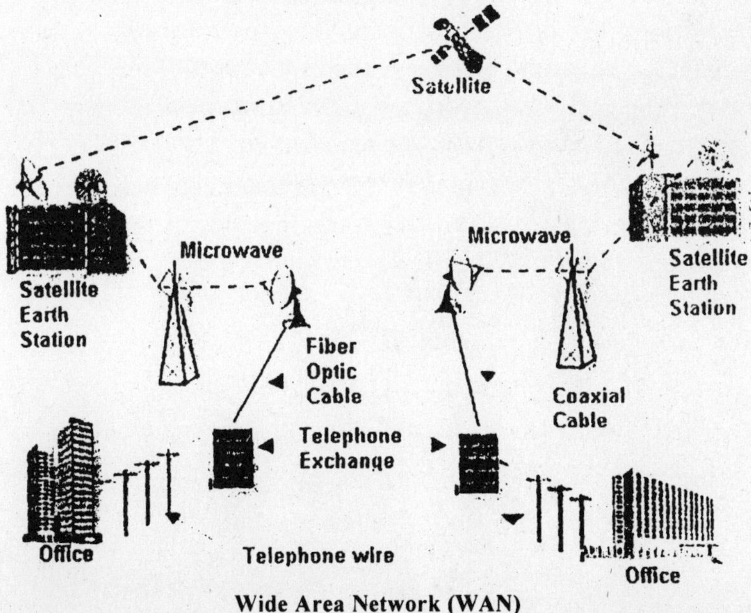

Wide Area Network (WAN)

(ii) Metropolitan Area Networks

These type of networks cover specific metropolitan area and provide to them all the services. As DELNET covers the network of Delhi Libraries and CALIBNET stands for Calcutta Library networks. The Metropolitan Area Network standards are sponsored by the IEEE, ANSI and the regional Bell Operating Companies. Although 802.6 was designed initially for a LAN to MAN support service, the telephone companies see it as a technology to provide for interconnecting LANs to its central office and even the interconnection of telephone switching facilities.

The MAN standard is organized around a topology and techniques called *dual queue/dual bus* (DQDB). This term means that the topology uses two buses. Each of these buses transmits traffic in one direction only. The implementation for MAN provides for transfer rates from 34 to 150 Mbit/s. The DQDB provides for two types of access. One access is called *pre-arbitrated services*, which guarantees a certain amount of "bandwidth" that is useful for isochronous services such as voice and video. The second service is called *queued arbitrated service* and it is based on demand and is designed to accommodate bursted services such as data transmission.

A MAN is designed with two unidirectional buses. Each bus in independent of the other in the transfer of traffic. The topology can be designed as an open configuration or a closed configuration.

(iii) Wide Area Network (WANs)

These are private networks linking equipment at several different sites and have much in common with conventional large scale data networks.

5. Network Topology Models

Prior to topology, it is better to understand what are the media through which computers are interconnected. In a network data are transferred or transmitted through different media or channels. The channels or media can be grouped into two main divisions. i.e., line and free space. In the line group, we have two metallic media; twisted pairs and coaxial cables and one optical medium- glass or optical fibres. In the free space category, we have radio propagation which includes broadcast (i.e., TV) and point to point (e.g., microwave signals).

(i) Twisted Pairs : The Twisted Pairs are the copper wire telephone lines. These are of low frequency, and support a limited bandwidth but can also be used for data communication at the lower speeds of 300bps. For higher speed or rates of data transfer, 4-wire leased lines may be used. The problems associate with this kind of transmission are; noise on the line, parity errors and so on. Twisted pairs are used for conventional voice telephone and telex services.

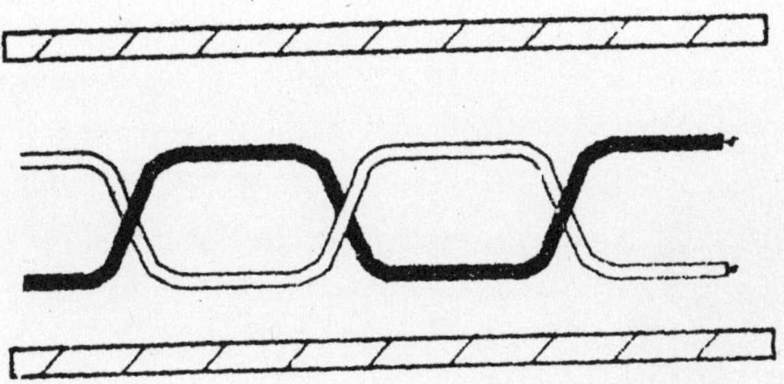

Twisted Pair Cable

(ii) Coáxial Cables : These are another metallic transmission media which can transmit data even at very high frequencies and hence they have much higher rate of data transmission than the twisted pair cables. A coaxial cable consists of copper wire surrounded by an insulation and over the insulation a cooper wire mesh is wrapped. This forms an electric shield around the main copper wire and reduces the electromagnetic interference.

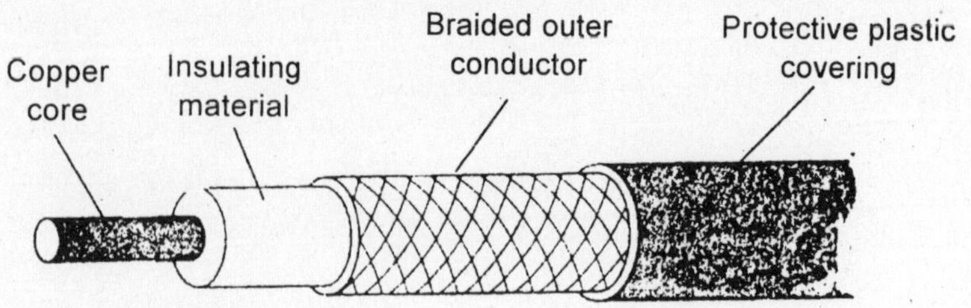

Coaxial Cable

The central cooper wire carries the data while the braided outer conductor prevents the electrical disturbances.

Further, Coaxial cables are of two types:

(a) **Baseband Coaxial Cable :** Baseband Coaxial cables are used for digital data transmission. Therefore, baseband cables are usually employed for LANs.

(b) **Broadband Coaxial Cable :** Broadband coaxial cables can work at frequencies as high as 450 MHz. Due to this, they can transit many simultaneous signals using different frequencies. The data carried in these cables is essentially analog in nature.

Data transmission through these coaxial cables is very fast and is of the order of gega bits per second. However broadband signals require analog amplifiers after certain distances to strengthen the signal.

(iii) Optical Fibres : These are superior over co-axial cables. These cables are very thin tubes made of glass plastic, mostly of silica. The diameter of a glass fiber is very small. Fiber optic transmit light pulses from the light source to the detector. Presence of light indicates a 1 bit and the absence of light indicates a 0 bit. Such a system is known as optical transmission system.

Transmission of data through fiber cables is very fast and most importantly is unaffected by electrical interferences. As compared to a copper telephone line, data transmission through a fiber optic cable is 75,600 times faster.

Fiber optic cables are much more expensive as compared to copper wires but another advantage they have is that they provide very high bandwidths.

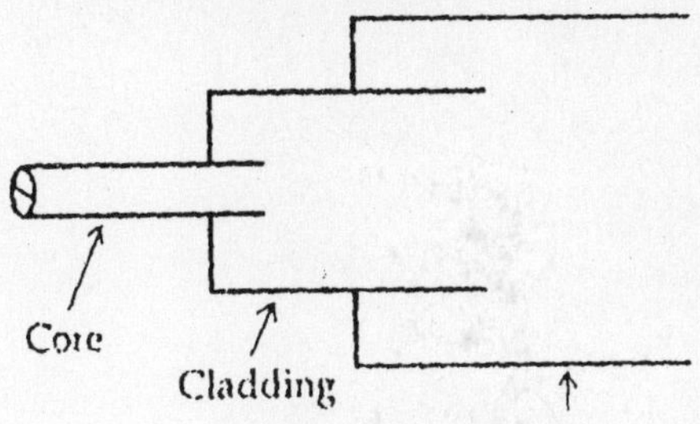

Optical Fibre

But, a repeater is required in fiber optic cables after a certain distances to boost the signal power.

A *topology* can be described by the way the workstations are physically connected to the network, or by the way the data appear to flow through the network – its logical topology.

It is generally agreed that there exists today several types of networks of which the following three types are popular and widely accepted-Star, Hierarchical and Distributed. The above three models are explained below with a 5 member hypothetical libraries in the network namely A, B, C, D and E.

The *star network* is one in which one member of network holds the majority of the resources while, at the same time, all other network members use the same resources. The figure illustrates such a network, with member A possessing virtually all the resources, while the other network members B, C, D & E use the resources.

In this type of network all the sites/participating libraries are linked to a central point/controller and exchange the data through it.

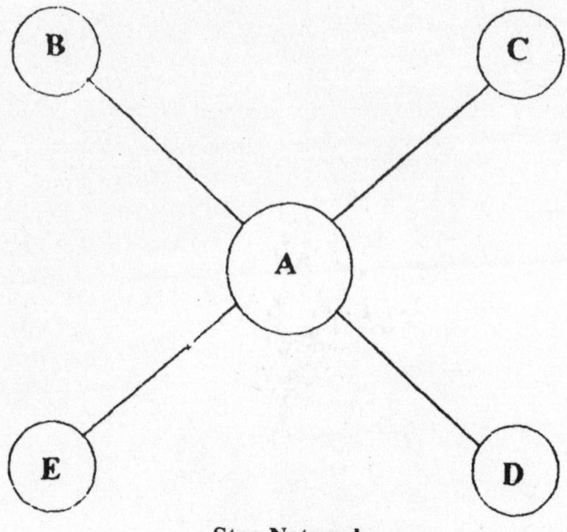

Star Network

The main advantages in this type of network are:

(i) It is the most common network and simple and easy to establish.

(ii) Better administrative control of the network.

(iii) Effective standardisation/uniformity in operations and services.

(iv) Optimum utilisation of expert services.

(v) Possibility for easy interlinking with other such networks.

(vi) Reduced communication costs.

The disadvantages in this type of network are:

(i) Increased cost for storage of data.

(ii) Failure of the central host collapses the whole system of network.

(iii) Since the database will be very large, search time and query processing time may be more.

The *hierarchical network*, on the other hand, is suitable for an environment where network members share resources locally, with needs request sent on to the next higher level in the system or, in effect, the next greater resource centre. This type of topology is illustrated in below figure.

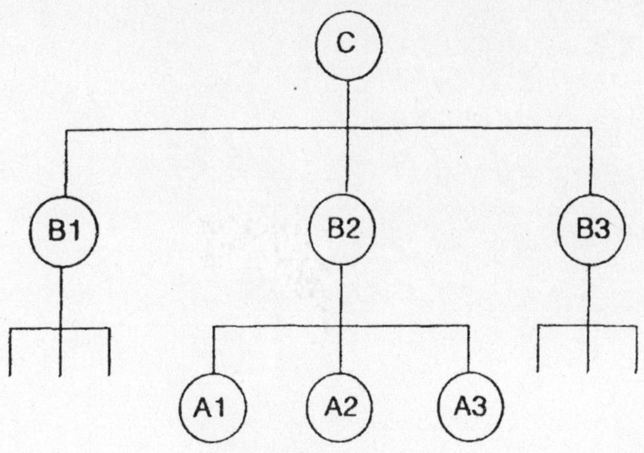

Hierarchical Network

From figure it can be seen that the network members A1, A2 and A3 are involved in resource sharing, finding that their resource needs can usually be met as a result of resource sharing activity among themselves. When necessary, these three members refer their requests to the next higher level or to the next greater resource centre-B2. If still an occasion arises where the requests of these members are not met, Unit C will then be contacted.

The main advantages in this type are:

(i) System failure at a given site will not effect the total system.

(ii) Since the databases are distributed, the size of the database will be less and results in faster processing of queries.

The disadvantages in this type are:

(i) Difficulty in maintaining the standardization of the data,

(ii) Lack of a centralised database.

(iii) Increased communication cost due to non-connecting of all the participants to every participant, administrative problems, etc.

In a *distributed or fully connected network*, members who have equal, but different, resources are connected with every other member. The foremost and basic rationale of the distributed network is the sharing of the different resources of the network members by each other. The distributed network configuration is given in figure below.

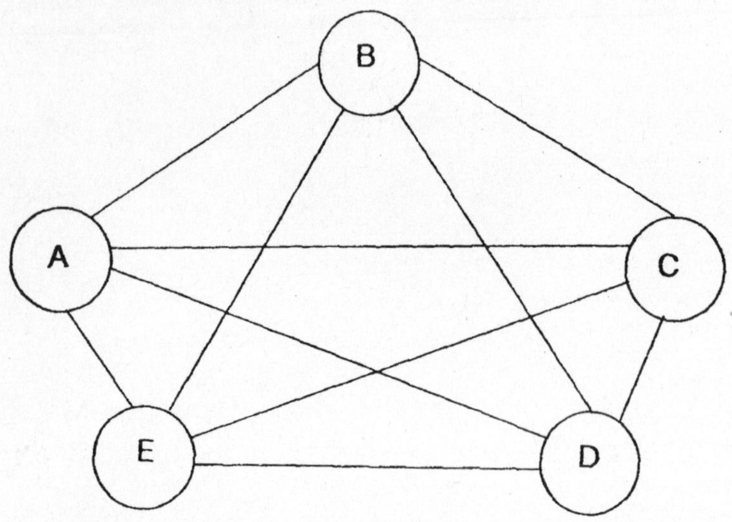

Distributed Network

The advantages in this type are:

(i) Failure at one node/site will not collapse the system.

(ii) Lesser cost for storage and maintenance of database.

(iii) Quick processing of queries.

(iv) Increased flexibility and reliability in the network.

The disadvantages are :

(i) Difficulty in maintaining the standardization of databases.

(ii) Requires more sophisticated software and communication infrastructure.

(iii) Administrative problems may arise among the participants/ sites due to non-existence of central controlling authority.

Whatever the topology may be but in the selection of a network topology, the following factors are to be considered carefully.

- *Installation cost* : Cost of hardware and software at various sites in the system and their interlinking.
- *Communication Cost* : Data transmission costs from one site to another site.
- *Reliability* : Possibility of failures in sites/links and the consequent effects on the network.
- *Flexibility* : Possibility in running the network even in the case of failures at one or two centres.
- *Geographical locations* : The distance between the sites and the communication costs.

Besides above, now-a-days, wireless networking is also emerging as a new concept in networking field.

Wireless Networking is one of the several ways to connect the computers. It creates a network by sending radio-frequency signals between your computers to share information It connects computers to computers networks without physical wire connections. A wireless network can provide network access to computers, databases, the Internet and OPACs both within and between buildings. The lack of a physical connection means that users are able to roam or work wherever they wish and still have access to the computer network. As a laptop with a wireless network card is completely portable throughout the library. A huge range of organizations in both the public and private sector enjoys the benefits of wireless networking.

The wireless networks send and receive data to and from laptops and handheld devices such as cell phones, PDAs and the cell phone/PDA hybrids like the Treo. The resulting nomadic computing environment allows for flexibility, unencumbered by the need to locate wall plugs and hardwired computers. Many libraries are using Wi- Fi to deliver library content to users. Wi-Fi or wireless fidelity refers to wireless local area networks. All wireless technologies use standard technology saddled over a wireless medium-airwaves.

The major advantages of the technology are that there is no cable between network access points. It requires a wireless access points, a wireless PC card, a wireless PC adaptor and a network connection for the access point. The important factor is that only the one access point needs a network connection, rather than each computer. If the wireless connection is over a WAN then the additional hardware would include antennas to boost the signal. The limiting factor of wireless networking is the distance versus bandwidth because the further the computer is from the access point the slower the speed of data rate transfer. Although the connection has the possibility of 11 Mbps it can be as 1 Mbps as the distance increases. However although 1Mbps would be very slow for an Ethernet network connection, it is still almost 30 times faster than 56K modem.

The significance of Wireless networking is:

(i) It provides access to multiple computers databases, the Internet and Library OPAC throughout the library;

(ii) It permits quick connectivity to the network and simplifies network Configuration;

(iii) Sharing of peripherals, files, multimedia resources and database are easier;

(iv) Using laptop computers library users can access electronic media and also be physically near whatever printed;

(v) Web OPAC is accessible from any corner of the campus through access point;

(vi) The transfer of information is normally faster resulting in better service and improved user satisfaction, location independent access for network administrators for easy on-site-trouble-shooting and supports;

(viii) The greatest significance is that while shifting the library building it can be shifted without affecting the Network System.

The advantage offered by wireless networks is the ability to provide computer network access in buildings not suitable for wired networks. But one may also face signal strength-concrete walls, foliage and trees etc. which can block the wireless radio signals, causing speeds of access to reduce or access to be lost entirely. Correct placement of access points may handle this problem.

6. Network Models

Library networks have grown with the main purpose of sharing resources so that the unnecessary wastage of limited finance with them can be avoided. In order to achieve this and the satisfaction of users, different types of networks came into existence. The following are some of the models at regional, national and international levels.

David Wood at the British Library Document Supply Centre ha developed several diagrammatic models which demonstrate the various cooperative situations.

Model 1 shows a very simple cooperative arrangement which is costly but can provide an effective international link as it provides only one main node per country. In this model each individual library (L) uses a national central library facility.

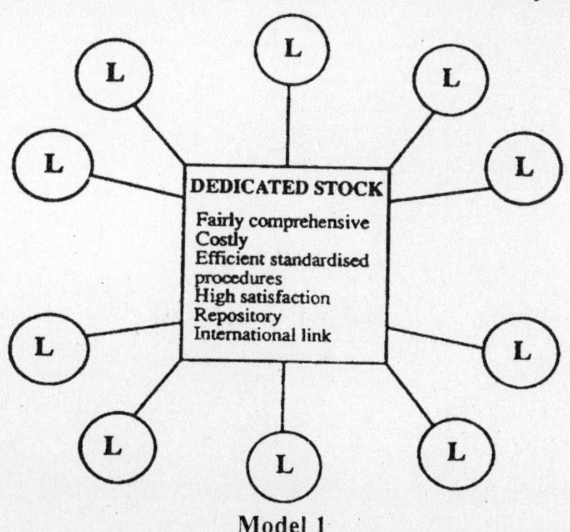

Model 1

Model 2 is similar to the first, with the central library also fulfilling a national service that is available to individual users as well as the libraries in the country. As the central library fulfils another function, it is less expensive. However, there could be a role conflict as the central library has to fulfil more that one function.

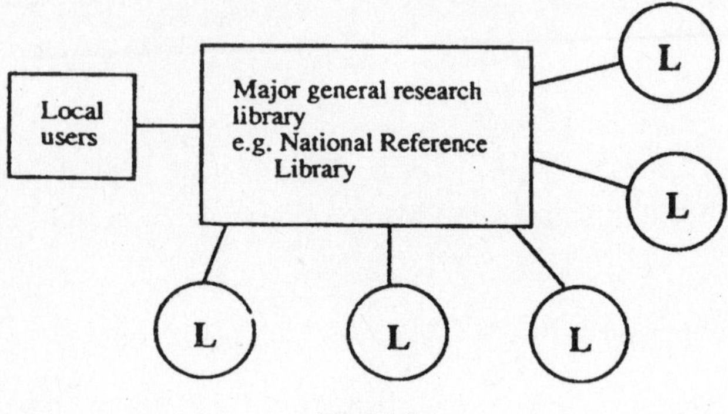

Model 2

A more complex plan - shown in Model 3 - is for several specialist libraries to provide services covering specific subject areas. Role conflict could again be a problem and there would be a need for coordination at the national level before coordination can be achieved internationally.

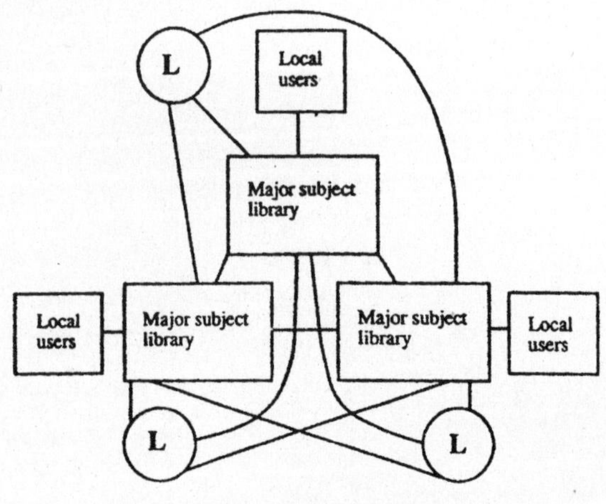

Model 3

International cooperation becomes more difficult in Model 4 where more libraries take the responsibility for collecting, conserving and acting as a repository for a relatively narrow subject area. Even more coordination is needed at the national level, users may be unsure about where to send requests and lines of access and communication become increasingly complicated. As a result, international cooperation is less easy to manage efficiently.

Unfortunately, according to Wood, the most frequently occurring arrangement is shown in Model 5. This model shows libraries functioning as individual entities, attempting to maintain discrete collections to serve groups of identified users. It is this unplanned model that is to be found in most countries.

It is based on the false assumptions that the libraries in the country will be able to collect and maintain the majority of the material needed nationally in spite of declining budgets, increased output of literature and shortage of space. It is also assumed that union catalogues will function effectively and that all libraries have efficient internal systems which will allow them to deal with ILL requests quickly. The problem with this system is that standards of service are difficult to agree and more difficult to achieve. Material in heavy or in low demand will frequently not be available and friction can develop between the users and lenders within the network. This is probably the most difficult national model for incorporation into an international network. As there is little or no national coordination, the problem of bringing individual libraries into a functioning national network is difficult. It is virtually impossible at a regional or international level.

Discussions on UAP and the establishment of a workable international cooperative framework have developed a model which combines the national network arrangements of Models 2, 3 and 5.

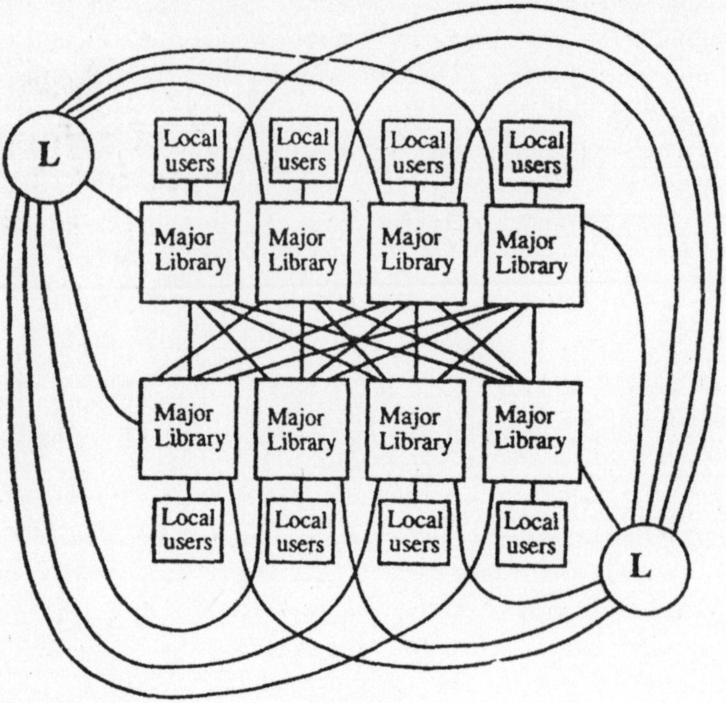

Model 4

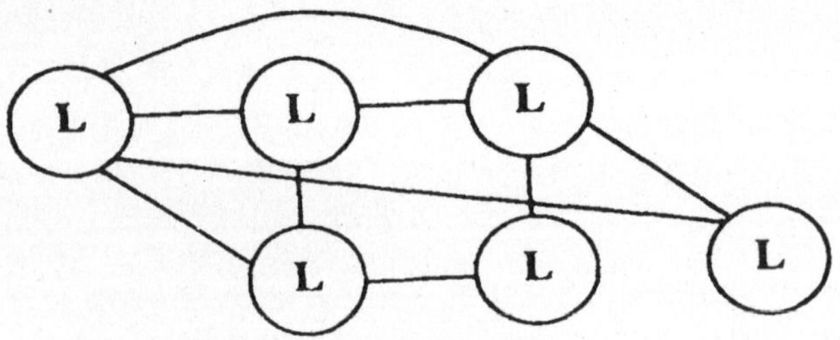

Model 5

In this structure (Model 6), countries with a single central library facility (A/B) and the dependant libraries (L) are shown in the left hand segment of the diagram. Countries with several specialized national libraries (C) are shown in the right hand segment, with the more common institutional 'loose' assembly of libraries occupying the bottom segment. This model also shows the communication links from single national libraries and specialist libraries going across national and regional boundaries to each other and to individual libraries in the network.

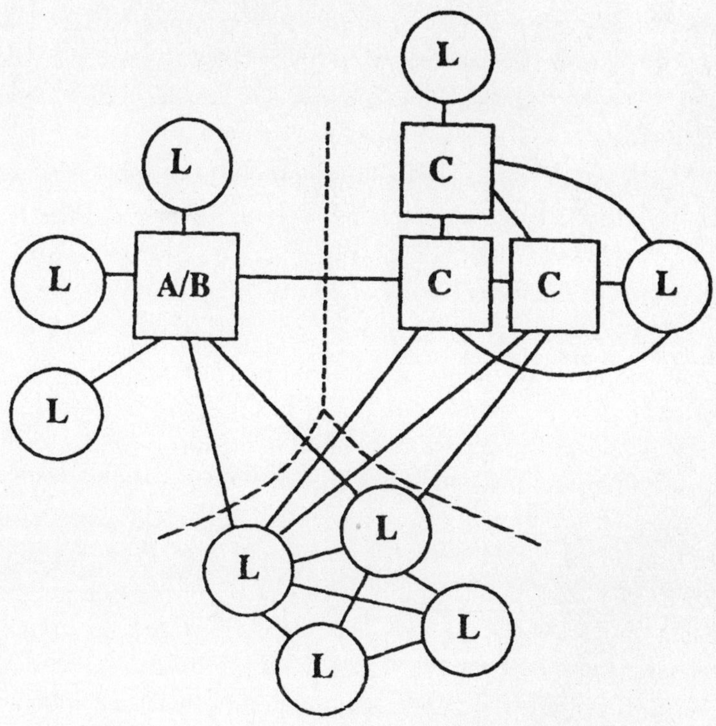

Model 6

This model may be slow to develop and will also function slowly. The role conflict will still be present. There will be currency problems in paying for lending and possibly high communication costs. In summarizing discussion of the various possible models, Dr. Wood says that it is likely that no system, even one planned from scratch is likely to emerge in a pure form and the optimum solution will probably lie in a combination of models and may change with time. He suggests that the best way forward for the development of optimum systems is for developing countries to examine their own 'history, politics, administration, population distribution, economy, education, research, transport, communication, climate, social factors, existing institutions, buildings, present demand and services, book output distribution, library budgets, existing local cooperation, regional links and international links- and see what sort of hypothetical system would best serve the users in your country - and at the same time make best use of existing resources'.

In effect, he is saying examine the basic infrastructure, apply it to the basic objective of serving the user and then see how national and international systems can be established to meet the needs of the users.

Recently various resource sharing networks have been observed at local, regional, national and international levels. Normally, three levels of national resource sharing networks exist: a) *Local*: Information is stored in the local libraries in the form of Union Catalogue for local collection available in local libraries. (b) *Regional*: Information is stored in regional libraries and services are provided on broad subject area basis. (c) *National*: National Union catalogue is prepared on national basis and services are provided to users based on national resources. Given the wide scope for exploiting resources and facilities available in the participating libraries, it is possible to work out a number of models for developing resource-sharing programs. There are four existing models, which have been presented in table on next page.

6.1. Centralized Collection Development and Services at National, or Regional Level

This model aims at providing the cooperation between libraries, which are geographically scattered within a region or the country. The resources, which the model intends to share, are acquired centrally and stored at a single site. For running the proposed facility, the participating libraries contribute towards

Table : Various Model to Resource Sharing

Model	*Aims and Funding*	*Examples*
Centralized Collection Development and Services at National, or Regional Level	Resources: acquired centrally and stored at a single site. Funding: Contribution by Participating libraries. Grants are also sought, from government and private agencies	National Lending Library, UK
Centralized Collection Development and Services By Subject	Resources: Subjects specific collection of documentary resources. Acquired centrally and stored at a single site. City, region, or country may limit the geographic distribution of libraries. Funding: Marketing of services and grants from the government and private agencies.	National Science Library at INSDOC (NISCAIR), New Delhi
Centralized Collection Development at Organizational Level	Resources: Libraries belonging to a single bigger organization collaborate. The shared collection is acquired centrally at a single site. Funding: Organization backing the Library provides funds. The participating libraries may also contribute towards the central funds	CSIR, DRDO, DOE, ISRO
Coordinated Collection Development at Institutional Level	Resources: Eliminates duplications. Serves at the level of participating libraries. The geographical area of cooperation could confine to a city, region, or country. Funding: The individual libraries determine their level of support. The higher their budget the higher their support. User libraries pay for the services they avail of.	DELNET, BONET and MAL1BNET

the capital funds and the recurring funds. Grants are also sought from the government and private agencies for raising capital fund. The facility provides for an organizational structure for its control and governance. The structure also includes an apex body. Creating a new facility is central to the concept of this model. National Lending Library, UK illustrates the example of such a model.

However, in true sense of the term latter is not the right example. National Lending Library, UK, is not based on the concept of library cooperation. It is a facility maintained and controlled exclusively by the National Library, UK. The subscribing member libraries are not its partners but its end users. They have no role to play in building its collections. Their role is limited to that of a consumer.

6.2. Centralized Collection Development and Services by Subject

This model aims at developing the specific subject collection of documentary resources on shared basis. City, region, or the country may limit the geographic distribution of libraries cooperating in such a venture. The subject collection is acquired centrally and stored at a single site. Membership fee and grants from the government and private agencies.

It constitutes the main source of funds to support and sustain such a facility. Examples of such a model result in consortia. National Science Library at INSDOC (NISCAIR), New Delhi (India), which once had the mandate to develop a complementary collection of journals in science and technology, is also cited as an example illustrating this model. However, this example is misplaced since this is not a venture used to provide funds for purpose. The user libraries are its consumers and not partners.

6.3. Centralized Collection Development at Organizational Level

This model aims at developing a shared collection of

documentary resources by limiting the scope of cooperation to libraries belonging to a single bigger organization such as the Defence Research Documentation Organization (DRDO), Department of Electronics (DoE), Indian Space Research Organization (ISRO) and Centre for Scientific and Industrial Research (CSIR).

The shared collection is acquired centrally at a single site. The participating libraries contribute towards the central funds for building the shared collections as well as for providing services.

6.4. Coordinated Collection Development at Institutional Level

In this model a group of participating libraries take the initiative to co-ordinate their acquisitions. Their objective is to eliminate duplication in acquisitions to the extent it is possible. Further, the member libraries undertake to give services such as information access and document delivery. This model leads to the concept of decentralized development of collection at the level of participating libraries and also to decentralized system of giving services. The individual libraries, participating in the programme, determine their level of support to the programme for building the shared resources. The higher their budget the higher is their support. User libraries are required to pay for the services they avail of. The geographical area of co-operation could confine to a city, region, or country. This model is in operation in most of the resource sharing programmes started by various library networks such as Developing Library Network (DELNET), Bombay Library Networking (BONET), Madras Library Network (MALIBNET) and Information & Library Networking (INFLIBNET).

7. Network Governance and Administration

William D. Mathews defines governance of a library network as:

Governance is the set of processes through which an

organization confirms its goals, establishes policy, selects its loaders, and insures the necessary resources to carry out its purpose. Selection of leaders is likely to be the most important role of governance, while insuring resources usually involves budgetary decisions and fund raising."

The specific types of governance and running of a network can be identified as :

- governance by a government,
- governance under a quasi-government body, and
- governance by the participating members under a legal charter and by laws or consortium of member libraries.

The advantages of governance emanating from a government is the fact that, as a result of that relationship, a continual flow of funds is usually assured and a major disadvantage under this type is that it is subject to satisfying a host of government rules, regulations and procedures. A library network under a quasi-governmental body implies that, in practice, the operational directions will come from a body that receives its powers of authority and regulations from the State or Central Government. Under this type also, the pros and cons of the first system will more or less prevail. In the third type i.e., governance by membership, all the governing powers are sustained within the network members. Under this type the advantages are that, the network retains the powers of accountability, authority to constitute its charter and bylaws, power to set standards, fix the fee and other financial matters. Moreover, the members of the network being the owners of the organization, the direction of the network will be monitored and influenced from within. The organization could be for a profit or non-profit one.

8. Network Functions, Services and Advantages

The knowledge that the primary reason for establishment of a network is to ultimately provide the users of member libraries more and extensive access to a universe of library materials, makes it possible to classify the functions of a network. James G. Williams and Roger Flynn list the following important functions of a network:

(a) Management Function in relation to network operations and financial accounting.

(b) Administrative Function to support coordination, resource allocation, planning, policy making, and funding.

(c) Acquisition Function to procure packages of information.

(d) Cataloging and Catalogue Production Function.

(e) Processing/Preparation Function.

(f) Information Retrieval Function.

(g) Circulation Function.

(h) Serials Control Function.

(i) Inter-library Loan Function.

(j) Delivery Function for transmission or transportation of a package of information.

(k) Storage Function.

(l) Referral Function.

(m) Communication Function.

(n) Education Function.

(o) Standaradization Function.

(p) Marketing Function and

(q) Systems Development and Support.

A careful perusal of the above functions indicates that the library networks perform a vast array of functions, including a mix of technological procedures, each of which requires varying degrees of skills and expertise.

A brief description of the services from networking are discussed hereunder.

8.1. Catalogue based services

Under this area, shares cataloguing service, union catalogue of books, serials and other non-book material, online catalogue access and catalogue production, book processing and preparation services are notable. Under shared cataloguing service, a librarian will use the catalogue information available in a major, nearby university library for cataloguing new publications added to his library. The union catalogue of books, serials and non-book materials, services will provide a union catalogue of books, serial and other materials held in different libraries with mechanism for maintaining it upto date all the time. From this, a user will be able not only to locate precisely the library where his required document can be had but also can limit his search to a particular geographical region which is proximate to him. The on-line catalogue access will provide identifying availability of one or more books and for the purpose of shared cataloguing among participating libraries. Catalogue production can be in the form of card book, magnetic tape/floppy/CD-ROM or DVD form.

8.2. Database Services

Under this head bibliographic database service, database of projects/institutions/specialists are important. The bibliographic database service would enable the library staff to search for the bibliography database developed/created at one or more libraries in order to disseminate current information and retrieve the retrospective information. These services can be classified into three types i.e., retrospective data bases in core areas built on the computer facility; retrospective databases in peripheral/low usage areas available through international search systems like DIALOG, BRS and ESA, etc.; retrospective databases on CD-ROM for secondary information. The number of searches of database of projects/institutions/specialists will make the participating libraries to capture the information from a unified database stored at one of the libraries through networking. The users and library staff will be able to search the database by various search elements.

8.3. Document Supply Service

Document supply service assumes a great importance in a network system as dissemination of information is of no use unless they are backed by actual provision of copy of source document. The user would be invariably interested in the original source document of his interest. This service can be met through inter-library loan requests, document delivery through fax; E-mail, etc. Under the inter-library loan request service, a librarian would be able to request another librarian through the network for one or more books of another library on loan basis for meeting the demand of his/her users. Success of this service will depend on the cooperative spirit of participating libraries. Through document delivery (fax service) a librarian would be able to request another librarian for copy of a document to be transmitted through tele fascimail. This service is generally used for transmitting a few pages from documents. The service of document delivery through non-fax refers to supply of hard copy of document required by users either in the form of xerox copies or through microfilm/micro-fitchi methods.

8.4. Collection Development

This service will help the libraries to identify and select publications which are worth acquiring. After examining the strength and weakness in a document collections in the libraries as well as duplication and based on the specialization of libraries, the network can be used to evolve a co-operative acquisition system. Through this, the libraries will be able to develop their collection on the basis of mutually agreed and assigned profiles to each of them and avoid duplication in their acquisition. The network can also assist the libraries in the process of procurement by providing vital information on purchases like supplier, cost, ISBN number, local agencies, currency conversion, discount rates, etc.

8.5. Communication based service

This service can be particularly classified into referral

service, electronic mail, bulletin board and academic communication. In the matter of referral service, the users are informed of the source to be approached to get the required information. To give this service, the libraries will be required to maintain a stock of referral directories and tertiary sources. The communication system of the network will be used to send referral queries and receive answers. Under the electronic mail service, the participants in the network would be able to transfer/ receive messages among themselves. This is a very important service and facility through which other services like inter-library loan requests, location searching, union catalogue, document delivery requests, transmission, referral and reference service are implemented. The service will reduce communication deals among the participating libraries. Under the Bulletin Board Service, a facility will be created to display on an electronic bulletin board, news, announcements, etc. with constant upgradation of information. Further, computer conferencing can also be carried out through the network and if more sophisticated and latest instruments are available in the network, facilities and services like teleconferencing can also be arranged.

9. Global and Indian Scenario of Networks

Library networks have grown mostly during the last thirty years in different geographical environment in order to cater to the specific needs of the users. In the United States there has been a proliferation of them. Library networks in other countries are also growing. Several models have emerged that provided specific services. Not all networks conform to the essential functions of library networks. However, the essential functions should include the promotion of Resource Sharing, creation of resource sharing tools like Union Catalogues, rationalization of acquisition and maintenance of International standards for creation of records uniformly. Libraries should be able to join different types of networks depending upon the need and select-a model, which conforms to its requirements.

In the developed countries resource-sharing networking was started long back. For instance the growth of networks in the United States can be traced from the mid of 1960. USA is the birthplace of library networking and by now libraries in each state is networked to local, regional and national network. It is important to note that the US Department of Education has been advocating a vigorous policy of promoting library networking. It offers networking grants, supports inter-library loan projects, automation and retro-conversion projects, resource sharing schemes, etc. besides providing regular federal grants annually to the public and academic libraries. Resource Sharing works in UK is also well established. The best example is Birmingham Library Co-operative Maintenance Project (BLCMP) in Birmingham, has 13 million bibliographic records of books, serials, music etc. in its database and its catalogues get a hit rate of above 90 per cent with more than 60 libraries comprising public libraries, college libraries, university libraries, national and special libraries. BLCMP has introduced EDI clearing house service in about 25 libraries. In Australia the resource sharing tools have grown from catalogue cards to national databases with the contributions of many older and larger libraries. In Australian Bibliographical Network, the national and central bibliographic databases are maintained and co-ordinated and maintained by a national agency. The Swedish Model for resource sharing is called the Consortium Model. This model is developed only for six major science and technology libraries in Sweden.

The developing countries like India are lagging behind in library co-operation. The reasons for the same are poor funding and the non-existence of the spirit of give and take or exchange is delaying the prospects of resource sharing programmes. The practice of resource sharing in the Republic of China (Taiwan) has been as limited in scale as has been in India. Greater efforts have been made in China for the development of documentary information resources because it was considered that these resources would work as China's knowledge reserve to promote the development of economy, science, technology and culture. The main effort was made on the rational distribution of the resources with the adoption of new technology. In some countries, resource sharing has become an important library programme such as in Thailand. In the 1970's work on the creation of bibliographic tools such as union catalogues and union lists of serials had begun but in the 1990s networking was considered to be the main tools for resource sharing. Best examples are MOSTE (Ministry of Science Technology and Environment) library network and CHULALINET.

It may not be possible to refer all the library networks in the world, but a brief review of the global and Indian scenario of networks has been presented here country-wise.

9.1. United States of America (USA)

As far as co-operation/resource sharing in university libraries in the United States (US) is concerned, Stuart Stubbs reviewed a number of co-operative arrangements attempted in the US prior to 1910 and Weber covered a century of such arrangements. According to Swartz, "Shared library resources and jurisdictions have prospered in the US based on the assumption that more is good and that a well-co-ordinated and well-financed more is even better."

Farmington Plan and the Latin American Co-operative Acquisitions Project were successful in the post-war era; but both were terminated at the end of 1972. The note-worthy arrangement of 1970's was formed by Harvard, Yale and Columbia Universities and the New York Public Library, under the banner of Research Libraries Group (RLG).

As early as in April 1976, Library of Congress' Network Advisory Committee (NAC) attempted to explore ways in which a more cohesive nationwide system might be developed for sharing of bibliographic information.

OCLC (originally Ohio College Library Centre) is the largest library network in USA, established in 1967, is a non-profit organisation and supports resource sharing among more than 6,700 libraries in USA, besides countries in Europe, Saudi Arabia and Australia. Its union catalogue database contains 13 million records and some 30,000 records are added every week. With the steady growth of OCLC, there has been a progressive decline in the amount of original cataloguing to be done by the participating libraries. The system hit rate has increased from 66% in 1971 to 94% in 1983. It caters to several regional networks. The chief among these are, Bibliographic Council, Dallas (AMIGOS), Illinois Library and Information Network (ILLINET), New England Library Information Network (NELINET), Midwestern Regional Library Network (MIDLNET), Wisconsin Library Consortium (WLC) and Michigan Library Consortium (MLC).

In addition to these networks, there are certain other networks prevailing in USA to promote resource-sharing activities in USA, namely the South Eastern Library Network (SOLINET), Washington Library Network (WLN), Research Library Group (RLG), Research Libraries and Information Network (RLIN) and California Library Authority for Systems and Services (CLASS).

WLN was established in 1972 and has a staff of 51 persons. It provides more than 250 libraries in seven states of USA, online computerised services to promote resource sharing and automated library functions. Its bibliographic file contains more than 3.5 million catalogue records.

RLIN, established in 1978 and which has a staff of 81 persons, supports the cooperative programmes of Research Libraries Group, comprising 36 major libraries and other research institutions. It maintains 6 databases online. The catalogue database holds more than 20 million records.

RLG was established in 1974 by four major American research libraries, namely, Harvard, Yale, Columbia Universities and the New York Public Library to share collection resources, to avoid unnecessary duplication of acquisitions, and to establish a single computerised bibliographic processing system. In 1978, RLG chose BALLOTS (Bibliographic Automation of Large Library Operation Using a Time Sharing System), a system developed in 1967 for the Stanford University Libraries, as its bibliographic processing system.

Lewis B. Mayhew described use of computers in college and universities for sharing the instructional resources. He considered sharing systems are necessary for handling of bibliographic information from TOXLINE, OCLC and Stanford University's BALLOTS. He isolated the problems and concluded the real problems are political, organisational and economic. James G. Williams reported at the 39th ASIS Annual Meeting on the use of simulation methods in designing a computer based library network at Pittsburg University to facilitate the resource sharing. The procedure can also be used to obtain data for determining hardware, software, communications and database storage requirements over a range of conditions. Allen Kent carried out a study in the University of Pittsburgh library system to determine the extent and full cost of use of library materials. The aim was to develop a foundation for improving the acquisitions, determine weeding policy and low-cost storage facilities for local library holdings.

At the 40th ASIS Annual Meeting James G. Williams reported that Pittsburgh University has designed and implemented the Western Pennsylvania Buhl Network (WEBNET), an experimental library resource sharing network comprised of six academic institutions. The objective of the network is to facilitate resource sharing by incorporating the major library functions such as acquisitions, cataloguing public service, ILL and management reporting system. A simulation model was developed to aid in the design of the regional network.

Ruedi Nothiger surveyed library automation and networks in the USA. The study on library networks involving OCLC, Ohio State University Library, University of Chicago Library, North-

West University Library, Stanford University Library and Biomedical Library of the University of California revealed that the libraries automated their routines in the order of loans first, then cataloguing and finally accessions. The libraries had co-operation on unified cataloguing rules and MARC data formats.

Bernard J. Hurley studied the automated resource sharing in Illinois. The library computer system (LCS) network in Illinois comprised of the three campuses of the University of Illinois and 14 other academic libraries in the state. The collective LCS database containing over 10 million volumes and the member libraries are allowed to search and borrow items from the collections of the other member libraries. Darrel M. Meinke described how three US college libraries are participating in a Tri College University Library Consortium by Concordia College, Moorhead State University and North Dakota State University. He concluded co-operation on a large scale has saved money and provide a rapid access to libraries with more knowledge than ever before.

Nancy C. McKeehan described the development of a state-wide computer based integrated library management system. The South Carolina Health Information Network (SCHIN) involving the libraries of the Medical University of South Carolina and the University of South Carolina School of Medicine developed circulation, cataloguing, acquisitions, serials control and online catalogue. Christine M. Roysdon reported that a campus-wide network was initiated in the Lehigh University, Bethlehem, Pennsylvania, to create an integrated electronic work place for users. A broader range of library services are available to the university community through the network which include electronic question negotiation and online search. Such campus network facilities are also available at the University of California, University of Kentucky, University of Maryland at Baltimore Health Sciences Library, Massachusetts Institute of Technology, Carnegie Mellon University as reported by Russel Shank and others.

M. J. McCallister and R.F.Gregory described the setting up of the Western North Carolina Library Network to facilitate library cooperation between three university libraries located in mountainous regions of North Carolina; Appalachian State University, North Carolina University at Asheville and Western Carolina University. The co-operation projects that were taken up by the networking group are a common database, union list of periodicals, Government documents union List, Co-operative Collection Development, etc.

So, it is clear that the university libraries in USA have been part of the resource sharing networks. These libraries have been benefitting from the larger network like OCLC or from the smaller regional networks.

Survey of literature shows tremendous work has been done in other countries also on resource sharing networks. The libraries in United Kingdom, France, Germany, Thailand, Canada, Japan, Netherlands, Brazil, Pakistan and other countries have also shown interest in the field.

9.2. Canada

Though co-operation among academic libraries started in 1960's, it was only at the provincial level and not at the national level. Tri-University Libraries (TRIUL), Ontario Universities Library Co-Operative System (OULCS), College Bibliocentre (CB) and University of Toronto Library Automation Systems (UTLAS) are the prominent networks among academic libraries in Canada.

Simon Fraser University, the University of British Columbia and the University of Victoria together established TRIUL in 1970. Collection development, Processing and Public Services were the highlights of the TRIUL consortium. Though the Council of Ontario Universities established OULCS in 1973, an informal arrangement was already working from 1965 itself. Shared automated library systems and the development of union files are among the objectives of OULCS.

The College Bibliocentre (CB) was established in 1967. The centre functions as a central agency for purchasing, processing and cataloguing for twenty two colleges of Applied Arts and Technology in Ontario. UTLAS was developed in 1967 as a computerised bibliographic system of the university of Toranto library.

The studies on resource sharing in Canadian Universities reveal that they are using mainly two networks namely Netnorth/ Bitnet and CDNnet. The office of the Educational Communications of the Association of Atlantic Universities studied the reactions of academic users of these two networks. Another study by L.Fritz and M.Baldock on Canadian Resource Sharing reveals that Saskatchewan University Libraries used resource sharing methods in support of distance education.

9.3. United Kingdom (UK)

Resource sharing in university libraries in UK has been studied by Burkett. He points out, "The universities have been acting cooperatively for quite a number of years, both in lending to each other and laterly through regional and local networking, including participation in the British Union Catalogue of periodicals and in permitting use of their collections by external scholars." As an example, he points out that the universities of Bath, Bristol, Exeter and Southampton are active members of the South Western Regional Network and they make substantial loans to other libraries both within and outside the region. The university libraries created regional data banks based on the MARC records generated by the British Library Bibliographical Services Division. Several university libraries are involved in Birmingham Libraries Co-operative Mechanization Project. Burkett further points out the contributions made by the Standing Conference of National and University Libraries (SCONUL) in stimulating the exchange of information and collaborative efforts of all the university libraries and major national libraries in UK.

Three major networks in UK are - (1) The VISCOUNT

Project; (2) LIBERTAS Project of SWALCAP; and (3) JANET.

VISCOUNT is an initiative of The London & South Eastern Library Region (LASER). LIBERTAS is the acronym for "Integrated Library System" developed by the South Western Academic Libraries Co-operative Automation Project (SWALCAP).

The United Kingdom Joint Academic Network (JANET) is a Wide Area Network (WAN), linking universities, polytechnics and research institutions. It was established in 1983 by the Universities' Joint Computer Board. JANET, which is an integrated, private, academic network linking all UK universities was developed in UK superseding all earlier regional networks.

Patrick J. Holligan made an in depth survey of 6 UK universities and two polytechnics on the implications of the current network developments for new categories of services and users. Peter Stone made another survey on JANET and respondents were asked if and how they used the network both to access other Online Public Access Catalogue (OPAC) to send e-mail. The OPAC of 15 universities were connected to JANET. There was little use of the network to send mail.

Marie Parkes described the installation of a New Integrated Information Network with fibre optic data and telephone lines at Oxford University. The data network allows easy inter-connection to a large number of asynchronous terminals, micros and host computer ports scattered among the university buildings. The data network is used by university library automation programme. May Katzen reported that the University of Leicester organised an information service on humanities through online bulletin board available on the JANET.

The other studies on library networks in UK indicate that JANET is the major network connecting the libraries of Universities and polytechnics. Its services include ILL, OPACs, e-mail, electronic bulletin boards, etc.

9.4. Netherlands

Alex Klugist reports the decision of several Netherlands' university libraries including Groningen and the Royal Library in the Hague decided to work together in the Project for Integrated Catalogue Automation (PICA). The Project developed library management system for purchasing, loans and online cataloguing, on PDP 11/44 computer system.

A local network is also proposed to connect important libraries in the locality to the computer system.

9.5. Australia

The Australian Government patronizes a modest Australian program of resource sharing by approving a special provison within the National Library's budget of resources.

The National Library of Australia (NLA) has promoted and maintained a wide range of resource sharing networks covering science and technology, industry, the social sciences, etc., offering traditional computer-based and referral services. Australian databases are available on-line through the Australian Information Network (AUSINET). NLA also participates in the international exchange of MARC data. NLA is the national agency for Cataloguing-in-Publication (CIP), International Standard Book Number (ISBN) and ISSN's; and is the designated focal point for the Australian Library-Based Information System (ASLIB) and also for UNISIST, NATIS and GIP of UNESCO.

College Libraries Activities Network of New South Wales (CLANN) and Co-operative Action by Victorian Academic Libraries (CALVAL) are the outstanding network ventures in Australia.

A communication and resource sharing network known as the Australian National University's Communications Network (ANUNET) was developed in Australia using distributed database management system with heterogeneous remote nodes.

There are two major networks in Australia, namely AUSINET and ANUNET, besides the regional networks.

AUSINET is general library and information network developed by National Library, whereas ANUNET is a resource sharing network of Australian National University.

9.6. Brazil

Janet Frederik described the national plan for university libraries in Brazil and recommended a Centre for co-operative cataloguing a standard format for computerized cataloguing and development of an on-line network.

9.7. Africa

The resource sharing in East African countries was described by B. M. Kawesa. Greatest amount of inter-university resource sharing was found among university libraries of Kenya, Tangenia and Uganda. It was found that gifts and exchanges were greater in number than purchases. The reasons were identified and attributed primarily to finance.

9.8. Arab World

A. Sharif in his article on "The Factors which effect the Development of Librarianship and Library Education in the Arab Countries", observed that despite the fact that Arab countries have many things in common to share (language, religion, culture, history, etc.) cooperation among Arab libraries is totally unknown.

The UNESCO Regional Seminar on Library Development in Arab-speaking States held in 1960 recommended the establishment of a regional scheme for the cooperative acquisition of foreign publications and a union catalogue of such publications. However, nothing concrete has emerged.

9.9. South-East Asian Countries

The International Federation of Library Associations (IFLA)/United Nations Educational, Scientific and Cultural Organizations (UNESCO) seminar on Resource Sharing of Libraries in developing countries in 1977 at Antwerp University made some proposals for the South-East Asian University

Libraries Network (SAULNET). The Association of South East Asian Nations (ASEAN) University Librarians favoured for regional co-operation in the creation of a union list of serials and inter library (IL) lending, periodical network models are also outlined for SAULNET by Lim Huck Tee.

The national libraries of South-East Asian countries, namely, Japan, China, Indonesia, Malaysia, the Philippines, Singapore and Thailand have shown great initiation to develop a co-operative resource sharing networks in the region.

The Congress of South-East Asian Libraries (CONSAL) suggested two important co-operative programmes, namely the National Libraries and Documentation Centres — South East Asia (NLDC-SEA) and International Serials Data System - South East Asia (ISDS-SEA).

9.9.1. Japan

The National Library of Japan (NLJ), through a bylaw, holds an advisory role in co-ordinating libraries in Japan; nevertheless, it did not promote or maintain nation wide resource-sharing networks. However, it planned to co-ordinate the distribution of machine-readable data as part of a national shared cataloguing system.

The NLJ was found to have been providing computer-based current awareness bulletins for general science and technology, social sciences, humanities and the arts.

The Ministry of Education, Science and Culture also established a central Inter-University Science Information Centre which aimed to provide bibliographic database information and database services including MARC and others. The university libraries assume a vital role in this Inter University Science Information Network.

Inter University Science Information Network (IUSIN) was developed by Kazuhiko Nayakama. He studied the use of network and concluded that the burden of computer use has shifted to online systems. Another study was made by E. Naito, A.

Miyazawa and H. Inoue on Centre for Bibliographic Information (CBI). The services of CBI include online cataloguing for union catalogue databases, online ILL, batch searching, etc.

Kenji Oyagi and Hideho Oikana described an investigation into the desirability of creating a co-operative network between different types of Hokkaido libraries and usefulness of Japanese Machine-Readable Catalogue (MARC) records. Morita observed, "Japan's information networks are characterized by their overall long-range planning and nationally coordinated development."

Inspite of technological development, especially in the field of electronics, it appears that Japan has not shown much interest in library networking. It is astonishing that national library has not promoted any network. Inter-University Science Information Network plays a vital role in sharing of bibliographic information among university libraries.

9.9.2. China

Wang and Seng described the programmes at the 45th Annual Meeting of ASIS in Columbus in 1982. They indicated that some plans have been "actively carried out to the effect that national bibliographic data-bases have been established with both Chinese and Western language materials" and that the present Chinese network "consisting of seven academic libraries will be made available to libraries at all levels."

The National Library of China has an advisory role in coordinating all libraries in China. Thus, it is the focal point for resource-sharing networks and it is authorized to contract with other organizations in the development and maintenance of resource sharing networks. The NLC also acts as the national centre responsible for meeting requests for foreign material from other countries, and therefore, it processed more than 90 per cent of inter-library lending requests sent to, or received from abroad.

The Chinese experiences in networking was revealed by Lian Huang at the International Symposium on New Techniques and Application in Libraries in 1988. Chong Qing University

Library in co-operation with the National Science and Technology Information Retrieval system (NSTIRS) developed a technique of long distance online information retrieval system. The objective of the NSTIRS was to set up three main sub-networks at Beijing, Shanghai and Chong Qing, connect the three sub-networks into a national network and build up a range of English and Chinese database and data-banks.

9.9.3. Thailand

Minaikit Nonglak surveyed the university libraries in Thailand for Ph.D. dissertation and proposed a plan for University Library Network in Thailand.

9.10. Pakistan

Anis Khurshid traces the status of library services in 15 universities in Pakistan and found no library co-operation existing. He stressed the need for resource sharing under the Central Government and suggested creation and maintenance of an updated union list of serials. University Libraries need to be connected with a telex system facilitating bibliographic uses, photocopying and loan of library resources. Establishment of a central agency for acquisition of foreign periodicals and specialization of subjects in universities, etc. are also suggested.

9.11. National Efforts

The growth of Indian library networks may be traced to the efforts made during the last four decades. The 1958 Scientific Policy Resolution adopted at the instance of Pandit Jawaharlal Nehru emphasized the fostering of scientific temper in people. In pursuance of this agenda, several committees and commissions were appointed to look into specific issues and come up with necessary recommendations, for e.g., the Sinha Committee's Report (1959), Ranganathan Report to UGC (1965), Peter Lazar Report and V. A. Kamath Report (1972). In the 1980s organized efforts were made to collect and disseminate information. The 1983 Technology Policy Statement emphasized the need for a technology information base. In July 1984, the Working Group of the Planning Commission headed by Dr. N. Seshagiri recommended to the Government the need for modernization of library services and informatics during the Seventh Five Year Plan of 1985- 1990.

However, in 1986 NISSAT had initiated the establishment of CALIBNET in Calcutta and supported the establishment of DELNET in Delhi in 1988, PUNENET in Pune in 1992, ADINET in Ahmedabad in 1993 and BONET in Mumbai in 1994. INSDOC supported the formation of MALIBNET in Chennai in 1993. BALNET in Bangalore was registered as a society in 1997.

The National Policy on Library and Information System submitted in 1988 recommended, among many other recommendations, using of information technology on a national level. As a result the Information and Library Network (INFLIBNET) was initiated by the University Grants Commission (UGC) as a cooperative venture for pooling, sharing, and optimization of library resources in the country. INFLIBNET proposed a mechanism to establish a network connecting libraries in universities, colleges, and institutions affiliated to the Council of Scientific and Industrial Research (CSIR), Indian Council of Medical Research (ICMR), Indian Council of Agricultural Research (ICAR), and Defence Research and Development Organization (DRDO), and government departments. It is designed to operate at national, regional, sectoral and local levels as a multi-service network to provide catalogue-based services, access to databases and document delivery services and facilities for computer mediated communication such as e-mail, bulletin boards, etc.

The National Informatics Centre of the Government of India has as one of its functions to provide Management Information Services (MIS) to various agencies in the central and state governments. This department is developing a network, NICNET, to promote communication among these agencies with mail and file transfer, and especially to provide access to databases kept on already installed computer systems. Hardware and software are to be shared to reduce overall costs. This is all in direct support of functions of the government such as monitoring projects involving the public, emergency relief, and dissemination of information to the public. NICNET is planned to be a four layer hierarchy corresponding to the levels of government of India and is designed primarily to be a government information network to promote the collection, storage, analysis, transmission and exchange of data at block, district, state headquarters and central ministries and departments at New Delhi for use in planning, management and monitoring of projects and government sponsored programmes. NICNET provides access to CD-ROM databases of the US National Library of Medicine, MEDLINE, Biotechnology Abstracts, COMPENDEX, etc.

Education and Research Network (ERNET) was initiated by the Department of Electronics (DOE), Government of India, as a thrust area for setting up a computer network for academic and research community with initial participation from the five Indian Institutes of Technology (IITs), Indian Institute of Science (IISc), Bangalore, National Centre for Software Technology (NCST), Mumbai, and the DOE, New Delhi. The development objective of ERNET is to enhance national capabilities in the areas of design, development, research, education and training in advanced concepts of computer networking and related emerging technologies. Today over 300 institutions in the country covering a cross-section of universities, government organizations, R&D organizations, research institutes are already using it extensively. Services available on ERNET are e-mail, database access, file transfer, remote login, and information retrieval tools, etc. Recently, ERNET is collaborating with INFLIBNET for UGC-INFONET.

Scientific and Industrial Research Network (SIRNET) interconnects all the CSIR laboratories and other R&D institutions in India to harness the vast science and technology information available with national laboratories and to promote resource sharing among them. The ultimate aim of the SIRNET is to link the entire scientific community of the country with the national library system and the Internet to achieve efficient scientific communication through e-mail, telnet, and FTP.

INET was established by the Department of Telecommunications (DOT), Government of India, as a nation-wide public Packet Switched Data Network (PSDN) with nodes in eight cities connected through high speed links. SIRNET operates through INET.

INDONET is a commercial distributed computer network to provide access to the computing power and software resources of the Computer Maintenance Corporation (CMC) Ltd. INDONET has mainframe computers distributed across the country and its Mumbai node is connected to Videsh Sanchar Nigam Limited (VSNL's) Gateway Packet Switched Services (GPSS), enabling computer-to-computer communication via networks abroad. The primary objective of the project is the establishment of a network of computing centres accessible from remote parts of the country so as to deliver the benefits of information resources management to a wider section of users in the country.

Business Subscribers Network (BSN) is planned for providing integrated and reliable facilities to business and industrial users. Services to be provided include voice and facsimile transfer, teletex, videotex, e-mail and access to remote databases. The central nodes are proposed at Mumbai, Kolkata, Chennai and Delhi with secondary nodes at Ahmedabad, Bangalore, Hyderabad, Kanpur/Lucknow and Pune.

Remote Area Business Message Network (RABMN) has been established by the Department of Telecommunications (DOT), Government of India, to facilitate exchange of messages in chosen user groups. The satellite based network has master earth station at Sikanderabad near Delhi and Very Small Aperture Terminal (VSAT) at user premises.

Under the Biotechnology Information System Network (BTISNET), ten specialized information centres in genetic engineering, cell culture, virology, plant tissue culture, immunology, bioprocessing engineering, etc., are being linked with micro-earth stations and X.25 protocols. Many more networks are likely to emerge in the near future such as the Defence Science Information Network, Transport Information Service Network, Oil and Natural Gas Commission Network, Coal Network, Steel Authority of India Network, Network for Business Communication, etc.

National Informatics Centre (NIC) is playing a vital role in data collection, organization, processing, analysis and accessibility. The databases available on the NICNET system are GIST (General Information to Public), TECH (Technology Data), ECO (Economic Data), CEN (Census Data), IMF (Member Countries Data) and ANAL (Analyst Software). Internet connectivity is available through the NICNET, ERNET and Videsh Sanchar Nigam Limited (VSNL) through its Gateway Internet Access Service (GIAS). The Information and Library Network (INFLIBNET) has linked all the participating libraries and its various databases, at national and international level. INFLIBNET has also its own network. It has Union Catalogue of periodicals and dissertations holdings received from participating universities and institutions in India. INFLIBNET in collaboration with National Centre for Science Information (NCSI), Bangalore, has introduced Contents with Abstracts of Periodicals in Science and Technology (COPSAT) service using the ISO 2709 format with a provision for photocopies of complete articles through document delivery service.

DELNET has emerged as the first operational library network in India with the support of the National Informatics Centre. No efforts have been made to network public libraries since it is becoming essential to provide networked information to the public. While funds are being made available for the literacy missions, public libraries which could serve as the backbones of these missions, suffer for want of adequate funds, trained staff, modern equipment, good and adequate collections, proper reading rooms, and stacking and users facilities. Not only is the number of users decreasing, but public libraries are turning out to be the decaying monuments in our information age. When access to global information is becoming almost instantaneous, there is a need to pump life into these monuments and reverse the trend.

Public libraries in India cannot afford to follow age-old systems when the computerization and networking have begun to transform many special, academic and institutional libraries. The growth of systematic modernization of libraries in the rest of the world, especially in Europe, North America and Japan is not only leaving an impact on the libraries in South Asia but is also doing so in the rest of the world.

There is a need to provide to the public, access to the latest information and educate them. The public libraries have not only to promote freedom of expression, but also the freedom to access information that may be available any where in the world. In order to do so, public libraries will have to be technologically advanced so that they have access to Internet and international databases and networks. The multiplicity in the types of documents, proliferation of literature, growth in specializations and new subjects and the increase in the number and types of users are forcing the libraries to change and adopt new methods of cooperation and new tools of information technology.

As far as rural libraries are concerned, rural settlements are generally scattered and their libraries are neither up-to-date or modern, nor are they well staffed or well equipped. The level of users is not of a high standing and therefore to connect rural libraries with the public libraries network for networking purposes in the first phase is not possible. However, as the telecommunications network has spread far and wide, it is now possible for institutions located in remote areas to join the network. With the use of satellite and radio communication technology and alternate power sources, selective institutions and libraries can make use of the public library networks.

10. Library Consortium

During the last two decades things have drastically changed due to more and more libraries automating their library catalogues, acquiring resources in electronic form, and getting connected to one or the other networks. This has resulted in easy accessing of the resources from the remote nodes adding new dimension to the nature of library-services, in a resources constrained environment, sharing of library resources among the libraries and providing services through the resource sharing practices is gaining considerable importance. With the developments and the application of information technology tools the sharing has become much easy. The consortia approach helps in improving the quality and standard of research in Indian universities by improving the access-base to literature. Forming a consortium of libraries -way of life to maximise resource base.

In the professional literature, the term consortium covers a great diversity of cooperation, situations and experiences according to the different contexts and times they were developed. The ideals and practice of library cooperation were progressively affirmed during the last century, giving rise to a considerable variety of activities and organizational forms with various names, often related to the most fashionable cultural trends or suggested by new technologies and innovative models developed in business contexts. The use of the term consortium became established in the North American library lexicon in the 1960s and it indicates forms of structured cooperation focused primarily on resource sharing and cost reduction. In some European countries, use of the term in library contexts has very remote origins. In Italy, for instance, the word *consorzio* has, with changing fortunes, been used in the area of public libraries throughout the twentieth century. The "Consorzio delle biblioteche popolari milanesi," set up in Milan in 1903 under the impetus of the social reform movements of the times to promote literacy among the working classes, is probably one of the oldest cooperation experiments to use this term in a library context.

A library consortium is a concept that facilitates the libraries to get the benefit of wider access to electronic resources at affordable cost and at the best terms of licenses. It is a group of libraries those are working together toward a common goal, whether to expand cooperation on traditional library services such as collection development, or electronic information services. The term is now used perhaps too broadly, and encompasses everything from formal legal entities such as incorporated or governmental agencies to informal groups that come together solely to achieve better pricing for purchasing electronic information. It is a community of two or more information agencies, which have formally agreed to coordinate, cooperate or consolidate certain functions, to achieve mutual objectives. The consortia may be formed on a local, regional, national, or international basis; on a functional or format basis; or on a subject basis

In the beginning, consortia focused on ILL and document delivery service based on union catalogues and locally held resources. Retrospective conversion and preservation initiatives followed. Today, emphasis is on buying, cooperatives, influencing policy, specifically scholarly publication patterns, research and development to improve content delivery and standards for developing and managing collections often through grants, and expanding access to specialized resources.

10.1. Aims of the Consortia

The primary objective of the Library Consortium is to encourage and facilitate interlibrary communication, education and resource sharing within its diverse multi-type library membership.

Today Consortium purpose is shifted from mere sharing of resources to sharing of expertise between libraries and also explores the need for libraries to make the most effective use of their funds collectively.

10.2. Salient Features of Library Consortia

A consortium may help :

(i) To eliminate the different problems faced by the libraries to provide various services to its users.

(ii) To meet the thrust of information of the vast people due to rapid growth of population all over the world.

(iii) To cope up with the newly generated knowledge published in different forms, such as, printed and non - printed documents, electronic media on various disciplines, multi-disciplinary and new generated subject areas.

(iv) To collect all the documents published at the national and international level, because of the library financial crunch;

(v) To overcome the language barriers i.e.:- primary documents are being published by the developed countries like USA, UK, France, Japan etc, and among them the non-English speaking countries produce majority of scientific literatures in their mother languages.

(vi) To single payment by one of the participants or through an agent and license has to be signed by all.

(vii) The members to maintain same level of subscription.

(viii) For initial minimum subscription.

(ix) Publishers to find it convenient to negotiate with members through an agent and agent raising individual invoices to all members and single payment to publishers.

(x) Institution-wise usage statistics to be provided to ascertain as to how often user's access to all titles subscribed.

10.3. Principles to Govern the Consortia

The important ones include :

(i) Flexibility to choose your own library management solutions vendor and select the member libraries with which you will share resources.

(ii) Flexibility to own, manage, and control your library's records and enforces its policies.

(iii) Flexibility to extend access to even more information with an information portal that shows your library's face.

(iv) Flexibility to share physical and digital resources.

(v) Flexibility to enable your library users to search and place holds on the resources of your own and other member libraries and

(vi) To enable users of other member libraries to search and place holds on your library's resources.

10.4. Functions of the Consortia

The major functions may be :

(i) Collection Sharing.

(ii) Electronic Content Licensing.

(iii) Electronic Content Loading/Presentation.

(iv) Inter - Library Loan / Document Delivery.

(v) Preservation.

(vi) Training.

(vii) Union Lists / Shared Online Catalogues.

(viii) Others such as new forms of scholarly and scientific communication.

10.5. Benefits of Consortia

The following benefits are observed of using a consortium.

(i) Consortia-based subscription to electronic resources provides access to wider number of electronic resources at substantially lower cost;

(ii) The Consortium, with its collective strength of participating institutions, has attracted highly discounted rates of subscription with most favorable terms of agreement.

(iii) The Consortium is proposed to be an open - ended

proposition wherein other institutions can join and get the benefit of not only highly discounted subscription rates by also the favourable terms of licenses.

(iv) The Consortia have been offered better terms of license for use, archival access and preservation of subscribed electronic resources, which would not have been possible for any single institution;

(v) Since the subscribed resources would be accessible online in electronic form, the beneficiary institutions would have less pressure on space requirement for storing and managing print - based library resources.

(vi) The Consortium is expected to trigger remarkable increase in sharing of both the print and electronic resources amongst participating library.

10.6. Elements of Library Consortium

Though, every library differs from one another according to its collection, information needs of users, working method, sources of finance, processing of information, etc., but the various steps of jobs/functions or elements can be adopted by a consortium for functioning standing on a common platform. These are:

1. Agreement for Establishment of a Consortium : A concrete agreement is needed to establish for the participating libraries in consortia to achieve a common target. Then, every library will be able to work in such a manner that they are mutually exclusive, but they follow the common mission of a consortium as a whole. As a result, a managing committee should be formed.

2. Administration of Library Consortium : To run the total functions of a consortium smoothly a statutory body is very much essential to be formed taking Chief Librarian / Chief Information Manager from every library / Information Centre and one of them will act as a Chief Coordinator on rotation basis. Each library has to inform about its collection, databases, user service, training of human resource for handling new equipments, etc. to the Chief Coordinator through hierarchical management level.

3. Financial Control : As due to financial crisis, libraries form a consortium for providing better service to the users, the crucial activities of the members of management committee is to take action on the following financial points like:

- Whether a consortium fund be created to subscribe the core journals in different subjects in multiple copies at a discount rate;
- How to manage the fund of a consortium and how much money is to be collected from each library as a contribution;
- Whether the participating libraries to whom the responsibility to negotiate with some publishes are vested by the managing committee, will send remittance to the publishers for multiple copies from its own fund and adjust it subsequently among the participating libraries.

4. Joint Work : Individual library has to prepare a list of titles for resource sharing among participating libraries looking into the user demand and may also initiate to contact with different publishers for negotiation. All the participating libraries under library consortia must work jointly just like a joint venture in business sector to make the consortium a total success. Each library will subscribe the core journals and prepare the union list of titles to be covered under resource sharing programme and the member libraries may also send full content page service of all issues of the title to another library.

5. Evaluation : After a certain period, the whole activities of a consortium, i.e. individual as well as co-operative, must be evaluated on the basis of the pre-determined objectives. If there is any lacuna in between the work performed and to be performed should be adjusted by taking corrective measures in activities in future. If there is a need for any change in the path of action, it should be changed immediately to achieve the objectives of a consortium.

10.7. Types of Consortia

Various consortia have been formed by different groups throughout the world, but there is no single model for consortium. However, different types of consortia may be observed on following points:

(i) From highly decentralized organization to highly centralized ones.

(ii) The degree of centralization of a consortium is the primary factor affecting not only how member institution interact each other, but also relationship with external part i.e., the publisher or vendor.

(iii) More decentralized the consortium, the grater the degree of autonomy each member retains.

(iv) Correlation between the amount of autonomy that the individual institution retains and the ability of the consortium to achieve set goals as a group.

(v) If the authority is highly centralized, the consortium is more likely to have dedicated staff to perform ongoing work.

Loosely Knit Federations : These possess following characteristic features:

(i) Local or Regional.

(ii) Governed by its members.

(iii) No central staff, no funding.

(iv) Very flexible with no bargaining power.

(v) With low common interest, no central authority, but limited or no group purchasing power.

(vi) Yields minimum return.

Multi-type State Network : These are with following characteristic features:

(i) Statewide or multiple states.

(ii) Low common interest.

(iii) Central staff but no funding.

(iv) Some what flexible.

(v) Little bargaining power.

Tightly Knit Federations : These possess following characteristic features:

(i) Statewide or single library.

(ii) High common interest.

(iii) May have sponsoring agency.

(iv) Have action agenda.

(v) Publisher discounts slightly high.

(vi) Central staff with possible central funding.

(vii) Fairly flexible with moderate bargaining power.

Centrally Supported Consortia : These are with following characteristic features:

(i) Single rate.

(ii) High common interest.

(iii) Significant action agenda.

(iv) Central staff and strong funding.

(v) Moderately inflexible.

(vi) Strong bargaining power.

Many international and national consortia of various types as stated above are working in the field of library science. To name few on international level are: *Arizona University Libraries Consortium* (United States), *Consortium of Academic Libraries in Manchester* (United Kingdom), *Co-operative Action by Victorian Academic Libraries Limited* (Australia), *Illinois Library Computer Systems Organizations* (United States), *Missouri Research Consortium of Libraries* (United States) and *Pennsylvania Academic Library Connection Initiative* (United States).

10.8. Existing Consortia Models in India

To begin with, a small group of libraries started coming

together and made headways for negotiating consortia terms and conditions so as to have access to large amount of information. As of now, we have a few consortia formed and each one is a model of its own as far as funding is concerned, viz :

(a) Model 1: Homogeneity of Subject : The Indian Astrophysics Consortium grew out of the efforts of handful of librarians from institutions specializing in astronomy and astrophysics in India. This consortium is also known as FORSA. Initially there were eight members but only five joined the consortium for negotiating licensing for astronomy journals. They had identified a subscription agent as a supplier of journals. Subscriptions for both paper and electronic format are paid through this supplier. The agreement is meant for only astronomy journals published by a particular publisher. The entire negotiation was based on the number of the print journals and hence the sales volume will dictate the price paid for the titles. As the number of titles increases, the price paid per title decreases by a few percentage points. This supplier has agreed to be a negotiator between the members and the publisher to provide access to the licensed materials. It is a win-win situation for both the members and the publisher in terms of the decreased cost for electronic access to members and an increased volume of sales for the publisher.

The Salient features of FORSA Consortium are :

- The journal titles for which the consortium license is negotiated are subject focused.
- The publishers find it convenient to negotiate with the members through the agent since the individual invoicing is handled by the agent for the individual members.
- The model is worked out for cross - e-access to the print journals subscribed to by the members of the consortium and hence gives equal access for all the members.
- No additional requirement of budget for the members in terms of subscription to new print journals is required since

the currently subscribed titles will be maintained which is subjected to the normal increase in subscription.

– The most important feature is that the members are not burdened with subscribing to peripheral and less important journals, which is a standard feature of 'bundling together' by publishers.

Problems : The FORSA consortium is not devoid of problems now that it is in operation. Since the consortium concept is still new in India, there are neither defined guidelines nor established models to help the librarians establish a formal consortium where the members are legally bound and their decisions protected. Secondly, the combined subscription to the print and electronic format through the same agent has created some confusion among the members since at least one member was subscribing to the printed journal through another agent. This member could not join the consortium in time to process the combined payment through the agent who is the negotiator. Even among a fairly homogenous consortium, there are differences that stem from institution size, funding, location in the same city, and differences in institutional culture and approach in management. At this juncture it has become very essential for the FORSA members to formalize the formation and functioning of the consortium before future consortia negotiations with other publishers are concluded. The idea of foregoing individual gain for greater overall benefit can be realised only if the consortium operates in a formal and coordinated manner.

(b) Model 2: Common Title Subscription : The same FORSA consortium has concluded a consortium deal recently, to access the journal *Nature.* The boundaries of the FORSA group have opened up in this case in order to include a few other libraries with mutual interests and at the same time, not to increase the size of the consortium beyond a certain number. At present there are six members who have formally committed to share the license fee to access *Nature* electronically.

A few interesting observations about this negotiation, are:

- There is no predetermined condition of the print subscription by the members.
- Independent invoicing to the members of the consortium will come directly from the publisher.
- The consortium negotiation is based on the total number of users.
- The calculation of the base price for the electronic access and the per site access fee is a standard offer made by the publisher worldwide in all the consortia negotiations.
- The more members in the consortium deal, the less the individual members will pay for the electronic access.

Problems : Since the publisher expects the members all to join at the same time, it is essential for them to start their subscriptions at the same time. The members are not free to join at any time of the year to access the e-journal, even if they already have active subscriptions to the same journal in print. When libraries commit institutional funds to participate in a consortium they not only expect their consortium to make intelligent use of their funds but also have flexible options to make use of the consortium negotiations.

(c) Model 3: Payment by a Parent Organization : Tata Institute of Fundamental Research is a premier scientific research organization which has five branches in the country. This is an ideal situation to work out a simple consortium model among the branches. They have negotiated with one of the major publishers for licensing a part of the serial collections. The main library of TIFR, at Mumbai, has acted as the parent organization for making payment on behalf of the branches. Initially, the agreement was signed for one year and later it was extended to the second year since the consortium is functioning smoothly. The members as well as the users are satisfied with the arrangement for accessing the essential set of e-journals among themselves. Since the negotiation was not based on print subscriptions by the members, one of the branch libraries has the benefit of accessing the entire group of journals in spite of not subscribing to a single print journal in the contract.

(d) Model 4 : Central Agency Funding Directly - MHRD-INDEST : An Indian National Digital Library in Engineering, Science and Technology (INDEST) was set under MHRD. Government of India, initially covering 38 major technological institute including IISc, all IITs, NITs, RECs and IIITs. It is an open ended system with provision for adding new members by shared subscription through a consortium of libraries. It hopes to increase access to e-journals and important databases on negotiation with major publishers.

10.9. Development of Consortia

Library & Information Center's networking in India have come to the existence almost two decade ago. In India we used the term "Inter-library Loan" in the parlance of library management. This scenario has extended from its limited basis to become fully grown consortia of various kinds. Since India is the developing country, we constantly work towards improving our infrastructure and technology to meet the demands of our scientists and researchers by taking the lead from the developed countries.

1. Library Consortia in Western Europe : The Nordic countries (Finland, Sweden, Norway, Iceland and Denmark) represent one of the areas where library cooperation experience is most widespread. With interwoven historical backgrounds and cultural roots (with the exception of Finnish, all the languages spoken in the area are from the same group), the five countries maintain solid collaboration relationships and have developed major library cooperation programs, some of which also include the Baltic countries. Among these, the best known is NORDINFO, the Nordic Council for Scientific Information, which carries on broad activities aimed at developing cooperation in the information and documentation sector and supporting innovative projects. Among programs supported by NORDINFO, NOSP (Northern/Baltic Union Catalogue of Serials) is to be mentioned in which 1000 libraries take part. This solid basis of common work and mutual exchange does not prevent the individual countries from displaying their own peculiarities in the development of consortium models. One common feature of the Nordic experience is the role that the libraries play in organizing cooperation, and the various degrees of centralization or decentralization in solutions adopted. Among these consortia, FINELIB, centering around the Finnish National Library, is the model with the highest degree of centralization but also a high level of participation in decisions, ensured by a fairly elaborate structure of governing bodies. This consortium, currently comprising more than 50 university and research libraries, is still expanding and is open to participation by public and other libraries. FINELIB's sphere of activities goes well beyond the negotiation of electronic licenses to cover also development of programs for access to miscellaneous resources and electronic publishing.

In Sweden, the main consortium initiative has been pursued by BIBSAM, the department of the Royal Library that coordinates cooperation and development activities at the national level. BIBSAM carries out various programs of activities to support the Swedish university and research library network, underpinned by central funding. It also has a fund to support access by libraries to electronic resources. Although not a consortium, BIBSAM acts like one, and in recent years has negotiated many agreements with publishers and suppliers of electronic information on behalf of libraries and supported the implementation of this program both financially and technically.

In Norway, consortium initiatives to purchase licenses at the moment are more fragmentary because they are handled by various central bodies: the National Office for Research Documentation, Academic and Special Libraries

(*Riksbibliotekstjenesten*), the National Library, and the B1BSYS library network.

In Denmark, consortium agreements were initially handled directly by the university libraries. Subsequently, some agreements with major scientific publishers were amended into national agreements with support from the DEF Programme (Denmark Electronic Research Library Project). Currently, collaboration is emerging between the decentralized approach pursued directly by the university libraries and the above-mentioned program, which now constitutes the framework for consortium activities to acquire electronic resources. DEF is an important innovative project at the national level supported by sizeable funds and run by the National Library Authority. It covers various programs, including creation of a high-speed network connecting the largest university libraries, the central purchase of modern, automated library systems, and the digitization of catalogues and relevant collections.

In Iceland, too, an agreement has been reached with a major supplier of electronic services; in perfect harmony with the other Nordic countries and with its relatively small dimensions, its consortium organization is centered around the National Library.

On the European scene, Great Britain is regarded as the most advanced in innovation in library services and development of advanced forms of cooperation. Helped by a language that is by now almost universally known, experience from that country is often regarded as a basis for comparison or even as a reference model. Established practice in the area of cooperation and the dynamism of relevant bodies at the national level are yielding good fruit in the digital age too. On the other hand, it is kept in mind that there is a strong position of autonomy among both universities and territorial units, resulting in a path to cooperation that seeks to balance the various requirements of coordination and decentralization. Consortium initiatives in Britain are numerous at both the national and regional level and in all library sectors. In the public library sector, mention has to be made of

EARL, the consortium born from the New Library (The People's Network) program, whereas in the university research library sector, one of the most well-established consortia is CURL, an organization not however primarily focused on handling electronic resources. But the main organization operating in the area we are considering is JISC (Joint Information System Committee), set up to promote development of electronic information in U.K. universities. JISC supports many projects concerned with education and research based on information technologies and has set up synergies and alliances with various organizations operating in the information sector. Among projects launched by JISC, we must mention the CHEST agency and NESLI (National Electronic Site License Initiative), the consortium today regarded as one of the main reference models beyond the United Kingdom as well. This consortium's operational structure is in the hands of two outside bodies: the "managing agent," a private company with the task of handling negotiations of electronic licences, and the computer center, which supplies technical support. The NESLI is directed by an advisory board where the participating institutions take part, and the management board on which the various components of the consortium are represented. More recently, to bring the various activities launched by JISC in the digital information area into a consistent pattern, the Distributed National Electronic Resources (DNER) program has been launched, aimed at promoting a national strategy.

In Ireland, consortium initiatives in the field of electronic resources, mainly between university libraries, are informal in character. Of these, the consortium for the acquisition of electronic periodicals, under the supervision of the 'Conference of Heads of Irish Universities' (CHIU), involves six universities.

In Germany, the federal structure means that cooperation is principally at the Lander level, but there are also national programs funded by the *Deutsche Forschungsgemeinschaft*, the German National Research Council. Since the 1970s, various cooperation programs have been developed to create collective catalogues. Activities associated with acquiring electronic resources have given rise to a variety of cooperation forms. "Only in the case of the Friedrich Althoff Consortium in Berlin-Brandenburg, a corporate body with deed of partnership does exist," stated Rein-hardt and Boekhorst. In the other Lander, consortia "are represented by an individual library (e.g., Baden Wurttemberg) or a central institution such as the *Bayerische Staatsbibliothek* or the *Hochschulbibliotekszentrum* NRW in North Rhine-Westphalia." Ways of funding consortia also differ considerably, even if the main sources are the Lander governments within whose jurisdiction, libraries fall. In some cases, the consortia are funded directly by participating libraries, but in most cases they receive substantial subventions or are entirely supported by central funds supplied by the Lander. There is an emerging need for programs to bring all the Lander together into a national strategy, but at the moment this prospect seems fairly impracticable. Nonetheless, there is a significant initiative by the leaders of the German consortia, who in 2000 started an association subsequently joined also by the consortia from Switzerland, Holland, and Austria: as well as exchanging information of mutual interest, this body—now named GASCO (German, Austrian, and Swiss Consortia Organization)—is intended to develop joint strategies for acquiring and handling publications, creating the pre-conditions for activating action plans at the supranational level.

The tendency to converge toward a national strategy, or at least link programs and instruments operating in a broader geographical dimension, is emerging with various patterns and orientations in many countries in central Europe. This is the case for the Dutch consortium—the UKB Association—in which 13 university libraries participate along with the Royal Library and the Library of the Royal Academy of the Science. This consortium, which has no legal basis and does not receive any ad hoc government funding, is supported by contributions from the participating libraries. Its activities are focused chiefly on negotiating electronic licences with major publishing groups, with which it has reached numerous agreements. More recently, the UKB Association has been preparing to update its objectives and strategies within a broader vision aimed at taking advantage of local academic and publishing output of the learned societies.

As far as the France is the case though the first consortium initiatives appeared only at the end of the 1990s, more recently university libraries there have been quickly catching up in this area. The first initiatives that emerged around a specific product or were developed by groups of libraries on a regional scale; among which the CAMPRA consortium, operating for some years in the Rhone-Alpes region should be mentioned; are giving way in the face of the rapid expansion of COUPERIN, a consortium initially promoted by a group of six university libraries including the Strasbourg University Library, aimed at purchasing academic journals. This is a decentralized initiative that has secured broad support from libraries throughout French territory, to the point of taking on a national dimension. In early 2001, COUPERIN had some 70 members, university and polytechnic libraries. Supported by the rectors of the universities that provided the resources in the initial stage of development, today COUPERIN is recognized at the national level and also enjoys ad hoc funding from the Ministry of Education. The success scored in the license-negotiating sector is compelling this consortium to broaden its mission and its programs and to integrate its digital collection development and management policy within the framework of a national strategy. To meet these new challenges, COUPERIN is today updating its projects and structures.

One interesting national library cooperation program is taking shape in Switzerland, despite the intrinsic difficulty of achieving an objective of this type in a country structured in 26 states, where three language communities (German, French, and Italian) coexist. The first consortium assemblages emerged at the local level, because the universities are financed by the cantons. Subsequently, in 1988, thanks to the commitment of the conference of university rectors, the Consortium of Swiss Academic Libraries (*Konsortium der Schweizer Hochschulbibliotheken*), 50 per cent funded by the federal government, was established. Today, some 60 libraries take part, in addition to the national library. The consortium's organizational structure, which also provides for potential members from among public and research libraries, is based on a central office and a fairly elaborate governing structure, at the summit of which is the conference of university rectors.

The linguistic and cultural barriers and the complications due to the political administrative system have to date still not been overcome in Belgium, where the libraries of the French and Flemish language communities organize separate consortium initiatives. The consortium initiatives of the universities and research institutes of the Flemish area come under the *Vlaams Overlegor-gaan inzake Wetenschappelijk Bibliotheekwerk* (Flemish Research Libraries Council) and the Flemish Ministry of Education, which supports the initiatives from central funds. The electronic resource-sharing programs of Francophone university libraries come under a nonprofit body: the BICfB (*la Bibliothequelnteruniversitaire de la Communaute Franchise de Belgique*), set up in 2000 under the auspices of the country's conference of Francophone university rectors.

Consortium experience under way in the countries of southern Europe is highly diverse, even in more culturally homogeneous areas where romance languages are spoken. In the Iberian Peninsula, much of the consortium activity aimed at shared handling of electronic resources is still in a start-up phase, although since the 1980s, Portugal and Spain have secured remarkable growth of library services and also a considerable development of cooperation activities. The turning point in Spanish interlibrary cooperation came in 1996 with the creation of the consortium of university libraries of Catalonia (*Consorci de Biblio-teques Universitaries de Catalunya*), more recently followed by other initiatives in Galicia (*CBUG, Consorcio de Bibliotecas universitarias de Galicia*), the Madrid region (MADRONO), and Andalusia. On the basis of the regional decentralization typical of the Spanish system, the consortia are financed by the universities and/or the government of the autonomous community to which they belong. Consortium activities concern acquisition of electronic resources and, in Galicia and Catalonia, also the development of other bibliographical utilities. The Catalan consortium undoubtedly represents the most advanced initiative in Spain. It is a consortium with a legal basis and solid institutional ties; of which the National Library of Catalonia is also a member, supported by a funding mechanism based on the contribution of the local government (Comunidad Autonoma) and equipped with dedicated infrastructures and staff. Thanks to the common technological platform used by participating libraries, this organization shows wide potential in integration of resources and development of value-added services. Although the administrative political systems based on local autonomy can in some cases be an obstacle to development of national strategies, the Spanish university libraries have in the last decade succeeded, under the auspices of the conference of university rectors, in creating a national cooperation body (REBIUN). This does not mean that there is a national strategy at the consortium level for handling electronic resources, but it seems clear that some of the premises for this sort of approach are present in the panorama of Spanish university and research libraries.

In Italy, initiatives to share electronic resources began to appear only in the late 1990s and are currently located chiefly in the center and north of the country. Of the three most important consortium activities, two are led by university computing consortia—CILEA in Milan and CASPUR in Rome—nonprofit organizations that supply computing services and, in the electronic information sector, act as intermediaries on behalf of the associated libraries. The third—CIPE (Inter-university

Cooperation on Electronic Journal)—was set up in 1999 on the initiative of some university libraries in the center and north including Padua, Bologna, Florence, and the European University Institute of Florence and was soon joined by other universities. CIPE—founded on an agreement among the member universities and governed by a committee made up of representatives of its members—does not enjoy special funds and does not to date have a central infrastructure. This consortium is in an expansion phase and is redesigning both its organizational structure and its mission. In Italy, there is no real national strategy in the area of electronic information, although the three consortia mentioned come together in INFER (Italian National Forum on Electronic Information Resources), a voluntary interconsortium coordination body that also undertakes awareness activity to develop cooperation in the area of access to digital information. In this context, collaboration has begun, enabling the three consortia mentioned to embark on joint negotiations with a number of publishers, laying the foundation for agreements on a national scale.

A country that differs in a number of ways, in both historical experience and geographical location, from the Mediterranean European countries, Greece today presents a very interesting experience of library consortia in Europe. Born on the initiative of a group of universities, including Thessaloniki, and with the support of European Commission technological library programs, HEAL Link (Hellenic Academic Libraries Link) currently includes 32 Higher Education Institutions plus the Athens Academy and the National Library. The sphere of activity and objective of this program are fairly broad, ranging from production of the union catalogue to operational standards and staff training, from periodical collections development policy to the acquisition and administration of electronic licenses. In conclusion, HEAL Link, which has reached many agreements with major academic publishers and is entirely supported from central government funds, is moving decisively in a national strategic perspective.

2. Consortia Initiatives in India : Several library consortia around the country have been formed on different lines and objectives. Presently many consortia are functioning viz. FORSA (Forum For Resource Sharing in Astronomy & Astrophysics), CSIR Consortia, HELINET (Health Sciences Library & Information Network), INDEST (Indian National Digital Library In Science And Technology) and UGC-Infonet E-Journals Consortium etc.

(i) Health Inter - Network (HIN) India

The Health Inter - network is a United Nations initiative created to respond to the challenges posed by the digital divide. The Health Inter - network aims to support and strengthen public health services and to provide access to high quality, relevant and timely health information. It further aims to improve communication and networking among public health care workers, researchers and policy makers.

(ii) HELINET Consortium

The Rajiv Gandhi University of Health Sciences has been working on collaboration and virtual resource sharing. In the past few year this has made a significant investment in hardware and content procurement for making International Journals and Databases available to its member libraries all over the Karnataka.

(iii) Indian Digital Library in Engineering Science and Technology (INDEST) Consortium.

INDEST Consortium is one the most ambitious initiatives taken so far in the country. Ministry of Human Resource Development (MHRD) has set-up the "Indian National Digital Library in Engineering Sciences and Technology (INDEST) Consortium" on the recommendation made by the Expert Group appointed by the ministry under the chairmanship of Prof. N. Balakrishnan. Initially, the Ministry provides funds required for subscription to electronic resources for 38 institutions including IISc, IITs, NITs, IIMs and a few other centrally-funded

Government institutions through the consortium headquarters set-up at the IIT Delhi. Besides, 44 Government or Government-aided engineering colleges and technical departments in universities have joined the Consortium with financial support from the AICTE. Moreover, the INDEST Consortium, as an open-ended proposition, welcomes other institutions to join it on their own for sharing benefits it offers in terms of highly discounted rates of subscription and better terms of agreement with the publishers. All electronic resources being subscribed are available from the publisher's Website. The Consortium has an active mailing list and a Web site hosted at the IIT Delhi. By now 91 engineering colleges and institutions have already joined the consortium on their own.

The INDEST Consortium, being an open-ended proposition, invites all AICTE-accredited / UGC-affiliated institutions to join the Consortium. While the expenditure on electronic resources proposed for subscription under the consortium for selected institutions is being met from the funds made available by the MHRD, the consortium welcomes institutions to join the consortium on their own for sharing benefits it offers in terms of lower subscription rates and better terms of agreement with the publishers. All electronic resources being subscribed are available from the publisher's Website.

Who is eligible to join : Membership of the consortium is open to any Private or Government-funded Engineering, Technological/ Educational institutions / Universities for one or more electronic resources. The members would be required to sign an agreement with the INDEST Consortium as well as with the publishers of electronic resources that they wish to subscribe. The consortium charges prescribed annual membership fee.

Why should you join : The consortium offers the best possible price advantage ranging from 12% to 95% (Average > 80% +) through its pricing agreements with publishers as well as terms of agreement for various electronic resources. Moreover, the consortium would also provide technical help and arrange for in-house training for optimal usage of resources subscribed.

Core Members : The Ministry of Human Resource Development (MHRD) provides funds required for providing differential access to various electronic resources subscribed by the consortium for 38 core member institutions. The members of core group of Institutions are as follows:

IITs and IISc (eight institutions)

NITs , ISM, SUET and NERIST (twenty Institutions)

HIT and IIITM (two institutions)

IIMs, NITIE and IIITM (eight institutions)

AICTE - supported Members : The INDEST Consortium is being expanded to include additional members with financial support from the All India Council of Technical Education (AICTE). The AICTE has identified 44 Government engineering colleges or technical institutions that offer programmes at postgraduate level. These institutions are being given access to a number of electronic resources including IEL Online Library, ASCE Journals, ASME Journals, Applied Science and Technology Plus (ASTP), ACM Digital Library and JGATE for Engineering and Technology (JET).

Self-supported Institutions : The consortium, being an open-ended proposition, invites AICTE-accredited and UGC-affiliated institutions to join hands with the leading Engineering and Technological Institutions in India and share the benefits it offers in terms of lower subscription rates and better terms of agreement with the publishers. 91 other engineering colleges and institutions have already joined the consortium on their own.

E- Resources : The INDEST consortium subscribes to the following resources for various categories of institutions. All electronic resources subscribed are available from the publisher's Web site. Local hosting of resources has not been considered at this stage.

Full-Text E-Resources

ABI / Inform Complete

http://www.il.proquest.com/pqdauto

ACM Digital Library

http://portal.acm.org/portal.cfm

ASCE Journals

http://www.pubs.asce.org/journals/jrns.html

ASME Journals (+ A M R)

http://www.asme.org/pubs/journals/

ASTM Standartds and Journals

Standards: http://enterprise.astm.org

Journals: http://journalsip.astm.org/

Capitaline

http://www.capitaline.com/intranet/INDESTconsortium.htm

CRIS INFAC Ind. Information

http://www.crisil.com/

EBSCO Databases

http://search.epnet.com/

Elsevier's Science Direct

http://www.sciencedirect.com/

Emerald Full-text

http://iris.emeraldinsight.com/

Euromonitor (GMID)

http://www.euromonitor.com/gmid

IEEE /IEE Electronic Library Online (IEL)

http: //ieeexplore.ieec.org/

Indian Standards

Intranet Version

INSIGHT

http://www.insight.asiancerc.com/

Nature

http://www.nature.com/

ProQuest Science (formerly ASTP)

http://www.il.proquest.com/pqdauto

Springer Link

http://www.springerlink.com/

Bibliographic Databases

COMPENDEX on EI Village

http://www.engineeringvillage2.org

INSPEC on EI Village

http://www.engineeringvillage2.org

J-Gate Custom Content for Consortia (JCCC)

http://jccc-indest.informindia.co.in/

MathSciNet

http://www.ams.org/mathscinet

SciFinder Scholar

http://www.cas.org/SCIFINDER/SCHOLAR/index.html (access through a Z39.50 Client to be installed on each PC)

Web of Science

http://isiknowledge.com

(iv) UGC-Infonet E-Journals Consortium

UGC-Infonet E-Journals consortium has launched by UGC, is one of the biggest and ambitious program in the history of higher education in India. The main objective of this program to facilitate the research and academic community of the country by providing them latest, authentic and scholarly literature from all parts of the world with the help of state-of-the-art technology. The program came into existence with the cooperation and co-ordination of UGC, Education and Research Network (ERNET),

Information and Library Network (INFLIBNET) Centre, and many prominent national and international publishers. Here UGC, is the main funding body, ERNET India is responsible for designing and maintaining the infrastructure within the each member university and, INFLIBNET Centre has the responsibility to execute the program in systematic and planned mode. The e-journals consortium has received 60 per cent to 90 per cent discount on subscription of these e-resources and varies from publisher to publisher. This effort enable the faculty and research scholars access to not only current issues of the journals but also getting access to 5 to 10 years back volumes and publishers like IOP and ACS are providing access to whole archive of their collections from volume 1 issue 1 almost the full text access from 1874. This will bridge the gap between the scholarly information, which was denied 5-10 years back and now they will have access to all of their collections. The access to scholarly literature has been made available from January 1st, 2004 to 50 universities start with. So far 100 Universities out of 171 Indian Universities, which come under the purview of UGC, have been provided access to these journals and it will gradually be extended to affiliated colleges as well. It covers almost all fields of learning like Arts, Humanities, Social Sciences, Physical and Chemical Sciences, Life Sciences, Computer Sciences, Mathematics and Statistics etc. The literature made available will include journals covering research articles, reviews and abstracting databases. Access will be provided to current and archival literature. Portals will be provided which will enable users to navigate easily through all the literature that is made available. And other subject fields have to be added in near future. The list of full text e-journals and bibliographic databases subscribed under this program are:

- *Chemical Abstract Services (CAS)*: CAS is the most important, strong and costly service tool in the areas of chemical sciences. As this e-resource needs a specialized training to access, therefore, in 48 universities specialized training program on STN access to Chemical Abstract has been conducted for proper and systematic utilization. The CAS access is given to 10 universities through Sci-Finder and other Universities having the Chemistry subject are getting this access through STN service. The archival access is made available since 1907 onwards.

- *American Chemical Society (ACS)*: Full text access to ACS titles is giving access to the prominent 31 full text e-journals from volume no. 1, issue no. 1.
- *Royal Society of Chemistry (RSC)*: Full text access to RSC titles is given access to 23 journals and 6 databases and the archival access is made available from 1997- onwards.
- *Institute of Physics (IOP)* : Access is provided to 36 full text topmost journals in the area of physics, and the archival access is made available from Vol. 1 issue. 1 of all 36 IOP titles.
- *Nature Journal* : World famous 1 full text unlimited simultaneous access for Nature Weekly from 1997 onwards is available.
- *Cambridge University Press (CUP)* : Access to 72 prominent full text e-journals of CUP are being subscribed under the scheme, and archival access is made available since 1997 onwards. Access to social science and humanities package of CUP titles are given from January 2005.
- *Project Muse* : The access is made available to 222 full text journals in the area of humanities and social sciences with the archival access mostly from 1999- onwards.
- *Biological Abstracts (BA)*: One database for biological sciences with more than 7.7 million archival records are available back to 1969.
- *American Institute of Physics (AIP)* : Access to 19 Full text journals with Archival access from 1997 onwards.

- *American Physical Society (APS)* : Access is made available to 8 Full text journals from 1997 onwards.
- *Encyclopedia Britannica*: Encyclopedia Britannica is one of the popularly used reference tool and can be used by Faculty and research scholars including colleges across the country. INFLIBNET has the National Site License for this reference tool.
- *Science Online* : This is a popular science magazine with 52 issues a year and provides access to the full text of all SCIENCE contents published from October 1996 through the latest issue.
- *Annual Reviews* : Access is made available to all 29 full text journals and archival access is provided up to 10 years back issues.
- *Kluwer Journals* : Access is made available for approximately all the 650 journals of Kluwer online for one year and after that members can access top 100 Kluwer journals. The archival access is provided from 1997 onwards.
- *Springer Online* : Access is made available for around 550 journals from Springer Link for one year and after that member institution will be continued to make access for 100 top Springer journals. The archival access is provided from 1997 onwards.
- *Emerald Journals* : Under UGC-Infonet e-journals consortium access is made available for 28 e-journals from Library and Information Science full text database and archival access is varies from journal to journal but mostly from 1994- onwards.
- *Elsevier Science* : One can access the 34 full text e-journals of health sciences from Cell Press, Current opinions and Trends. The access is made available through the www.sciencedirect.com and archival access is provided from 1995 onwards.

– *J-STOR* : This most awaited e-resource is dealt with back volumes of social sciences, humanities and to some extent with natural science subjects. For accessing JSTOR each university perform the Network Performance Test (NPT). This test is essential for getting access to the JSTOR. JSTOR access is presently given to 24 universities selected by the committee. Member universities can access to 319 full text e-journals from Vol.1 issue 1- onwards up to last two-three years gap depending on the moving wall period of original publisher rights.

– *Ingenta and J-Gate* : 2 subject gateway portals are also available and both of these are gateways for more than 20,000 journals. One of these portals is provided to each university in the first year, however five major universities have been provided both the portals to get the feedback on these portal services. The portals provide one stop solution to all publications and get access to full text access for the above titles from single window.

Present situation of Subscribed E-Resources under UGC-Infonet, E-Journals consortium

Name of the Publisher	***No. of Journals / Database***	***No. of Universities***
American Chemical Society	31	100
Royal Society of Chemistry	23 Journals + 6 Databases	100
Chemical Abstracts Services (Sci-finder Scholar)	One Database	10
Chemical Abstracts - STN service	One Database	100
Nature Publishing Group	One Journal	50
Institute of Physics Publishing (IOPP)	36 Journals	100
Cambridge University Press	189 Journals	100

Name of the Publisher	*No. of Journals / Database*	*No. of Universities*
Project Muse	222 Journals	100
Biological Abstracts - BIOSIS	One database	100
Encyclopedia Britannica	National site Licensing	All academic Institutions
JSTOR - Archival Access	317 Journals (Arts & Science I, II & III. including Languages & Linguistics)	24
American Institute of Physics	19 Journals including AIP society package-II titles	100
American Physical Society	8 Journals	100
Science Online	One Journal	50
Springer and Kluwer Publications	Subscriptions to 200 Journals but the access for all 1200 Journals in the initial one year	100
Elsevier Science-Life Sciences	34 Journals in current trends, opinions, cell press	70
Emerald Library Science Collections	28 Journals	50
Annual Reviews	29 Journals	100
Taylor & Francis	Subscription to 100 journals and access to 1030 journals in the initial one year	100
MathSciNet	One Database	50
Portland Press	4 Journals	50
Gateway Portals	Cover more than 10,000 journals up to abstract level	100

Besides discussions are in progress with several other publishers and their publications are expected to become available in stages.

Probably for the first time in the history of higher education system in India, higher education has been given prominence and access to many scholarly purnals is made available from the support of University Grants Commission. Presently the system allows universities covered under the purview of UGC out gradually it will be extended to colleges and different R & D Institutes of the country. The ultimate goal of this program is work on the virtual philosophy of libraries i.e., right information to the right user at the right time with the help of state-of-the-art technology.

5
Barriers of Resource Sharing

1. Introduction

Kaul has defined some of the laws for smooth functioning of resource sharing. These Seven Laws of Resource Sharing are:

- Library Resources are for Sharing.
- Documents in Standard Database Form are the Dynamic Resources for Global Sharing.
- Every Resource its User.
- Every User His or Her Share of the Resource.
- Minimize the Non-use Period of Documents-in-Demand.
- Automated Delivery Mechanisms of Resources will Progressively Grow.
- Resource Sharing is a Global Phenomenon.

Each author creates a work for the use by others. In this act of creation the author generally keeps in mind the users with whom he wants to share his ideas. He produces a paper, an article, or a book. In case of a book if it is purchased by an individual it may remain locked in his or her collection but if it is obtained by a library, it can remain independent of control and can become a source for sharing by others.

Another factor which forces libraries to share their resources among each other is the economic factor. Libraries cannot afford to buy all documents that are published in the areas of their interest.

Therefore it is noticed that the acts of resource sharing are inherent in the creative and mechanical processes that give birth to publications. Thus the First Law of Resource Sharing could be defined as "*Library resources are for sharing.*" By promoting the sharing of resources the libraries are fulfilling the basic wishes of authors. They enable the books written by authors to be read by others and make sharing possible by using the resource sharing methodologies. As resource sharing is important for libraries, we try to analyse the ways the resource sharing can take place. For each type of document available in the library resource sharing techniques vary in some degrees.

When we examine the types of documents which were produced in the past like books, articles, periodicals, grey literature, including reports and also look into the present day additions such as CDs, video recordings and sound recordings, full text databases, etc., it is noticed that there has been a gradual shift from the physical form of presentation to the mechanical and electronic forms. Today, we have important documents in digital form. In the past, when resources had to be shared, books had be borrowed from one library to another and this process is still happening and will continue to happen. But at the same time the other types of documents are coming in like CDs or the online databases. In case of online databases we notice that the same database can be used by a large number of users simultaneously. Therefore, there is a paradoxical shift from the document being used by one person at one time to the same document being used by several users simultaneously. That is a major development.

And therefore there is a continuous development taking place from the publishing of ideas in the print form to the publishing of ideas in the electronic form. The reason being, the ideas, the basic components of knowledge are moving towards an environment where sharing takes place simultaneously by a large number of users who are stationed in different parts of the world. The electronic form covers distances between the document and the users, and it also covers the concept of simultaneous use as well.

This growing scenario, makes us able to define the Second Law. It is "*Documents in standard database form are the dynamic resources for global sharing.*" If we have to create a document and make it a dynamic resource for global sharing and not only for local sharing, we have to convert the document into the standard database form. Once it is done it is available through INTERNET and through other communication media, and it becomes a dynamic resource for global sharing.

It is also noticed that once an author creates his or her work, that work plays a role on its own. A document forms a part of the universe of knowledge and it contributes to the universe of knowledge in some form or the other. As authors want that their ideas be propagated, authors seal their ideas in words. Once printed and published, they are available for use. Once they are available in a library in document form, they get on to the shelves after some use. If they are just kept on the shelves and not used, the purpose for which the documents/resources were created is defeated. The contents of the documents have to be available for use around the globe. It is the librarian's duty to find out who could be the proper user of a particular document. Thus we get on to the Third Law of Resource Sharing which is "*Every resource its user.*" If the resource is available in the digital form it is very easy or comparatively easier to make it available globally. Greater possibilities of its use become available anywhere in the world. The Third Law gets partly satisfied if the document is available in the digital form.

Once we look at resource sharing from the users' point of view, it is noticed, that users all over the world have their own choices and maintain interest in certain types of publications/ documents. The users are unable to obtain everything they need. It is very important that the system of resource sharing is such that each user gets the document of his or her choice. Then only can we feel that the resources that exist are shared and are made best use of. The Fourth Law of Resource Sharing "*Every user his or her share of the resource*" comes into force. Each user just wants his or her share of the resource. They are not interested in the whole universe of knowledge. No single individual is interested in the whole universe of knowledge because it will not be comprehensible. It will not be possible to assimilate and accommodate all that exists in terms of knowledge and information. But if each person gets his or her share from the universe of knowledge, we are able to satisfy the genuine needs. It is therefore a major obligation on the part of the librarians and information specialists to make such facilities and systems available so that each user is able to get his or her share of the library and information resource.

Another issue that concerns the librarians is the non-use of valuable documents. There is no differentiation between a document which is likely to be used and the document which has lost its utility. In fact, it is very difficult for a librarian to find out which document is valuable and which is not. Since the librarians are involved in the dissemination of information, the librarians should be able to ascertain the life of a document, see that the documents which are in demand are not left without use on the shelves. Today, the librarians mostly feel that once the book has been classified, catalogued and kept on the shelves or at the most listed in the regular lists, the job of the librarian is over. Few librarians make special efforts to see that the books and documents recently acquired are made known to the users so that the users can come and use them. It may happen that a librarian may circulate the list of new books or keep new books closer to the circulation counter so that the members or users may see them and borrow them. This happens mostly for new books, but nothing happens to the books which are old, which stay on the shelves for occasional readers to come and refer to them. There is a need to make the wealth of information available in such documents reach the users.

In several countries, including the United States and the European countries efforts are being made to develop digitized collections. Once the document is digitized there is every possibility of minimising the non-use period of a document because if the document is made available on the INTERNET it can reach a large number of users any time if information about it is well indexed and publicised. Digitization therefore could, to a greater extent, minimise the non-use period of a document. Other methods could also be adopted. It is therefore noticed that there is a need to see that a document-in-demand is always in circulation. The Fifth Law therefore is: "*Minimize the non-use period of a document-in-demand.*"

Now when we talk of minimizing the non-use period of a document-in-demand, we have also to think of efficient delivery mechanisms that exist today or those that could be developed in future. The use of photocopying, fax, post, courier, etc. are being utilized today to a larger extent and the use of sending information through E-mail or passing on digitised data through INTERNET is also growing. There is a shift from the delivery of documents physically to the delivery of documents electronically.

This is an evolutionary shift. More and more documents are becoming available on the INTERNET in the digitized form through automated delivery mechanisms. The physical delivery of documents is slowly taking second place. The Sixth Law of Resource Sharing thus is: "*Automated delivery mechanisms of resources will progressively grow.*"

With the increase in use of better resource sharing mechanisms there is increase in resource sharing work. The patterns which existed in the past for resource sharing in different parts of the world are growing further giving rise to local, regional, national and global resource sharing links. Every country is making an effort to share the resources of the libraries. We have come a long way from the days when books were locked on shelves to the days when the books are becoming available in the digitized form and getting accessible globally. These developments confirm that resource sharing is taking a new shape. Digitized books are available for more and more sharing. The concept of owning information is being replaced by the concept of sharing information. Thus the Seventh Law comes into force: "*Resource sharing is a global phenomenon*."

So above laws are the ideals for a proper resource sharing system. But there are some hurdles which obstruct or act as hinderance in proper functioning of resource sharing. Any barriers to the access of resources will prevent communication and proper flow of information, which in-turn, may cause serious problems and losses for the user.

2. Barrier's Types

Several scholars and experts have identified them in different contexts but it may be necessary to refer to some of them.

2.1. L.B. Woods et. al., state that there are four sources of resistance to resource sharing :

- economic resources;
- political decisions and neglect;
- personal and professional concerns; and
- social and cultural pressures.

They maintain that lack of resources would have promoted resource sharing if the basic structures of sharing were in place. In the Third World countries these basic structures may not be in place for many years. They further add that:

(a) Many countries do not have modern library postal and telecommunication network;

(b) Access to photocopy and facsimile machine is rare;

The protective attitude by institutions in Third World countries is because of (a) and (b) above;

(d) Library planning in developing countries is either sporadic or nonexistent,

(e) Libraries within the same campuses do not exchange documents or the same catalogue standards;

(f) Little support is available for learning; and

(g) Lack of national bibliographies and union catalogue.

2.2. Barriers to resource sharing take various forms and concern different departments of a major library. Sharon C. Bonk reminds us that before one looks into the barriers as such one should understand "what is known and what is still conjecture or myth or unsubstantiated wishful thinking before the promises and potentials are realized or not as the case may be." She lists the following barriers to resource sharing:

1. The belief that the technical infrastructure is not complete and is becoming more fragmented rather than complete;
2. It will move the locus of control of collection development off campus; it will change priorities in collection development;
3. Faculty will not be well served;
4. Document delivery time is too slow to meet local needs;
5. Staff attitudes: Extra work; it won't work;
6. It is too costly of staff time and operations dollars; it is not worth dollars saved or deployed within the acquisitions budget;
7. Library users lack education on the scope of local collections and the extent of document delivery services available and their efficiency;
8. Procedures developed to support resource sharing do not exist or are too difficult to institute across department lines;
9. Administrative structure and support are lacking;
10. There is often difficulty in locating suitable partners;
11. There is a lack of common language for collection description and common definitions for cost studies; and
12. Politics at a regional or national level may prohibit or undermine efforts.

2.3. Joseph A. Bramin looks into this subject and lists following obstacles to resource sharing :

1. A desire for everything here and now;
2. Changing priorities for collection development;
3. Control of collection policies and priorities;
4. Staff and faculty attitudes;
5. Document delivery time;
6. Lack of awareness among users about cooperation;
7. Lack of needed support services;
8. Lack of required administrative structure and support;
9. Non-conducive political environment;
10. Reluctance to yield autonomy; and
11. Lack of common language for analysis and description.

2.4. Several barriers hamper resource sharing activities. While we are able to remove some of the barriers, we can reduce the impact of some others. R. G. Prasher lists the following factors that hamper resource sharing:

1. Attitude of some of the librarians is conservative and they are unwilling to part with the material for resource sharing or do not take up additional responsibilities;
2. Restrictions, mainly local in lending the library materials to others;
3. Due to limited resources, libraries may not participate in ILL;
4. Lack of adequate funds can hamper resource sharing programme;
5. Shortage of staff for handling ILL requests;
6. Lack of reprographic facilities;
7. Distances between the libraries and lack of proper communication system; and
8. Lack of awareness about the usefulness of resource sharing.

2.5. In addition, some of the other barriers that come up in the way leave resource sharing a concept at times. Mr. Prasher refers to the following regulations that are important and need to be introduced:

(a) Interlibrary Loan :

1. Borrowing library will bear the expenditure;
2. Books taken on loan are to be returned within the stipulated time;
3. The books on loan should not be issued out by the borrowing library;
4. The reader for whom the book has been borrowed should use it within the library;
5. If necessary, reproduction of any part of the document may be made permissible;
6. Lending libraries may not loan rare materials;
7. Request for a book which costs less than five rupees and is easily available for purchase should not be made; and
8. Borrowing library will be solely responsible for the safety of the document.

(b) Cooperative procurement of books and other documents, which could be economically desirable does not happen.

(c) Cooperation for centralized system for classification and cataloguing which would reduce duplication does not happen.

(d) Preparation of union catalogues could be done cooperatively for resource sharing.

(e) Cooperative storage could also be achieved if the institutions retained the weeded out books and journals at one place both for storage and reference.

(f) Non-cooperation in documentation work results in duplication in documentation work by the institutions specialising in the same subjects. This barrier of non-cooperation needs to be removed by:

1. Allotting subjects for documentation work in a discipline to different institutions to avoid duplication; and
2. offering all documentation lists to the users through a network.

(g) The exchange of surplus/duplicate copies of journals and books can fill vital gaps in the libraries. Cooperation in this regard is very scanty and it can be promoted only if the management have liberal policies and the librarians make an extra effort to inform intended libraries about their surplus stocks.

(h) The exchange of experts in the library and information science field is becoming increasingly important as information technology is changing very fast.

2.6. Besides, Improvements in international relations, on the one hand, and tighter economic pressures, on the other, demand greater cooperation at many more levels than was previously thought necessary or deemed desirable. Now vastly different world entities, including both newly emerging and reconfigured ones, each recognize a greater need for international interaction and perceive their potential of being able to bring a unique contribution to the world's information-access bargaining table.

Several long-existing barriers to resource sharing seem to be gaining renewed attention as major issues are considered. Some of those factors are easily identifiable for deeper scrutiny.

1. Lack of Technological Sophistication : Serious international considerations and cooperation have been delayed because of network unreliability and erratic electrical supply; limited reprographic equipment with concomitant insufficient maintenance and inadequate climate control, lack of technical know-how; shortage of paper and spare parts; inadequate printing and binding equipment. The lack of equipment to use microfilms, audio-visual media and computerized services caused frustrations.

2. Physical and Economic Barriers : Distance and costs have limited services and hours of opening, have prevented full utilization of resources: currency conversions and restrictions prevented serious negotiations, and the shortage of resources-human, financial and material—-limited the international services that could be provided. Such fiscal limitations have curtailed the ability to publish enough local materials, and even postage and shipping regulations have presented barriers.

3. Politically Acceptable Efforts : Ideology has dictated that censorship of materials was often arbitrarily administered and restrictions for reasons ofreligious belief, national security and other political considerations became obsessions. Sharing of resources was discouraged for economic as well as political reasons

4. Sociological/Cultural/Educational Impacts : High illiteracy and poor motivation to use services produced varying service objectives; poor presentation of information or lack of identified need; language barriers; lack of training and tradition in the use of information, resistance to change; and the intangibility of many of the benefits of information access were detractors.

5 Information Policies and Plans : Lack of a suitable infrastructure and established national information policies produced conflicting ad-hoc decisions; ineffective performance of systems; lack of effective procedures, and inadequate bibliographic control by both book trade and libraries presented major barriers. Semantics prevented both natural and machine language interaction.

6. Legal Considerations : Unnecessary restrictions and procedures associated with the use of published materials including copyright, censorship, and photocopying restrictions produced frustrations.

7. Personal Skepticism : Prejudice and value differences held by those responsible for action promoted suspicion and distrust. The lack of vision and interest on the part of librarians and information professionals acts as a major barrier in resource sharing. Even if the information is available and the information professional is not willing to help a user, nothing can be done. This missing link can create a great deal of loss or irreparable loss to a user. The information professional has to have faith in serving the users as service to the nation or humanity as such or should at least consider fulfilling his moral obligation by providing the best service possible to the users. The information service professionals should follow a code of conduct and if need be, should be educated about their obligations to the society or the users in their libraries in particular. This will minimize the impact of this barrier.

8. Financial Implications : It is a well-known fact that because of the limitations of finance and space, no library can afford to house every document. As such efforts are made to share resources. But it becomes necessary to see how we save finances by resource sharing. Therefore, our attention gets drawn to the jobs the resource sharing networks take for coordinating the processes of packing besides infrastructures and staff. As such, ILL service can be priced. The job thus involves the pricing of the service and the recovery of costs. In this connection, a reference may be made to the pricing of ILL service by the University of New South Wales (UNSW) and the controversy it created. CD. Marshall of Riverina Community Library Service claimed that UNSW did not consult fellow professional colleagues, did not "carry out proper research into either the costs of ILL or the impact of charging on the end user." He also maintains that cost-recovery is a difficult job to perform in academic libraries. He was against charging as he considerd: "To charge for ILL is penalizing the many of the benefit of the academically privileged few." But in the modern world information is considered as a commodity and the efforts made for sharing it and for facilitating its use has to be compensated in order to see to it that the resource sharing networks run on a no-profit-no-loss basis.

The advanced technology is reducing slowly the impact of obstacles in resource sharing and it is likely that one day the role of the librarian and nature of resource sharing will be redefined. Librarians could help the user in selecting the right information from thousands and thousands of items. Thus the resource sharing and accessing techniques will change and so will the economic parameters.

Michael J. Carmel has presented the method for calculating the economic benefit of a resource sharing scheme. This is a method to compare the cost of cooperative interlibrary photocopying using a union list of serials with that of using the prepaid British Library Document Supply Centre (BLDSC) forms.

Step 1: *To compare costs between a scheme and use of BLDSC*

Let C=the sum of all those costs which are specific to the system; i.e., excluding those which are also incurred when using BLDSC by prepaid form

Let B = the cost of each BLDSC form

Then if C<B the system is cost saving (although not guaranteed to be worth doing)

If C = B the system is viable

If C > B the system has a net cost, which may be worth bearing if the organizational or service benefits are sufficient.

Step 2 : *To calculate C*

Let O = the fixed annual overhead costs incurred at the centre administering the scheme.

Let N = the number of times the list is successfully used each year

Let Cr=the specific costs incurred at the requesting library

Let Cs = the specific costs incurred at the supplying library

Then C=Cr+Cs+O/N.

Step 3 : *To calculate O/N*

"O" comprises all the capital, labour and materials costs assignable to the maintenance of the system itself (agreeing procedures, training, etc.) and the collection, processing, reproduction and distribution of information about holdings, availability, location, and both temporary and long-term amendments.

This calculation can be substituted by an estimate of 1,500 UK pounds pa +/-500 UK pound p.a. However, this does depend on the infrastructure that already exists. Data on N is available in regional systems, and would need to be collected for others.

Step 4 : *To calculate Cr*

Let I (look-up) = time in minutes spent looking up each item in the union list and recording the information on the form

Let h (hit-rate) = the proportion of items searched for that are actually in the list (if half the items are found, h=l/2). (This element is extremely important)

Let t = cost per minute of staff time, averaged over the staff doing the work

Let o = cost to library of keeping the union list up-to-date (sending in own amendments, writing in amendments, etc.)

Let n = number of successful uses

Then Cr = t 1/h + o/n

Step 5: *To calculate Cs*

Let r = average time in minutes spent receiving, identifying and sorting each request

Let w1 = average time in minutes spent walking to the shelves and finding the item

Let h (hit-rate) = proportion of items found on shelves each time

Let w2= average time in minutes spent walking to the photocopier, and then returning the item to the shelves

Let c = time spent copying the item

Let d = time spent dispatching the item

Let p1 = cost of copy paper etc.

Let p2 = postal cost

Then Cs = t (((r + w1)/h) + c + w2 + d) + p1 + p2

Comment on important variables

"t" i.e., cost per minute is central. It must allow for the full annual cost of employment, divided by the actual number of minutes worked per year. Most authorities agree that after allowing for leave and sickness, "wasted" time, breaks, overheads and essential but unproductive tasks, 1,500 hours per year is the average actually worked in white collar occupations. Where posts arc graded lower than they should be, it would be sensible to calculate 't' according to preferred rate of pay rather than actual rates. This would show librarians valuing their own time at a proper rate.

'h' is a decisive variable in both Cr and Cs and can tip the balance of the equation. The viability of the present regional systems rests partly on the similarity of the libraries' subject interests, which produce a high hit-rate for low costs. Extensions to the system would probably involve a high marginal cost per hit. So would any system involving either general libraries or a wide range of special interests.

'w1' and 'w2' both show up very large differences between supplying libraries according to their physical size and level of development, 'w1' is highest in bigger libraries (where the effect is further emphasized because 'h' is often lower)." w2' may be high in a small library that does not have its own photocopier.

However, according to Kaul in an Indian scenario in which DELNET is offering both online ILL and ILL reference service through its unions lists and catalogues, the following scenario emerges:

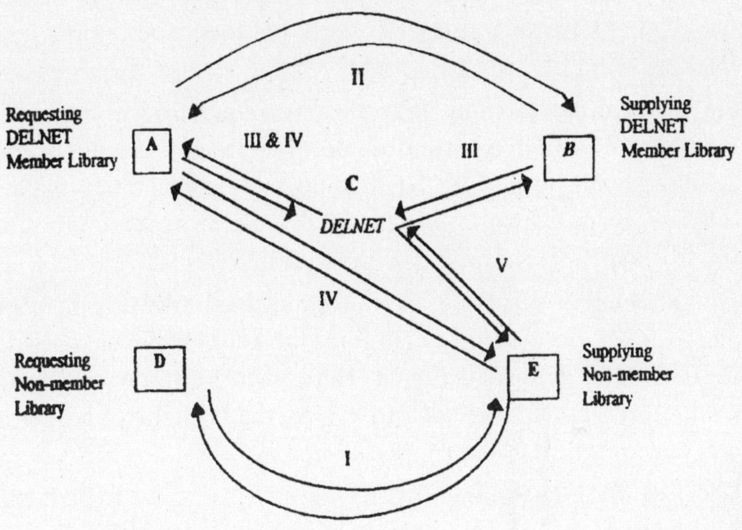

DELNET ILL Scenario

Scenario I : In this case a library is not a member of DELNET and for borrowing a book, it makes several telephone calls before locating a book or deciding not to pursue the search further. In case it locates a book in a library, it sends its person once to collect the book and again to return it.

Scenario II : In this case both the requesting library and borrowing library are members of DELNET. The requesting library searches the union catalogue of books and then gets the book itself and later returns it to the library.

Scenario III : In this case the requesting library and the supplying library are both members of DELNET and the requesting library has paid Rs. 4,000/- as online ILL charges. As soon as the requesting library finds the book in the DELNET union catalogue, it enters the request in the DELNET online ILL facility. DELNET immediately sends its courier, collects the book and delivers it to the requesting library. After the borrowing period, the DELNET courier collects the book and returns it to the supplying library.

Scenario IV : In this case the requesting library is a member of DELNET but it does not find about one tenth of the required books in the DELNET union catalogue and thus makes the search on its own to find the book, collect it and return it to the library.

Scenario V : In this case the requesting library is a member and uses ILL online facility but finds the book/document outside the DELNET union catalogue. Here also the library requests DELNET to collect the book from a particular library, deliver it and later return it to the supplying library.

In these five scenarios, it may be of interest to find the expenditures incurred by the requesting library, supplying library and DELNET in the promotion of ILL facility.

Requesting/Borrowing Libraries

a = Membership fee

b = Expenditure on staff

c = Miscellaneous expenditure Rs. 5 per book

d = Expenditure on phone

c = Courier

f = Books borrowed per year

g = Number of users

h = Number of books available in library

i = Number of professional staff

a. Membership fee of DELNET is Rs. 5000/-. Membership is used for searching 14 databases and for reference work, including 7 databases for full text and INTERNET services, i.e, for Union Catalogue of Books alone Rs. 357/- are spent if we divide Rs. 5000/- by the number of databases.

b. Expenditure on staff: On an average if a library spends Rs. 7000/ on a person for reference and ILL work.

Expenditure Made by Requesting Libraries

Scenario I

b = Expenditure on staff: Rs. [x]. This is a variable. The salary will depend upon the type of library and the quality of services offered.

f = books borrowed per year. It is estimated that on an average 10 books arc borrowed per month, i.e., 120 per year on an average per year

d =	Expenditure on phone		
	@ Rs. 10/- per book = 10 × 120		1200
e =	Expenditure on courier		
	@ Rs. 40/- per book each time (i.e. Rs. 80/-		
	per book (two trips, both sides) = 120 × 80	=	9,600
c =	Misc. expenditure Rs. 5 pet book = 5 × 120	=	600
	Total: x + d + e + c		= x + 11,400.00

Scenario II

a =	Expenditure on account of membership		
	for ILL = 5000/14	=	357.00
b =	Expenditure on staff	=	x
d =	Expenditure on phone = 1 × 120	=	120.00
e =	Expenditure on courier = 80 × 120	=	9600.00
c =	Misc. Expenditure = 5 × 120	=	600.00
	Total: x + a + b + d + e + c		= x + 10,677.00

Scenario III

a =	Membership expenditure = 5000/14	= 357.00
b =	Staff	= x
d =	Phone = 1 × 120	= 120.00
e =	Courier	= 4000.00
c =	Misc. Exp.	= 0
	Total: x + a + b + d + e + c	= x + 4477.00

Scenario IV

a =	Membership expenditure = 5000/14	= 357.00
b =	Staff	= x
d =	Phone 10 × 12	= 120.00
	1 × 100	= 100.00
e =	DELNET Courier	= 4000 00
f =	Local Courier =12 × 80	= 960.00
c =	Misc, = 5 × 12	= 60.00
	Total: x + a + b + d + e + f + c	= x + 5597.00

Scenario V

a =	Membership Exp. = 5000/14	= 357.00
b =	Staff	= x
d =	Phone = 10 × 12	= 120.00
	1 × 100	= 100.00
e =	DELNET Courier	= 4000.00
	Total : x + a + b + d + e	= x + 4577.00

If we sum up the above analysis and consider the value of x (the staff) as the same for all types of libraries, we get the following picture of the expenditure involved during one year on ILL for 120 titles:

Scenario :	I	Rs 11,400/-
	II	Rs. 10,677/-
	III	Rs. 4,477/-
	IV	Rs. 5,597/-
	V	Rs. 4,577/-

From the above analysis it is noticed that the use of DELNET's online ILL facility (Scenario III) is the cheapest. It saves the borrowing library from all the botheration of handling DLL requests.

2.7 Technology

Three major areas of information technology—computing, communications, and contents, all developed during the last decade—have made dramatic technological changes in libraries. During this short period of time, the advent of personal computers; worldwide packet networks; optical disc and other mass storage media; interactive video technology; and the growth both in size and number of public and private databases—first bibliographic, then numeric, and now multimedia—are observable forces in library services. Indeed, it is fair to say that the use of computing and information technologies in the library workplace is not only widespread but is becoming mandatory. These are becoming integrated and international in scope and impact.

Access to a worldwide on-line information bank, is an essential component for national and international advancement and cultural understanding as well as industrial and economic development. This trans-border interaction benefits everyone. Technology has removed geographic barriers to communication Both satellites and broadcast capabilities to an entire continent and other telecommunications capabilities allow instantaneous communication throughout the world. The ability to communicate has created a library marketplace not limited to a single country, area, region or even continent. The information revolution has helped shape this global dimension and at the same time have presented new challenges and issues to be explored indepth.

Recently some of those barriers have begun to crumble, while others remain unaddressed and unresolved. For instance, on-line database development, CD-ROM technology, Fax machines, and particularly the Internet are technologies which have removed some physical barriers. The rapid expansion of knowledge and technology and the growth in worldwide literacy have greatly enhanced the library's role and its potential function. All of those factors noted must now be explored in a systematic manner to put into place a context for international cooperation.

There is no doubt that the educational, social, cultural and political climate of each country has had influence on the development of libraries and library service. An acronym, PEST (political, economic, social and technological), captures the various pressures which influence information access.

The readiness and ability of a nation to support an expanded library programme is key to the further interaction across borders. This is fertile ground for comparative research. If library science is truly the global discipline strategically best suited to bring about one world of understanding in a world of conflicting cultures no longer apart by time and space then it is important to speculate on that point of time in the life of a nation that libraries and librarianship begin to play a vital role in the development of each individual country. Identification of the manifestation of this role is important in individual countries – are there in existence basic services including an indigenous library science programme; a national library; a national library association; a system of public libraries; a national bibliography? If not, how can cooperation be effective without developing that common base? If so, how does it vary among nations and how can it become compatible with others? International research studies on those aspects could add greatly to the knowledge base of librarianship.

2.8 Networking Aspects

International networking has begun to create a world bibliographic database of library holdings and information resources management. But coupled with this bibliographic access is the need to establish a centralized source of each country's total information output. This is a complicated task deserving concentrated study. Cooperative ventures, utilizing such technologies as CD-ROM, promise easier access by more international users to national bibliographies and realize cost-savings in cataloguing on both the local and international scene. The bibliographical holdings of major libraries, now available on the Internet, enhances this development. Those transborder ventures, as they develop, are likely to make access less costly and more timely. Issues of who owns what and whether or not it is copyrightable are questions still to be resolved on the international scale, and will surely impact the sharing of databases.

A number of on-line library catalogues, local databases, network newsletters, interest group fora on specific library topics, and innumerable text, graphic, image, and sound files, as well as executable programmes, are currently available on the Internet. These are but examples of international library networks developing. Indexing and abstracting databases now provide access to the world's research literature; full text systems enrich the information access process; work stations provide conversion of printed materials into electronic forms; and mass optical storage systems support local network desktop delivery of electronic images to users. The library's place in this information rich milieu is a researchable theme.

For promoting resource sharing networks of libraries, it is necessary to look into the following important facets of library networking.

(i) Participating Libraries

For efficient resource sharing work, the selection of

libraries joining a network should be based on the following criteria:

(a) Each library should be willing to buy its own hardware, software and at least have one telephone connection, either a direct line or a line with zero dialling facility.

(b) The library should have at least two professional staff with a degree in library science and familiarity with bibliographic standards;

(c) It should undertake to pay the necessary participation fee to a network or more networks.

(d) The participating library should follow rules and regulations of the network and be willing to create bibliographic records according to standards laid down.

(e) It should pool its bibliographic records that it creates in machine-readable form in the Central Host of the network. The copyright of the records created by the library should vest in the library but the copyright of the records so pooled in the Central Host of the network should vest with the network.

(f) The librarians specializing in any subject should be able to join a library network in a city.

(g) The gradation of libraries should not be made on the number of books they hold, but the rate at which they convert their records into machine-readable form, and the number of transactions they have or are likely to have in a graded form through the automated system.

(ii) Institutional Autonomy

Resource sharing among libraries is based always on an understanding among the libraries that they will share their resources. This needs decisions to be taken and such decisions are taken fast by the institutions when they are autonomous. Otherwise, it has been noticed in DELNET that the institutions that are dependent financially upon others or sponsoring organizations cannot take decisions on their own. As such the absence of autonomy in an institution can act as a barrier in resource sharing activities.

(iii) Locating Suitable Partners

Resource sharing can be done best by the institutions acquiring the same type of material so that they can rationalize their acquisition programmes. It becomes very essential to locate suitable institutional partners that are ready to cooperate in acquisition and sharing of resources. As a result, collection development work becomes smooth and reciprocal.

(iv) Geographic Proximity

The location of suitable partners is an important factor in resource sharing, for, until all resources are not converted into electronic form, it is necessary that the documents, other than those that could be faxed, are physically transported fast. As such close proximity of the locations of institutions facilitates resource sharing work.

(v) Role of Librarians

Resource sharing is not possible unless the librarians cooperate among each other and with their management. It has been noticed in DELNET that some of the librarians who were not interested in resource sharing with other libraries managed to send notes to their management against resource sharing on one pretext or the other. It is therefore considered that the librarians themselves could act as major barriers in resource sharing if they were not interested in it.

(vi) Training of Librarians

Lack of proper training in the use of online catalogues, INTERNET and network databases for locating materials and making online ILL requests, would hamper the speed of acquisition of materials. As retrieval commands change from time to time, officials in charge of resource sharing would have to remain in touch with the changes and update themselves regularly.

(vii) Participation in Resource Sharing Networks

Resource sharing is not possible unless the participating libraries begin to agree to share and this sharing takes different forms. The agreement to share depends upon the compulsions of the participating libraries and their desire to help other institutions and users. An interesting example of this is seen in the resource sharing networks started by the Committee on Institutional Cooperation, USA in which they agreed to cooperate in:

(a) Microfilming project;

(b) Reciprocal borrowing facility for faculty;

(c) Telecommunication/networking infrastructure;

(d) Free loans and photocopies and waive interlibrary loan fees;

(e) Five of the eleven CIC libraries agreed to lend materials including dissertations/theses, bound serials, fragile materials and audiovisual materials; and

(f) Eight CIC libraries agreed to send all article requests by fax.

The non-participation of libraries in a network can act as a major barrier in resource sharing. But, if the participation is full, the barrier vanishes to a greater extent. A typical example that needs a mention is from Illinois Libraries Computer Systems Organisation (ILCSO) which according to B.G. Sloan, has three levels of participation.

1. Forty libraries use the system in support of local operations, and for resource sharing and interlibrary circulation. This group includes the libraries of each state-supported university, 19 privately supported colleges and universities, four community colleges, one state-supported high school for mathematics and science, and the Illinois State Library, the state library agency and library to state government.
2. Eight hundred libraries contribute catalogue records to the database through their subscription to the State's ILLINET/ OCLC services. The University of Illinois receives weekly

subscription tapes from OCLC, and these records are processed through a series of programmes that prepare the data for entry into the ILLINET Online database.

3. Twenty-six hundred Illinois libraries participate in the Illinois Library and Information Network (ILLINET) and may connect to ILLINET Online via dial access. ILLINET Online borrower IDs have been assigned to each of those twenty-six hundred libraries, and may be used to inititate requests for materials held by the forty ILCSO member libraries.

It is noticed that the large participation of libraries in the network have promoted the network for effective resource sharing. The large scale participation of libraries has greatly reduced the impact of obstacles which could have affected resource sharing.

One of the major concerns of a network for better network participation is to introduce services so that the access to various types of databases becomes possible. An example of ILLINET Online system is worth noting. The system first started with providing access to its online union catalogue, but later began offering access to CARL Uncover, a current contents database; and to the Illinois Bibliographic Information System (IBIS), a collection of online journal indexes including ERIC and a selection of W.H. Wilson databases covering several subjects. The role of networks as the experiences of established networks go, is to introduce a large number of relevant databases among its users so that the dark chamber of ignorance which acts as a barrier between the resources and the users is diminished.

(viii) In-House Functions

In-house functions like acquisition, cataloguing, classification, series control, circulation, SDI, current awareness service, etc. should be left to the libraries. The network software should support these operations of the libraries and the libraries should use the data in Central Host for this purpose.

(ix) The Hardware

Hardware includes following aspects :

(a) The network should be able to recommend to participating libraries the type of hardware they need for their in-house functions and for networking purposes.

(b) It must be noted that the use of microcomputers in networking is going to grow further.

(c) Hardware should be selected considering the number of entries the participating libraries can generate within the next 3-5 years which will also dictate the configuration.

(d) The size of collection at a library should never be regarded as the norm for hardware selection.

(e) The hardware should be able to accommodate the need to be raised in next coming 3-5 years. So latest configuration must be purchased. And it should be upgradable.

(f) The hardware at the Central Host may be upgraded depending upon the speed with which participating libraries generate records and pool them into the Central Host.

(x) The Software

Software includes following aspects.

(a) A common software must preferably be used by all the participating libraries.

(b) The network should be able to provide a networking software for creating bibliographic databases.

(c) Commercial software that has not been internationally tested on large databases should not be used.

(d) A networking software should be able to handle in-house operations of libraries including SDI and CAS, promote database creation and accommodate communication interfaces.

(e) The network should maintain or arrange to see that the software in use is upgraded from time to lime.

(xi) The Standards

The absence of common standards creates incompatibility problems and stops the flow of bibliographic and related information. The standards, protocols and the software that convert data from one format to another should essentially be of international standing.

Format compatibilities are necessary for computerized catalogue data and these are being standardised by the ISO standards. ISO 2709 has been adopted the world over and the efforts to harmonize MARC formats are on. Reference may be made to the efforts made by the British Library, Library of Congress and National Library of Canada who achieved a major milestone in harmonising their MARC formats in January 1997. According to the joint communique published on INTERNET: "The benefits of a harmonised format include easier and more efficient record exchange between the users and procedures of MARC records, elimination of the need for conversion programs, and potential reductions in the expense of format maintenance and documentation. Whereas full harmonisation of USMARC and CANMARC has been accomplished, the three libraries recognize that UKMARC must retain certain features of particular value to the UKMARC user community, and therefore full harmonization is not achievable in the short term. Partial alignment is being pursued immediately with full harmonization as a long-term goal."

DELNET has been successfully using CCF (Common Communication Format). This format incorporates only necessary and sufficient fields, and conversion of databases in this format is possible at international levels. For compatibility with international and national bibliographical databases DELNFT has now started the use of MARC format.

Maintenance of bibliographic standards uniformly is essential for quick exchange of records.

(a) AACR-II is the widely accepted code for cataloguing. It helps in the creation of standard records.

(b) LCSH is used by DELNET and many networks in the world. It should be used as a guide for creating subject descriptors. Other thesauri available on specialised subjects could also be used whenever needed in specialised libraries.

(c) A network should also maintain the authority and thesaurus data. DELNET has already begun authority data on its MARC database.

(d) DDC is commonly used as the classification scheme.

Todays, MARC format is used mostly in libraries.

(xii) Language Barriers

Intellectual barriers include language, subject heading lists, authority files besides descriptive cataloguing rules.

A language acts as a major barrier in resource sharing as it does not allow the use of information to be made by users who do not know that particular language. The system designers need to consider not only the accessibility of text but also screen displays, documentation, character sets, etc. for the users who may not know the language of the text. In the bibliographic database which is interconnected with housekeeping functions in order to ascertain the availability of a particular document the system search is more complex, especially if it has to cater to bibliographic data in several languages.

Rowland C. W. Brown adds: "Acceptance of vernacular non-roman alphabets and characters along with multiple transliteration schemes present significant obstacles which will not be overcome by cooperative action of interested international partners."

In this regard reference may be made to GIST technology developed by C-DAC in Pune and adopted by DELNET for bibliographic databases. It is being used successfully for Indian languages, except for Perso-Arabic scripts.

The rendering of subject headings in a standard way and terminology that is comprehensible to the users all over the world becomes very essential in bringing the right users closer to the right documents. The use of Library of Congress Subject Headings is growing although the use of (PRECIS Preserved Context Index System) and specialized indexes are also in vogue.

The authority files like those of the Library of Congress have to grow so that we develop an authority file and system acceptable to users all over the world. But all this has to be done in conformity with the standard cataloguing rules. Anglo-American Cataloguing Rules, 2nd edition are being used in major libraries in the world.

(xiii) Promotion of Database Creation

It includes following activities :

(a) The maintenance of centralised databases are good when the communication facilities are not reliable. A Central Host machine should be installed for creating a union catalogue, comprising catalogues of all participating libraries.

(b) A Central Host that can accommodate about 10 lakh bibliographic records with work space for data handling, system software, communication software, application software, etc. may be used.

(xiv) Electronic Mail and INTERNET

It should comply :

(a) Electronic mail is a must for each participating library.

(b) Besides E-mail, the use of INTERNET is essential as it enables wider access to international databases.

(xv) Classification

The following conditions must be fulfilled :

(a) As libraries in India use mainly DDC, UDC and CCC for classification of books, it would not be within the means and worth the effort to have one classification scheme in all participating libraries.

(b) One class number, preferably a Dewey number should be given in machine-readable bibliographic data.

(c) As search requests would mostly be by authors, titles, editors and subject descriptors, the network would offer a commendable service. For the few classification based search requests the network staff could make special searches using class numbers.

(d) For the National Bibliographic Database Pilot Project, it is must to give class numbers of a record in each library along with the standard Dewey Decimal class number.

(xvi) Interlibrary Loan

For this following condition must be sought :

(a) A network should promote the online interlibrary loan service.

(b) Rationalisation of foreign periodicals should be attempted. As far as possible foreign exchange should be saved on avoidable duplicate titles.

(c) A courier facility should be established by the network to support the sharing of resources.

(xvii) Network Topology

Network topology include :

(a) A centralised topology may be preferred in India due to limitations in the communication facilities. Whereas in big cities a mix of distributed-cum-centralised topology may be preferred.

(b) Efforts should be made to develop union catalogues in a central database.

(xviii) Communication Links

For this, following aspects must be seen :

(a) The network operation should be established on circuit switching principle.

(b) Packet switching data network should be used.

(c) Transactions between libraries and the Central Host could be in online mode.

(d) The user in a network should be able to log into the Central Host or his request should be sent to the system.

(e) Network specifications as recommended from time to time may be considered for a city network in India with suitable adjustments.

(xix) Legal Issues

Copyright issues are acting as major barriers in the free flow of information. In case of bibliographic records, their exchange and use has to be authorised by the copyright holder or the licensed authority. In the international scenario data protection laws and transborder dataflow regulations affect online access and exchange and transfer of information. OCLC has successfully met several issues through a variety of solutions.

(xx) Governance

Governance include following aspects :

(a) A network should have a clear aim of resource sharing as a guide for all activities.

(b) The constitution should be democratic with scope for participation of libraries in the Governing Board of a network.

(xxi) Agreements

Agreements between libraries are essential for resource sharing. A reference may be made to the increasing pressure on university libraries in South Africa for rationalising INTERNET operations and improvement of mutual resource sharing. The recommendations made by E.D. Gerryts and H. de Bruin on improving resource sharing and rationalisation have given considerable support to the idea of formal, cooperative service, agreements between university libraries for the possible establishment of a cooperative organization.

2.9 Information Policy

One further remaining barrier to politically acceptable cooperative ventures is the paucity of information policies which, by implication, have international ramifications. Such policies, now being recognized as necessary to support economic, industrial, social and educational development, have been naively ignored until recently. Further, it is being recognized that information policies are vital to address and facilitate regional or geographical area policies Such policies have the potential of promoting "the free flow of all non-proprietary non-confidential information to each individual, regardless of location, level of comprehension, economic status, or other circumstances".

Resource sharing policies come into existence at several points policies of international agencies like IFLA, national governments, resource sharing networks, institutional members of networks and institutions outside the networks all act as agents of resource sharing. Their policies or non-policies either promote resource sharing or act as barriers thus slowing down or stopping genuine efforts for the execution of resource sharing work.

(i) International Concerns

International Federation of Library Associations and Institutions (IFLA) has been undertaking various projects for resource sharing. The latest in its efforts for resource sharing has been the creation of IFLA Training Database which helps in locating suitable partners the world over for resource sharing purposes. Such efforts and policies have to grow more. This is becoming possible through INTERNET and electronic publishing programmes.

There is a great deal of duplication going on in the cataloguing all over the world and as a result, non-existence of universal union catalogues result in either delays in resource sharing or no resource sharing at all in case of a majority of publications, IFLA's core programmes, Universal Bibliographic Control and International MARC (UBCIM) promotes the production of internationally compatible bibliographic records and their exchange on internationally accepted standards. There is a need to share catalogue records. In order to do so electronically OSI is considered to work as an effective tool for the transfer of bibliographic records.

Cynthia J Durance and Neil McLean note that barriers exist in resource sharing. "First, the citation/verification and the location process. As electronic abstracting and indexing databases and bibliographic union files proliferate, ones ability to search multiple databases is restricted by several things: different proprietary terminals are sometimes required and if so, there are costs associated with maintaining these separate terminals; there are difficulties of unconnected databases; there are separate billing mechanisms for each; and finally, different search arguments and language must be used to search different databases to find either the desired citation or location, or both".

(ii) National Policies

The national policies should be such that all information except confidential or classified should become available online for public use. Also, each country should have at least one library or a centre which holds at least one copy of all documents that are relevant to that country. Information has become a world resource and participating of each nation in the creation of the world information infrastructure is necessary and useful. In each country, centres need to be promoted for maintaining libraries in specific disciplines and such libraries should play roles for the dissemination of information in that discipline nationally and globally.

The following six points are recommended for consideration while go for designing a national policy for resource sharing.

1. Each country should create a national centre for establishing and administering interlending norms and procedures. This centre would also be responsible for

handling requests and providing the documents requested within a national structure based on simple procedures and clear and uniform policies.

2. There should be a better understanding of new information technologies, for example, INTERNET and electronic mail, so that they can be used to improve service.
3. There should be a systematic acknowledgement of copyright of requested materials.
4. New policies for the application of standardized photocopying costs of documents should be implemented.
5. A uniform approach to the collection of ILL statistics should be collected on satisfied requests, failed requests, speed of service, requesting organisations, type of material requested, etc.
6. Seminars and formal or informal courses on interlending should be held in the region in order to promote the fundamental rale in which this service plays a part in the universal availability of a publications programme.

2.10. Recently, Gatenby and Goldner studied barriers to deep resource sharing among libraries. The responses from the French studies library group (FSLG), London, are listed below :

1. Is there currently significant sharing of resources (which could be stock, staff, expertise, technology, space, etc) in this subject area of LIS?

Access : Reciprocal agreements such as the M25 Consortium scheme or UK Libraries Plus; also various reciprocal agreements negotiated between individual libraries.

Specialist staff and expertise : Sharing of expertise via our FSLG discussion list and other mailing lists; also sharing of experience sessions on particular topics. This is the most frequent and hitherto most useful form of sharing.

We are not aware of any subject specialist appointed to two or more libraries in our field.

Note that CURL has recently conducted a survey of language expertise.

Stock : Some exchange of stock takes place in the context of disposals where other institutions are given the opportunity to take over the material e.g. via the FSLG mailing list.

BLDSC makes available material to other libraries from its own stock or from backup libraries, thus saving them from having to purchase it themselves. DSC also currently lends post-1950 non legal-deposit material from the BL London Collections (DSC ceased purchasing books in foreign languages in 1996).

The SCOLMA Acquisitions Specialization Scheme in the cooperative acquisition of material, wherever published, relating to African subjects and regions.

HE DNER deals for electronic resources.

Storage : In London the University of London Depository Library (both cooperative and collaborative storage).

2. Are there areas in which further resource sharing would benefit the work of LIS staff and users in this subject area?

Access : Enhanced reciprocal access to collections: at least for onsite reference and ideally offering access to other library services such as borrowing rights.

Stock : Assumption is that the aim is to increase the national provision of research-level materials, to rationalize holdings where appropriate and to identify current gaps in provision.

Pre-requisites for any cooperative collection development are:

– a union catalogue of books and of serials.
– effective mapping of collections. There may be transferable lessons to be learnt from the current RSLP collaborative collection management projects, especially COCOREES and Mapping Asia.
– survey of needs of researchers.

- agreed collection description standard.
- publishing and publicizing individual libraries' collection development policies.
- improved promotion and exploitation of existing collections.

Preconditions for successful implementation are:

- Ongoing commitment and funding from Government and partner institutions to meet the costs of:
  - Long-term collecting and retention.
  - Making material promptly available (acquisitions and cataloguing).
  - Cheap and quick document delivery (hard copy and electronic).
- Selection of focused and clearly defined area for coordination:
  - expensive purchases in all formats; also possible development of consortial purchasing of this material; lobbying e-providers for more foreign-language/ foreign-related material.
  - and/or by area/subject (e.g. Caribbean, minority languages (Occitan, Breton, etc); also coordination on disposals, especially cancellation of serial subscriptions.

There is scope for the cooperation in other areas:

- *cataloguing.*
- development of *subject gateways and portals.*
- selection of material for *digitization* to identify rare/unique material and provide one-stop online access to collections dispersed in different institutions.
- cooperative/collaborative *storage* of older, lesser-used material. The facility should offer onsite access, inter-library loans, an online catalogue and preservation facilities.

3. What barriers have you experienced or would you expect to arise in further resource sharing in this subject area?

Access : Allowing enhanced access to external users is difficult in institutions experiencing pressures in space and staffing.

Staff and expertise : There is a decline in the number of subject specialists as staff are increasingly being asked to take on extra areas of responsibility with a consequent dilution of expertise. This has a negative impact on releasing the necessary staff time to work on collaborative projects.

Stock : Collection development in university libraries is typically driven by current teaching and research needs. These are liable to change as academic staff develop new courses or new research interests or move to a different institution.

In practice, collaborative collecting is likely to centre on the national and legal deposit libraries and the major university research libraries. This could be politically sensitive if the result is to further reinforce the gap between the majority of institutions and the elite few. Subject to the caveats below improved resourcing of specialized collections would be desirable. This should not, however, be at the expense of diverting funds from the London and Oxbridge golden triangle which constitutes a world-class resource. London is the most accessible destination from the rest of the UK. The licensing agreements for electronic resources usually restrict access to the staff and students of the institution buying in the service. Non-HEIs are currently excluded from HEDNER deals.

Funding : Institutions are typically keen to guard their autonomy and may have very different missions. Most university libraries are experiencing funding constraints. There are three main flinders in England: DfES (HEIs via HEFCE), DCMS (British Library) and DTLR (public libraries via local authorities). Different arrangements are in place in Northern Ireland, Scotland and Wales. There are also research collections funded by a wide variety of host institutions. Some institutions rely on funding or donations from overseas for material (e.g. the Centre de Recherches Francophones Beiges at the University of Edinburgh).

Users : User buy-in is essential. There may be a reluctance to travel since this impacts on the researcher's own time and often his/her own money. This is a real barrier as academics are under increasing pressure to publish but have heavy administrative and teaching commitments.

So, it can be stated that the developments are changing the lives of librarians and the profile of libraries They impact a global educational and research community are being concentrated into a single life span. New information technology now makes possible the development of a truly working electronic library, an institution that is committed to basic principles of the widest possible access to information; and the use of electronic technology to increase and manage information resources.

Several issues of international networking and resource sharing, present interesting research challenges which could effect:

- Changing national policies that tightly control, discourage, or even prohibit trans-national data flow;
- Developing common standards, both bibliographic and technical;
- Resolving issues of distance, availability, and costs of the physical items, as well as the need for foreign exchange to purchase equipment, software, and data from outside the country; and
- Increasing interest and decreasing mistrust regarding exchanging information. This negative attitude is perhaps the greatest barrier of all.

Resource sharing in the sense of sharing printed documents is largely based on scarcity of financial resources, which resulted in reductions in the range and depth of information resources individual libraries can make available. Traditional co-operative projects do not offer a real solution to the problem of deteriorating collections. The changes being experienced in the transition to a digital environment offers new opportunities for cooperative action in making information available to users. However, the shift to a predominantly digital environment will occur at different rates in different fields.

6

User Expectations, Needs and User Education

1. Introduction

Resource sharing is primarily done to provide the necessary and adequate documents to the users in such a way that the users' time is saved.

Users tend to live under the shadow of ignorance and they pick up bits of information that become available to them through known or unknown sources. They are never sure about the ultimate resources available on the topics of their interest. Thus their search and research is mostly relative in nature. The users create for themselves small worlds of information aournd their topics. These worlds expand provided the users have the resources or information disseminators that help users in moving closer to objectivity by providing the necessary and adequate information to them. So librarian and library staff have to understand and help the users in getting their desired needs. In order to fulfill the needs of the users and achieve better results in this task, it is important to be familiar with :

(a) the user's behaviour; (b) the user's exact information requirements; (c) the informaton resources, both indigenous and foreign, and their locations within a library and outside in other libraries and centres; and (d) the document delivery facilities etc.

As suggested by S.V. Sangameswaran and M.V. Gopinath, P.S. Dwatra, B. Guha and R. Subbaiah for considering the needs of Indian users following activities are supposed to be essential.

Users

1. Identify the potential users and their categories;
2. Identify the levels of involvement of users with network services;
3. Identify the different approaches of the users in collecting information.

Informaton Requirements

4. Identify the information requirements of users; categorize them by levels and type of communicaton media, etc. and match them with the available resources and kind of user's needs;
5. Identify the priorities of users' needs;
6. Design the user orientation/instruction/education programme;
7. Orient the user with network services and databases;

Training

8. Provide training to the users in accessing information;

Existing Resources

9. Identify existing resources and services, for better performance and avoidance of duplication of efforts and saving of finance;
10. Develop databases and services that meet the users' needs and approaches.

Discouraging Factors

11. Identify the limitations and problems which discourage the use of network services.

Evaluation

12. Evaluate the various existing services in relation to the users' needs and introduce changes and new services;

13. Develop an information system which gives regular feedback from users for introducing effective improvements.

2. Understanding the User

Though the future of scholarly publishing lies in a grey area somewhere between all-print and all-electronic forms, print media will survive because of the things print does best:

– *Print is portable* : it can be read in a comfortable chair or carried along on a trip. Current computer technology restricts the user to a workstation or an expensive portable computer.

– *Print is tactile* : many readers prefer printed pages to a computer monitor, keyboard, and mouse. Print publications can provide high-quality graphics that would be time-consuming to download online.

– *Print is browsable* : the reader can make serendipitous discoveries by paging through a journal's articles and book reviews. The term *browsing* reveals an important way in which online media are both like and unlike print. One of the key arguments advanced by proponents of digital media is the ability to *browse* from one web page to another. Hypertext makes it possible to move among documents in non-linear fashion, ideally making the same kind of serendipitous connections that journal reader's desire. For this reason, software programs used to navigate the web are called *browsers.*

But convenient access and quick printing of e-journals allow students to accelerate their research process. The advent of e-journals can best be understood, then, as depending on the level of knowledge and subject expertise of the student. From the freshman who has no grasp of what a "journal" is, in whatever format, to the doctoral student who needs the latest, cutting-edge research in a given field, the range of expertize in the accessing and evaluating of journals varies enormously.

Faculty members who gain some sense of their students' research sophistication at the beginning of each semester will be able to guide them, with the assistance of librarians, through the mazes of the research process and will be able to promote the use of e-journals at the appropriate point in that process.

An undergraduate candidate in academic libraries, may expect following from e-environment.

(i)Understanding the concept of a journal and its related concept of peer review : Most undergraduates do not know the basic concepts of e-journals. Explaining these ideas in class at the time an assignment is given may clarify some misconceptions. But requiring students to see and handle some print journals initially will elaborate on the basic idea and may help them to grasp more completely what e-journals are when they start using them from the libraries' web page.

(ii) Distinguishing E-journals from other web-based information : The seamlessness of the web environment, with no quality control and filtering at a global level, creates a rich but very uncertain, messy information world. Undergraduates often do not yet have the knowledge or background to differentiate e-journals, with their quality control through peer review, from many websites that appear authoritative but are suspect, produced by special interest groups or others with agendas. The web category of "E-zines" adds to this complexity because these may appear to be journals but are popular press publications.

(iii) Finding E-journals within the range of knowledge and understanding : E-journals contain highly technical vocabulary describing advanced research projects and processes. Students in introductory courses may have difficulty with these resources, but students in subject majors may have learned enough to make better use of them. Increasingly, some databases intended for interdisciplinary undergraduate use such as Expanded Academic Index contain links to full-text articles, but this practice is done selectively and students will need guidance in selecting the best and most appropriate journal articles, electronic or in print.

(iv) Students' Use : For graduate students and others, e-journals offer rich possibilities for expanding their research. Because graduate students work within a disciplinary knowledge base, some journal titles in their disciplines are already familiar to them and others are assimilated very quickly, just as graduate students learn the landmark works and best-known schools of thought in their fields. The pedagogical and research issues for graduate students can best be thought of as ways to enhance and enrich their research options.

(v) Keeping up-to-date with new research : E-journals make research articles available relatively quickly and graduate students need to know which groups of e-journals will be most productive for them. Many publishers such as Academic Press make tables-of-contents for e-journals available online so that quick scanning of the latest journal issues is possible. Users can set up an "ALERT" service at this website (http://www.idealibrary.com/news/ideal-alert.jsp) This entails setting up a profile so that the user receives by e-mail tables of contents from specific journal titles or a digest of article titles from more than one journal. Other vendors and publishers such as the Institute of Physics (http://www.ioppublishing.com/) show "forthcoming article" citations, another way of becoming very aware of current research topics and seeing new trends in research.

(vi) Facilitating interdisciplinary connections : Although graduate students necessarily specialize, much advanced research and thinking now seeks out and draws upon research in related fields. The sheer ease with which tables of contents in e-journals can be browsed allows graduate students to see interdisciplinary connections. For graduate students, e-journals can therefore become vehicles for sharpening awareness of new research and deepening understanding of one's own discipline within the context of other disciplines.

In a network environment the actual users are generally at a distance. They access information through the member-libraries of a network. In each member-library, either the staff can help them to access network information or an intelligent user may use a terminal himself and access information. The users generally may not know what may be available through a network. The management of a network may also be unaware of the precise needs of the users and therefore a wide gap emerges between the networked information and the needy user. How can this gap be filled? Various facets that strengthen this correspondence need to be examined:

In a network environment databases are not in close proximity. They are at a distance. Therefore, the databases of the network should be easily accessible and affordable. Users' approach to collecting or accessing information is determined by their socio-economic and educational backgrounds, their behavioural patterns, reading habits and their dedication to research. But in a network environment easy access to databases is necessary to help the users who approach information under different compulsions and limitations. Research studies show that remote access to the library's online catalogues helps users to become familiar with the availability of resources. If the remote access is online and interactive, it is preferable, but if it is off-line and e-mail based, it is second best. In such an environment the network should increase the number of databases considering the interests of the users and make them available to him.

The foremost issue that stands out in this regard is the behaviour, educational background and the precise need of the user. It is important to know whether the user is casual or serious in seeking information, or whether the user wants general or in-depth information.

There are studies made of users' needs vis-a-vis a particular library or a discipline, but in a network environment only those needs of users come into prominence that are able to establish a direct or indirect contact with the network.

The information needs of the users of member-libraries of a network, can be very large. The more the member-libraries of a network, the greater would be the needs of their users. They would be diverse in scope and content. The assessing of these needs can be done by the library staff that provide service to users in each member-library. In India this is done only in very specialized libraries.

3. User Studies

The user studies are analogous to the efforts of a manufacturer who surveys his market for the product that he proposes to produce. In the context of a library and information system, it is extremely important that in-depth studies are conducted to acquire the actual and potential needs of users. On the basis of user studies, the collection building, processing and organization and service are assessed to justify itself for its existence. The following methods are used for user studies.

3.1. Direct Methods

The efforts in user studies so far have been confined to studying the user needs in the context of research and development in universities and industrial.research units. The direct methods have emerged in recent decades to supplement the data acquired by indirect methods, that is, to analyse library records, to obtain data in the use of materials and user categories. Direct methods can be broadly studied under the following broad groups.

(i) Information gathering habits

(ii) Reading habits

(iii) Service preferences

(iv) Flow of information among users

(i) Information Gathering Habits : Information gathering habits are studied in the context of research and development. It is generally noted that researchers gather information in a number of ways such as :

— browsing current journals and also noting down the latest references to research papers.

— consulting, indexing and abstracting periodicals.

— contacting and obtaining information from persons in the same field.

— seeking information from tutors, guides and senior co-workers.

— writing to information supply centres and so on.

The efforts in trying to find out how a user obtains his information is to study the researcher's dependence on libraries, technical staff in the library and the main journals through which the researcher obtains the information. These studies have enabled library and information professionals to know the general behaviour of the researchers in obtaining their information, which in turn help them to organize their acquisition programmes, oriented towards actual requirements and to generate appropriate services.

(ii) Reading Habits : Reading habits of users of libraries throw considerable light on the types of documents a user studies, his relative preferences to the different categories of documents, frequency of borrowing and such other data. It is also possible for the library staff to study the time taken by a user for searching literature, browsing and reading. The data obtained in such studies help the organization to operate the library, in terms of user needs, physical location of documents, display of current journals, identification of intensive users of libraries, the types of documents frequently consulted and many others.

(iii) Service Preference : The library offers a variety of services which have evolved in the course of several decades. The normal lending, reference, bibliographic, hard copy supplies, etc. have been offered conventionally for a long time. More recently libraries and documentation centres have been offering Current awareness Services, Selective Dissemination of Information Services (SDI), Consolidation and Repackaging Services and so on.

It would be a waste of time, if these special services are organized indiscriminately without knowing the user preferences. It has now become, therefore, a practice to ascertain what kinds of service would be preferred by the users. Presently only those services which are of any consequence to the users are offered.

(iv) Information Flow : Research information generated by an individual or a group, gradually gets disseminated through personal correspondence, meetings at national and international conferences, publications in current journals or in the form of pre-prints and so on. It would be useful to know what medium is preferred by the generators of information for their propagation, to what extent conventional media like printed periodicals helping the dissemination and whether languages pose any barrier in communication, etc. These aspects are studied in information flow from generation to its final destination. These studies have thrown considerable light on the distribution of responsibilities among the different groups of disseminators, such as, the generator of information, the researcher and the editor, the publisher and the printer, the documentalists and information specialist and librarians. This has enabled these groups to organize their efforts with a sense of understanding of their responsibilities and ensuring smooth flow of information.

In the study conducted by the Operations Research Group of the Case Institute of Technology, USA in 1958 and by the Advisory Council of Science Policy in association with the department of Scientific and Industrial Research (UK), some interesting facts were found, which are given here.

(I) User requirements are of four types:

   (a) current approach

   (b) everyday approach

   (c) exhaustive approach

   (d) catching-up or brushing-up approach.

Current approach implies search for current literature. Every day approach means browsing through literature arrived at the library every day. Exhaustive approach entails search for exhaustive coverage of literature. Catching-up approach is the one that updates the knowledge of the user in any particular discipline consulting current journals and review journals.

(II) Library resources, library staff and the library services are generally revealed to be under-exploited by the users.

(III) Researchers spend about half of their working time in activities such as, browsing, reading, collection of references, talking or listening to co-workers, or fellow scientists.

(IV) The average number of journals scanned regularly by the researcher is less than 10.

(V) Scientists gather information mostly from their colleagues, teachers, group leaders, etc., and very less from libraries or secondary sources of information.

(VI) Scientists prefer review periodicals more than abstracting and indexing periodicals.

3.2 Indirect Methods

While direct methods of assessing user needs involve interface of investigators with users; the indirect methods analyse various types of records of a library, maintained on the use and users of the library. Another useful data which pertains to the bibliographical references that a researcher appends to his paper, provides considerable scope for analysis to get indicators for the management of the library. Indirect methods further can be sub-divided as under :

(i) Analysis of Library records : Libraries generally maintain statistical records on the different services it provides, such as, lending including inter-library loan, reference services, compilation of bibliographies, supply of facts, etc. Analysis of these records reveals the nature of use and documents, users needs, types of question posed, gaps and redundancies in book and journal collection, efficiency of reference and documentation services and similar others. This method has been used for a very long time to determine the policies of library in relation to collection building, organization of reader services, introduction of modern gadgets for speedy and efficient service etc.

(ii) Citation Analysis : Bibliographic citations appended to articles contributed by an author in a journal article, provides very useful data on the types of documents cited. This type of analysis helps in determining the acquisition policy, particularly of journals, and in weeding out less important ones. The citation studies also provide very useful indicators for identifying institutions of excellence, individual experts and similar others.

3.3 Survey Methods

To explore information needs of users, their information gathering habits, reading habits, etc., various survey methods are prevalent. Some of the more important methods are :

(i) Questionnaire

(ii) Interview

(iii) Diary

(iv) Observation

(i) Questionnaire : In questionnaire method, the objectives of the survey are converted into simple and unambiguous questions. The questions posed relate to the user with reference to his name, designation and qualifications, experience and place of work etc. The other questions relate to the sources of information that the researcher consults and the way in which he obtains information from documentary and non-documentary sources. Preference is given to any type of information service and similar others, The questions are framed in such a way that the answers to most of them can be more or less 'yes or no' type without any necessity for detailed descriptions.

In this method, the cost of conducting a survey is very low and a large sample scattered over long distances can be covered. But sometimes, the response is usually poor and very often replies are incomplete, illegible and also manipulated. Besides, quite often the respondents fail to understand the merit of the questions properly and hence give incorrect replies.

(ii) Interview : Here, the investigator personally contacts the respondent and elicits the required information from him. The interview is taken either through a structured or unstructured questionnaire. In the structured questionnaire, all the questions are set prior to the interview, and the respondent is asked by the investigator to give replies to the questions. Either the investigator notes down the replies or the respondent himself writes down the replies. Whenever the respondent does not understand a question, the investigator explains the same, and the correct answer to the question is obtained.

In the unstructured questionnaire, the investigator does not possess a set of questions already framed. On the other hand, he goes to the respondent keeping in view his objectives, and accordingly asks questions and notes down the answers. This methods is found to be more flexible than the structured one. This method however, is costly, labourious and time-consuming, since one has to contact·personally or through representatives, all the respondents spread all over the country. Of course, it won't prove costly if the respondents are the users of a single library.

(iii) Diary : In this method, a diary of all the information activities by the user for a specified period of time is studied. Initially a diary form is framed indicating all possible information activities of a user, i.e., literature search, browsing, reading, library use, discussion with experts etc., and supplied to the users. The users maintain the diary for the specified period and then hand this diary over to the investigator for analysis. The method proves to be successful if the diary keeping period is short, say one week or ten days.

(iv) Observation : Two types of observations methods i.e., participants and non- participants are known. When the observer participates with the group under study, it is called participant observation, and when the observer observes the activities of the group/ individual from a close distance, it is call non-participant observation. A particular observer makes himself a part of the group and takes part freely in the activities of the group and observes them in their natural behaviour, without allowing the individuals in the group to know that they are being observed. The information required is noted down and finally analysed.

A non-participant observer on the other hand, observes a selected number of user from a close distance and keeps a record of their information activities like time spent by user in library, types of documents he consults, number of documents he takes on loan and so on. Data gathered in this way are finally analysed.

3.4 Other Methods

These comprise of following sub-methods.

(i) Feed-back Service : A library can acquire feedback information on the variety of services it provides. In the organization of Selective Dissemination of Information Service, every document supplied to the customer is appended with a feedback data card which contains questions as to the relevancy of information, timeliness of supply and the descriptors use, etc. The analysis of such feedback data cards throws light on the efficiency of service and also provide considerable clue to build up pertinent user profiles.

(ii) Information Days : Information days are organized in many libraries which provide the occasion for the users to come in close contact with the library staff. This creates a better understanding between the users and the suppliers of information in the library and creates a sense of cordiality and brings a certain amount of credibility to the library. This practice is seen in the Soviet Union (now Russia), where on a particular day of a month, the library has an 'open day' and obtains direct feedback from the users on its services and collection. This method had enabled the libraries in the Soviet Union to improve their quality of service.

(iii) Unconventional Methods : Autobiographies or

accounts of library users, such as scholars and writers provide useful hints as to their own experience in the collection of information. This study throws interesting light on the users' approach to information and provide pointers which may not be possible to obtain through any investigation. It should be noted, however, that this method is rather unusual and may or may not fetch any additional data at all.

In this way, opting any one or the other methods, user studies are done in the libraries.

4. Understanding User Needs

Over the past decade there have been many new initiatives in scholarly communication, digital libraries, and the development of educational, scientific and cultural heritage institutions with significant commitments to online resources and online services.

In electronic or digital environment, following approaches may be helpful in understanding user needs, bringing organizational capabilities to bear on these needs, and engaging a broad spectrum of community members in design and governance. These approaches fall into three broad categories:

- user-centered design
- participatory design
- shared governance models

Each of these are discussed further below in detail.

4.1 User-centered Design

The central tenets of user-centered design, originating from human factors, are the early and continual involvement of users in the design process, a focus on real users and their tasks, and iterative design guided by frequent formative evaluations. Numerous user-centered design methodologies based on these tenets have been proposed, including task-centered design, goal-based design, and scenario-based design. All of these methodologies draw on suites of common design practices and formative evaluation techniques, e.g. interviews, observations, prototyping, usability inspections, and usability studies. Many efforts have investigated how standard design and evaluation techniques can be modified to better serve the specific needs of digital libraries and other information technologies such as hypertext/hypermedia for education.

Irrespective of the particular methodology chosen, the objectives of a user-centered design process are to develop a deep understanding of user requirements for technology design and planning, and to get systematic user feedback on evolving library systems throughout the design process. It is the responsibility of library designers to generate possible design options and to devise appropriate protocols and studies to elicit user feedback on these options.

In this issue Shreeves and Kirkham describe an early pilot study to test the viability of a search portal created specifically for discovering primary source materials by K-12 teachers-in-training and for use in a classroom. They tested their portal early with users and are candid and blunt in their assessment of the challenges that aggregation of heterogeneous metadata, despite being OAI-compliant, poses to users and service providers. Focus groups, written evaluation, and transaction logs were used to gather data and understand actual usage and user needs. They found that multiple levels of intervention are necessary if aggregation of metadata is to lead to successful user experiences. These findings, because they were early in the development of the portal, helped them redesign it to offer a more successful user experience to a specific community.

4.2 Participatory Design

Participatory design methods seek to involve users more deeply in the process as co-designers, i.e., users also propose and generate design alternatives as opposed to simply providing feedback on designer-generated options. An important ideal of participatory design is industrial democracy, which implies that users should be politically empowered with a broad design remit that includes: co-designing the technology, co-determining the nature of the design process itself (schedules, processes, outcomes), and co-designing the social conditions of technology use (i.e., work practices, organizational structures and responsibilities). Contextual inquiry, where the designer works or interacts with the user in the work environment, is a particular technique and is intended to support the development of products that support, extend and transform user work.

Participatory design requires significant and ongoing collaboration between designers and users throughout the design process. A key challenge to any participatory design process is access to users: it is difficult organizationally, logistically, and financially to bring users and developers together to engage in collaborative design on a frequent and sustained basis. As such, participatory design has historically been most successful in in-house software development contexts where users and developers ate part of the same organization and are often co-located.

In this issue Bartolo *et al.* describe the work being done to integrate material from scientists/researchers' workspaces within a digital library (MatDL). Their project is an alliance of many geographically distributed institutions, and they are adapting open source tools such as CVS to enable collaboration on tasks. At the same time as tools are modified and developed, use and users of the library are supported using techniques such as kernel groups and student feedback from courses. A kernel group is an interesting form of participatory design as it encompasses notions of collaboration (access to designers and users among different partners), interdisciplinarity and multidisciplinarity (partners come from many disciplines) and practice and use environments (partners and users include teachers, students, researchers, etc.).

Unsurprisingly, many have seized on the Internet and Web as offering the technical means to enable wider user participation in the design process. Collaboration systems based on these ubiquitous technical infrastructures could, in theory, provide a virtual commons where distributed stakeholders overcome cultural and geographic separation to get together and engage in collaborative design on a regular basis, without having to travel to distant locations and without taking large chunks of time away from their other work responsibilities. Needless to say, given the inherently distributed nature of digital library users, approaches that enable such users to participate meaningfully in the design and planning of library systems would be invaluable. Despite the promise, results to date have been mixed, with some groups reporting reasonable success and others reporting little participation by users.

Khoo's contribution to this issue provides valuable insight into the formidable barrier posed by the variable understanding of developers and users about the same artifact they are building together. A study in organizational communication, individual participant understandings about the word 'resource' are described in detail in order to highlight the different tacit understandings that existed among participants of the same digital library project. The human-based effort to create concept maps that represented the collection development process also resulted in the creation of an online communication tool, the DWEL WorkHub, to represent the knowledge of the developers to the users and increase understanding between both groups.

While participatory design embraces the importance of co-designing the social conditions of technology use. Its projects tend to focus on technology innovations as opposed to emphasizing social change. Participatory action research builds on the participatory design tradition, but instead emphasizes working with community groups to effect immediate social change and building capacity within these groups to frame and investigate issues of their own concern. Thus, the design and use of library technologies and services takes a back seat to helping community groups affect local change. Participatory action research contexts can often yield invaluable, possibly profound, insights in the design and planning of library technologies and services as this approach requires designers to focus on the transformational needs of specific community groups.

Bishop *el al.*, emphasize participatory action research with the goal of effecting change through the use of Inquiry Labs (iLabs). This approach is about stimulating, motivating, improving, integrating learning within a community, often a marginalized group by infusing library technologies and capabilities into community organizations rather than bringing users to the library. They describe the iLabs suite as "simultaneously a Web site, a community of learners, and a locus for knowledge construction". A simple blend of informational and communication tools is offered for diverse sets of users: users of iLabs inquiry activities come from all walks of life such as neighbourhood activism, university courses, research projects, committee work, K-12 education, conference presentations, developing international professional associations, and art projects. iLabs reflect the successful fulfillment of user needs that have surfaced in many different arenas over and over again, and are helping in the transformation of people's ability to process and use information on both sides of the digital divide.

This is especially relevant in view of a report about the digital divide that claims the Internet has no social impact on low-income adults but may increase learning motivation and cognitive competencies.

4.3 Shared-governance Model

The third model for negotiating the future has its roots not in design research but in educational administration and, more broadly, organizational development. "The process of consultation", wrote John J. Corson in 1941, "strengthens the allegiance to the institution and their individual zeal and satisfaction". In a nutshell, that is the essence of the shared governance model: respect for the different roles played by students, faculty, staff, administrators, and the general public, and ensuring that all continue to feel a sense of ownership for the institution through the process of consultation, with the benefit of greater excellence and improvement for all. While shared governance is an idea that is generally considered to have originated in academic governance, it has been found to be effective as a business management strategy for services such as IT security risk management, and is promoted as a tool for global and sustainable management of our environment. Shared governance is also practised by another venerable academic endeavour: the publishing of scholarly journals. Considering the peer review process: most scholarly refereeing is unpaid labour that the individual offers as a service to the discipline and as part of his responsibility and commitment to help maintain the quality of the work published in the discipline.

In using shared governance quite innovatively and in different ways from each other to inform the design of the digital library, deliver needed services to users, and to ensure sustainability, they are also effecting social and educational changes. Foulke *et al.* describe the creation of Connecticut History Online (CHO), a new non-profit entity to support cross-institution collaboration, incorporating different advisory groups, including one for teachers and one for educator specialists, into a formal governance structure. Partnership is a core value, while ownership and consensus building are integral to all the project's efforts. CHO holds promise for changing the digital futures of libraries, archives, museums, and educational institutions from objects on separate trajectories to partners in a more seamlessly integrated world of multimedia information.

McMartin emphasizes how shared governance is an inherent part of MERLOT's business model, perhaps even a direct influence on its sustainability. Again, partnership is emphasized: in sharing the governance of the MERLOT collection among a large and distributed group, the responsibility for the integrity and quality of the collection is distributed among the faculty, similar to the scholarly journal's editorial and peer review model. Besides encouraging digital library research projects and initiatives to incorporate shared governance models for long-term success and sustainability, MERLOT could influence changes in social processes such as academic peer review and the promotion and tenure process.

5. Users' Attitude and Behaviour towards E-Journals

This can be better understood under following heads :

(i) People don't like reading from screens

Some computer screens have a very low resolution, a black background and the characters are white — the reverse of the ink on paper to which people are accustomed. Since then, screen design has improved immensely and now the typical screen has relatively high resolution, has a white background and black characters. The recent trend in mounting e-journals in Adobe's PDF format also discourages screen reading and encourages printing. Though now-a-days coloured monitors had dominated the scenario, but sometimes they also create problems.

(ii) People like to annotate

The average academic's collection of offprint and photocopies usually they are annotated in one way or another. Some people use a highlighter pen, others underline sections and some write comments in the margin. These annotations are an important part of our research process. Annotating electronic articles is certainly possible.

(iii) People know how to manipulate paper

A paper journal article is more easily manipulated than an e-version. It is easier to turn the page of a paper journal. Regular journal readers understand the structure of journal articles and use that knowledge to aid manipulation, providing rapid access to the information in an article. Watching a reader pick up an issue of a journal, skim through the contents, turn to an article and skim through it and then turn back to the contents, all in a matter of seconds. it is clear that such skills are largely automatic.

Watching people trying to do the same thing in an e-journal system, it is clear that people will have to learn a different set of skills.

(iv) People don't read journals at their desk

The issue of portability is also important when it is remembered that academics and researchers donot typically read journals at their desk. The majority of reading is carried out while travelling on trains or planes. Hence, the aim of publishers to provide delivery of journals to the academic's desktop computer again encourages printing.

(v) People do not sit still while they read

No matter where they read, people often move around while reading paper articles. They shift position in the chair or even change chairs in order to maintain a comfortable position, moving the paper nearer or further away in order to find a comfortable reading distance. Usually the paper is held in a near-horizontal position with the head bent slightly forward in order to look down at it. Reading from a screen, it is usually necessary to maintain a single position, although some movement in the chair is possible. However, the screen is usually near upright and viewing distance is generally constant.

(vi) People like to browse

Most people browse by subject because that is how libraries are arranged. Hence, it is easy to look at the library sections of current journals and see a wide variety of library and information resources. E-journal systems such as Academic Press's IDEAL can present readers with a list of journals in a particular area, but in order to browse at the title and author level it is necessary to go down several levels of the hierarchy before an issue's contents can be viewed. Even then, it is only possible to view journals published by Academic Press. To read another publisher's journals, one has to go to their website and go through another login procedure. Typically, an academic library will deal with more than one subscription agent and may also deal direct with certain publishers. However, as a library user one need not know any of this. As an electronic journal user, one has to know which subscription agent supplies which journals.

(vii) People like to find things by accident

No matter how sophisticated the search engine, no matter how many Boolean operators it supports, no matter if it incorporates relevance ranking, academics often report finding things serendipitously. What is more, they seem to enjoy this process. Typically they go looking for a known article in a journal and then notice another interesting article in the same journal. They may have missed it on previous visits or it may not have been relevant at that time and so was forgotten.

(viii) People use more than the current issue

One of the reasons often cited for lack of use of e-journals is that there is rarely a large enough corpus of information in experimental systems. The half-life of information clearly differs between disciplines and publishers have yet to put any significant effort into making e-versions of their back run, concentrating instead on the most recent issues. For a PhD student, it is important to trace through the literature no matter what the discipline.

(ix) People like stability

One can pick up the current issue of a journal, again select an article published a hundred years ago and read it. The same is not true in the case of an e-journal — ironically, when the computer on which it was mounted was decommissioned. Also users accustomed to their site suddenly found themselves confronted with a completely different interface design, users running Netscape version 1 suddenly found themselves unable to read the site because the new version was based on frames and required Netscape 2.

So what do people think of e-journals? The e-version offers

easier access, readily available at any time, whereas the paper version might be in use by another person. A journal is published because its authors wish to publish. Publishers and editors know that if they can attract the best authors in a field then academic libraries, which are the major market for such journals, will be under pressure to purchase them. Most libraries purchase their journals through subscription agents so the publisher is even further removed from readers. This raises the interesting question of where and with whom; publishers are conducting their market research into e-journals.

6. User Education & User Education Programmes

The education of users in accessing information has been in vogue for more than a century now but year after year the process of user education have becoming increasingly complex. To Ian Malley user education is : "A process whereby the library user is firstly made aware of the extent and number of the library's resources; of its services and of the information sources available to him or her, and secondly taught how to use these resources, services and sources."

The above definition over twenty years old still stands the test of time, though the concept of the library's resources has widened to world resources because of the roles played by library networks and the INTERNET. A network has two types of users. Firstly and chiefly, they are the libraries and secondly, the users of the participating libraries. Though the main purpose of networking is to help the users, the networks have to educate the users and also the librarians who serve them. Elizabeth Orna observes that users should:

(i) be aware of what the information service can do;

(ii) identify their information problems;

(iii) communicate them to information staff and discuss with them;

(iv) give feedback to the service;

(v) keep information staff aware of their changing subject interests; and

(vi) involve the service in projects which have information implications.

So, a library network has to provide training in using information to the libraries and to their users, bearing in mind the type of user, type of library and ensure that the human resource available at each participating library develops a healthy relationship with their users. It is therefore necessary that user education material on a network should be given to the library staff so that the users are able to fulfil the above conditions.

As far as user education programmes in general are concerned, for helping the users in using library resources, reference service is given at personalized level. But, apart from providing assistance to users the reference librarians or reference assistants are expected to orient the users in the library mechanism, because libraries are these days mechanized things. One needs orientation to exploit the resources to their fullest extent. The activities to be carried out by the reference staff within the library to orient or educate the users are called 'User Education Activities' or 'Internal Extension Activities. Such 'user education' or 'orientation' programme not only help the users in exploiting the resources of a library, but also, help the library staff in better organization and management of the libraries. Some of these programmes discussed below:

(i) Orientation into the Library Mechanism : The reference staff may orient the users either formally or informally into the library systems. In an informal way, the user may be taken to the Library Map/ Plan and explain the various sections, special collections and services. The reference staff may take the user personally to various sections and explain the type of material available, kind of information one can get, etc. It will be more effective if it is demonstrated to the user as to how to locate the information from various types of source material. In the formal system of orientation, the structured orientation programme may be planned wherein one can combine lectures supported by audiovisual aids; tour around the library demonstration etc., can be used effectively.

(ii) Formal Programmes : In the formal programmes, the following areas may be comprehended:

(a) **Introduction to the Library :** Concept and role of the library; types of libraries; kinds of documents; sections of a library; services provided, etc.

(b) **Documents :** Sources-Primary, Secondary and Tertiary, Kinds-Books, Periodicals, Audio-Visual, etc.

(c) **Parts of a Book :** Preliminaries- Half title page, Title page, Back of the title page, Table of contents, Preface, Introduction, Body of the Book-parts, Chapters, Paragraphs, Sectional headings, References, Notes, etc., End matter - Notes, References, Index etc.

(d) **Care of Books :** How to pick-up a book from the shelf, opening of the book for consultation, protecting books from its enemies, improper way of handling, etc.

(e) **Arrangement of Materials :** Books-textbooks, reference books; pamphlets; pictures; clippings; periodicals; films and film strips; slides; wire; tape; phone; cassettes - audio-visual; floppies; CDs, DVDs; etc.

(f) **Location of Documents :** Use of catalogues - kinds of entries; arrangement of entries; location in the catalogue; Call Number -Parts and role of each part; Arrangement of books on the shelves-Bay guides, shelf guides, inclusive numbers on the tier, arrangement and spine labels; identification of the book; etc.

(g) **Reference Books :** Characteristics, Kinds - Encyclopedias; Dictionaries, atlases, almanac, guide books, gazetteers, biographical dictionaries, indexes, etc.

(h) **Bibliography :** Selection of items, arrangement, preparation of index cards etc.

(iii) Other Activities : Other extension activities or user education programmes that a library may take-up to bring books and users together are:

(a) **Organization of Exhibitions :** This will help in bringing to the notice of the users the richness of the collection of the library. Topical exhibitions will attract large number of users and will provide an opportunity to discover books which were not expected of.

(b) **Display of New Additions :** Many libraries display the jackets of the new additions at the entrance of the library so that they can draw the attention of the users and thus tempted to read. Some libraries may start a 'Monthly Book Exhibition' wherein, books added in the previous months are displayed from 1-10 of every month. This may provide an opportunity for users to have a look at books on all subjects at one place. Inter-disciplinary nature of the research support such displays.

(c) **Lectures :** Libraries should arrange topical lectures suitable to different sections of the users - men, women, children, students, etc. This opportunity should also be utilized for arranging suitable exhibitions/display of books and other reading material which help the users to select the right book for extended reading. Dr Ranganathan used to bring out topical bibliographies also on such occasions and distribute them among the listeners so that they can easily select literature on their choices of subject.

(d) **Other Extension Activities :** Many public libraries also organize dramas, musical concerts, film shows, quiz programmes, elocution and essay competitions, etc. to attract the public to the library and finally become beneficiaries of its resources.

(e) **Mass Media and Communication Technology :** In this context, mass media can be exploited in spreading the message - by writing articles in newspapers and magazines; radio and television talks; organizing public lectures; demonstration tours; attractive sign boards; organizing exhibitions; observing library weeks; publishing brochures; leaflets; bulletins; etc. The CDs etc. of user education programmes can be created and be shown at periodic occassion to the users to educate them.

(f) **Adult Education Programmes :** As a part of the extension programmes, library enthusiasts were organizing adult education classes to make the public literate so that they could make use of the libraries. Even today many of the public libraries conduct adult education programme.

(h) **Local Broadcasting :** Village libraries may organize film shows, audio and videobroadcasts, lecture programmes, etc., in order to enlighten the illiterate public in terms of health, hygiene, family welfare, agriculture, culture and heritage, contemporary politics and economics, etc.

7. Methods of Instruction in Network Environment

It is important to throw some light on the methods of instruction in a network environment so that we could get better results. The methods of instruction can be :

Direct; Semi-Direct; and Indirect instructions.

7.1 Direct Instructions

The network can arrange the direct instructional programmes, which can be in the following forms:

- Lectures
- Demonstration/Workshop
- Film, Videotape, Slide/Tape
- Slide/Lecture

Since direct instruction is a familiar mode of instruction, it is comfortable. It is time conserving and better organization and presentation of data can facilitate learning through this method. But, as each user wants to obtain practical knowledge, demonstration or participation in a workshop would be preferable.

7.2 Semi-Direct Instructions

This method helps users to do practical work after lectures. The initial presentation should be such so that users are led to practical work soon after. This kind of training is generally done in groups in workshops.

7.3 Indirect Instructions

In a network environment the users are scattered and are directly in touch with the member-libraries rather than with the network. The network has to facilitate learning and therefore discussions, brainstorming sessions and the use of videos and films on the activities have to be arranged at the individual libraries.

It is important for a network to mix and match instruction methods in order to achieve the desired results. The use of online access, INTERNET, slide shows, video and film demonstrations, etc. would be highly useful. In the West users are generally satisfied with the network performance as there is a major shift towards automating networking of libraries.

As inability of users to understand and apply the changing tools of information technology act as one of the major barriers in resource sharing, the users have to depend upon the service of library and information professionals in this regard. Grace Saw and Vicki Williamson argue that management policies should place higher priority upon the quality of user education programmes, because exponential growth of knowledge and databases was making it difficult for users to access necessary and sufficient information.

8. Internet Search Strategies

Internet has become a household name now. The tremendous growth doubling in size is really exciting and it is an unexplorable ocean. No one could have foreseen the explosive growth in the Internet usage. A user can be guided as given below for finding information from Internet.

Finding the web documents you want can be easy or seem impossibly difficult. This is in part due to the sheer size of the WWW, currently estimated to contain more than 3 billion documents. It is also because the WWW is not indexed in any standard vocabulary. Unlike a library's catalogues, in which we can use standardized Library of Congress subject headings to find books in most large libraries, in web searching you are always guessing what words will be in the pages you want to find or guessing what subject terms were chosen by someone to organize a web page or site covering some topic.

When you do what is called "searching the web," you are not searching it directly. It is not possible to search the WWW directly. The web is the totality of the many web pages which reside on computers all over the world. Your computer cannot find or go to them all directly. What you are able to do through your computer is access one or more of many intermediate search tools available now. You search a search tool's database or collection of sites — a relatively small subset of the entire world wide web. The search tool provides you with hypertext links with URLs to other pages. You click on these links, and retrieve documents, images, sound, and more from individual servers around the world.

8.1 Internet Search Engines

A search engine indexes a portion of web documents as a full text database. The function of a search engine is an as locator of information available on the Internet via the world wide web. It contains references to thousands of web documents. It provides an interface between a user and the related database. To provide information to users is composed of two parts; available information with data and method of indexing of information. The user interface by asking his query. The response of the search engine comes in the form of "result", listing addresses of matching and relevant resources. For giving the matching results, it runs the query terms or the search string, against databases. Many a popular search engines are Yahoo, Alta Vista, AOL Search, AskJeeves, Direct Hit, Google, Hot Bot, Excite, Lycos, and MSN Search.

8.2 Search Engines - How Do They Search?

Before a search engine can tell you where a file or document is, it must be found. To find information on the hundreds of millions of web pages that exist, a search engine employs special software robots, called spiders, to build lists of the words found on websites. When a spider is building its lists, the process is called web crawling. In order to build and maintain a useful list of words, a search engine's spiders have to look at a number of pages.

How does any spider start its travels over the web? The usual starting points are lists of heavily used servers and very popular pages. The spider will begin with a popular site, indexing the words on its pages and following every link found within the site. In this way, the spidering system quickly begins to travel, spreading out across the most widely used portions of the web.

Once the spiders have completed the task of finding information on web pages though the task is never actually completed — the constantly changing nature of the web means that the spiders are always crawling), the search engine must store the information in a way that makes it useful.

Searching through an index involves a user building a query and submitting it through the search engine. The query can be quite simple, a single word at minimum. Building a more complex query requires the use of Boolean operators that allow you to refine and extend the terms of the search.

The Boolean operators most often seen are:

- *AND* : All the terms joined by "AND" must appear in the pages or documents. Some search engines substitute the operator "+" for the word AND.
- *OR* : At least one of the terms joined by "OR" must appear in the pages or documents.
- *NOT* : The term or terms following "NOT" must not appear in the pages or documents. Some search engines substitute the operator "-" for the word NOT.
- *FOLLOWED BY* – One of the terms must be directly followed by the other.
- *NEAR* : One of the terms must be within a specified number of words of the other.
- *Quotation Marks* : The words between the quotation marks are treated as a phrase, and that phrase must be found within the document or file.

8.3. How to Prepare for Search?

The points to be considered while preparing for a search are :

1. Formulate the search question carefully;
2. Identify the important concepts within the question;
3. Identify the keyword related to the topics and think of related synonyms.

(i) *Wildcard Searches* : A special symbol which allows you to search simultaneously for several words with the same stem (*).

For example: educat* gives the following words or more - educator, educators, education, educational.

(ii) *Boolean Searches* : Boolean searches allows you to broaden and narrow a search. It is search engine specific and is designated differently in each search engine.

The Operators and Syntax in Boolean Searching :

- *AND* : terms on both sides of this operator must be present somewhere in the document in order to be scored as a result.

  For example : teaching AND learning
- *OR* : terms on EITHER side of this operator are sufficient to be scored as a result.

  For example : course OR class
- *AND NOT* : documents containing the term AFTER this operator are rejected from the results set.

  For example : course OR class NOT schools
- *NEAR* : similar to AND, only both terms have to be within a specified word distance from one another in order to be scored as a result.
- Learning how to construct this Boolean syntax structure is easy. You only need to remember four things.
  1. You define a Boolean expression through use of an open parenthesis ['(']to begin it, and a closed parenthesis [')'] to end it;
  2. Make sure the first search concept you want evaluated is at the inner most level of your Boolean expressions; followed by subsequent expressions in your desired order;
  3. Make sure you have a balanced (equal) number of open and close parentheses in your entire query;
  4. Expressions at the same "level" are read in order, from left to right.

(iii) *Use of Parentheses* : The simple rules of the usage of parentheses can be illustrated as follows:

- THIRD expression (SECOND expression (FIRST expression evaluated) evaluated) evaluated;
- ((education* AND medic*) AND (reform OR revision)) AND ("united states" OR USA).

(iv) *Typical Search Strategies* : Understanding how search engines work and combining multiple search engines in a given search can increase the likelihood of finding the information desired by a factor of 3.5 or more.

(v) *Search Recommendations* : These include :

1. Use nouns or objects as query keywords;
2. Use 6 to 8 words in query;
3. Truncate words to pick up singular and plural versions;
4. Use synonyms via the OR operator;
5. Combine keywords into phrases where possible;
6. Combine 2 to 3 concepts in query;
7. Distinguish concepts by parentheses;
8. Order concepts with main subjects first;
9. Link concepts with AND operator; and
10. Issue query to full Boolean search engine and query searchers.

Though different search engines accomplish their task through different methods but some common ways of providing information to users can be explained as under:

1. Searching information on the basis of important and defined keywords.
2. Indexing of keywords and related URLs (Uniform Resource Locators).
3. Making available the keywords or pages to users.

Earlier search engines used to index some thousands of web pages and documents and served 1-2000 queries but in today' scenario any popular search engine indexes billions of web pages and satisfies millions of queries. Some search engines use web-spiders which list out used terms used in web pages. This process is known as web crawling. These "spiders" read hundreds of pages in a second.

Besides there are Subject Directories which are smaller than search engines and Internet sites are usually organized by subjects. Yahoo, the largest subject directory has only 1.2 million pages indexed, whereas the smallest search engine contains at least 50 million pages. There are human editors involved who review and categorize the sites. Subject directories are mainly used to find specific information. But there is no hard and fast rule that what should be used for searching. Much depends on the personal preferences of the user. Some people like directories because the user can control the search pattern. Search engines leave the searching pattern to the computer program and can be used to find more specific resources. Knowing how to conduct searches is a skill. With any search strategy, effective searching becomes a matter of matching the particular information needed with a strategy that can answer it.

9. User Satisfaction

User satisfaction is a relative term. A user becomes satisfied when he uses all the material that he is aware of and which becomes available to him, at a given time and place. His satisfaction is relative and not absolute. Although it is the highest objective of a service provider like a library or library network, the service provider also works within the limitations of resources, time and space.

In order to get better user satisfaction, the observations of Peidad Dector may be referred regarding the steps taken towards user satisfaction at the Scientific and Humanistic Information Centre (CICH) of the National Autonomous University of Mexico. Serving about 150,000 students, 27,000 professors and researchers, CICH undertakes research on the following five topics in order to increase user satisfaction.

1. Social Sciences in Latin America through the class database;
2. The importance of the services of a magazine/periodicals library in an information centre;

3. Coverage of biomedical information by international indexes and abstracts;
4. The impact of new technologies on services in a library of an information centre; and
5. Scientific dissemination as part of university dissemination.

All the above projects provided inputs for offering better services and user satisfaction.

In conclusion as suggested by Kaul, a library should perform the following task for better services :

1. Provide necessary and adequate documents to the users;
2. Provide the documents/information fast so that the users' time is saved;
3. There is a need to promote values which ensure respect for scholarship;
4. Identify the potential users and categories of them;
5. Identify the levels of involvement of users with network services;
6. Identify the different approaches of the users in collecting information;
7. Identify the information requirements of users; categorize them by levels and type of communication media, etc. and match them with the available resources and kind of users' needs;
8. Identify the priorities of users' needs;
9. Design the user orientation/instruction/education programme;
10. Orient the user with network services and databases;
11. Provide training to the user in accessing information;
12. Identify existing resources and services, for better performance and avoidance of duplication of efforts and saving of finance;

13. Develop databases and services that meet the users' needs and approaches;
14. Identify the limitations and problems which discourage the use of network services;
15. Evaluate the various existing services in relation to the users' needs and introduce changes and new services;
16. Develop an information system which gives regular feedback from users for introducing effective improvements;
17. The information needs of users of a network are large and therefore all kinds of databases and services should be introduced to satisfy them;
18. At this stage the users interest in books and periodicals is the maximum, but slowly it is going to shift towards electronic and full text documents;
19. Training of users of IT and INTERNET should be a regular activity;
20. Extra information services and extension activities should be introduced in order to achieve better user satisfaction.

In above conditions are fulfilled, users of the library will definitely be satisfied in modern environment of the technology.

7
Management of Resource Sharing

1. Introduction

'Resource management' is a phrase often used in library and information work. It can be defined in many ways but much depends upon the context and the culture in which those who are responsible for a given set of resources are allowed, are able and wish to manage. There is no single or obvious definition of resource management perhaps because libraries, as public rather than private institutions, have not traditionally been fully in control of all the resources which are used to provide the total service. A study of standard thesauri suggests that 'to manage' involves administering, directing, engineering, overseeing, controlling, handling, manoeuvring, manipulating, coping, faring, functioning and simply surviving.

The standard synonyms for the term 'resource' are perhaps less obvious to academic librarians. They relate to assets, capital, fortune, riches, wealth, means, property, substance and similar words, terms and concepts. They are the words from commerce, business and accounting. Yet, increasingly, they symbolize attitudes and approaches which higher education will have to adopt. The library becomes an asset to the university, college or other institution of which it forms a part. The building, equipment and collections are assets. The whole provides a service which attracts resources and which properly' the library is. What is the 'resource' to be managed? It may be money or people, buildings or furniture, books or journals, networks or standalone workstations, remote databases or in-house CD-ROMS. It may only be some of these, depending upon the extent to which the individual resource manager has control over the allocation and management process relating to the unit being managed. Resource sharing has been taking place before the five laws of Dr. Ranganathan which were published in 1931. These Laws are :

1. Books are for use
2. Every reader his/her book
3. Every book its reader
4. Save the time of the reader
5. The library is a growing organism

But, all aspects of resource sharing are getting embodied in them directly or indirectly. If we replace books by documents or information which in effect are synonymous, we find that these principles have an enduring role to play in making resource sharing functional in terms of :

(a) Improving the quality of publications and their effective use;

(b) Arranging documents from any part of the world which are needed by a user;

(c) Locating the right type of users for each document and making the use possible;

(d) Taking all such steps which the current technology and financial resources permit by which a user gets the needed document and the document becomes available to the user for whom it was created, without any loss of time; and

(e) Considering that information is a growing organism, it is becoming multidimensional and interdisciplinary and it is becoming available in all sorts of formats, steps need to be taken to promote resource sharing in such ways, including electronic methods, so that the guiding principles of the first four laws become operational.

These principles are meant to overcome all types of barriers that obstruct the use of information or sharing of resources. Whether these barriers are international or national, social or political, technological or scientific, economic or psychological, information specialists will have to cross them, as far as possible, to fulfil the obligations these principles bestow on them. It may therefore be noticed that in times to come these principles will periodically evolve new and newer in built mechanisms to balance the level of information among each set of users.

2. Resource Management Strategy

Having a resource management strategy in place, together with the appropriate tools for implementing and adapting that strategy over a period of time and to suit changing conditions, will act as an 'insurance policy' against the worst effects of any sudden and/or drastic changes within the parent institution or the library itself.

2.1. Aims of a resource management strategy

The first aim must be to attract the necessary financial resources to fulfil the aims and objectives set down by the parent institution and, in consequence, those determined by the librarians themselves in respect of the library and its role. The second should be to allocate and manage those resources efficiently and effectively. The third must be the monitoring of the effects of the resource allocation and management process with a view to making changes to improve efficiency or effectiveness and/or to increase the likelihood of fulfilling the library's and the parent institution's aims and objectives.

2.2. Characteristics of a resource management strategy

It is argued here that a resource management strategy, like any other strategy within the academic sector can be applied across a wide range of institutions. The following key and common characteristics of a successful strategy are suggested:

(i) There must be commitment 'from the top' and widespread support within the institution : A library-specific resource management strategy which is not actively supported by the institution's senior management is unlikely to be successful, at least not on the scale necessary to justify the inevitable input of time. In this context, the nearer the library's resource management strategy can approximate to the philosophy and approach of the parent institution the more likely it is to be supported by that institution and accepted by those who have to live with the results; typically the academic departments.

For example, the Library chose to introduce a formula to divide up the acquisitions budget between subject areas. This was after years of 'historic' funding and in order to respond to considerable academic change within the institution - new subjects, growth in some existing areas and contraction in others-together with differential price increases between subjects and types of material. The University was looking to central budget managers who could control expenditure and re-allocate it strategically. The Library's initiative was applauded centrally. Departments were harder to convince initially, though transitional funding and a high degree of consultation with and involvement of, academic staff resulted in a general approval of what was seen as a 'firm but fair' allocation process.

The University itself subsequently adopted a formulaic approach to resource allocation across the academic and central support units. This took as its basic principle the distribution of resources to academic units in direct relation to the units' contribution to the University's overall income. As with the Library formula, there was a good deal of frank debate, but an eventual 'ownership' of the result. The Library then revised its own formula to ensure that it mirrored the basic philosophy of the University's resource management model, whilst maintaining a subject distribution of the funds, once the school-level allocations had been determined.

(ii) The strategy must grow out of the organization's overarching strategic plan : The success of a resource management strategy, and the performance of those charged with implementing it, will in large part be measured by the extent to which the strategy aids the fulfillment of the institution's broader objectives. If, for example, a university has decided to improve its research ratings, then the library must aim to contribute to that drive for improvement, reallocating resources accordingly. The recent research assessment exercises have concentrated effort in many universities on the targeted use of resources to improve performance in subsequent exercises. The university library will have to seek, and be given, a clear indication of the ways in which research activity is to be developed and supported. Even with selective support of given areas, the resources available to the priority areas is unlikely to be sufficient to fulfil all the demands that researchers might reasonably or unreasonably place on the library service, the strategy will also need to encompass modes of delivery, i.e., on-site versus remote; hard copy versus electronic, etc. as well as level of support postgraduate taught course; postgraduate research; research group; individual academic research requirements, etc.

(iii) The critical issues identified by the parent institution will drive the strategy at any one time and the order of priority for any particular activities associated with it : A 'critical issue' might be the drive to research excellence in given subject areas, or a new subject area, an emphasis on excellence in teaching, of particular types of delivery of teaching or of learning support or some other area, whether locally or nationally led. In some institutions, the effective use of existing space consequent upon the institution's inability to acquire additional quantities of this resource might be a particularly important 'critical issue'. This will inevitably affect the library's resource management strategy and, space will naturally be seen as a resource. The library resource manager will ensure that use of library space is - and is seen to be an effective and integral part of overall management of the unit.

(iv) The strategy will recognize the diversity within the institution and the importance of 'ownership' of its aims and objectives : It is clear that ever more difficult decisions will have to be made. It has not always been easy to allocate funds. A resource management strategy must make life easier in this respect, even if the decisions continue to seem harsh to those who are at the receiving end. Whether or not a formula is adopted, there must be a clear and widely-owned approach to the disbursement of resources at the librarian's disposal.

(v) The longer-term development of the strategy will be informed by major national initiatives : There can be very few academic institutions which do not need to take account of national level activity, whether in relationship to teaching quality assessment, research selectivity, initiatives leading to regional cooperation and many more areas where national guidelines or directives have been issued in respect of the way in which an individual university or college might or must allocate and manage its resources. In this context, the most important national 'initiative' is likely to be the way in which funds are allocated centrally to individual institutions. A higher education system which, for example, explicitly separates out the funding of teaching or of research or consistently top-slices for 'central' initiatives such as networking provision is likely to be mirrored, at least to some extent, at individual institutional level and, hence, at library resource management level. Even if the end results do not overtly affect the library budget distribution, an awareness of the ways in which the income has reached the library is important, as is early warning of any major changes in the shape and nature of the broad income streams.

(vi) The strategy should be a flexible, rolling plan : The futures in education are uncertain and technological changes are equally unpredictable. It is noted that the main reason for success or failure in achieving high quality business systems depended on the state of readiness of the organization: that is, on a combination of circumstances that encourage or even determine success at four key levels - in the organization overall, in the development team overall, in the specific project teams allocated to particular areas of work and amongst individuals themselves. As far as is humanly possible, the strategy should be adaptable to rapidly changing circumstances. To use the example of the University of East Anglia's formula approach to resource distribution: both at library and institutional level, there is general acceptance that a formula model is the best way of allocating resources and as a base for measuring the effectiveness of targeted allocation. However, the formula has changed over time to take account of changes in central funding (e.g. the gradual withdrawal of separate capital funding) and allowed for the creation of separate 'pots' of money which could be used for new initiatives-new subjects, major infrastructural change, and so on.

The computer and communication technology has stepped up the growth, storage techniques and methods of disseminating information, and given birth to information technology (IT) in the last quarter of the 20th century. The age-old manual operations in the libraries are getting replaced by automated systems and the processing of information is becoming a specialized art, including in its ambit, both the science and technology of information. With the increase in use of better resource sharing mechanisms there is increase in resource sharing work. The patterns which existed in the past for resource sharing in different parts of the world are growing further giving rise to local, regional, national and global resource sharing links. Every country is making an effort to share the resources of the libraries. We have come a long way from the days when books were locked on shelves to the days when the books are becoming available in the digitized form and getting accessible globally. These developments confirm that resource sharing is taking a new shape. Digitized books are available for more and more sharing. The concept of owning information is being replaced by the concept of sharing information.

3. Resource Dependence Systems

Resource sharing can take place when information about the resources is available or is made available. Resource sharing is therefore dependent not only on the resources but also on the information about the resources. Each resource sharing network or an agency which maintains shared databases can also facilitate the actual sharing of documents. The better the size and quality of information of immediate interest to the users, the best a network can perform. H. M. K. Dunbar considers that the survival of a resource sharing organization is contingent upon its ability to engage in advantageous resource exchange relationships. The term advantageous is not to be considered as a financial advantage but rather the success the network gets in users' satisfaction each time a resource sharing transaction is conducted. It becomes important because it provides a basis for using a specialist's subject knowledge and ideas for fast professional interaction. It offers view points that make inroads in the universe of knowledge from diverse angles around the world. This gives rise to various resource dependence systems as each system tries to cater to a group of users with specific requirements. The resources could be in the form of union catalogues with locations data, bibliographies, biographical databases, articles databases, full text databases either on specific subjects or general in nature. The creation of these resources will define collections as well.

3.1. Membership Patterns

For participation in a resource sharing network it is important that the libraries understand the commitments they are supposed to make in terms of finance and resource sharing. The benefits and obligations of a participating library should become clear to it for a long range fruitful association. The network should have a participation plan for each participant. It should be realistic.

Participation in a resource sharing network for cooperative collection development and sharing of resources becomes more effective if the participating institution is a member and not a casual participant. John Rutledge and Luke Swindler have made a survey evaluating the role of membership in the Centre for Research Libraries (CRL), which unlike other library networks develops collections for use by member libraries. They observe :

(a) A large membership base is essential to support expanded programmes.

(b) Research libraries have a duty to provide highly specialized and low-use materials. CRL represents one means of achieving this goal.

(c) Cooperation among libraries is an ideal with many adherents. It is difficult to speak against cooperation.

(d) Libraries regarding CRL as an extension of their own libraries have a strong philosophical commitment to CRL, while others value membership in terms of items borrowed.

(e) The competition to CRL is growing due to other networks. Joseph A. Rosenthal comments on this issue: "Although the Centre's collections are large and extensive, it is only in a very, very few areas that they are sufficiently comprehensive to be relied upon by North American research libraries to the point where libraries can discontinue collection development in specific fields of publications."

(f) CRL is regarded as a "Library's Library" and therefore is treated as a collection that complements and supplements the collections of its member-libraries.

(g) Membership enables a user to participate on a continuing basis, and advise on collections and services offered.

(h) An institution can make savings if it uses membership, compares its collections with CRL and reevaluates its collection development programme.

(i) CRL also acted as a cooperative storage warehouse, enabling members to use the warehouse facility.

The CRL experiment has been a unique experiment in resource sharing as it depended more on developing collections itself on behalf of member-libraries and did not exclusively specialise only in the preparation of resources such as union catalogues. This system has disadvantages and it may be worthwhile to highlight some of them.

1. To withdraw from a membership is difficult as it can pose political problems for the library and withdrawal will require careful explanation.
2. The deposit function is one theoretical argument in favour of membership that seems to have diminishing practical value.
3. CRL does not excite donors and benefactors without special promotion it may remain an invisible asset.
4. Special collections in definition serve a different purpose than do primary programmes, and their justification and support cannot be based upon the principles used in austerity budgeting.
5. Based on the experience and documentation the cost per transaction for using CRL is shocking. It ranges from $200 to $400.

So it is considered that resource sharing through the CRL approach has some benefits for the libraries that are approachable easily say in a campus, but this system cannot be effective in a wide area environment. Yet, even those libraries that are situated at a reasonably convenient distance from CRL should take individually decisions for achieving tangible benefits from such a resource sharing system. This model in toto or with some modification can be adopted in Indian Libraries.

3.2. Managing Services

In a library network the important services include off-line/online access to database, e-mail and INTERNET services, ILL and document delivery and trouble-shooting due to the failure of communication hardware like modems, etc. Access to the union catalogues, assistance to libraries for creating catalogues, customisation of softwares and databases has to be available 24 hours and in order to maintain the services the systems manager has to be efficient. In addition to online access off-line access has to function smoothy.

Efficient use of e-mail by the participating libraries needs to be monitored so that those who are not able to access INTERNET are helped. It happens that those library professionals who are new to accessing INTERNET and using e-mail need guidance and this the network needs to provide.

Searching documents and their delivery is an important service. For example, DELNET offers online booking of requests for ILL and delivers such documents to such users who have registered for online ILL service. Otherwise the libraries after finding the location of a document arrange to get it collected themselves. In the major networks in the West, requests booked for a document online, automatically reaches the first location where it is available and the library after receiving the request sends the document by post or courier or online, in an electronic form. ILL protocols, a communications standard permits the exchange of ILL messages between institutions that use different computers and systems.

3.3. Managing Copyright

A network has to see to it that the commercial interests of the authors/creators and publishers of intellectual property are protected and are not violated under the copyright rules in force for fair remuneration needs to be paid to the copyright holders. In order to do so the network has to develop the mechanism for identifying copyright owners of resources that are being copied beyond the fair limit, the payment schedules and the modes of payment. The network has also to be able to get due copyright payments from the users for this purpose. Major copyright and licensing issues need to be resolved under the copyright rules.

3.4. Managing Technology

Management of existing technology and its replacement by new and better technology in terms of hardware, software, communication facilities, INTERNET use, ILL protocols, etc. has to be an ongoing process. The transition has to be so smooth so that the member-libraries only find themselves introduced to new features without disruption in the coming time, multiple users of the electronic mail, efficient use of union-list based system with links to lull-texts and multimedia applications, access to INTERNET databases, with subject approaches rather than database approach, etc. are going to be the areas where smooth transition is necessary. The following areas need to be considered for such a change over.

(a) Improving access through new technologies;

(b) Guidance for utilization of the new technologies;

(c) New services with new technologies;

(d) Sharing of resources and services.

3.5. Managing Finance

Networks cannot be run without recurring financial assistance. The assistance may be inadequate but it should cover all running costs on maintenance, staff, hardware, software, communications and miscellaneous expenses. Its membership fee must be kept low to attract more members. As the number grows, the membership fee becomes a regular source of income.

The role of products can also generate finance. These products could be the software or the databases. The services such as retro-conversion of records, and access to international databases can also generate revenue for the networks. In order to streamline managing of finance, the following may be considered:

(1) ILL costs must be determined honestly to be fair to members.

(2) Pricing of data, used online or off-line must be affordable and competitive;

(3) An equitable approach be taken for the compensation to libraries that provide more lending but made effective after the network is financially sound.

3.6. Managing Manpower

Using IT is the continuous growing facet of librarianship of the present era. Education and Training activities have been instrumental in the adoption of information technology in order to maximise a powerful searching mechanism. The optional use of offline and online information retrieval through IT requires a good training on the part of the user. With the increase in the number of databases available in various disciplines the need of user education and training has become obvious.

It is not always easy to make a clear distinction between education and training, but educational objectives may some time will require training components and viceversa. The objectives of education and training in terms of IT can be observed as follows:

Education is concerned with foundations, principles, and basic knowledge of information science and disciplines as they relate to such things as database structure, database management system, file structure, logic, formulation of search strategies in the generic sense, system analysis and design, vocabulary structure and users' needs.

Training is concerned with the contents and structure of specific-database, design of search for specific online system, techniques for utilizing service offers by individual centres.

In order to attract the best manpower to the library or the network, the Network Manager or the Chief has to play the following roles :

Roles of Network Manager

(i) Personnel role	***(ii) Welfare role***	***(iii) Clerical role***	***(iv) Fire fighting role***
(a) Advisory	(a) Research in personnel and organizational problems	(a) Time-keeping	(a) Grievance handling
(b) Manpower planning	(b) Group counselling motivation, leadership	(b) Salary and wages	(b) Settlement of disputes
(c) Training and development		(c) Maintenance and records	(c) Standing disciplinary acts
(d) Measurement and assessment of individual and group behaviour		(d) Human engineering, man-machine relationship	(d) Collective bargaining
			(e) Joint consultation

Management of trained manpower for a resource sharing network involves the following :

Assessment of the trained staff needed in each division of the network such as given below needs to be done periodically:

(a) Database Division

(b) Software Division

(c) E-mail and INTERNET Division

(d) ILL Division, etc.

The assessments have to be done keeping in view :

(a) New databases introduced.

(b) Managing and upgrading of existing databases and union catalogues.

(c) Introduction of new technology including software.

(d) Availability of new databases on INTERNET, etc.

After each assessment, we need to take into account the continuous training of the existing manpower and training of the librarians and users in the use of the network services.

For updation in fast changing environment, e-learning and on-line learning could be the best solution. E-Learning material is available at a variety of levels. At the simplest level, it could be purely text oriented. The concepts are presented as text pages, which are followed by quiz to test the understanding of learners. Use of product screen dumps to provide look of the product in various usage conditions. More advanced products provide a look and feel of the product to the learner. The learner is demonstrated a certain feature and them asked to perform a simple task using the product interface.

Online learning constitutes just as part of technology based learning and desirable via internet, intranet and extranet. This includes text and graphics of the course, exercises testing and record keeping such as test score and bookmarks. A sophisticated online learning program includes animations, simulations, audio and video sequences, peer and expert discussion in group.

Nevertheless, in an environment where changes are taking place in the information technology, continuous training of library staff is essential. After training is imparted it is important to see that:

(a) the supervisor provides a continual learning environment for the trainee.

(b) the trainee and the coach agree about what will be practized.

(c) the trainee's coach balances criticism about what was done wrong with praise about what was done right.

(d) the trainee gives the supervisor periodic progress reports.

(e) the administration repeats the training programmes until a critical mass of employees competent in the desired skill is stained.

Ronald Powell and Sheila Creth after conducting a survey found that librarians had more of a theoretical than practical knowledge, and there was an urgent need for them to harness technology and management tools. With the spreading of modernization of libraries and library networks have to function, there is a need to fill the jobs available with suitably qualified manpower.

Besides, the following guidelines, may also be kept in mind for effective management of a network by the Network Manager.

(i) *Resource Sharing* : Dependence on resource sharing is going to grow and become an essential activity of a library. Working together makes us learn from one another and share resources. Cooperation has to be achieved by a network at all costs.

There cannot be a single best way to do resource sharing to satisfy all users and handle all information. Resource sharing methods should get evolved on a continuous basis. The resource sharing terms listed in the MOUs between network and the participating libraries should be simple in order to induce more libraries to join.

Resource sharing values should be introduced through critical example and dependable record of interdependence and ILL. Distances between the participating libraries should be reduced by providing efficient and fast document delivery service. Sharing of information on specific needs on the basis of the resources available in participating libraries will help in creating new databases and services.

Resource sharing responsibilities should ensure:

(a) subscriptions to specific serials;

(b) maintaining back files of certain newspapers;

(e) developing retrospective cataloguing of certain collections;

(d) maintaining collections in certain languages.

(ii) *Network Management* : Network management should be transparent, all agreements in written form and the management should be accountable for each decision taken by it. Effective management decisions should plug in economic uncertainty and infuse faith in the network. Extension activities should be undertaken to educate libraries that believe in an independent style of functioning. The objectives should be realistic and the terms for participation and the rules for executing them should be clear. A reward system should be introduced among participating libraries. Responsibilities should be assigned to the libraries to promote resource sharing and rationalization work be held periodically.

Perceptions of the heads of participating institutions should be ascertained. The burden of running a network should not be left to one institution or entirely to all the participating institutions. Efforts should be made to raise resources from other governmental and other agencies.

In the governance, participation of a few elected members on the network's Governing Board would be essential. Pilot projects be introduced on the basis of reciprocity and complementarily in specific areas.

(iii) *Knowledge/Information* : A library network handles knowledge by acquiring, creating, transferring and accessing it. Due care should be taken of each facet of knowledge and information in these areas by approaching it from the broader aspects to the narrower ones.

The behaviour of knowledge growth should eventually get monitored by a network. The impact of multiple languages of cultures on the free flow of information should be reduced by a network.

(iv) *Technology* : Communication and network technology is far ahead of human capacity to use it at a given point. The information explosion, and unbelievable growth in information technology will force operational networks to adopt the latest technology. Network technology should be backed by a reliable human network. Therefore each network should maintain cordial relations with all its members.

(v) *Users* : The analysis of the users' needs should be done periodically and should become part of the planning process. The users are most neglected as far as the education and training is concerned, because user education had been a good subject for conferences, workshops and seminars but actual groundwork is still invisible. Least consideration is made for user education for conventional libraries and the education and training programme of IT in India is still to be considered sincerely. Library and Information users in India are also grouped. Some users' demands are met through conventional type of libraries and some users need sophisticated information products, which are met by special libraries, information centres and documentation centres. But the well-equipped and modern libraries and information centres are not giving the proper education and training to their users as they should.

It is observed that there is no single user education programme that exists which includes orientation about online and offline facilities. To what extent users can access a system, where searching can be carried out easily. And instruction in how to prepare and carry out search by the users must be thought out in a programme. Three types of skills are necessary for carrying out interactive computerised information search, i.e. (i) subject knowledge; (ii) skill in using the system; and (iii) knowledge of the information system to be used, appropriate command; type and quality of information available, database structure, etc. The last two skills can be given with proper user education and training programme. The capacity of each participating library to share resources should be evaluated periodically and exploited for better use of the resources. Meetings with actual users should be held from time to time.

Concludingly it can be said, Resource sharing methods have to be functional and evolving as resource sharing technology evolves periodically. Maximum use of existing resources and maximum information to the users on their topics within a short period of time has to be the motive of a functional resource sharing. INTERNET has already made the exchange of information possible internationally. Resource sharing is as much dependent upon the information about resources as it is on resources in libraries. But for effective participation in resource sharing programmes, a library can only develop a resource management strategy within the context of the parent institution's strategy. The library has to be accountable for the resources made available, not simply in terms of their deployment but also in relation to their origin. The service provided has to be one which is perceived as being relevant to the needs of the parent institution as well as being one which is efficient and cost-effective. The academic library resource manager must be aware of the perceived dispensability of support services in times of financial restraint.

A resource management model has to begin with the library's fundamental role. It could be argued that the role of the academic library is to be what the parent institution wants the library to be, and especially to appear to be so. It must be a positive factor in the continued survival and growth of the organization rather than an expensive and unpopular millstone round the administration's financial and strategic plans and ambitions; to be cheap, cost effective, responsive and proactive.

Key questions need to be asked as part of the process of managing resources in the academic library, which include the following:

- Is the library supporting study and teaching or research?
- Is it providing just-in-time information or long-term research collections?
- Does it exist for the scientist or the humanist, the scholar or the teacher?
- Is it an archive or an information centre?

– Does it have a hard copy or a technology base?

Only when these questions have been asked and answered can the assessment of effective performance be properly undertaken. Good resource management presupposes a long-term strategic plan, a well-run accounting system and effective financial reporting mechanisms. It also presupposes estimating and budgeting systems which feed into the longer-term plan and which are capable of being well and easily managed and changed at relatively short notice if strategy dictates it. Good resource management implies a high degree of freedom within the budget to transfer resources to where, in the opinion of the library manager, they are most needed and where they will bring the greatest return on their allocation. That freedom will, of course, be in the context of clear lines of responsibility and accountability for decision-making, monitoring and control in relation to available resources.

Increasingly, effective resource management also requires detailed and as far as is possible precise information on the cost of all library activity, enabling the resource manager to plan ahead in terms of future expenditure requirements in new and existing areas and to identify relative levels of efficiency within the library.

Finally - it requires people to make it work. Being a good resource manager is not just about being good at managing resources. To be a good one must also have leadership skills and an ability to motivate others. Senior resource managers must also have leadership skills and an ability to motivate others, not least at times and in areas where perhaps those who collect the data which makes effective resource management possible are less than convinced of the need to do so.

8
Resource Sharing : Future Prospects

1. Introduction

Resource sharing is most often discussed in the context of bibliographic materials and is achieved through the process of inter-library loan-an extension of circulation, the primary resource sharing function. Although resource sharing in this traditional conception is important today, it cannot continue to be justified, much less supported, as an important means of sharing resources because: (1) It is labour intensive and therefore quite costly and such costs will only increase; (2) it causes resources to be out of the reach of everyone but the client to whom they have been lent in fact, they are out of the reach of everyone during transit; (3) it involves distribution costs, i.e., packaging, shipping, receiving, record-keeping; that are significant and increasing; and (4) it is not timely, frequently taking a week or two to get materials into the hands of a client. Traditional resource sharing also reflects too limited a view of what resource sharing should encompass.

But how do you organize and manage a library in which your users expect service 24 hours a day? In which most of your technical services staff and some of your public services staff are not even in the building? In which many of your heaviest users may never enter the building or may be located in another town or state? What kinds of budgeting does this require? What kinds of buildings? What kinds of librarians? These changes and the questions they inspire will result from the growing dominance in our society of digitized information delivered over electronic networks. The changes libraries face will be profound, and many librarians fear them, sometimes with good reason. And yet these changes offer many positive opportunities to libraries as well. The future of libraries and of librarians is not yet determined; by understanding technological change and by anticipating some of its effects in the workplace, we can shape our future as well as be shaped by it.

We are in the early stages of a transition from a print-based to a digital society. The effects of this transition will be just as revolutionary as the effects of the transition from a world based on the oral transmission of information to a world grounded on the printed word and just as profound as the transition from an agrarian to an industrial economy during the industrial revolution. That said, no one can know or predict precisely what the course of this revolution will be? No one knows what will really happen because we are in the midest of the chaotic business and technical environment that always accompany such periods of change, but looking at the course of the print revolution 500 years ago or at the course of the industrial revolution 200 years ago can help us understand the kinds of changes we can anticipate.

Revolutions depend on the conjunction of a need and a technology. In the late fifteenth century, the new technology of moveable type met the rapidly-expanding knowledge base of the Renaissance and the Age of Exploration. The two developments fed on each other. The new technology made the broad dissemination of new information possible; the copiousness of the new knowledge made the new technology necessary. This new technology, the printed book, was as threatening in its time as digital information is today. Lovers of literature and of illuminated manuscripts thought books were ugly; the Catholic Church thought books were subversive. Both were right. Books were less attractive than illuminated manuscripts, and they were in fact used to spread the Protestant revolution. There were even laments about the lack of bibliographic control of these new "ephemera"!

We stand today at the beginning of another revolution in the delivery of information. When this revolution is complete, most information will be delivered to users in digital format over high speed telecommunication links. This revolution, like the revolution which led to the printed book, also depends on the fortunate conjunction of new technologies with a rapidly expanding knowledge base. The technologies that make this revolution possible are the development of cheap computer processing power, cheap mass storage, inexpensive and ubiquitous access to high speed telecommunications networks, and convenient retrieval devices.

These technologies give us the ability to create, to manipulate, to store, and especially-to transfer large quantities of information in digital form at low cost. The products of these technologies are today as primitive and as imperfect as the book was in 1494, but the abilities they offer will have profound effects on the academic world and ultimately on the larger society.

We know this because we can see the effects of digital technology in industries where it has already become dominant. It has proved thus far to be a reliable general rule that when paper-based information systems come up against electronic information systems, electronic systems always prevail.

2. The Changing Scenario

The library profession has never been exposed so much in the past to the changing information scenario as it has been exposed now. In this age of information explosion the technology has progressively replaced the old methods of information collection, storage and retrieval. Today the walls of a library are giving way to electronic environments to establish links with information and virtual libraries that are getting shaped on the INTERNET. Each individual library is acting as a place for storage and service to the users while the trend is to provide shared information to the users. This advanced scenario is not firmly entrenched in India yet, although a number of libraries have INTERNET connectivity and access to other electronic resources.

In the changing scenario, the multidimensional nature of knowledge is going to make access to information more complex but the technology is equally becoming increasingly powerful and user-friendly. While the growing information resources on the INTERNET are going to expand further the libraries that hold the printed documents will be busy converting the important ones into machine readable forms. They will act as switching centres for accessing computerized databases for a limited period of time and gradually the users' focus is going to shift from libraries to their places of work at home. Databases are going to grow out of the libraries and in fact all transactions will be made in machine readable forms.

3. Libraries and Networked Information

Libraries are one of the institutions that stand to gain most from the networked information revolution, but, paradoxically, they are one of the institutions that stand to lose most as well. Public libraries, which have the greatest need for the expanded resource base that networked information already provides, are least prepared financially and by training and inclination to access it. Smaller academic institutions are in much the same position as public libraries, while larger academic libraries are already beginning to observe the workings of a kind of intellectual Gresham's law whereby users reject superior print resources in favour of inferior but more accessible electronic resources. Such institutions are pressed to spend scarce resources to convert resources to electronic formats if they are to get any reasonable return on their investment.

Fortunately, libraries are at a point where their future is not yet determined. What are the factors that will determine what their future looks like? What will the consequences of these factors be? And how shall we cope with them?

First, and most important, in a world of ubiquitous

networked information, librarians will have infinite new resources at their command. We will be working, as far as information is concerned, in a post-scarcity environment. All our expectations and most of our practices in librarianship are based on information being a scarce commodity. We limit access with hours and user categories and collection development policies. Our public services are based on helping people find information in local resources that are always inadequate to the task and our service points like circulation and reserve are based on controlling access so scarce resources will be available to the largest number of people.

We will have to make profound changes in the way we think about what we do if we are to survive as institutions because users experienced with electronic information have almost infinite new expectations. If libraries are unable to meet these expectations, resources will inevitably flow away from the library to other institutions that do. Librarians who don't understand this will see their libraries wither away.

More interesting perhaps are the implications of the revolution for the way librarians work. In the first stage of technological revolutions, we apply the technology to improving the efficiency of what we already do. Thus OCLC replaced printed LC cards and fax replaced mail for delivering ILL. In the second stage, we do things differently. In the third stage, we do different things. In libraries, we are currently in the second stage of technological change. We are just beginning to do things differently. We are exploring just-in-time models and the idea that access to information is more important than ownership of it. We are allowing end-users to do online searches and initiate their own interlibrary loan requests. Will empowering users to do their own searches turn out to be as profound in its effects as allowing people to have their own Bibles?

There is still plenty of room to do things differently before we begin to do different things. Twenty-four hour online reference service is not only possible, it is easy to achieve. There is no technical reason for a copy cataloguer ever to come to the library except to understand how users relate to information. Most *Index Medicus* indexing is done by freelancers working at home, and in an electronic environment, the cataloguer might as well be at the beach as in the office. At the University of South Florida, a number of copy cataloguers work at home and come to the library only for weekly meetings. More radically, there is probably no real reason why most libraries should do their own cataloguing at all, and copy cataloguing will almost certainly migrate to centralized services. Similarly, document delivery is already cheaper than ILL in most circumstances, and technology like OCLC's Guidon or Bell Labs' RightPages, and the growth of electronic publishing will quickly supplant both in certain applications.

A more glaring example of the kind of inefficiency that can be eliminated by electronic information resources is the wasteful duplication of materials and services between public and school libraries. School libraries are open seven or eight hours a day for eight to ten months a year to a limited clientele, and yet many of their resources duplicate those of public libraries. Why should citizens continue to tolerate the cost of duplicating materials and services when both schools and public libraries could have access to the same information sources through dial-up services? It is immoral to ask taxpayers to invest in separate school and public libraries when their collections and services should and can be integrated electronically if not physically. And yet the political barriers to integration are enormous because we are not used to thinking in ways that are empowered by the new technology.

What will libraries be like when librarians do something really radical-when we do different things? It is a bit early to predict, but certainly in a post-scarcity information environment, the task of the librarian becomes at least partly one of filtering and evaluating a flood of information, and these are tasks for which many librarians at present are singularly unprepared. We are taught in library school not to label information. We are taught to present choices to users, not to make choices for them. In a post-scarcity environment, there is likely to be little patience with these values.

With rise in the number of digital information systems, more preference will be given to systems that are accessible from any part of the world than to the collections that are not accessible. Financial support will become available for outstanding collections to be digitized but with the hope to recover costs through users. It is likely that in the first half of the 21st century two parallel information systems, one based on totally digitized information and the other on printed collections, will be in use. The important trends that are likely to emerge in this regard include:

(i) information services will become globally accessible;

(ii) scholarly communications will make radical changes in the universe of knowledge;

(iii) local print collections will become outdated fast;

(iv) provision centres will emerge to serve regional, natural or specialized collection needs; and

(v) access to global collections will become increasingly necessary.

The creation of new methods of classifying and cataloguing internal resources, developing such search engines, which specialise in certain subject areas only and interlink each bit of information which has relevance to anything else in the universe of knowledge is going to be an ongoing process.

4. The Challenges

The obligations of librarians towards the world, towards the country, towards the institutions, users and themselves for playing positive roles as library professionals are actually going to place the challenges before them in a wide variety of contexts in the near future. Contributions to the universal bibliographic control and the universal availability of publications, will become essential for providing better information to the users. Every day it is becoming necessary that bibliographic, biographical, statistical and full text information should get so standardized around the globe that a librarian anywhere in the world can contribute to this resource and any user anywhere in the world can access this information smoothly. This global compulsion is going to become increasingly compelling in the 21st century because no longer will wastage of effort by creating non-standard databases be appreciated and accepted.

Creation of standard databases and networking them in the early decades of the 21st century in a developing country like India is going to be a common feature. But it is expected that national and international agencies and vendors will create databases and make them available against a fee to all the libraries, and users at home or in offices. This next phase of the challenge is going to be far more difficult for the librarians because two schemes are likely to emerge. One that a growing number of the documents will begin to get published in digital form and will be available online. The librarians will not have to house full text journals and books, as they do the printed volumes. And second, there will be no need to classify and to catalogue documents in the present form because data will be accessible online. As a result of this, the existing libraries in each country will slowly have the tendency to become archival in nature and unless the library professionals create a role for themselves in information retrieval and dissemination out of the growing number of databases and networks they will have a major problem to face.

There are other barriers that stand between librarians and success in the emerging digital world. Most of us are not comfortable with technology because most of the current technology has only been developed since we were in library school. We have learned to cope with it through self-education, and we understand that reaching the next plateau of knowledge will push us harder than we have hitherto been pushed. Similarly, we have had little exposure to and less instruction in budgeting and financial planning in our professional education, and yet it is a major activity for many of us. We have not even developed the tools to measure accurately the new services we can provide.

Besides, the standards for creating, storing and accessing information have to become universal, which are not so at present. When standards become universal and they are maintained throughout the world, any change in them may not be adopted uniformly at the same time due to the limitations of staff, finance and the motivation of the administrators unless the benefits of change are convincing and of interest to them. Therefore, the process of transformation will be ongoing.

INTERNET or INTRANETS will be frequently used for accessing information, exchanging files and even for publishing of information electronically. The use of new standards is also going to be important for transfer of articles, books, etc. on word processing so that the text is not rekeyed again by publishers, for flagging contents of documents accurately for easy and precise indexing, for creating permanent storage banks on INTERNET for uniform global accessing, etc. In this regard, the comments of Marsha Ra can be preferred "The day is not far off when systems will be linked through Common Communication Protocols, and bibliographic and other text files will be searchable by an accepted common command language, over a national education and research network, with lax machines sharing the same common and subsidised communications network. Powerful communications lines will permit the sending of digitized illustrations directly to workstation screens. Resources will be created and shared dynamically without the involvement of librarians."

Advances in multimedia applications are going to add a new dimension to a librarian's work. The librarian will have to qualify to provide greater inputs for the creation of multimedia editions of books.

The World Wide Web is going to be more interactive and multidimensional, incorporating multimedia presentations. And all this data will be accessible through the Information Super Highways. Microcomputers will have the capacity to process more instructions per second than now. As data grows beyond the controlling capacities, librarians will be using compression and other techniques of optical storage. A wide variety of technology options that exist now are already ahead of what librarians can use today and as the trend reveals, the technology is going to change even more rapidly. Coping with the technology is going to remain a continuous challenge.

5. Resource Sharing

Collection development is going to be a specialized art. With documents getting published electronically and the INTERNET resources growing at 18 per cent a month, the selection of documents is going to be a difficult job. Libraries may have to subscribe to a package rather than to journals in the 21st century.

The reason why print material is going to be much in demand during the first half of the 21st century is because still in the U.S. major university libraries utilize a good deal of subjects on print material. A survey made of the University of Minnesota Library reveals that only 10 per cent of the library's total budget goes into the maintenance and acquisition of digital library services. However, there will be a marked increase in the expenditure on digital resources as more and more digital databases and services become available.

The Web is doubling in size every 30 days. The existing methods of ILL will recede in functionality due to rising costs, growing demands and the frequent changes in the technology. Dependence on new service agencies that have access to global resources will become a necessity for researchers and knowledge seekers.

It is therefore apparent that the 21st century libraries will basically become the centres for resource sharing with resources which will have no local, national or international boundaries. Library networks therefore, will play major roles as partners in the global networking of information. Library professionals will have to be closely associated with the networks and also be contributing information to a network or a number of networks as considered appropriate and necessary.

Inter library Loan will take different shape in the 21st century, especially with regard to the documents available in machine readable form. Any document can be delivered to anyone at any time regardless of the location and also the same document can be presented in various forms including the hard copy. James Rush adds that "for entire books, articles, sound recordings, music scores, maps, and other forms of material, on-demand publishing for use in hand-held or lap-top readers designed for single or multimedia presentation can be achieved. Although some would argue that the printed book will never cease to exist, the number of books produced in their present form will decline dramatically as personal readers are developed and become popular."

The resource sharing is going to take place in various other spheres of activities in the libraries. Circulation which is the basic method of sharing resources with the users is likely to have links through ILL and other networks. This will enable the networks to know which books are in circulation or available for borrowing or for reference. The cooperation is also possible for acquisitions. Since more and more publishers' works will be available via data communication networks, the acquisition activities will not exist in the present form. There will be no need of physical storage place and no staff needed to man the acquisitions in the present form. Cataloguing will be centralized and can be done by the network or by the library for data maintained in CDs or DVDs. It is likely that most of the cataloguing will be done with greater preference for deep subject indexing and consistency in use of notation.

As the serials data will be available through networks there will be no need for local cataloguing of serials. Most of the cataloguing will be handled by the library networks. The library networks could also link serials data with the full text and with appropriate hyperlinks for other necessary information to the users.

It is likely that computer facilities available in the campus could be shared and the need for having a separate facility in each library and in each room could be avoided in order to save on cost. James Rush observes that computer operations for 3-4 libraries would cost 10-15 per cent more than providing a facility to one library. Furthermore, it may also provide better operating conditions and fail-safe capabilities. Even if extended hours of coverage by operations personnel were required, a facility shared by four libraries could afford around the clock coverage, whereas an individual institution probably could not. James Rush also notes that the libraries could gain economically and in terms of services if they shared integrated systems. It is likely that institutions will begin to appreciate the information of shared systems by which they will not only significantly improve access to information but also reduce the financial burdens considerably.

Besides, it is also possible that language barriers will get eliminated slowly. The documents in machine readable form can be translated and communicated in other languages as well.

6. Consortia-Subscription

The phenomenon of consortia or group of libraries buying e-information together has become very important in the last few years. Todays :

- The days of building an independent reference library is over.
- The days of selling single subscriptions to one institution at a time are past.
- The days of providing online access exclusively through large centralized vendors are gone.

The days of networked information are upon us.

But are any of us ready? The answer is no! Reevan had explored the potential and the pitfalls of implementing shared electronic information services. He has pointed out the future of consortia under following heads :

6.1. Why Consortia Licensing?

Many electronic products are priced out of reach for a single institution. As budgets become tight, libraries look toward consortia as a way of reducing costs by subscribing as a group to commonly used databases, relying on the economics of scale to bring prices down. Furthermore, consortial licensing often serves the "greater good", in that larger partners carry some of the cost for the smaller ones, for e.g., in the case of Academic Press electronic journals. The technological capacity of the group frequently jumps to that of the most advanced partner. There should be much less duplication of effort for even such products that could be afforded individually, e.g. in developing a single contract, in negotiating all customization of products together, and in joint implementation, publicity, problem solving, and training. Consortia are also more likely to be able, utilizing the expanded resources among the membership, to add value to the products that they purchase, e.g. by adding local holdings to citations. Traditionally, libraries networked products locally, but more and more people agree the CD-ROM LANs may be a thing of the past. As a recent quote puts it: " CD-ROM has always been more suitable as a publishing and distribution, rather than a retrieval, medium. Libraries have stretched the retrieval capabilities of the little discs right to the limits of the network, and in many cases, transferred the resource to hard disks to mimic more closely the on-line system that they really wanted but could not afford." As a member of a consortium, a library is much more likely to be able to afford, for instance, access to a flexible client/server search and retrieval system, preferably via the Internet.

6.2. Are there any Successful Licensing Consortia ?

Yes and no, there are good outcomes from a number of consortial efforts:

- **Example: Public Libraries :** The North of Boston Library Exchange (NOBLE), a consortium of 15 area libraries, are implementing consortial access to EBSCOHost's MasterFile index and fulltext database. Something they could not afford individually.
- **Example: Multi-type Library Consortium :** OhioLINK, is the almost legendary alliance of many types of libraries cooperating statewide to purchase licenses to electronic products centrally. It is a consortium of Ohio academic libraries in both the public and private sector ranging from major research institutions to community colleges. This is the first major attempt in the US to create a virtual, statewide library system. More than just linking the holdings of participating libraries within the context of a 48-hour delivery system for books and journal articles, OhioLINK provides the platform as well for statewide delivery of commercial and other databases, Internet access, and experimentation with the development and testing of new information tools, and joint licensing.
- **Example: Digital image rights licensing :** The Museum Educational Site Licensing project (MESL) is a collaborative exercise to reengineer the distribution of art. MESL has established terms and conditions for the educational use of museum images and associated information from six museums, seven universities, and the Library of Congress. This is an example of educational institutions licensing their own products in a responsible and reasonable way.
- **Example: Phased consortial agreements.** The Council of Prairy and Pacific University Libraries (COPPUL) in Canada allows members to join initiatives progressively;

first the "big three", then middle-sized libraries, and so on.

- In Canadian Census Data, the raw CC data was mounted on a central server at one member site; another site developed an interface to search this data and to generate reports.
- Electronic Reference Library® (ERL), Silver Platter's platform for mounting their databases was being considered as the "generic" way to deliver bibliographic searching.
- Current Contents® on OVID® was explored as a consortial license after the two largest libraries in the consortium had already purchased it. The negotiations with ISI broke off after it became clear that they expected these libraries to continue to pay the same as members of a consortium. This is an example of using the "fatal flaw" system for making joint decisions.

– **Example: Subject and Project based consortium :** The Library Service Alliance of New Mexico ("Alliance"), is an alliance of six Sci/Tech Libraries; three from Universities and three from the local National laboratories. Members of this group has been successful in obtaining access to subject databases that would be impossible to afford singly and has created the opportunity for other members to share in these if and when they can afford to do so. They are currently working on consortial licensing for electronic journals. Having Los Alamos National Laboratory Library as a member brings tremendous added benefit to the rest of the group in which can help underwrite the customization and enhancement of the products they purchase. One of these is to link citations found in the Science Citation Index (SciSearch©) to full text articles of jointly purchased electronic versions of sci/tech journals.

6.3. Can Consortia make timely Decisions about Networked Electronic Products?

Can groups really get their act together to do the job? Yes, if due process is followed in establishing a legal entity and if bylaws are clarified before making consortial decisions. Also, keeping to the time-honored rules for conducting good meetings will make difficult decisions easier, especially if each member gets an opportunity, early on, to describe their local systems operation; what's good about it, what their machine and people strengths are, and what the organizational infrastructure and funding obstacles might be. In deciding on any joint purchase, decision making will be easier if there are clear goals and priorities for the group, e.g., priority is given to products serving undergraduates/the public/ researchers, or priority is given to products which require minimal implementation effort, for instance, access via the internet using a standard browser.

6.4. Is there such a thing As a Good License?

Possibly. One thing is for certain, it can only be as good as the group's planning and preparation, i.e., how many questions you ask and how assertive and cohesive the group is in negotiating with experienced commercial vendors. A great psychological "prop" for members is a list of what would constitute a "Fatal Flaw" in any contract - three Fatal Flaws and the deal is off.

1. Know as much as you can. That means asking questions and the best way to do so is to develop guidelines to measure a contact against.
2. Have criteria that MUST be met, as well as preferred criteria. There are the guidelines to be written into a Check List to ensure that we do not miss anything in the excitement of acquiring a new product. These should preferably be written into more detailed questions for those contract clauses that cause the most concern.

   For instance, "Does the license allow the library to define

the user population ...?", can be refined into the following questions:

- who is an authorized user?
- what type of user would not fit the given definition?
- how are users counted?
- are number of USES counted?

Refining questions regarding legitimate uses could be :

- what are acceptable uses?
  - noncommercial vs. commercial use?
  - is it okay to incorporate specialized library uses, like cataloguing and Interlibrary loan?
- are there restrictions on printing, downloading, ftp-ing, or sending to e-mail addresses?
- can we keep and use older versions of the product?
- what is the library's liability for the way our users use the information acquired?

The latter is such an important issue that is decided to adapt a rider regularly attached to all licenses by Loyola University of Chicago for our own use.

Ultimately, the best solution to getting consistent licensing will be through the use of "License Brokers" somewhat like the current journal vendors. Tony Ferguson of Columbia University, one of the negotiators for the Northeast Research Library Consortium (NERL) said: " ...what I hunger for is a vendor who will do all the work commercial e-journals seem to be requiring and let me get back to worrying more about user needs and collection content."

6.5. Is it Really Possible to Negotiate Better Conditions and Prices?

Consortia has leveridge; the larger and/or wealthier and/or more influential the consortium is, the more leveridge it has. It is important to let the vendor know, early on, that the group will be tieing the fees they are prepared to pay to the degree to which their criteria has been met. Tough bargaining stances are also more creditable coming from a group, e.g., could you as an individual say the following to a vendor like ISI or Elsevier: "We can only afford a network license for your product if the price is within the X dollar ballpark" ? Probably not! As a well organized group with more financial clout, we could and should. The vendor then has the option to choose to get some money or none!

6.6. How Does Consortial Licensing get Done?

The best way to start negotiations is to ask for a free trial or offer to be a beta test group for an evolving product. This should be free to members of the consortium, except for their local investments of people's time and the use of existing hardware at each site. If members and their local users are satisfied with the product, the group should begin planning the contract negotiations, especially what the product is "worth" to them. Decide on the amount which will be the bottom line. Then ask for a draft contract and invoice from the vendor. Insist on a dedicated sales representative to whom the consortium's negotiators will direct all communications and questions. Explain the major issues and concerns to this person; being honest about whether and how these issues will affect the purchase decision. It is also important to try to find out if other organizations or consortia have signed licenses recently or are in a similar negotiating phase. This information is hard to get - using the library. Internet grapevine and informal networks may be the best way to do this. Vendors are loath to divulge such information as they see this as weakening their bargaining position.

Responding to the contract: this is the most problematic phase as individual members will have to "sell" and get approval for the contract and subsequent changes and additions from their "home" organization's decision makers. This is made easier if such persons or committees were kept informed at each step of the process and funds were identified in advance. Once a suitable contract is negotiated with the vendor, the group should decide on the best way to invoice members for their portion of the licensing fee. Either, directly from the vendor to each member, or as a single invoice to the consortium, to be paid from membership fees.

6.7. What Happens to Copyright Under a Consortial License?

The short answer is: you negotiate a license that over-ride copyright. Other speakers will be dealing with some of these issues at the conference, but for all intends and purposes, with the right license you should not have to worry about copyright. It is, however, prudent to protect the consortium members from third party liability, i.e., what your users do with the information they retrieve. An appropriate waiver should be attached to the contract.

6.8. What is the Potential for Consortial Licensing and from Where we can Get Funding?

Potential exist, especially for investing in a standard platform to mount common databases, like the Wilson databases. SilverPlatter's ERL platform would be ideal for this purpose. Where can we get funding? "The Government!" Seems to be the obvious answer. However, good consortia look at their joint resources first, exploring how reallocation can help provide the needed funds or some of it.

6.9. Can the Organization take the Risks Necessary if We are not in Sole Control?

This last point is actually not a question, but a hard reality consortia have to deal with. It is an issue of organizational culture and our ability to take managed risks in an uncertain environment, in uncertain times. Our options, however, are fairly clear: we can choose trailing edge technology which is individually affordable but ultimately pleases no one, or we can be part of a potential, that pool resources and take risks to serve its users better. If such risks pay off, State and other funding would be secured. If we fail as a Consortium, at least we are in it together and the political fall-out is distributed among the members! As a group we can have the potential to look more objectively at the lessons learned from both failure or success. What Barbara Steissand said about money in "Hello Dolly" is also true for success and failure: "Money [or failure, or success] is like manure if you spread it around, it makes things grow!"

He said finally, if you are now convinced that consortial licensing has greater benefits than going it alone, be prepared to compromise and let go of control and/or preferred ways of working or preferred platforms, when the greater good is served. Also, be prepared to say no when your local customers or conditions makes it impossible to join the group, and do it in such a way that it does not prevent the rest of the group from pursing the project further; you may be able to join at a later date.

Consortia in India are still in their infancy and there is a need to study these models and establish guidelines and methodologies. It is felt that the concept of 'Consortia' can work well among similar organizations having similar situations such as sufficient additional funds available for the libraries of the consortia members and above all the committed mindsets of the library administrators. However, in reality the idea of consortia is still far fetched as many university libraries have yet to experience the power of information technology applications. In India it is the right time to develop models for consortia, so that when the information technology applications are introduced in university libraries they can be prepared for participating in consortia which are already in practice in other libraries. UGC-INFONET is one such step in this direction.

7. Changing Role of Librarians

The librarians, especially reference librarians, and those handling resource sharing work will have to gain competence in interviewing skills so that they are able to locate the precise needs of the users. In the past, the librarians used to offer mostly bibliographic references, but in future it will have to be supplemented by full text access. In a study made by Joan C. Durrance, it is found that only 27 per cent of professional librarians could find what the users actually needed. This means that the librarians will have to ascertain a new the methods by which users' needs were closely monitored. As users' needs become known, the librarians will have to provide information rather than bibliographies. This role demands total transformation of the librarians. They have to become knowledge brokers rather than document brokers.

Dependence on the librarian becomes more important as the librarian's role grows as the provider of knowledge. The librarians will have therefore to be more dependable so that they do not disclose the purpose for which a particular user obtained information, though the librarians will not stop the flow of the same information to other users. The Librarian is going to work more as a:

- Disseminator of digital information rather than the custodian of information;
- Trainer in information technology than as a passive learner;
- Researcher in information technology to compete with the rest of the professionals than a user of age-old library techniques;
- Promoter of extension activities in regard to the creation of manuscripts, publication of multimedia and other documents and the distribution of documents than simply a user of published documents; and
- Master of the contents of the world resources than a librarian of a single library.

Resource sharing of the electronic materials will go together with the resource sharing of the materials in print for the transformation of the print material in the electronic form is going to be a really difficult job, never complete, or entirely satisfactory. 21st century is going to witness the struggles between the print and the electronic documents, the document libraries and the knowledge libraries, computer and communication specialists and the information specialists and many more among a variety of users and information providers.

The creation and analysis of information, synthesis of knowledge, and the applications of knowledge in multiple scenarios will be so rapid that the existing libraries that remain struggling to survive will find their resources becoming less relevant as electronic databases will be in a constant influx of sharing and exchanging information. The existing resource sharing methodologies will slowly be replaced by concept based sharing of digital resources.

9

Important Library & Information Networks

Due to advancement in information and communication technology, various Library & Information Networks have emerged in India. These are working well in providing information to its users. Some of the important library networks working in India are briefly discussed below :

ADINET
(Ahmedabad Library Network)

Introduction

ADINET, the Ahmedabad Library Network, is a network of libraries located in and around Ahmedabad and it was established with the sponsorship of NISSAT.

Objectives

(i) To bring about cooperative mode of working amongst the libraries and information centres in and around Ahmedabad.

(ii) To integrate the economic, scientific and technical information systems into an effective network in and around Ahmedabad.

(iii) To facilitate and promote sharing of resources amongst the libraries and information centres in and around Ahmedabad by developing and maintaining a central online union catalogue containing bibliographic information on books, serials and non-book materials of all the participating libraries.

(iv) To coordinate with other regional, national and international networks, libraries, information and documentation centres for exchange of information and documents.

(v) To offer technical guidance to member libraries on selecting, storing, sharing and disseminating the information.

(vi) To coordinate efforts for suitable collection development and reduce unnecessary duplication wherever possible.

(vii) To develop databases of projects, specialists and institutions in and around Ahmedabad.

(viii) To create awareness amongst all users' groups and to educate them in the utilization of information.

(ix) To develop resources and to propagate in ways appropriate to the needs of users in and around Ahmedabad.

(x) To help library and information centre users and also individuals who practice different professions in getting specialized information of their interest.

Functions

A centralised database of periodicals , books and non-book materials available in the libraries of Ahmedabad is being created. Records collected from participating libraries are being suitably formatted and merged to generate the Union Catalogue of Ahmedabad Libraries. This database is being updated regularly. At present this database includes only the present/current holdings of libraries. Retrospective conversion will be taken up later. It is planned to procure some databases on special subjects and mount them in the host computer.

Services

Online Information : Information can be searched by the

participating libraries by accessing the Union Catalogue. Presently, the database of periodicals is searchable online. This facility will gradually be extended to other databases also.

Inter-Library Loan : ADINET enables a user to locate a periodical/book/report of his interest. Once located the document including the audio-visual material can be borrowed on inter-library loan basis.

Photocopying Service : Librarians of the member institutes and library professional members regularly get photocopies of the contents pages of library and information science journals. They get full text of the selected articles from the contents pages. For meeting the requests for other journal articles, the journal is procured from other libraries in and around Ahmedabad, the required article is photocopied, and then sent to the customer on payment basis.

Current Awareness Service : This service can also be provided using commercial databases that are available in machine-readable form in some libraries.

Information Service : All the members are provided access to databases generated and procured by the network.

Internet Service : Individuals can come to ADINET and access Internet with e-mail, downloading and printout facilities.

Publications

ADINET Newsletter: It is published quarterly, and is distributed free.

Union List of Periodicals: It is published annually and contains unique titles subscribed by libraries of institutes and colleges located in Gujarat and Gandhinagar and the universities of Gujarat.

Directory of Institutions in Ahmedabad and Gandhinagar: It includes postal addresses, e-mail addresses, telephone numbers, fax numbers and other relevant information about the activities of the institutes and colleges situated in

Ahmedabad and Gandhinagar and universities of Gujarat. It is updated annually.

Directory of Library and Information Science Professionals in Ahmedabad and Gandhinagar: A database is being created providing details about the professionals, i.e., names; official and residential addresses, phone numbers, e-mail addresses, URLs of the organizations and the libraries, etc.

All the publications are provided free to the members.

Other Activities

Training Programme: ADINET is providing computer training to library professionals on CDS/ISIS and Internet. For member institutes, one participation is free.

Study Circle: Under the auspices of ADINET, the study circle is held on the last Friday of every month during 5 PM to 6 PM at MJ Library, Ellisbridge, Ahmedabad. One of the member initiates the talk on a particular topic by presenting a paper which is followed by discussions and suggestions.

BONET
(Bombay Library Network)

Introduction

Bombay Library Network (BONET), which is sponsored by the NISSAT, aims at promoting cooperation among libraries in Mumbai.

Bombay now Mumbai, has many wonderful libraries whose enormous and comprehensive collections are of great value to academic and R&D communities. BONET, has simplified accessing these collections and services by offering links to all libraries in and around Mumbai. The aim of the Bombay Library Network Project is to make information available to researchers at low cost, using computer networking facilities and at the same time, enhancing inter-library cooperation. Information made available rapidly and as cheaply as possible, will improve the quality of research in India. So it is not surprising that Bonet was initiated and is funded by the National Information System for Science and Technology, NISSAT, part of the Government of India.

The nucleus of Bonet is people and technology. A small team of staff at the National Centre for Software Technology, Mumbai (NCST) manage the human and methodological side of the network. Existing datacom arrangements NCST has in operation, play an important role in promoting BONET's growth as does the Education and Research Network (ERNET) Project, whose international gateway is operated by NCST. ERNET connects 170 teaching and research institutes throughout India and is sponsored by the Department of Electronics with assistance from UNDP.

Affordable Technology

BONET offers a low cost library network system that can be considered as a model for similar services outside Mumbai. A library can participate with nothing more than a PC and a modem card. Dialling into the BONET computer, a VAX 8600 running Ultrix - DEC's implementation of Unix, the newcomer can access a whole range of network services. The VAX 8600, named sangra (the Hindi word for database), has a 9600 BPS leased line linked to ERNET's international gateway, sangam.

Sangam is in turn, connected to the Internet through a 64 KBPS leased line. Sangam is also connected by ERNET's leased lines to Bangalore, Delhi, Chennai and Pune. Another leased line links Kanpur to ERNET's node in Delhi. All this adds up to excellent E-mail connectivity for BONET members many of whom are acquiring leased lines to sangra or sangam, thereby increasing manifold the volume of services they can provide to their readers.

Services

Services offered by BONET include:

(i) An online catalogue of periodicals in member libraries, named Unicat.

(ii) Access to online information on books in member libraries. Currently, NCST has its catalogue on the network and is encouraging other libraries to put their catalogues on too.

(iii) Inter-Library Lending Service (ILLS) for books and periodicals, with sangra providing a simple forms based request facility integrated with E-mail and book keeping functions.

(iv) Inter-Library Request Service for photocopying, and a book ordering service offering facilities very similar to the ILLS.

(v) An online Information Retrieval System for Computer Science and Software Technology.

(vi) Online access to foreign library catalogues. Since this is usually free of charge, a number of libraries find it very attractive.

(vii) Online access to commercial databases such as Dialog.

Many of these services are yet to be fully exploited as participating libraries require good datacom facilities. But, the exploratory use with dial up facilities means that a good deal of learning is going on. BONET also runs a monthly seminar that is usually very well attended. In fact, exchange of know-how and information may turn out to be the greatest benefit of Bonet membership.

Arrangements are also being made with a number of overseas sources for supply of photocopies of articles not available in India. Bonet is keen to have reciprocal arrangements with libraries in Asia who would like access to Indian material and the extensive back runs of journals from all over the world held by member libraries.

Centralized versus Distributed Services

In the long run, members are expected to operate their own computerized catalogues and access the network from their workstations or terminals. The basic model is one of an heterogeneous network of information sources. However, centralized facilities on sangra will continue to be available for meeting some of the needs of libraries that are not computerized. Some facilities may continue to exist in a centralized form, for instance the catalogue of periodicals of member libraries for which a general format for data entry has been disseminated along with PC based software. Member libraries can also use datacom links to keep information on their holdings up to date on sangra. Clearly, it is easier for everyone to access Unicat on a central computer than on a dozen computers spread all over the network.

Courier Service

Mere knowing where a particular journal can be found, is not enough. Researchers need rapid access to the journal itself. One of the comforts of a city oriented library network is that inter-library lending can be promoted by a courier who calls on member libraries two or three times a week. BONET offers this service for delivery of photocopied articles and inter-library loans entered into sangra.

Booksellers too, have been invited to participate in the project. Orders and inquiries can be sent to them directly by participating libraries, using software on Sangra.

UNICAT helps libraries to stretch their budgets

Besides helping to locate journals and articles, BONET is enhancing the value of library budgets by encouraging libraries to service each other, for example the provision of photocopies for scholarly use. UNICAT helps to locate requested titles and also enables members to coordinate the ordering of journals thus reducing the duplication of titles from library to library.

The current set of members reads like a Who's Who of R&D, higher education and business houses in Mumbai. They include the Cancer Research Institute, Credit Rating Information Services of India Ltd, Garware Institute of Career Education, Bombay University, Hindustan Lever Research Centre, Indira Gandhi Institute of Development Research, National Addiction Research Centre, National Centre for Software Technology, National Centre for Information which publishes current contents of 250 Indian journals, Narsee Monjee Institute of Management Studies, S. P. Jain Institute of Management, Tata Consultancy Services and the Victoria Jubilee Technical Institute.

Finally, as the momentum of BONET increases, many other libraries are on the point of joining and several have provided data for UNICAT. They are Mafatlal Polytechnic, Bhabha Atomic Research Centre, Inter-University Centre for Astronomy and Astrophysics, Tata Institute of Fundamental Research and the National Centre for Radio Astrophysics located in Pune.

Internet users can log in to the BONET catalogues using the command telnet sangra.ncst.ernet.in. The IP address is 144.16.1.100. Users can log in as "bonet". No password is required. You will be able to look through:

- The catalogue of periodicals, UNICAT.
- The NCI database, a current contents service to 250 Indian journals.
- The NCST library catalogue.
- Information about BONET including a list of members and their addresses.

CALIBNET
(Calcutta Library Network)

Introduction

The formation of Calcutta Library Network (CALIBNET) is the result of the efforts made by NISSAT (National Information System for Science, and Technology). The Department of Scientific and Industrial Research initiated action for this purpose. Accordingly a feasibility study report for networking of about 40 libraries in Calcutta (now Kolkata), was prepared by the CMC Limited. As per the details contained in the report, an amount Rs. 233.8 lakhs was to be spent during the two phases of its implementation. CALIBNET has made significant strides towards fulfilling its dual objectives, i.e.,

(i) launching its library network programs, facilitating remote online access to the holding data of Kolkata libraries, and other specialized databases as well — a significant step towards bibliographic resources sharing amongst Kolkata libraries; and

(ii) providing electronic access to globally available information, imbibing its 'information centre approach'.

Both are essential for advanced learning and scholarship. In the process, CALIBNET aims at covering a wide panorama of information end-user interests, with diffusion of new electronic information technology as the primary concern.

Software Developed & Library Network Launched

Intense in-house research and development efforts have now achieved the Library Network capability by three significant strides:

- a multi-user storage and retrieval software 'SANJUKTA' to support CALIBNET's Centralized Database (CDB), and to provide online access to it from remote locations;
- a conversion software package 'PARAPAR' to support

interchange of bibliographic data between USMARC, UNIMARC and CCF files, and also from non-standard formats to standard ones; and

– evolution of a Centralized Database (CDB) of holdings data of Kolkata libraries, and specialized databases as well.

Apart these, CALIBNET's pioneering study and research led to its publication of the "Guidelines for Implementation of UNIMARC in Indian Libraries". This will be an invaluable aid for the national database development programme under consideration, that favours adoption of UNIMARC format.

With the support of SANJUKTA, the CDB, hosted on CALIBNET server and located at the Network Service Centre, can be accessed and searched online by any one from a remote location, provided one is equipped with a computer, a telephone, a modem and a password from CALIBNET. The efficacy of SANJUKTA has been tested by successful remote logging of the CALIBNET server at Jadavpur, hosting the CDB, from a Workshop venue at Great Eastern Hotel, Kolkata. Online access to the locational information of bibliographic resources via the CDB and sharing of such resources amongst the libraries of this metropolis is now a reality.

The capability of PARAPAR was established through exercises and/or tests on sample records furnished by a major library in New Delhi, and conducted in-house at Kolkata at their instance and eventually demonstrated at a Workshop-cum-Meeting in New Delhi.

Centralized Database

Now that the library network capability has been established, the most crucial and indispensable activity is to develop the basic resource — the Centralized Database (CDB), that constitute the very backbone of the any library network — by inputting the holding data of Kolkata libraries.

The CDB, launched only recently, currently holds around 30,000 records covering:

- conference documents held by Kolkata and contiguous libraries;
- social sciences: management and economics, behavioural sciences, quantitative methods, computer science, etc. including predominantly journals held by management libraries in South Asia, libraries of Indian Statistical Institute, and Indian Institute of Management, Kolkata; and
- index to contents of serials published by Asiatic Society in previous two centuries.

Library Network: A Cooperative Movement

The CDB is the bedrock of CALIBNET, and its development essentially calls for a cooperative movement, whereby each library partakes in the movement by contributing its own holdings data to be incorporated in the CDB and thereby enrich it. The CDB needs to be now augmented by inputting holdings data of as many libraries as possible and getting the data continuously updated. Optimum coverage of libraries, which alone will progressively transform the CDB into a truly resourceful online searchable central pool of Calcutta's bibliographic holding data, is now on with the cooperation of libraries.

Participant Libraries

The responses from institutional libraries are very encouraging. The libraries of following institutions have extended cooperation by way of furnishing their respective machine-readable database and/or current journal subscription lists:

- Calcutta University
- Jadavpur University
- Indian Statistical Institute
- Indian Institute of Management
- Central Research Institute for Jute & Allied Fibres
- Anthropological Survey of India

- Botanical Survey of India
- Geological Survey of India
- Zoological Survey of India
- Bengal Engineering College (a deemed university)
- National Atlas & Thematic Mapping Organization
- Bose Institute, and
- University College of Medicine (Calcutta University)

These are being now inputted into the CDB. By the advent of the new millennium, holding data of many more libraries are expected to go into the CDB. Priority is being accorded to holding data relating to current journals subscribed and new additions from January 1, 1999.

Electronic Access to Global Information

CALIBNET has added to itself, under its 'information centre approach', a new dimension that of a purveyor of global information, a phenomenon that now pervades international information market.

With online access to Internet and in-house CD-ROM resources, CALIBNET can explore a wide spectrum of the knowledge base and corporate and professional enterprises, and meet the information requirements of researchers, academics and other scholars, professionals and any other practitioners engaged in a wide gamut of subject interests.

On-demand Information Services

CALIBNET has several attractive information packages. CALIBNET's *ConFile* service reaches at one's desk contents of any journal of one's choice out of over 20,000 high-impact journals. Libraries can now prune their journal subscription list or even forego subscribing to new ones, when budgetary constraints so demand, and still get exposed to their contents from ConFile. ConFile helps libraries in economizing on journal subscription and reducing the drain on precious foreign exchange resources. On demand, *CalibOrder* offers the requisite back-up service by way of delivery of full-text of any article, and even patents.

CALIBNET services are well defined and could be customized as well. Once can go with CALIBNET just keywords defining his subject interest and get at regular intervals via *ConAlert* service the current and tailored bibliographic information at his desk. *RetroFile* offers least status and trend of research on any specific topic. ConFile, ConAlert and RetroFile, in combination, offer the latest information and advances in the entire spectrum the subject interest.

CalibLink

A special feature of CALIBNET is the CalibLink, an e-mail connectivity (from its ERNET hub) installed and working fine at four institutions.

Institutional Resources Development Services

Some of the key institutional resources development services offered are:

- retrospective conversion of existing card catalogue in libraries into computerized local databases via electronic mode by downloading from international databases;
- consultative services on LIS automation;
- manpower development for operating and manning automated LIS environment through a wide range of graded training programmes, and customized courses for individuals or groups at client's site.

Immediate Focus

Indian Resources Database

Development of Indian Resources Database of historical value covering manuscripts and rare books, and personal collections, has already been initiated with porting on the CDB and index to serials published by Asiatic Society during the last two centuries.

CALIBNET on Internet

The design of CALIBNET Web page is almost complete and will be available on the Net very shortly. The web page will facilitate access to bibliographic information resources available through hosting of CALIBNET's Centralized Databases. Apart this, the CALIBNET web site would provide:

(A) Active links to access

- Indian Library & Network Resources,
- Overseas Library Resources on India, including rare documents — printed and manuscripts,
- Worldwide Library Catalogues,
- National Libraries of the World,
- Newspapers and Journals,
- Electronic Reference Tools,
- Factual Information Sources, and
- Book-Trade Databases.

(B) Varied CALIBNET programs for

- On-demand Information Services,
- Electronic-mail Connections,
- Consultative Services for Library Automation,
- Manpower Development; and
- R&D in IT Applications.

SGML-Mediated Conversion of Free-Text into Standard Structure

This is one of the areas of research which should contribute enormously in developing machine-readable databases speedily and cost-effectively. The experience in bibliographic conversion available in-house will greatly help in using the relative software once those are sourced from Internet and / or commercial agencies.

SANJUKTA

A multi-user storage and retrieval software has been developed in-house to support CALIBNET's Centralized Databases and to provide online access from remote locations. SANJUKTA has been designed and implemented by A. Mukhopadhyay, Technical Consultant, CALIBNET, and his associates, based on MOD+, a software he developed earlier to support management of small/medium-size libraries.

Database Structure : The database, designed after network model, consists of several inter-operative data files, and implemented on FoxBase platform under UNIX environment. The design supports variable-length fields, multi-valued fields, variable record structure, and storage of variant types of bibliographic records concurrently.

Software Feature : The software has been developed, using 4GL code, and designed to provide the user with options and flexibility in generating records, organizing and searching information, viewing the search outputs, and interchanging data files with external databases with least manual interference.

Search Facility : End-users can search databases in two ways. If so desired, one can view a table of search terms, including personal and corporate names, title keywords, subject descriptors, and then select those of interest with the help of highlighted navigation bar. Alternatively, the user can key-in the search terms directly. Along with the search terms, the relevant field-selectors may be assigned to restrict search within the specified fields. The terms can be connected with each other with boolean operators to narrow down the search. It also permits truncation to include all terms with a common stem. The software employs techniques and methods capable of searching databases with precision and speed, and prompting the number of hits on screen instantly.

Display of outputs : The users have option to specify the range of records for display by inputting the starting and ending hit numbers. The next option they have is for viewing the records in a format of their choice. While the default is Labeled Display, as commonly found in OPAC, the alternatives are AACR II, USMARC and UNIMARC formats.

Record Generation : The records can be generated programmatically by converting bibliographic data imported from external databases, or alternatively, by keyboarding manually. The manual procedure is user-friendly and does not require inputting of any data element twice. The Classification Codes and Subject Descriptors can be assigned by switching predetermined values from an updateable thesaurus.

Data Transportation : Since the centralized databases are populated with records originated in the participating libraries, the import of bibliographic files from external sources is the primary means for database building. The imported records are often dissimilar in structure and required to be converted before transferring into the centralized database files. To support such requirements, a series of utility programs have been created and bundled into a separate package PARAPAR.

PARAPAR

A conversion software package, PARAPAR, has been developed in CALIBNET to support interchange of bibliographic data between USMARC, UNIMARC and CCF files, and also from non-standard formats to standard ones.

Objectives : Its primary objective is to convert data files, received from the participating libraries in variant formats, into a ISO-2709 compliant implementation through which the files are merged into the Centralized Database of CALIBNET.

Apart this, PARAPAR provides necessary means for generating machine-readable catalogue by converting records downloaded from USMARC databases available online or in CD. Its capability of cleaning data, by stripping off the special characters and punctuation marks prior to actual conversion, ensures high quality of data that should require no or little editing. This feature helps the libraries in computerizing their catalogues cost-effectively.

The utility also helps those libraries who prefer to develop special databases in CCF by enabling them to convert records from non-CCF files.

Environment : Most of the libraries in India are using CDS/ISIS or some commercial systems for developing their databases. Only a few follow standard specifications. PARAPAR could be much useful in upgrading them to a standard format with a bit of customization. This can be done in two ways. Firstly, when the internal structure is known, as in the case of CDS/ISIS, the conversion can be executed on the internal data. Otherwise, when the internal structure is not known, as in the case of some commercial proprietary DBMS, the conversion can be executed on the data-strings extracted from the output files.

Operations : PARAPAR works at three levels for data extraction, organization and transportation. The middle level file holds processed data elements ready for being transferred to the target file. The user is allowed to browse the processed file for previewing the data representations in their redefined formats for validation, before the transfer finally takes place.

User Interactions : The program assumes that the source file be fully compliant to one of the ISO-2709 implementations, and therefore there should be no need for the end-user to supply processing parameters, like tags, subfield-code, indicators. Users' intervention, though often considered user-friendly, can be idiosyncratic field-designators to creep in. PARAPAR requires its users only to specify the special characters used for the Record Separator, Field Separator, Subfield Delimiter, and to indicate if the Indicators are used in the source file.

The software package is also designed and developed by A. Mukhopadhyay, a Technical Consultant of CALIBNET.

Guidelines for implementation of UNIMARC

It has been brought out by CALIBNET to provide the library professionals in India with a working tool for developing their databases in a mutually exchangeable format. The document has been prepared in 1994, based on UNIMARC Manual (1987), by A. Mukhopadhyay, Technical Consultant, under a project sponsored by the National Information System for Science and Technology (NISSAT), Department of Scientific and Industrial Research, Government of India. The Guidelines has made an attempt to take care of the special requirements of the Indian libraries.

The document consists of five sections. Its introductory section deals with the objectives and scope of the document, the purpose and role of UNIMARC, the physical aspects of UNIMARC, and highlights some significant issues relating to successful implementation of the system. A glossary of related terms has been provided for the benefit of those not familiar with bibliographic database parlance.

The core document enumerates field-by-field specifications of the data elements. Every UNIMARC field has been represented with a definition in terms of the data elements it holds, an indication of its status in terms of occurrence, the proper form of data rendering, and examples of the field -contents filled with actual data. In addition, a number of illustrations of coded records have been given in an appendix for helping the users to understand the specifications and build confidence in working with the standard.

A separate section has been devoted for enumerating various codes to be used in UNIMARC-fields for depicting language, country, currency, role designations, textual formats, GMDs, etc.

The document also offers recommendations, under the section 'Implementation Notes' for synchronizing the physical database structure and application software with the UNIMARC specifications, particularly keeping in view the application of Micro-CDS which is being used commonly in India and neighbouring countries.

Its appendices include citations of the standards and references relevant to the study of UNIMARC, and a supplementary note on the changes taken place in the UNIMARC format incorporated since 1987.

UNIMARC has been developed with the initiative of the International Federation of Libraries and Institutions (IFLA), and maintained by its Universal Bibliographic Control and International MARC Programme (UBCIM). Besides its use as a common exchange format, the UNIMARC has been adopted by countries like France, Portugal, and South Africa, as their national standard. The scheme has been preferred to other implementations of ISO-2709 due to its relatively sound logical base and comprehensiveness of treatment. It is important to note that the UNIMARC has been accepted by the Library of Congress as a standard alternative to USMARC for distribution of LC Records. In India, it is now being adopted as the national standard for bibliographic database.

The Guidelines is expected to serve the Indian libraries in upgrading their databases to the international standard.

Publications

(i) **Union List of Current Serials held in Kolkata Libraries:** A union list of current serials held in Kolkata libraries has been prepared. Search can be made through Title, and by the host library.

(ii) **ASJI Database :** A union list of journals subscribed by Asiatic Society has been prepared. The search can be made by Title, Publication year etc. The database contains indices to the Serialized Publications of the Asiatic Society.

(iii) **Conference Proceedings :** A database of conference proceedings of the seminare/conferences held by the

CALIBNET is prepared. The search can be made through Title, Venue and Year of the conference.

(iv) **Union Catalogue of Social Science Serials :** This contains holdings of select management and development libraries in India, and one each of Bangladesh, Pakistan, Sri Lanka and Bhutan. It is developed in continuation of the database built under AMDISA Project. Search can be made by Title and Host Library Name.

DELNET
(Developing Library Network)

Introduction

The DELNET is established in 1988 by India International Centre with the initial financial support of NISSAT and later official registered as a society in June 1992. Current, it is being promoted by the National Informatics Centre, Department of Information Technology, Ministry of Communications and Information Technology, Government of India and India International Centre, New Delhi. Though DELNET was started to cover the libraries in and around Delhi but latter it changed the motto and now is covering most of the Indian libraries. Todays it is much known as Developing Library Network rather than Delhi Library Network.

DELNET has been actively engaged with the compilation of various Union Catalogues of the resources available in member-libraries. It has already created the Union Catalogue of Books, Union List of Current Periodicals, Union Catalogue of Periodicals, CD-ROM Database, Database of Indian Specialists, Database of Periodical Articles, Union List of Video Recordings, Urdu Manuscripts' Database, Database of Theses and Dissertations, DEVINSA Database, sample databases of language publications using GIST technology and several other databases. The data is being updated in each of these databases and is growing rapidly. All the DELNET databases have been resident on DELSIS, an in-house software developed on BASISPlus, an RDBMS, the product of Information Dimensions Inc. of USA which has been provided to DELNET courtesy National Informatics Centre, New Delhi.

DELNET provides an array of facilities including E-mail to its member-libraries including both institutional and associate institutional members. DELNET'S relentless efforts in resource sharing have proved extremely effective. It has indeed been a big leap towards the modernization of libraries in India.

Objectives

DELNET has been established with the prime objective of promoting resource sharing among the libraries through the development of a network of libraries. It aims to collect, store, and disseminate information besides offering computerized services to users, to coordinate efforts for suitable collection development and also to reduce unnecessary duplication wherever possible. Its main objectives are :

(i) to promote sharing of resources among the libraries by developing a network of libraries, by collecting, storing and disseminating information and by offering computerised services to the users ;

(ii) to offer guidance to the member libraries on cataloguing, database services, circulation, acquisition, serials control, online services, selection of hardware and software, etc.;

(iii) to coordinate efforts for suitable collection development and reduce unnecessary duplication wherever possible;

(iv) to establish a referral centre, to monitor and/or facilitate catalogue search and maintain a central online union catalogue of books, serials, and non-book materials of all the participating libraries;

(v) to facilitate and promote delivery of documents manually and mechanically;

(vi) to develop specialist bibliographic database of books, serials and non-book materials;

(vii) to develop database of projects, specialists and institutions;

(viii) to possess and maintain electronic and mechanical equipment for fast communication of information and delivery of electronic mail;

(ix) to coordinate with other regional, national and international networks for exchange of information and documents; and

(x) to undertake, facilitate and provide for the publication of newsletters and/or journals devoted to networking and sharing of resources.

Services of DELNET

Online Databases

- Union Catalogue of Books in CCF Format
- Union Catalogue of Books in MARC Format
- Union List of Current Periodicals
- Union Catalogue of Periodicals
- Database of Periodical Articles
- Indian Specialists: A Who's Who
- CD-ROM Database
- Union List of Video Recordings
- Union List of Sound Recordings
- Union List of Newspapers
- Union List of Serials : Management Libraries
- Union List of Serials : Petroleum and Natural Gas
- Union Catalogue of Hindi Books
- Multilingual Books : Sample Database
- Urdu Manuscripts Database
- Database of Theses and Dissertations
- DEVINSA Database

Other Services Include

- ILL Online
- Retro-conversion
- Referral services
- Creation and maintenance of bibliographic databases
- Document Delivery Services
- Training programmes
- Lectures and Workshops
- Newsletter

Products

DELSIS (DELNET System for Information Services)

DELSEARCH : An Offline E-mail Based Remote Database Access System.

DEL-DOS

DEL-PLUS

DEL-MARC

INTERNET

Electronic Mail

Full INTERNET (TCP/IP)

Some of the major services are discussed below.

Online Databases

DELNET had created a Web-page on INTERNET HYPERLINK http://www.nic.in/delnet. In addition to the above services, DELNET main objective is to promote sharing to resources among the libraries located in Delhi and outside Delhi. It is the first operational library network in India and has developed databases mentioned below :

(i) Union Catalogue of Books in CCF: DELNET maintains an online union catalogue of books available in its member-libraries. This union catalogue is continuously updated. The information can be retrieved by author, title, subject, conference, series, etc. The request for inter-library loan can also be placed through the online system.

(ii) Union Catalogue of Books in MARC Format : MARC is an internationally used format for machine-readable bibliographic records. DELNET has introduced CCF for the creating of records in MARC format. DELNET has separately created a union catalogue of books for MARC records.

(iii) Union List of Current Periodicals : DELNET has created union list of current periodicals in science and technology, social sciences and humanities. This databases is available online to DELNET users. It is regularly updated and new titles are added annually.

(iv) Union Catalogue of Periodicals : DELNET maintain a union catalogue of periodical which contains full holdings data of the libraries.

(v) Databases of Periodical : The database has details of articles, which can be searched under the title, author.

(vi) CD-ROM Databases : A bibliographic database of CD-ROMs available with the member-libraries has been started recently and is available online.

(vii) Union list of Video Recordings : This is a database of video cassettes available in DELNET member libraries.

(viii) Union List of Sound Recordings : This union list consists of audio-cassette records available in member-libraries.

(ix) Union List of Newspapers : This database lists newspapers being subscribed by Delhi Libraries. It contains information about the newspapers including title, name of the editor, published from e-mail address and also the web address of the INTERNET edition, if available.

(x) Union List of Serials of Management Libraries: DELNET has recently constituted as Sub-Committee for rationalizing the periodicals in the Management Sector Libraries in and around Delhi.

(xi) Union Catalogue of Hindi Books : The database contains records in Hindi and can be retrieved thorough the GIST compatible system.

(xii) Multilingual Books Sample Database : DELNET has also prepared a sample database of language publications of various Indian and some foreign languages using GIST technology. This acts as a guideline for member-libraries wishing to create databases other than in English.

(xiii) Urdu Manuscripts Databases : DELNET has created an Urdu manuscripts database, which is available, online to member-libraries and lists manuscripts. It contains a descriptive bibliography on a variety of subjects such as animal husbandry, astronomy, teaching techniques, ethics, Arabian history, letter writing, literary criticism. Islamic sects, Jehad, theology, sports, etc. The maximum number of entries are on poetry, fiction and Islam.

(xiv) Database of Thesis and Dissertations : DELNET has recently started the database on theses and dissertations available in various member-libraries. This database is steadily growing in size.

(xv) Serial Database of Petroleum and Natural Gas : A serials database on the current periodicals available in Petroleum Natural Gas libraries in India has been started recently and is available online.

Other Services

Its other services include :

ILL online : DELNET members can place their inter-library loan requests through our ILL Online facility, which is available on the union catalogue of books database. The members' requests appear on the main server, which are monitored by DELNET staff at regular intervals and the books are acquired and supplied to the requesting library through the courier. This is charged service. Photocopying charges for journal articles and courier charges for sending books to member-libraries outside Delhi are extra.

Retro-Conversion : DELNET offers retro conversion facilities to the libraries for the creation of MARC records.

Referral Services : DELNET maintains a referral centre that provides reference facilities to participating libraries. The referral centre also looks after the access to the central databases and monitors access to international databases.

Creation and Maintenance of Bibliographic Databases: DELNET helps the participating libraries in the creation of bibliographic databases. It is considered that for effective networking, standard bibliographic data should be available in machine readable form to the libraries. Periodic meetings of the member-librarians are organised to discuss their problems.

Document Delivery Services : DELNET provides the Document Delivery Services to its users and it is a very popular.

Training Programmes : DELNET has been organizing in collaboration with NIC Monthly Training Programmes since September 2001 on the topics covering MARC-21, Web Page Designing & Hosting, Internet Searching Strategies, Library Resources on the Internet and CDROM Networking. A large number of library and information science professionals from different parts of India had attended these programmes.

DELNET also conducts training programmes in the use of DELNET services, software, E-mail, AACR-2 and LC Subject Headings, Internet, etc. from time to time. Information about future training programmes is available on request.

Lectures and Workshops : DELNET organizes lectures by networking specialists working in different parts of the world. The lectures are open to members, specialists and users in general. It also organizes national workshops, seminars and meets on library networking periodically.

Newsletter : DELNET publishes a Newsletter in order to spread the message and increase the awareness about library networking in India. Through this Newsletter, DELNET communicates to its members the progress it is making in various fields. The Newsletter is also a forum for communication on the advances, achievements and needs of the libraries and their services.

INTERNET : Internet can also be surfed at DELNET by the members.

Electronic Mail : DELNET provides RENNIC e-mail facility to its member-libraries which is introduced by National Informatics Centre. This gives them access to both national and international e-mail users and also to INTERNET users. E-mail service is very efficient, fast and effective.

INTERNET (TCP/IP) Connectivity : DELNET is provides INTERNET TCP/IP Connectivity which is given to member-libraries in Delhi through NIC at Rs. 5,600 per year for 500 hours of connect time. These rates are subject to change by NIC.

Products

Its various products are discussed below :

DELSIS

A major breakthrough has been achieved by DELNET with the launch of DELSIS, a powerful library networking software. DELSIS (DELNET system for Information Services) is an integrated modular system which supports DELNET online databases.

DELSIS has been developed by DELNET on a Relational Database Management System called BASISplus provided by NIC. DELSIS handles not only the Online Public Access Catalogue but also has the administrative tools for building up the union catalogues on BASISplus. It provides powerful and extensive facilities for online enquiries for books, serials, biographical details about the specialists and supports the cataloguing of books in Indian languages.

DELSIS has following features :

- It is a user-friendly, menu-driven package.
- Its versatile options allow the users to retrieve the information quickly.
- It contains the modules for Online Public Access Catalogue as well as the modules for the creation of databases, e.g. addition, deletion, importing of records, etc.
- The Online Public Access Catalogue (OPAC) components of DELSIS can meet the needs of the users, irrespective of whether the user has negligible computer experience or is familiar with using computers to perform various library tasks.

DEL-DOS

DEL-DOS based on DOS platform is used for creating MARC records of books published in English as well as for creating records in Indian languages using GIST card technology. Some of its salient features are :

- The software is very simple and easy to use.
- The records can be stored in MARC format.
- Deletion and printing of selective and range of records is possible.
- Global values can be defined during the worksheet entry.
- The search results can be displayed in the Tag Format. AACR-II or the brief summary can also be displayed and stored or printed out.
- The name authority database is maintained.
- Import/Export into and from ISO 2709 is possible.

DEL-PLUS

DELNET has also released of DEL-PLUS Version 1.0.0 after the successful creation and implementation of DELSIS Unix version. It is an efficient tool for creating and retrieving bibliographic databases and catalogues. DEL-PLUS can convert the simple PC into a powerful management information system. Some of its salient features are:

- It is simple and easy to use. Library professionals and end users can interact with the software without any prior training.
- It is user-friendly with adequate window-menus for data inputting and search capabilities.
- It provides the option for creating the bibliographic records either using Common Communication Format (CCF) or the MARC Format.

DEL-PLUS provides the following operational modules:

(a) Database Creation and Maintenance : This is used to create and store the bibliographic records in a machine readable format using CCF or MARC format so as to facilitate the easier exchange of information. Salient features of its operational *modules are* :

1. The desirable formats worksheet, i.e. CCF or MARC worksheets can be chosen for data storage purpose.
2. The MARC worksheet consists of two levels, viz. fixed field entry and variable field entry. To save the user's time and also the system space, the required field tags along with the indicators can be chosen.
3. The online assistance is available for data inputting through the help menus.
4. Data validation check is possible in order to avoid the data errors.
5. Provision for duplicate checking is available while inputting or importing a record into a database.
6. The authority database is maintained.
7. Data Import/Export into and from MARC as well as CCF is made possible.
8. The option for printing the desired records is also available.

(b) Online Public Access Catalogue (OPAC) : This module helps the librarians as well as the end users to retrieve the information available in the database in a very user-friendly manner. The salient features of Del plus OPAC are :

1. Browsing facility is available for beginners. They can search a book by title, author, subject, etc.
2. Word or phrase searching is available.
3. Full text searching is available.
4. Search Term is not case sensitive.
5. Brief as well as detailed bibliographical information can be retrieved.
6. Displays records in AACR II format is available.
7. Print search results in standard AACR II format or other formats as desired.

Hardware Requirements for DEL-PLUS : The following hardware configuration under Windows 95/Windows NT is required to run DEL-PLUS.

Hardware Platform: PCAT 486, Pentium or above

Main Memory: Minimum 16 MB RAM

Disk Space: 20 MB

Microprocessor speed: 66 MHz or above

DEL-MARC & DEL-MARC VER 1.0.0

This is basically for the bigger libraries which are complex entities with a large collection and serving a huge clientele. To carry out various operations in a library effectively, there is a need for automation. This software has been designed after a comprehensive study of different library- related functions performed in different kinds of libraries. This software is quite easy to work with.

Hardware and Software Requirements : Minimum requirements are as under :

Server

Pentium @233 MHz with 64 MB RAM

4.1 GB HDD

40X CD ROM Drive

1.44" Floppy Drive

Colour Monitor (SVGA)

WINDOWS-NT Operating system

MS-SQL Server 7.0

Client

Pentium @ 233 MHz with 32 MB RAM

1.2 GB HDD with 15 MB free space

1.44" Floppy Drive

Colour Monitor (SVGA)

Windows-95 Operating system

Benefits of Using DEL-MARC 1.0.0

Various benefits of using this software may be observed as under :

1. It is available at a greatly reduced cost.
2. Software designed and developed exclusively to work under all kinds of libraries such as public, academic and special libraries.
3. Multi user facility of this software will allow different branch libraries/sections/nodes to function together.
4. Free updation/modification is given.
5. Free technical assistance is available.
6. It follows internationally recommended standards and formats such as :

US-MARC, UNI-MARC, UK-MARC, MARC-2, CCF, AACR- II

Modules: The software comprises of the following modules:

- Acquisition
- Cataloguing
- Circulation
- OPAC
- Administration
- Export/Import
- Authority Control
- Article Indexing
- Reports

Acquisition : The acquisition module enables library staff to handle the following major functions related to acquisition of library material:

Suggestions management

Approval

Ordering, cancellation and reminders

Receiving

Accessioning

Management of vendors, publishers and currency tables.

Cataloguing : The cataloguing module enables you to catalogue any type of material in any of the MARC formats.

Circulation : This module will take care of all possible functions like issue, return, reissue, reservation, etc. Member enquiry, maintenance of status of material can be handled. Complex functions like fare management for each category of user and material can also be effectively carried out.

OPAC: It facilitates three types of functions :

Individual search (Search by Author, Title, ISBN, Accession Numbers, Subject, Class Numbers etc).

Boolean search (Search by Author, Title, ISBN, Accession number, Subject, Class No. etc in combination).

Special search for cataloguing purposes.

Results can be seen in AACR-II format or any MARC format described above.

Administration : Here you can define the categories, group, and their exchange, sales, acquisition modes, MARC tags, holidays, user passwords etc. that will be used throughout the functioning of the software.

Export/Import : Here you can export/import your data into/from any standard MARC format described above.

Authority Control : This module enables you to maintain author, title, series and subject authorities.

Article Indexing : This module is developed to maintain various articles in the library or out of the library.

Reports : Here you will get each and every type of report such as vendors' list, material ordered, material received, order due, overdue charges, stock verification, etc. Reports can also be generated datewise.

Environmental Information System (ENVIS)

Introduction

India, a large and old civilization, has inherited a vast area with a variety of flora and fauna. It is one of the largest reservoirs of bio-diversity, along with other natural resources. To preserve and sustain such precious resources, scholars and missionaries are trying to understand the environment and its related issues. The information generated all over the world is very important for these scholars. There was a need to develop a network using the latest technologies and share the wealth of information. Various steps have been taken in this direction by the Government of India and by other institutions with the help of World Bank under its Environmental Management and Capacity Building Programme. At the Government level, the Ministry of

Environment and Forests of Government of India established Environmental Information Systems (ENVIS) centres across the subcontinent act as communication bridges to reach out to the masses. The basic premise was to empower people through the powerful tool of information by evolving decentralized information paradigms and make them sensitive towards environment.

ENVIS is a decentralised network consisting of a focal point in the Ministry coordinating the activities of a chain of 25 subject-specific nodes located in various Prestigious Institutions/ Organisations all over the country. The Focal Point of ENVIS and its network partners laid emphasis on the development of its information-base by creating comprehensive databases and strengthening information resource repository in the concerned subject area. Major activities of the ENVIS Focal Point and its various centre are as follows:

Objectives

The objectives of ENVIS are classified into two broad categories- long-term and short-term objectives. The long-term objectives of ENVIS are as follows:

(i) To build up a repository and dissemination centre in Environmental Science and Engineering;

(ii) To gear up the modern technologies of acquisition, processing, storage, retrieval and dissemination of environmental information;

(iii) To support and promote research, development and innovation in environment information technology.

The short-term objectives are as follows:

(i) To provide national environmental information service relevant to present needs and capable of development to meet the future needs of the users, originators, processors and disseminators of information;

(ii) To build up storage, retrieval and dissemination capabilities with the ultimate objectives of disseminating information speedily to the users;

(iii) To promote national and international co-operation and liaison for exchange of environment related information;

(iv) To promote exchange of information amongst the developing countries.

Responsibilities

The responsibilities of the ENVIS Centres are as follows:

(i) Building up a good collection of books, reports and journals in the particular subject area of environment.

(ii) Establishment of linkages with all information sources in the field of environment.

(iii) Responding to users' queries.

(iv) Establishment of a data bank on some selected parameters relating to the subject area.

(v) Co-ordination with the focal point for supplying relevant, adequate and timely information to the users.

(vi) Helping the focal point in gradually building up an inventory of information material available at the Centres.

(vii) Identification and filling up of the gaps in the specified subject area.

(viii) Bringing out newsletter/publications in their subject area for wide dissemination.

Based on the functions of the ENVIS, it has been designated as a National Focal Point (NFP) and a Regional Service Centre (RSC) of INFOTERRA of UNEP for the South Asia sub-region, a global environmental information network which stimulate and support exchange of information within and between the nations. Almost all member countries of United Nations are partners of this network.

ENVIS maintains a close liaison with various national information systems like National information System of Science and Technology (NISSAT), Biotechnology Information System (RTIS) and several other similar networks for exchange of environmental information as well as to avoid duplication of efforts in the concerned fields. ENVIS also makes use of a large number of computerized databases developed by scientific institutions all over the country. In order to search the various databases both nationally and internationally, ENVIS has created a Web site, which could be browsed at *http://www.nic.in/ envfor/ envis*.

ENVIS Focal Point in the Ministry has been identified as an implementing agency for UNDP's Sustainable Development Networking Programme (SDNP). The SDNP has been initiated with financial support from United Nations Development Programme (UNDP) and International Development Research Centre (IDRC), Canada for a period of three years (1998-2001). The goal of the programme is to promote the process of sustainable development through organised accessibility to and exchange of information among all concerned parties, viz. academic and research institutions, NGOs, government bodies and business establishments. The ENVIS Focal Point in the Ministry networks with twenty-five ENVIS Centres located in various parts of the- country. These Centres have been collecting, analyzing and disseminating information on their specialized subject areas related to environment.

It is important to note that both ENVIS and SDNP have to work together to avoid any duplication of efforts and set up a common goal which can be met by joint efforts of the ENVIS Point in the Ministry and the SDNP Secretariat.

Activities of ENVIS Centres

All the ENVIS centres continued their activities related to collection, storage, retrieval and dissemination of information on the subject areas allotted to them. Besides strengthening the data bases and responding to various national and international queries, all the ENVIS centres carried out a variety of activities aimed at disseminating information to wide range of users. Highlights of some of the activities of the ENVIS centres are given below:

(i) The ENVIS Centre on Control of Pollution at the Central Pollution Control Board (CPCB) continued to publish thematic issues of the Newsletter 'Parivesh' on themes such as air pollution and its control, ground water quality, coastal pollution, bio-monitoring, etc. CPCB brought out nearly 20 publications/booklets/reprints under various series and two new series on "Groundwater Quality" and "Information Manual on Pollution Abatement and Cleaner Technology" were added during the years.

(ii) Apart from continuing its regular activities, the ENVIS Centre on Toxic Chemicals functioning at ITRC, Lucknow has developed a computerized data base on toxic chemicals including information on some chemicals. On the basis of information and literature provided by the ENVIS Centre, the U.P. Department of Environment has developed guidelines for assessment and identification of waste disposal sites in Lucknow district. The Centre also helped the U.P. SPCB to identify various categories of hazardous wastes. Publication of ENVIS Newsletters and Abstracts of Current Literature in Toxicology was continued.

(iii) DAINET, the Development Alternatives Information Network operated by the ENVIS Centre at the Society for Development Alternatives (SDA), New Delhi continued to collect, store and disseminate information related to environmentally sound appropriate technology and environmental management. During the years existing database of the ENVIS Centre were parted on the RDBMS platform. A NGO directory is also being designed and developed on the RDBMS platform. A web page of the SDA has been set up on the Internet.

(iv) Computerization of the data base is being continued at the ENVIS Centre on Biodegradation of wastes and

Environmental Impact Assessment functioning at the Centre for Environment Studies, Anna University, Chennai. The database includes a listing of over 5000 papers on the two subjects allocated to the Centre. The ENVIS Library has over 800 books/reports on the subjects. E-mail facility is operational.

(v) A new journal "TERI Information Monitor on Environmental Sciences" has been launched by the ENVIS Centre on "Energy and Environment" functioning at the Tata Energy Research Institute (TERI), New Delhi as the ENVIS Newsletter. The journal contains review articles, bibliographies, abstracts of recent literature, book reviews, etc. relating to the subject area allotted to the centre. The ENVIS centre at TERI also contributed to the preparation of the project proposal on "Environmental Management Capacity Building" assigned to TERI by Ministry.

(vi) The "Third Environmental Status Reports of Madhya Pradesh" was brought out by the ENVIS Centre at EPCO, Bhopal during the year. It also published three issues each of "Madhya Pradesh Paryavaran" and ENLAW and circulated them among NGOs, government departments, educational institutions, etc. Information about NGOs functioning in the state of Madhya Pradesh, has been stored in the computer and is made available to users on request. Several camps and workshops were also organized jointly with EPCO for different target groups.

(vii) The ENVIS Centre on 'Desertification' functioning at the Central Arid Zone Research Institute (CAZRI), Jodhpur has created a database on "Desertification and Soil Science" using CDS/ISIS software package, which is being updated regularly. Searches on the database can be made through author(s), title, subject, keywords and serial numbers. A fortnightly 'Current Awareness Bulletin' relating to soil conservation and desertification and newspaper clipping service are being provided. A

Bibliography on Desertification, Soil Conservation and Environment (upto 1995) has been compiled. The centre also provides material for inclusion in the "Paryavaran Abstracts" being brought out by the Focal Point at the Ministry.

(viii) Information are to be added to the EE bank being maintained by the ENVIS Centre on Environment Education functioning at the Centre for Environment Education, Ahmedabad. Workshops were held at Ahmedabad, Bangalore, Guwahati and Pune to help educators access the information, adapt it for their use and develop locale-specific EE material. Six issues of the networking newsletter "News EE", and a bibliography of "Readings on the North East" have been brought out by now. Work on updating the Directory of NGOs in EE in the North East has also been completed.

(ix) The subject alloted to the ENVIS Centre at the Zoological Survey of India, has been changed to 'Faunal Bio-diversity" from Animal Ecology to reflect the scope of its subject coverage. Application software for storage, retrieval and dissemination of data has been developed by the staff of the ENVIS Centre. Data of 12 species of vertebrates listed in Schedule I of the Wildlife (Protection) Act 1972 and all the genera of butterflies belonging to the family Lycaenidae occurring in India, Pakistan, Sri Lanka, Nepal, Bhutan, Bangladesh and Myanmar have been entered into the computer. Over 4000 bibliographic references on bio-diversity and ecology of Indian animals have also been stored electronically.

(x) The ENVIS Centre on Solid Waste including hazardous waste at NEERI, Nagpur actively disseminates information on the subject by regularly publishing the highlights of the R&D work carried out at NEERI on Solid and Hazardous Waste Management. The Centre has also acquired several national and international databases on the subject which are searched regularly to provide service to the users.

(xi) The bibliographic database developed by the ENVIS Center on Himalayan Ecology at the G.B. Pant Institute of Himalayan Environment and Development has more than 500 abstracts, research papers & technical reports on the subject, collected from the universities/institutions/ research stations located in the 12 Himalayan States of the Country. Records of more than 200 scientific and technological personnel working on various aspects of Himalaya have also been collected. Socioeconomic data of the region is being collected from the Information Centres of the District Statistical offices of 72 districts spread over 12 states. It also publish ENVIS Bulletin.

(xii) The ENVIS Centre on Human Settlements functioning at the Centre for Environmental Studies, School of Planning and Architecture has collected data spanning four decades pertaining to six mega cities of the country with a view to studying the trends of development in these cities. City profiles and trends of demographic growth of cities/urban areas of the country in the more than one million population are also being studied. Data has been collected on various parameters to determine the human environment and quality of life in the four metropolitan cities. A seminar on "Environmental Quality of Human Settlements" was organized by this centre and an report of the presentations has been published.

(xiii) The ENVIS Centre on Biogeochemistry and Environmental Law located in the School of Environmental Sciences, JNU has so far loaded 7942 references on Biochemistry and Environmental Law, in the computer. An "International Workshop on Environmental Legislation and Management for SAARC Countries" sponsored by the Ministry of External Affairs was organised by the Centre during 23-25 October, 1996. CD-ROM's related to Biogeochemistry and Environmental Law are proposed to be acquired to under the scope of its databases.

(xiv) The ENVIS Centre on Floral bio-diversity, previously known as plant ecology; located at the Botanical Survey of India (BSI), Kolkata is engaged in collecting data on plant diversity, plant econology and on plants of coastal and marine ecosystems. An applications software has been developed for the database on rare and endangered plants. E-mail connection has been set up and publication of the ENVIS Newsletter was continued.

(xv) The database on Eastern Ghats, being developed by the ENVIS Centre at the EPTRI, Hyderabad consists of non-bibliographic and bibliographic components. The non-bibliographic database is being developed using remote sensing data and GIS and mapping of the entire Eastern Ghats of Andhra Pradesh in 1:1 million scale has been completed. During the past years mapping of a few selected areas in 1:50,000 scale has been undertaken, based on which a model decision support information system will be developed. The bibliographic database has been developed using CDS/ISIS, which consists of records and references of all literature on Eastern Ghats available at EPTRI.

(xvi) The ENVIS Centre on Avian Ecology and Inland Wetlands at BNHS, formally inaugurated by former Secretary (E&F) in June, 1996 has initiated the creation of a database on the subjects allotted to it. Bibliographic data are being entered into the computer using both d-base and access software. The first issue of the ENVIS Newsletter was published in September 1996.

(xvii) The ENVIS Centre at Annamalai University in the subject area of mangrove, coral reefs, estuaries and lagoons continued to publish the ENVIS Newsletter in the subject area disseminating information to all concerned. The draft state-of-the-art report on estuaries, mangroves, coral reefs and lagoons have been prepared by the centre during the past years which will be published shortly. Besides the centre continued to strengthen its data-base in these subject areas by procuring the latest ASFA (Aquatic Sciences and Fisheries Abstracts) diskettes and other abstracts of literature in the specified subject areas.

(xviii)The ENVIS Centre at the National Institute of Occupational Health, Ahmedabad continued to publish its quarterly publication namely, "Environmental Information" to disseminate the latest information on various aspects of occupational health. Monographs on different compounds having health hazardous index were also published by the centre in the past years.

(xix) The ENVIS Centre at WWF-India, New Delhi has established an Internet Website for WWF-India on an experimental basis. Data relating to the questions and answers on environmental handled in both the houses of Parliament from 1994 is being entered with a view to publishing the same.

Publications

ENVIS publishes the quarterly journal namely 'Paryavaran Abstracts' reporting information on environmental research in Indian context. More than 600 national and international environmental related journals are referred to for compilation of relevant abstracts for inclusion in this publication. The abstracts are arranged under major categories like air pollution, water pollution, noise pollution, environmental management, ecology, health and toxicology, environmental legislation, forestry, wildlife, etc.

ERNET
(Education & Research Network)

Introduction

ERNET (Education and Research Network) has made a significant contribution to the emergence of networking in the country. It practically brought the Internet to India and has built up national capabilities in the area of networking, especially in protocol software engineering. It has not only succeeded in building a large network that provides various facilities to the intellectual segment of Indian society—the research and education community, but it has over the years become a trendsetter in the field of networking. UNDP has lauded ERNET as one of the most successful programmes it has funded. The Govt. of India has committed itself to further strengthen the project by including it in the 9th Plan with the allocation of funds and by creation of a new organisational set-up in the form of a Society. Science community of the country has also recognised ERNET's contribution—both for infrastructure services as well as for R&D. Scientific Advisory Committee to the Cabinet has adopted ERNET as the platform for launching an S&T network in the country.

ERNET was initiated in 1986 by the Department of Electronics (DoE), with funding support from the Government of India and United Nations Development Program (UNDP), involving eight premier institutions as participating agencies—NCST (National Centre for Software Technology) Mumbai, IISc (Indian Institute of Science) Bangalore, five IITs (Indian Institutes of Technology) at Delhi, Mumbai, Kanpur, Kharagpur and Chennai, and the DoE, New Delhi. ERNET began as a multiprotocol network with both the TCP/IP and the OSI-IP protocol stacks running over the leased-line portion of the backbone. Since 1995, however, almost all traffic is carried over TCP/IP.

Objectives of ERNET India

Its main objectives are :

(i) ERNET operations, i.e. providing state-of-the-art communication infrastructure and services to Academic and Research institutions, Govt. organisations, NGOs, private sector, R&D organizations, and various other non-commercial organizations;

(ii) Research and development;

(iii) Training and Consultancy;

(iv) Content development.

Achievements

The foundation of national capability building in the area of computer networking laid through :

(i) Setting up of a chain of core groups at the participating agencies with a minimal set of lab facilities and creation of skilled manpower to carry out R&D.

(ii) Generating man power at different levels

(iii) Making the world of standards (TCP/IP, OSI etc.) well understood.

(iv) Providing an insight into emerging issues such as ATM networks, networked multimedia, and information infrastructure.

Its Network infrastructure and services set up, include :

(i) Installation, maintenance and operation of large Campus LANs;

(ii) Design, commissioning and testing of SATWAN hub and the installation of VSATs;

(iii) Seamless interconnection of LAN-WAN segments, and multi-protocol capability provided;

(iv) Provision of the whole range of Internet services; and

(v) Deployment of TDM/TDMA based VSAT network for Internet access.

Research & Development

Research and Development in the area of computer networking has been the forte of ERNET. The ERNET backbone is a judicious mix of terrestrial and satellite-based wide area networks.

The satellite WAN, using VSAT technology, has facilitated reliable and quick access from remote areas. Its VSAT network acts as an overlay for the terrestrial WAN by providing backup links between the backbone sites. International connectivity is achieved through gateways at New Delhi, Mumbai, Bangalore and Kolkata. ERNET architecture is based on industry standard TCP/IP protocol, ensuring connectivity from heterogeneous computer systems and local area networks (LANs) at user sites.

ERNET International Gateway : ERNET Head Quarter , New Delhi ERNET HUB, Bangalore NCST JUHU, Mumbai Inter University Centre for Astronomy and Astrophysics (IUCAA), Pune, IIT Chennai, University of Hyderabad, IISc Bangalore, NCST Mumbai, Variable Energy Cyclotron Centre (VECC), Kolkata.

ERNET Backbone (Including PoPs) Sites

ERNET is supported by the following backbone sites which enable organisations located at different geographical locations to access various services:

ERNET Head Quarter , New Delhi

National Centre for Software Technology, Mumbai

Indian Institute of Science, Bangalore

Indian Institute of Technology, Chennai

Inter University Centre for Astronomy and Astrophysics, Pune

Variable Energy Cyclotron Centre, Kolkata

Indian Institute of Technology, Kanpur

University of Hyderabad

Centre for Advance Technology, Indore and

Orissa Computer Application Centre, Bhubneshwar.

Communication is the key—in more ways than one. And a prerequisite for communicating is a connection. ERNET India supports different connectivity options to connect wider user bases located even in remote areas. The various connectivity options available to ERNET users are :

- Dial up UUCP
- Dial up IP
- Leased lines (analog or digital)
- VSAT and
- Radio link.

Dial-up UUCP **:** Services accessible are e-mail, news group services. It requires telephone connection, high speed modem, a PC 386/486 machine running Windows/UNIX, or a LAN. It is ideal as a starting point, especially for small user sites, at a close distance from the ERNET backbone. It provides a store-and-forward system, and can be programmed for dialing at night, to minimize STD cost.

Dial-up IP **:** Services accessible are full range of IP services. It requires telephone connection, high speed modem, a PC 386/486 machine running Windows/UNIX, or a LAN. This is more of a stop gap before a leased line/VSAT/radio link becomes operational.

Leased line (analog or digital) **:** The services accessible are full range of IP services. It requires leased line between the site and the nearest ERNET backbone, a pair of high performance modems for analog lines, or a CSU/DSU pair for digital lines, PC 386/486 system running Windows or UNIX, and TCP/IP protocols, a router to provide access to LANs interconnected at user site. It provides a cost-effective link and economy of on-line access to network resources.

VSAT **:** It is of following types :

(a) TDM/TDMA : The services accessible are all IP services. It requires VSAT terminal installation, router, high performance modem V.32 bits, system running UNIX or Windows NT with TCP/IP, or a cluster of such systems. It is recommended for large organizations or sites requiring high level of reliability especially when distance to ERNET backbone is large. Also the only feasible option for remote areas where leased lines are not practical.

(b) SCPC (Single Channel Per Carrier) : Its advantages are High Speed of 64Kbps to 2 Mbps.

(c) Radio link : Its services accessible are all IP services. It requires radio modems, router, system running UNIX or Win/NT with TCP/IP, or a cluster of such systems.

It is recommended for large organizations or sites requiring high level of reliability especially when distance to ERNET backbone is well within the line-of-site.

ERNET broadband TDM/FTDMA (Time Division Multiplexing/Frequency and Time Division Multiple Access) VSAT network is based on the most recent, advanced and the industry-leading product, the SkyBlaster 360E - from Gilat Satellite Networks.

The SkyBlaster 360 E, The Broadband VSAT network is with high speed, quality and reliability, which leads to increased operational efficiency and provides a competitive advantage. The architecture of the network is a two- way, star topology using C-Band transponder on INSAT-3C. Its two-way functionality allows for high levels of interaction, feedback and access to resources. ERNET SATWAN Hub, located at Bangalore, is DVB compliant and enables outroute bandwidth, which is capable of reaching up to 52.5 Mbps. The salient features of TDM/FTDMA Broadband VSAT network are as follows:

(i) The network facilitates high speed Internet access. It is based on industry standard TCP/IP protocol and operates in two-way star architecture using C-Band transponder on INSAT-3C satellite.

(ii) ERNET SATWAN hub is located at Bangalore and consists of 9.2 m antenna, 700W HPA (High Power Amplifier) & SkyBlaster 360 E TDM/FTDMA base band equipment of Gilat.

(iii) Broadband TDM/FTDMA consists of one Out-route and many In-routes.

(iv) Out-route is DVB equivalent and data rate of Out-route is capable of reaching 52.5 Mbps. One 2 Mbps video channel stream is also available in the same outbound. With DVB capabilities, the network supports virtually any data and IP multicast applications (multimedia, video and audio).

(v) Incoming streams are with FTDMA access mechanism & QPSK modulation and one incoming stream is of 307.2 Kbps.

(vi) Network management is carried out from the hub. Remote terminals are monitored from the ERNET central hub located at Bangalore.

(vii) Remote VSATs consist of a 1.8 m antenna with linear feed. The supported features of VSAT IDU (Indoor Unit) are:

- Plug n Play simple, compact, robust & proven standalone box with embedded OS;
- In-built transparent routing capabilities;
- 10BaseT Ethernet LAN Data Interface;
- In-built TCP spoofing with TCP header compression;
- IP prioritization, UDP broadcast, IP multicast (IGMP);
- Fast Processor with 16 MB RAM;
- Flash PROM;
- Classless addressing;
- Port Filtering;

- Low Power consumption < 35 W; and
- Enhanced Environmental parameters etc.

(viii) Complete network is designed with built in redundancies in (1+1) configuration maintaining the network availability of 99% at remote sites & 99.9% at hub.

(ix) Main applications supported on the Network are:

- Voice Over IP
- Two way interactive IP communications
- IP multicast
- Reliable software distribution
- Internet/Intranet access
- FTP
- E-mail.

Information and Library Network (INFLIBNET)

University Grants Commission (UGC) in its attempt to establish networking has taken the initiative and decided to develop a network of academic libraries to manage effectively and administer the resources of these libraries and to provide efficient library services to a large number of users, using modern computer and communications technologies. As a consequence of UGC's efforts, INFLIBNET, a network of university and college libraries in India was established in 1988, which became functional in 1991.

Information and Library Network (INFLIBNET) is an autonomous inter-university centre of the University Grants Commission (UGC) located at Gujarat University Campus, Ahmedabad. It is directed towards modernization of libraries and information centers for information transfer and access, to support scholarship, learning and academic pursuits by establishing a national network of libraries and information centres in universities, institutions of higher learning and R & D institutions in India. It is basically a co-operative endeavour in resource development, sharing and its utilization at national level. Since May 1996 it is an independent autonomous Inter-University Centre under UGC, and it is set out to be a major player in promoting scholarly communication among academicians and researchers in India.

Major Objectives

Its major objectives are :

- To promote and establish communication facilitates to improve capability in information transfer and access, that provide support to scholarship, learning, research and academic pursuits through cooperation and involvement of agencies concerned.
- To establish information and library network - a computer communication network for linking libraries and information centres in universities, deemed to be universities, colleges, UGC information centres, institutions of national importance and R&D institutions, etc. avoiding duplication of efforts in acquiring resources.

Major Activities

Its major activities are :

(i) Automation of University Libraries : Realizing the importance of automation as basic necessity, INFLIBNET Centre, through University Grants Commission, has provided grants (initial and recurring) to the universities identified under the programme. About 142 universities were provided with this grant. Non-recurring grant enabled the university libraries to purchase computers, modem, telephone, printer, air-conditioner, softwares (OS) etc. They were also provided with recurring grant for the first five years after the installation of systems to help them maintain the same and convert the collection into machine readable form. With this INFLIBNET has been able to create an IT conscious environment in the university libraries.

(ii) SOUL Software : To facilitate automation functions of the participating libraries, SOUL Software has been developed. This software Works in Client/ Server mode in Windows environment using MS-SQL server as back end tool. It also provides web access. SOUL software supports barcode technology to generate labels. It supports international standards such as MARC 21, CCF, AACR 2, ISO 2709 etc. This software is attracting many libraries and has more than 540 installations so far, and many installations are in pipeline. The software is very economical as it is developed and distributed by non-profit organization INFLIBNET, and the features of the software suit any type of library. INFLIBNET has also established SOUL service centres at four different places viz. Mumbai, Ahmedabad, Delhi and Kerala to serve the respective and neighbouring states. Many more such service centres are likely to be established to support and promote SOUL activities.

(iii) Human Resource Development and Consultancy : Training of manpower working in the universities and colleges in the use of Information Technology (IT) is an important objective of INFLIBNET and as such it has been given due priority. Twenty training courses of four-week duration for operational staff working in the university libraries and seven workshops of one-week duration for senior library staff, focusing on the managing automation and networking have been conducted. INFLIBNET Regional Training Program on Library Automation (IRTPLA), a new series of training programs are conducted at different locations in collaboration with universities across the country to train library professionals from college and university libraries at regional level with emphasis on regional languages. More than 44 IRTPLA training programs have been conducted by now. More than 1100 College library professionals have also been trained under these training programs.

With technological advancement, the Centre has conducted

specialized workshops on Network Management for Libraries, Website Designing and Hosting, Network Configuration and Management, E-Resource Management in using UGC-infonet, Orientation programme on awareness of access to e-resources. All programmes have received good response from professionals and there was heavy demand for conducting such special kind of training programmes/workshops on regular basis. Similarly various types of training courses are conducted from time to time to suit the requirements of the professionals. Centre has conducted workshops on Library Automation in Hindi for the benefit of Hindi speaking states in the country.

Apart from these courses, several other collaborative training programmes were conducted for All India Radio Libraries, ICSSR/ NASSDOC, ICAR-NATP and Kendriya Vidyalayas Sanghatan. Centre has also conducted collaborative training/workshop on Digital Library using D-space at Osamania University, Hyderabad, Birla Institute of Technology, Pilani and Aligarh Muslim University, Aligarh. Centre has conducted two days duration of five National Seminars on UGC-Infonet and E-Resource in collaboration with universities for benefit of faculties, Research Scholars and Students. More than 1000 participants were benefited from these seminars.

Centre also conducts every year the national convention viz., CALIBER (Convention on Automation of Libraries in Education and Research Institutions) which helps the library professionals, as well as IT professionals to interact with each other and discuss the burning issues for mutual benefit. Twelve such conventions have been held on various topics of interest to profession.

Though all the libraries in north eastern states have been covered under INFLIBNET program, in order to provide special attention to the problems and issues of these states, the centre is conducting two days annual program called PLANNER (Promotion of Library Automation and Networking in North Eastern Region) for the benefit of north eastern region libraries.

The first PLANNER-2003 was successfully conducted at North Eastern Hill University Shillong in November 2003; the second PLANNER-2004 was held at Manipur University, Imphal in November 2004 and third PLANNER-2005 at Assam University, Silchar in November 2005.

(iv) E- Journal Gateway and Archival Library : The INFLIBNET Library is also maintaining a National Archive for the print version of e-journals subscribed under UGC-Infonet E-Journals Consortium in its 'E-Journal Gateway and Archival Library". This collection is computerized using SOUL software and can be accessed on OPAC. Academicians can make use of this facility.

(v) Development of Union Databases : The development of union databases is one of the major activities of the centre. Following are the databases developed, which are updated on regular basis.

- **Books Database:** Received around 80 Lakh records from more than 100 universities and has around 20 lakh unique records processed from 70 universities and remaining are under process. These records representing holdings of participant libraries under the programme covering both old as well as current books.
- **Theses Database:** It has more than 1.5 lakh records of doctoral theses submitted to various Indian universities till date. Efforts are in progress to include abstracts in this database also.
- **Serials Holdings Database :** It has more than 14,250 unique serial titles having over 54.000 holdings of various universities in the country.
- **Current Serials Database :** Current serials database is created to provide access to journals currently subscribed by the university libraries. Efforts are in progress to link this database with e-Journals consortium.
- **Experts Database :** It provides useful data relating to the

name (s) of the experts in different disciplines. This database has more than 15,000 records, and is growing steadily.

- **Research Projects :** It gives information about ongoing and completed projects funded by government agencies. It has over 10,000 records.
- **Experts Database (Science & Technology) :** It has more than 20,000 experts profiles in the area of Science and Technology. It is funded project of NISSAT and this database can be accessed from the URL http://nissat.inflibnet.ac.in.

All the above mentioned databases can be accessed from URL: http://www.inflibnet.ac.in.

(vi) Bibliographic Standards : To maintain consistency and quality in databases created by the participating libraries, each participating library follows the standards adopted by INFLIBNET, which is an effort of the task force comprising experts in this area. The Document "INFLIBNET Standards and Guidelines for Data Capturing" is made available to all the libraries. The other standards recommended for this activity are:

- Anglo American Cataloguing Rules 2 (Revised)
- Library of Congress Subject Headings

Libraries following the INFLIBNET Standards and SOUL software will not have any difficulty in converting their records in to CCF/MARC-21 format.

Information Services of the Centre

To facilitate free flow of information to the end users and develop interaction among academia, various services have been started. These include:

(i) Access to Union Databases : All the bibliographic and factual databases developed at the centre have been mounted on the server and can be accessed from URL: http://www.inflibnet.ac.in

(ii) CD-ROM based services to Academicians : To provide the information on literature published in their areas of interest to the academicians, the centre subscribes to a large number of bibliographical databases in CD-ROM mainly in the areas of Social Sciences and Arts & Humanities. This service is provided free of cost to promote the use of electronic resources.

(iii) INTERNET Based Service : This service is provided to limited number of academic users who do not have access to the Internet resources.

(iv) UGC-Infonet and E-Journals Consortium Website: Centre has developed a website of UGC-Infonet and e-Journals consortium. Users can get information about the UGC-Infonet and usage statistics etc. Academicians can access the e-Journals subscribed under UGC-Infonet by Subject, Publishers etc and they can get all the required information about the e-resources.

Publications of the Centre

INFLIBNET Centre publishes following publications :

- Quarterly Newsletter titled 'INFLIBNET Newsletter' is being published since 1995 to create awareness among the professionals about the activities of INFLIBNET.
- Guidelines for Data capturing manual.
- CALIBER Proceedings are brought out every year.
- PLANNER Proceedings are brought out every year.
- Information Brochures, Course Material.
- Union Catalogue of Serials.
- Union Catalogue of Secondary Serials.
- Union Catalogue of Current Serials of Document Delivery Centres.
- Annual Reports and
- INFLIBNET Directory of Indian Universities accessible through INFLIBNET Website (http://libserver.inflibnet.ac.in:8080/wwwisis/add.01/form.htm).

INFLIBNET Repository

Centre has digitized all the proceedings of CALIBER and PLANNER, Course Materials, Newsletters, Centre's Press Clippings and articles published by INFLIBNET staff using D-space open source software. It has been customized based on INFLIBNET requirement. In future it can be customized and installed on request for all participating universities to digitize their doctoral theses as well articles and other publications to provide access to full text within the campus also on the internet. Presently INFLIBNET digital publications can be accessed through its website and also from the URL: http://dspace.inflibnet.ac.in/

Major Projects

(i) UGC-Infonet : University Grant Commission has launched an ambitious programme to bring about a qualitative change in the academic infrastructure, especially for higher education. Under this initiative UGC is modernizing the University Campuses with State-of-the-art campus wide networks and setting up its own nationwide communication network named UGC-Infonet. Under this programme it is proposed to use information and communication Technology (ICT) and Internet to transform learning environment from a mono-dimensional one to a multi-dimensional one. UGC-infonet will be a boon to the higher education systems in several ways:

- UGC-Infonet will become a vehicle for distance learning to facilitate spread of quality education all over the country.
- UGC-Infonet will be a tool to distribute education material and journals to the remotest of areas.
- UGC-Infonet will be a resource for researchers and scholars for tapping the most up-to-date information.
- UGC-Infonet will form a medium for collaboration among teachers and students, not only within the country but also all over the world.

- UGC-Infonet will be an Intranet for University Automation.
- UGC-Infonet will encompass entire University Systems for most efficient utilization of precious network resources.
- UGC-Infonet will establish a channel for globalisation of education and facilitate the universities in marketing their services and developments.

UGC-infonet is overlaid on ERNET Infrastructure in a manner so as to provide assured quality of service and optimal utilization of bandwidth resources. The network is run and managed by ERNET India. The project is funded by UGC with 90 percent capital investment and up to 100 percent of recurring costs. A joint technical and tariff committee (JTTC). consisting of leading experts in the country has also been setup to guide and monitor the design, implementation and operations of UGC-Infonet. INFLIBNET will be monitoring the network to provide assistance to universities for setting up IT infrastructure. This would help in optimizing the overall data traffic and improve performance. 124 universities have been provided grant till date under the scheme to connect under UGC-Infonet with bandwidth ranging from 64 Kbps to 2 Mbps.

(ii) UGC-infonet E-Journals Consortium : University Grants Commission (UGC) has initiated a programme to provide electronic access, over the Internet, to scholarly literature in all areas of learning to the university sector in India. The programme is wholly funded by the UGC and administered and monitored by INFLIBNET. All universities which come under UGC's purview will be members of the programme and it will gradually be extended to colleges as well.

The programme will increase in a very fundamental way the resources available to the universities for research and teaching. It will provide the best current and archival periodical literature, from all over the world, to the university community. This programme will go a long way in mitigating the severe shortage of periodicals faced by university libraries for many years, due to the ever widening gap between the growing demand for literature, and the limits of available resources.

The E-Journals programme aims at covering all fields of learning of relevance to various universities including:

- Arts & Humanities
- Social Sciences
- Physical and Chemical Sciences
- Life Sciences
- Computer Science, Mathematics, Statistics.

Future Programmes

Its future programme aim at following :

- Developing Modules on E-Learning, E- Education and Teleconferencing.
- To make facility to access our website by visually challenged persons.
- To conduct specialized training programs on Digital libraries, Website Design & Hosting, Standards and other emerging subjects.
- Collaboration with national documentation centres and other resourceful libraries.

Besides, the centre aims to provide the widest possible access to the e-resources to the academic community.

Madras Library Network (MALIBNET)

Introduction

To face the challenges and meeting the growing information demands of the user community and obviating the problems of resource crunch in libraries, MALIBNET a registered society was formed in 1993, through an MOU. INSDOC (now

NISCAIR) has been entrusted the responsibility of setting up and provides technical support for operating the network.

Presently nearly 50 libraries in Chennai are contributing actively to the creation of various databases on MALIBNET. With the help of communication links and sophisticated information technology, the resources of the member libraries are shared and made available to the users.

Achievements

The major achievements of MALIBNET are :

(i) **Directory of Databases of Current Serials :** It contains information of 5200 serials currently subscribed by 50 libraries in Madras (Chennai). It covers journals of basic sciences, applied science and technology, medicinal science and life science disciplines which is available online and on diskette and can be searched by title, subject and by library options.

(ii) **Contents Database :** It holds article index of nearly 500 journals online, and is searchable through author, title and keyword options.

(iii) **Specialized Database for Automotive Industries :** This database covers valuable National and International journals in the field. It has currently around 10000 records and is updated regularly. Search options are available-by journal, keywords and author.

Mysore Library Network (MYLIBNET)

Introduction

The NISSAT, Department of Scientific and Industrial Research (DSIR) took up initiation for the design and development of library networks in India in 1985 in order to share the resources available in the libraries in various parts of the country. Mysore city is unique compared to any other metropolitan city due to the richness in information resources. It is also unique in a way where one can find information on many areas like food science, sericulture, speech & hearing, pharmacy, dentistry, polymer, medicine, archeology, anthropology, Indian languages and engineering at one place. Considering this uniqueness, the Mysore Library Network was set up during May 1995 in the city of Mysore under the financial assistance from NISSAT.

CFTRI is one of the premier Sectorial Centres of NISSAT in the area of food science and technology. With this added advantage, MYLIBNET is working closely with MCLC to promote information services in Mysore city.

Objectives

MYLIBNET is also having the same objectives like other library networks in India but with a difference. One of the main objectives of this network is to prepare a union catalogue of periodicals subscribed by the member libraries. Accordingly, most of the library networks have been compiling the catalogue either in hard copy or in electronic form. Due to information technology advancement, this catalogue is now made available on the Internet.

MYLIBNET has also compiled this catalogue in the year 1996 in the machine-readable form and developed a software package (floppy disk version) for searching this catalogue either by institution name, journal title or by keywords. This software was released to its members in July 1996.

In order to have faster communication among libraries, MYLIBNET has been subscribing to electronic mail service of Education and Research Network (ERNET) of Department of Electronics (DoE), Govt. of India. Since the mail hub was located at Bangalore, which is 140 km away from Mysore city, all the members were provided with telephones with STD facility by their parent institutions to access e-mail service. Library and information science professionals from member institutions were trained on e-mail operation.

Programmes

MYLIBNET is organizing various programmes regularly for the benefit of library and information science professionals. Some of them are:

- Workshop on Multimedia Applications in Library and Exhibition of Multimedia Products;
- Seminar on Bar Code Applications in Library and Demonstration of Bar Code Products;
- Workshop on Internet Concept and Techniques and Live Demonstration of Internet Access over STD Line;
- Training Programme on Common Communication Format for the Creation of Databases;
- Seminar on Digital Library;
- Technical Seminar on Library Management System;
- Workshop on Internet and Web Publishing in collaboration with Academy of Information Science; and
- Workshop on Bandwidth Management.

MYLIBNET has established its Web server www.mylibnet.org to provide services globally. A radio link with the local earth station of Software Technology Parks of INDIA (STPI) has been established. The union catalogue of periodicals compiled earlier has been ported on this Web server for easy access over network.

Achievements and Services

MYLIBNET has many achievements to its credit. Some of them are:

(i) First library network to have its own e-mail node under ERNET.

(ii) First to introduce Internet technology to the people of Mysore City.

(iii) First library network to have its own Web server.

(iv) First library network to have dedicated link with ISP for providing various services on Internet.

A new wave has brought into its activity with the hosting of variety of information on the Web in addition to the library networking services: The issues of *Information Today and Tomorrow* from volumes 14 to 20, are now available on its Web site.

Information related to food patents, newsletter, NICFOS publications, etc are also available on the Web site. On-line directory of manufacturers, consultants, professionals, doctors, associations, various service providers, etc. can be accessed on-line through the Web. It has also developed the following databases :

(i) Vidyanidhi : Vidyanidhi is a Digital Library Interactive currently underway at the Department of Library and Information, University of Mysore, India. This initiative is sponsored by NISSAT, DSIR, Government of India. The full texts of thesis are available online submitted in Indian universities. Full text search allows user to search theses by author, keyword, language and university etc.

(ii) Serials Catalogue : A unit catalogue of S & T serials in Mysore City Libraries with the financial assistance from NISSAT was completed. The catalogue is available online. Search can be made by the title/keyword in the title of the journal. For institutions, a drop-down list it is given from which it can be selected.

No database will be useful unless it is updated regularly. Initially the data for the union catalogue was collected manually from each of the participating libraries. Now MYLIBNET is bringing reality to its networking activity by providing Web-enabled facility to its member libraries to modify the union catalogue database online. Now member libraries can login to this database sitting in their library by entering their ID and password. Once their identity is authenticated and validated by the server, they can view the records provided by them only. If the record needs any modification, it can be done immediately. Proper authentication has been incorporated so that only a member library can modify their records.

After updating their records, the member library has to send a confirmation .message to the database administrator for its implementation. With this facility, libraries from across the country can become a member of MYLIBNET and join their hands to build a national database.

One of the objectives of the library network is to provide e-mail facility to its members. A Web interface for the e-mail server has been developed and made available on the Net. A member can login to his mailbox from anywhere in the world using the standard Internet browser like Internet explorer or Netscape.

In addition to the above services, MYLIBNET is also providing specialized service whenever the situation arises.

Information Portal for Mysore city

Since Mysore city is well-known for its cultural activities and tourist attractions and is a crafts centre, information on these has been compiled and made available on the Web. This section is updated regularly. The Web site contains information about seminars, workshops, short-term courses, camps, competitions, etc. to be held in Mysore city. Important news like awards, nominations, etc. will be displayed on the main page.

PUNENET

Pune Net is a joint programme of the university of Pune, Centre for Development of Advanced Computing and the National Chemical Laboratory. The project is also funded by NISSAT. Its main objective is to open the door to the information available in the libraries and other resource centres in Pune.

PUNENET maintains centralized book, periodicals and professional databases of the participating libraries. The other objective is to help increasing cooperation among the participating libraries holdings and coordinates their activities, so as to serve the user community effectively.

Achievements

At present PUNENET hosts the database mentioned below. These databases are updated annually. Users can search these databases online using its website.

(i) **Database of Books :** This database contains 1,08,835 records from 20 participants libraries of PUNENET. A user can conduct simple or Boolean search to locate the desired item.

(ii) **Union Catalogue of Periodicals :** The Union Catalogue of Periodicals database contains 6425 records pertaining to various libraries in the Pune city. Currently data from 60 libraries are available online.

By accessing these databases, the user will know the availability of information source in the participating libraries. Thus the user gets up-to-date information at one place and can avail the facilities of the participating libraries. PuneNet databases are accessible over the INTERNET thus giving the project a world wide accessibility. The user will therefore know whether a particular book is available in any of the libraries in the city. PuneNet, therefore, acts as a gateway to the INTERNET.

Services

Presently following services are in operational mode :

- Search Library Database
- Online Data Entry
- Member Library Information
- Bulletin Board
- News Channel

- Training Calendar
- Student Section
- Book Seller Channel
- Consultancy Services and
- Web based e-mail service.

UGC-INFONET
(A Network of Indian Universities)

Introduction

With globalization of education and competitive research the demand for the journals has increased over the years. Due to scarcity of financial resources, libraries have been forced to withdaw the scholarly journals, which have great impact on the search community. University Grants Commission has initiated an ambitious project called UGC-Infonet for modernizing the University campuses with state-of-the-art technology. This programme is launched to bring about a qualitative change in the academic infrastructure, especially for higher education. Under this initiative, UGC is modernizing the University Campuses with State-of-the-art campus wide networks and has set up its own nationwide communication network named UGC-Infonet. INFLIBNET is responsible for executing and monitoring the entire project. Its sailent features are :

(i) UGC-Infonet is a vehicle for distance learning to facilitate spread of quality education all over the country.

(ii) UGC-Infonet is a tool to distribute education material and journals to the remotest areas of the nation.

(iii) UGC-Infonet thus becomes a resource for researchers and scholars for tapping the most up-to-date information.

(iv) UGC-Infonet forms a medium for collaboration among teachers and students, not only within the country but also all over the world.

(v) UGC-Infonet becomes an Intranet for University Network.

(vi) UGC-Infonet encompasses entire University Systems for most efficient utilization of precious network resources.

(vii) UGC-Infonet establishes a channel for globalization of education and facilitates the universities in marketing their services and developments.

Intranet for Universities

Availability of reliable and stable network infrastructure will facilitate increased usage of computers in the university campuses. Campus Management will be more efficient and student friendly. Interlinking of the universities will expand the reach of students and faculty to other universities providing them with better avenues for wider horizontal growth.

UGC-Infonet will establish a seamless link between the UGC and the universities. This will help to provide a more accurate and up-to-date picture of the universities, while at the same time it will enable universities to have timely information about various schemes of the UGC. Consequently, this will bring a qualitative change in the UGC-Universities interaction. The huge and multi-faceted Indian Education system would achieve greater efficiency through e-governance of UGC.

Technology Partnership

Information Technology is evolving at a rapid pace worldwide to cater the need of providing information in any form, at any time, anywhere. The trend is to set up networks which are device independent, thus enabling flexibility of access, and also to meet the requirements arising out of convergence of technologies. Regular technology input would be required to upgrade the network infrastructure to ensure delivery of upcoming applications and content to the education and research community in the country. UGC, INFLIBNET and ERNET have come together to meet the challenges that may face academic community with respect to real time information.

Implementation Technology

UGC-Infonet is overlaid on ERNET Infrastructure in a manner so as to provide assured quality of service and optimal utilization of bandwidth resources. The network is managed by ERNET India on turnkey basis. The project is funded by UGC with 100 percent capital investment and up to 90 percent of recurring costs. Towards this end, an MoU has been signed between UGC and ERNET India for implementation of UGC-Infonet and also for long term technology partnership. A Central Connectivity Monitoring Committee (CCMC), consisting of leading experts in the country has been setup to guide and monitor the design, implementation and operations of UGC-Infonet. INFLIBNET, as autonomous IUC of the UGC, is the nodal agency for coordination of the UGC-Infonet and is a linkage between ERNET and the Universities.

Network Architecture

UGC-Infonet is based on open IP platform, employing state-of-the-art technologies like IP Multicast, TCP Spoofing and other Internet tools that provide interactive education on PC or TV, enabling on-line response to queries. Open systems architecture ensures support for current and future applications. Users from Educational Institutions would enjoy high data rates while accessing Intranet and Internet resources.

Connectivity Options for the Universities

UGC-Infonet is overlaid on ERNET Infrastructure including a nation wide terrestrial backbone and a complimentary satellite Wide Area Network (WAN). As such ERNET can provide a complete range connectivity options to the universities depending upon their location and bandwidth requirements. Since terrestrial media offers greater scalability and performance, efforts are made to connect the universities on the terrestrial media. Alternately, a Satellite connection is provided through VSAT.

Digital Leased Lines (LL) : In the localities where telecom network is well-developed, dedicated leased lines are hired from basic telecom service providers. Such links are primarily for 256 Kbps to 2 Mbps speeds.

Radio Link (RF) : The universities located within 30 kms of the ERNET PoPs are provided with dedicated radio links operating from 256 Kbps to 2 Mbps speeds.

Satellite based Wide Area Network (SATWAN) : ERNET operates a Satellite based Wide Area Network (SATWAN) using C-Band transponder on INSAT-3C. SATWAN hub, located at Bangalore, supports Broadband VSATs with up to 45 Mbps shared bandwidth. Single Channel Per Carrier (SCPC) VSATs are used for establishing dedicated two-way channels of 256 Kbps to 2 Mbps from Hub. SCPC VSATs are ideal for those universities, which are located in remote areas but wish to host their own Internet server for providing access to their information through Internet from all over the world. A number of Universities are provided with FTDMA VSATs.

Network Access Centre

For maximum benefits of UGC-Infonet, the universities are advised to set up campus wide network and ensure uniform access all over the campus. Wherever campus LAN is not in place it is suggested that the university sets up a network access centre, which is open to all students at the university. This will work on lines similar to the terminal rooms in traditional computer centres.

Network Trained Manpower

Trained manpower is one of the most critical resource for successful implementation of high-tech programmes like UGC-Infonet. ERNET India has setup a modern training laboratory to train network system managers and users of UGC-Infonet. Technical staff from each of the participating universities are trained to take maximum advantage of the infrastructure.

By now 150 university had received the grant and 145 of them have been connected under this programme. And from 129 universities, manpower have been trained to be acquainted with the UGC-Infonet technology.

INFLIBNET Centre is also monitoring bandwith utilization of each participating university with help of ERNET. Now all these universities are receiving E-Journals in a consortium mode through INFLIBNET free of cost.

Bibliography

Abraham, A. 1992. Resource Sharing in University Libraries : A Myth or Reality. In G. Devarajan et al., edited 'Resource Development in Academic Libraries'. Ess Ess Publications, New Delhi. Pp. 77-85.

Agarwal, V. 2000. Library Networking : Challenging and Opportunities. Rajat Publication, New Delhi.

Allen, B M and Hirshon, A. 1998. Hanging together to Avoid Hanging Separately: Opportunities for Academic Libraries and Consortia. *Information Technology and Libraries*. 17: 36-44.

Arora, J. and Agrawal, P. 2003. Indian Digital Library in Engineering Science and Technology (INDEST) Consortium : Consrotia - Basesd Subscription to Electronic Resources for Technical Education System in India : A Government of India Initiative. In T.A.V. Murthy edited 'Mapping Technology on Libraries and People' (CALIBER-2003). Inflibnet Centre, Ahemdabad. pp. 270-90.

Allen, B, M. 1999. Consortia and Collection: Achieving a Balance Between Local Action and Collaborative Interest. *Journal of Library Administration*. 2 : 85-90.

Baker, D. 1997. Resource Management in Academic Libraries. Library Association Publishing, London.

Barua, P. and Saibaba, B. 1992. A Plan for Cooperation and Networking among Engineering and Technological Libraries in India. *Annals of Library Science and Documentation*. 39 (3): 101-05.

Becker, J. and Becker, J.F. 1983. Technology Trends in Library

Resource Sharing Networks. *Australian Special Libraries News.* 16 (4): 121-24.

Billings, H. 1989. Governing Library Networks. *Library Journal.* 11 (4): 49-54.

Biswas, B.Ch. and Dasgupta, S.K. 2003. Opportunities for Libraries in Managing and Resources Sharing through Consortia : A New Challenge for Indian Librarians. In T.A.V. Murthy edited 'Mapping Technology on Libraries and People' (CALIBER-2003). Inflibnet Centre, Ahemdabad. pp. 291-97.

Bose, K. 1994. Information Networks in India. Problems and Prospects. Ess Ess Publications, New Delhi.

Bouazza, A. 1986. Resource Sharing among Libraries in Developing Countries : the Gulf between Hope and Reality. *International Library Review.* 18 (4): 373-87.

Cakewell, A.E. 1988. Electronic Information Delivery Systems. *Critique.* 1 (1): 1-12.

Chandel, A.S. and Saraf, V. (Eds.) 1987. Planning in Library Resource Sharing : Proceedings of the Seminar on Coordination in Resource Sharing held at Isabella Thouburn College, Lucknow. Print House (India), Lucknow.

Chandel, A. S., Mezbah-ul-Islam M. and Gupta, S. 2003. Use of Resources by Research Scholars in University Libraries with Special Reference to Electronic Media. In TAV Murthy edited 'Mapping Technology on Libraries and People (CALIBER-2003 Papers)'. INFLIBNET, Ahemdabad. Pp. 522-34.

Chandler, G. 1980. Development of Resource Sharing Networks in Australia. *International Library Review.* 12 (4): 369-80.

Cholin, V. and Karisiddappa, C.R. 2002. Library Consortia for Academic Libraries in the E- Publishing Era. In H. Anil

Kumar, P. Upadhyaya, S.R. Ganpule and P.C. Shah edited 'Internet Engineering for Libraries and Information Centres (Ninth CALIBER-2002 Papers). INFLIBNET Centre, Ahemdabad. Pp. 362-74.

Chopra, H.R. 1991. Resource Sharing in University Libraries in India. In S.P. Sood and C.L. Sharma edited 'Outstanding Studies in University Librarianship'. RBSA Publishers, Jaipur.

Choudhury, B.K. 1989. Inter Library Loan Services in University Libraries in India : An Assessment. *Lucknow Librarian.* 21 (2): 68-72.

Devadson, F.J. and Karisidappa, C.R. 1984-85. International Information System for the Agricultural Sciences and Technology (AGRIS) : An Outline. *Libra.* 22-23 : 33-47.

Dastidar, P.G. 1989. Educational and Research Network of India, *Lucknow Librarian.* 39 (3): 173-84.

Dhiman, A. K. 1997. Computers and their Applications in Libraries. *Lucknow Librarian.* 29 (1-4): 11-15.

Dhiman, A.K. 1998. Modern Technology in Resource Sharing for Information Handling. *Library Progress.* 18 (1-2) : 19-21.

Dhiman, A.K. 2000. LAN: An Overview. In R. Vengan, H.R. Mohan and K.S. Raghvan edited 'Information Services in a Networked Environment in India (Caliber-2000)'. INFLIBNET, Ahemdabad. pp. 2.106-111.

Dhiman, A.K. and Sinha, S. C. 2000. Computer Education Centre at Roorkee: A Survey. *Indian Journal of Information, Library & Society.* 13 (3-4) : 257- 64.

Dhiman, A.K. 2001. Usefulness of Performance Appraisal in Library & Information Centres. In S.M. Dhawan edited 'Quest for Quality : Strategies and Applications in Library and Information Services' (46th All India Library Conference Papers). Indian Library Association, Delhi. Pp. 333-39.

Dhiman, A.K.2001. Role of Library Professionals in the Era of Information Technology. *Indian Journal of Information, Library & Society.* 14 (1-2): 81-85.

Dhiman, A.K. 2001. Impact of Information Technology (IT) on Library Management. In Kalpana Dasgupta edited 'Library Practices for Effective Management' (47th All India Library Conference Papers). Indian Library Association, Delhi. Pp. 191-202.

Dhiman, A.K. 2001. Restructuring LIS Curriculum: A Need of the Hour. LIS Education in the Internet Era & Assessment and Accreditation of LIS Schools (XVII National Seminar-2001 held from 7 - 9th February 2001). DLIS, University of Kerala, Thiruvanthapuram. Pp. B5.1-5.4.

Dhiman, A.K. 2002. Resource Sharing in Digital Environment through Internet: Problems and Prospects. In H. Anil Kumar, P. Upadhyaya, S.R. Ganpule and P.C. Shah edited 'Internet Engineering for Libraries and Information Centres' (Ninth CALIBER-2002 Papers). INFLIBNET Centre, Ahemdabad. Pp. 43-54.

Dhiman, A.K. and Sinha, S.C. 2002. Academic Libraries. Ess Ess Publications, New Delhi.

Dhiman, A.K. 2003. Internet Based Library Services. In Pandey S.K. Sharma edited "Electronic Information Environment and Library Services: A Paradigm' (48th All India Library Conference Papers). Indian Library Association, New Delhi. Pp. 99-106.

Dhiman, A.K. 2003. Intellectual Property Rights in Digital Environment. In Y. Singh et al., edited 'New Challenges in Information Management and E-learning in the Age of Globalization' (SIS - 2003 Papers). IIT, Roorkee. Pp. 292-98.

Dhiman, A.K. 2003. Basics of Information Technology for Librarians and Information Scientists. 2 Vols. Ess Ess Publications, New Delhi.

Dhiman, A.K. 2004. Acquisition, Preservation and Retrieval of Digital Resources: Role of Library Consortia. In Ashu Shoukeen edited 'KODEL : Introspect and Prospects' (50th All India Library Conference Papers). Indian Library Association, New Delhi. Pp. 116-26.

Dhiman, A.K. 2004. Cataloguing of Non Book Materials. Ess Ess Publications, New Delhi.

Dhiman, A.K. and Rani, Y. 2004. Library Management: A Manual Book for Effective Management. Ess Ess Publications, New Delhi.

Dhiman, A.K. 2005. Consortium Based Library Subscription : Some Issues. In T.A.V. Murthy et al., edited 'Digital Collections in Development and E-Journal Management in Libraries (PLANNER-2005 Papers)'. INFLIBNET Centre, Ahemdabad. Pp. 294-300.

Dhiman, A.K. and Rani, Y. 2005. Learn - Library and Society. Ess Ess Publications, New Delhi.

Dhiman, A.K. and Rani, Y. 2005. Learn - Library Management. Ess Ess Publications, New Delhi.

Dhiman, A.K. and Rani, Y. 2005. Learn - Information and Reference Sources and Services. Ess Ess Publications, New Delhi.

Dhiman, A.K. and Rani, Y. 2005. Learn - Computer Basics and its Application in Libraries. Ess Ess Publications, New Delhi.

Fielding, D. 1988. Inter-Library Loans and Resource Sharing. *Australian Library Journal.* 37 (1): 34-44.

Flanders, B. and Zuck, G. (Eds.). 1992. Wide - Area Network Applications in Libraries. Meckler, Westport, CT.

Fredrick, J. 1989. The Birth of a Network : the Brazilian Struggle. *College and research Libraries.* 50(1): 76-82.

Galvin, T.J. 1979. The Structure and Governance of Library Networks. Marcel Dekker Inc., New York.

Gatterman, G. 1985. Shared Cataloguing Networking in the Federal Republic of Germany : Some Problems of Plaining Realization. *Libri.* 25 (3): 191-201.

Ghosh, B.K. 1979. National Information Network in Developing Countries with Special Reference to India. *Herald of Library Science.* 18 (1-2): 105-12.

Govan, J.F. 1986. Preservation and Resource Sharing : Conflicting or Complementaries. *IFLA Journal.* 12 (1) : 20-24.

Gupta, P.K. and Pawan, U. 1986. Library and Information Science: Current Trends in India. RBSA Publishers, Jaipur.

Hanif, A. 1987. Library Resource Sharing in Pakistan : Problems and Prospects. *Pakistan Library Bulletin.* 18 (1): 7-17.

Holligan, P.J. 1986. Access to UK Academic Networks. *Information Processing and Management.* 22 (4): 353-56.

Hurley, B.J. 1981. LCS : Automated resource Sharing in Illinois. *Resource Sharing and Library Networks.* 1 (1): 67-77.

Huston-Sommerville, M. and Wilt, C.C. (Eds.). 1995. Networks and Resource Sharing in the 21st Century : Re - engineering the Information Landscape. The Haworth Press, New York.

Jefferson, G. 1977. Library Co-operation. 2nd Revised Edition. Andre Deutsch, London.

Joshi, S.C. 1990. Resource Sharing. *Indian Journal of Information, Library and Society.* 3 (3-4): 153-60.

Kamath, V.A. 1993. Evolution of Information Technology : An Overview. *IASLIC Bulletin.* 28 (4): 178.

Karki, M.M.S. 1983. Library Resource Sharing though Online Network : Problems and Prospects. *IASLIC Bulletin.* 28 (3): 135-39.

Katezan, M. 1988. A National Information Network. *Scholarly Publishing.* 19 (4) : 210-16.

Kaul, H.K. 1988. DELNET : the Network of Delhi Libraries. *IASLIC Bulletin.* 33 (4) : 125-28.

Kaul, H.K. 1990. Library Networks in U.K. and Spain : the Projections for India. *Herald of Library Science.* 29 (3-4): 179-82.

Kaul, H.K. 1992. Library Networks : An Indian Experience. Virgo Publications, New Delhi.

Kaul, H.K. 1999. Library Resource Sharing and Networks. Virgo Publications, New Delhi.

Kaul, H.K. and Rama Reddy, E. 2002. Library and Information Networking (NACLIN-2001). DELNET, New Delhi.

Kaul, H.K. and Baby, M.D. 2003. Library and Information Networking (NACLIN-2002). DELNET, New Delhi.

Kent, A. (Ed.) 1974. Resource Sharing in Libraries : Why, How, When- Next Action Steps. Marcel Dekker, New York.

Kent, A. 1978. Library resource Sharing Networks : How to Make a Choice. *Library Acquisitions : Practice and Theory.* 2 (2): 69-76.

Kent, A. 1990. Library Networks. In S.S.Murthy Anuradha Ravi and A. Lakshmana Moorthy edited 'Bibliographic Databases and Networks' (Proceedings of the International Conference, held during 22-25 Feb 1989 at New Delhi). Tata Mcgraw Hill Publishing Company Ltd., New Delhi. Pp. 3.19 - 3.29.

Kent, A. and Galvin. T.J. (Eds.). 1979. The Structure and Governance of Library Networks. Marcel Dekker, New York.

Kent, A., Lancour, H. and Daily, J.E. 1978. Resource Sharing. In Encyclopedia of Library and Information Science. Vol. 25. Marcel Dekker Inc., New York. Pp. 293-307.

Khandawala, V.K. 1989. Resource Sharing in Indian University Libraries. In N.B. Inamdar and L.S. Ramaiah edited 'National Policy for University Libraries in India'. Concept Publishing Company, New Delhi. Pp. 155-61.

Khanna, J.K. 1985. Advances in Librarianship. Ess Ess Publishers, New Delhi.

Khanna, J.K. 1996. Handbook of Library Information Systems & Services. Beacon Books, New Delhi.

Khurshid, A. 1982. Resource Sharing of University Libraries in Pakistan. *Herald of Library Science.* 21 (3-4): 169-82.

Kilgour, F.G. 1990. Planning and Design of Information Networks. In S.S.Murthy Anuradha Ravi and A. Lakshmana Moorthy edited 'Bibliographic Databases and Networks' (Proceedings of the International Conference, held during 22-25 Feb 1989 at New Delhi). Tata Mcgraw Hill Publishing Company Ltd., New Delhi. Pp. 3.7-3.18.

Konnur, M.B. 1992. Resource Sharing in University Libraries : the International Scene. *University News.* 31 August, pp. 93-97.

Koop, J. 1998. Library Consortia and Information Technology: the Past, the Present, the Promise. *Information Technology & Libraries.* 17(1): 7-12.

Kumar, P.S. G. 1987. Computerization of Indian Libraries. B.R. Publishers, New Delhi.

Lahiri, A. and Singh. S. 1990. Bibliographic Databases and Networks : Indian Scenario. In S.S.Murthy, Anuradha Ravi and A. Lakshmana Moorthy edited 'Bibliographic databases and Networks' (Proceedings of the International Conference, held during 22-25 Feb 1989 at New Delhi). Tata Mcgraw Hill Publishing Company Ltd., New Delhi. Pp. 1.41-1.66.

Lahiri, R. and Subramanian, K. 1991. NELIBNET : A Promise of prospect for Northeast India : An Outline. *University News.* 26 August, pp. 9-13.

Lang, B. 1994. The Electronic Library : Implications for Librarians : Academics and Publishers. *Libri.* 44 (4): 265-71.

Lee, S.D. and Boyle, F. 2004. Building An Electronic Resource Collection : A Practical Guide. 2nd Edition. Facet Publishing, London.

Liu, D.T. 1985. Co-operative Sharing of Library Resources in America. *Journal of Library and Information Science.* 10 (1) : 36-52.

Luquire, W. (Ed.) 1983. Library Networking : Current Problems and Future Prospects. The Haworth Press, New York.

MacDougall, A.F. and Prytherch, R. 1997. Handbook of Library Cooperation. Jaico Publishing House, Mumbai.

Mahajan, S.G. 1992. Resource Sharing and Networking of University Libraries. *University News.* 31 August, pp. 79-85.

Martin, S.K. 1987. Library Networks : Trends and Issues. *Journal of Library Administration.* 8 (2): 27-33.

Martin, S.K. 1989. Information Technology and Libraries : Toward the Year 2000. *College & Research Libraries.* 50 (4) : 397 - 405.

Martin, W.J. 1990. The Network Market Place and its Implications. *ASLIB Proceedings.* 42 (6): 165-70.

Meera. B.M. 1993. Wide Area Networks : a Facilitator for Library resource Sharing. In I.K. Ravichandra Rao edited 'Seminar on Library Networks' in India held during 12-13 August 1993. Paper - 1. Documentation Research and Training Centre, Bangalore.

Moody, P. 1982. Resource Sharing in Universities and Polytechnics : Possibilities and limitations. *ASLIB Proceedings.* 34 (4) : 209-13.

Mukherjee, A.K. 1965. Inter - Library Loan and Exchange of Publications in India. *Indian Librarian.* 29 : 144-48.

Murthy, T.A.V., Kembhavi, A. and Cholin, V. 2004. Access to Scholarly Journals and Databases: UGC-INFONET E-Journals Consortium. *University News.* 42 (34): 1-5,8.

Natrajan, M. and Kalivaperumal, R. 1989. Impact of New Information technology on Document Provision and Supply. *ILA Bulletin.* 24 (4): 214-20.

Ojha, D.C. 1989. Resource Sharing in Agricultural Libraries. In CD. Sharma and D.C. Ojha edited 'Advances in Library and Information Science'. Vol. 2. RBSA Publishers, Jaipur. Pp. 86-95.

Pandian, M P, Jambhekar A. and Karisiddappa, C. R. 2002. IIM Digital Library System: Consortia Based Approach. *Electronic Library.* 20 : 211-214.

Parekh, H. 1993. Library Networks : Moving from Informal to Formal. *University News.* April 5,: 4-7.

Paskoff, B. 1989. Networks and Networking : How and Why should Special Libraries be Involved. *Special Libraries.* 80 (2): 95-100.

Payne, L. 1998. The Working for Research Library Consortium: a Real Organization for Virtual Library. *Information Technology & Libraries.* 17 (1): 13-17.

Rahelamma, A.V. 1990. Library Computerization in India. Ess Ess Publishers, New Delhi.

Ramaiah, L.S. 1990. Resource Sharing among the Indian University Libraries : the Need for a Network. In H.A. Khan and S.R. Ijari edited 'Current Problems and Trends in Library & Information Services'. Indian bibliographic Bureau, Varanasi. Pp. 294-300.

Reddy, Y.J. 1991. Manpower Planning for University Libraries: An Analysis. *Indian Journal of Information, Library and Society.* 4 (1): 112.

Reynolds, M.M. 1964. Inter-Library Loan : A Reference Service. *Library Trends.* 12:1-13.

Robinson, B. 1980. Funding for Library Networks : Types and Sources for Available Funds. In B. E. Markuson and B. Wools edited 'Networks for Networks'. Neat Schumann Publishers, New York. P. 246.

Rogersons, CM. and Lee, E.L. 1988. Electronic Integration of Library Services through a Campuswide Network. *RQ*. (28 (1): 82-93.

Rouse, W.B. and Rouse, S.H. 1980. Management of Library Networks : Policy Analysis, Implementation and Control. John Willey & Sons, New York.

Saha, J.C 1985. Resource Sharing in Libraries : A Fresh Look. *Lucknow Librarian.* 17 (1 & 2): 1-6.

Sethi, A.R. 1983. Library Co-operation in India. *ILA Bulletin.* 28 (4): 51-58.

Sinha, S.C and Dhiman, A.K. 2001. Citation Analysis of the Research Field and Information Technology Development. Ess Ess Publications, New Delhi.

Sinha, S.C. and Dhiman, A.K. 2000. Information Chaos and Conflicts with Contradictions in Information Science and Information Technology : Some Factors and its Remedies. Proceeding of XIX IASLIC Seminar. Pp. 85-88.

Srinivasan, K. 1987. Data Network for India. *Library Science with a Slant to Documentation.* 24 (3): 155-56.

Srivastava, A.P. 1989. Development of Information and Library Network (INFLIBNET). *University News.* April, 24, pp. 1-3.

Stuart-Stubbs, B. 1974-75. An Historical Look at Resource Sharing. *Library Trends.* 23 : 649-64.

Subbarao, V.S. 1999. Library Management through Automation and Networking. Allied Publishing Ltd., Bombay.

Sujatha, G. 1999. Resource Sharing and Networking of University Libraries. Ess Ess Publications, New Delhi.

Tadsad, P.G. 2003. University Library Consortia in India- From a Vision to Reality; One will not get a Chicken by smashing Egg open. In T.A.V. Murthy edited 'Mapping Technology on Libraries and People' (CALIBER-2003). Inflibnet Centre, Ahemdabad. pp. 396-406.

Taneja, S.A. Resource Sharing in Science and Technology Libraries in India. *INSPEL.* 20 (1): 34-46.

Thiagarajan, R. 1984. Networks and National Information Systems. *INICAE.* 3 (4): 144-65.

Tikekar, A.C. 1989. Co-operation in Indian University Libraries. Inamdar and L.S. Ramaiah edited "National Policy for University Libraries in India". Concept Publishing Company, New Delhi. Pp. 177-88.

Tsuda, Y. 1985. Library Co-operation Network and Library Sharing in Japan. *Journal of Library and Information Science.* 10 (1) : 18-23.

Wiggins, B. 2000. Effective Document Management: Unlocking Corporate Knowledge. Gower Publishing Limited, Hampshire, England.

Wilson, T. C. (Ed.) 1992. Impact of Technology on Resource Sharing : Experimentation and Maturity, The Haworth Press Inc., New York.

Appendix-1
Other Important Library Consortia

M25 Consortium of Academic Libraries

The M25 Consortium of Academic Libraries (http://www.m25lib.ac.uk/) was formed in 1993 with the aim of fostering cooperation amongst its London-based, higher education member libraries in order to improve services to users. The Consortium now has 52 member institutions. Contacts for each institution can be found at http://www.m25lib.ac.uk/m25sec/about/people.htm. A list of over 150 member libraries is available at http://www.m25lib.ac.uk/Guide/directory.

In June 2001 the Consortium agreed to open up membership to other institutions find groups outside of the Higher Education sector in the light of its constitution. Full subscription based, membership is now open to

- Higher Education Institutions located in and around the M25 region (defined as London within the new regional boundaries) who are eligible for membership of SCONUL.
- Other academic and academic related institutions in the M25 region which may be invited to join, including groups of libraries with similar interests.

Observer status may be offered to such institutions or professional bodies, as are recommended by the Steering Group.

The emphasis of the Consortium is clearly centred on London and the early members came from within the London Boroughs. There followed a gradual growth in the number of Higher Education Institutions joining the Consortium from outside the London area, which added to the diversity and richness of the Consortium. In June 2001 it was confirmed that, despite the new regional boundaries, membership of the Consortium should remain open to members from outlying regions around the London area but without seeking to dilute regional representation. The Consortium does not seek to represent those members located outside the London Boroughs within their local region.

From the HEFCE South East and East regions the following are members to date: University of Hertfordshire, University of Kent, University of Surrey, University of Sussex and University of Brighton along with 2 HE Colleges: Buckinghamshire Chilterns UC and Canterbury Christ Church UC.

Mission

The mission of the Consortium is to:

(i) Act as a co-operative, and inclusive, organization which recognizes the diversity of missions amongst its constituent members, and seeks to build on them to further their common objectives and to co-operate with other bodies having similar objectives.

(ii) Co-operate in the effective enhancement of library and information services, in order to improve availability of, and access to, information and learning resources for the combined constituencies of publicly-funded higher education and related institutions located in and around the region defined by the M25.

(iii) Develop, manage, market and publicize resource discovery, sharing and co-ordination and access to services so as to enable a greater use of libraries and other information resources across the region to the benefit of learners, researchers, academics and members of the public.

(iv) Provide a collaborative forum for innovation, partnership and mutual support, and through collaborative staff development to facilitate the exchange of experience, the transmission of expertize and improved professional development.

(v) Monitor developments in Higher Education and related sectors in the region, assess the implications for member libraries and represent the views of its members to policy making bodies.

Aims

The aims of the Consortium in support of this are:

(i) To provide high quality, cost effective services and mutual support for member libraries and to enable services to learners and researchers to be improved.

(ii) To act as a voice for higher education and related institutions' libraries in the region and play a positive role in influencing regional, national and professional agendas including those particularly relevant to learners and researchers and delivering practical solutions.

(iii) To work with other organizations to create an environment whereby the richness and diversity of library, museum and archive provision within the region can be accepted as a single distributed collection for London as a World city, and for the surrounding area, for the benefit of learning and research, economic development, culture and social inclusion.

Goals

The four key goals of the Consortium are in relation to:

(i) *Resource discovery, sharing and co-ordination* : The development of effective resource discovery and sharing tools that reflect the diverse and varied missions of the member libraries and the complexity and diversity of London's library resources.

(ii) *Access*: The delivery of defined services to its users with optimal access to scholarly resources.

(iii) *Mutual support*: The promotion of continuous improvement of services to users, dissemination of good practice and provision of professional support to the staff.

(iv) *Collaboration and partnership*: The development of mutually beneficial cross-sectoral, cross-domain, and other alliances.

Members meet twice a year as a full Consortium. A Steering Group meets about six times a year to take the medium-term strategy and Development Plan forward. Working Groups address specific operational issues.

Resource discovery, Sharing and Co-ordination

Its InforM25 service provides users with simultaneous searching of member libraries' catalogues using standardized protocols. It also provides users with information about member libraries and their collections both by subject and geographic location, opening hours and access arrangements. Consortium is a partner in AIM-25 (Archives in London and the M25 region) which provides electronic access to collection level descriptions of the archives of over fifty higher education institutions and learned societies within the greater London area.

The Consortium is a partner in MASC-25 (Mapping of Access to Special Collections), a cross-sectoral project in partnership with public libraries involving the construction of a web-enabled database with collection-level descriptions for special collections.

The Consortium is a partner in Find it in London (FiiL), working with partners from the public, higher education and further education college library sectors, as well as archives and museums to design a web-based look-up tool. This will allow users to find an answer to the question: 'Where in London will find strong collections in my subject?' Essentially a prototype, the vision is to extend Fill to cover over 450 libraries, museums and archives in London.

The Consortium, through its M25 Systems Team, was involved in the development of the "What's in London's Libraries" service, made possible by a grant from the People's Network which is Lottery-funded by the New Opportunities Fund. It has opened up the collections and community information resources of a range of libraries, museums and archives across London and gives a range of information about facilities like location, opening times, services. The London Libraries Development Agency manages the service on behalf of the 33 London boroughs. It has also been supported by the London Museums, Archives and Libraries partnership and the British Library Co-operation and Partnership Programme.

Access

These 'resource discovery' projects are all underpinned by a national reciprocal access scheme called SCONUL Research Extra, which gives researchers physical access to libraries within the Consortium and allows staff and researchers of member libraries to borrow material.

UK Libraries Plus includes many of the member libraries as participants. It is a national co-operative venture between HE sector libraries which permits access and borrowing facilities for part-time, distance, and placement students. It includes provision for full-time students and staff to use other libraries on a reference only basis.

M25 a partner in Libraries and Learners in London. This is a mutually beneficial, reference access scheme to facilitate access by public library users to academic libraries within the Consortium. Many M25 libraries also participate in the Lamda service which provides speedy electronic document delivery of journal articles at a competitive price.

Collaboration and Partnership

The Consortium actively seeks and develops partnerships with other organizations within the region. M25 has strategic links with a number of cross-sectoral and cross-domain organizations for mutual benefit. The Consortium also acts as a focal point for the delivery of national initiatives within the region.

The Consortium is a subscribing member of the London Libraries Development Agency (LLDA) which is developing a coordinated, strategic vision for information services across London. This also supports the work of Archives, Libraries and Museums London, a partnership which promotes co-operation between museums, archives and libraries in the region.

The Consortium has ongoing links with the Association of London Chief Librarians who represent the public libraries in the region. There is reciprocal attendance at meetings and other regular discussions that have led, for example, to the Learners and Libraries in London scheme mentioned above.

This is also seeking to develop links with further education libraries and the Learning and Skills Councils, the NHS and the libraries of learned societies and government departments.

The Consortium is keen to support the work and agenda of the London Higher Education Consortium, the London Development Agency and the Greater London Authority's cultural strategy for London. This also engages with the work of the London Metropolitan Network and London Connects which is helping to drive forward the e-government agenda for the London Boroughs.

Other Activities and Mutual Support

The M25 Consortium is involved in a range of other activities including:

- A flourishing staff development and training group.
- A positive move towards promoting a student centred focus which builds on activities already in place to support staff and researchers.
- A scheme for mutual support in the event of a disaster occurring in a member library and advice on disaster preparedness. The scheme promotes the exchange of information and good practice, notably the award-winning web site.
- Ongoing work to review current practice and potential collaboration activities in member libraries in support of users with disabilities or special needs and to identify good practice at regional and national level.
- Active involvement by members in a wide range of projects funded by the Research Support Libraries Programme and BL Co-operation and Partnership Programme.

World Wide Web Consortium (W3C)

In 1989, Tim Berners-Lee invented the World Wide Web. He coined the term "World Wide Web," wrote the first World Wide Web server, "httpd," and the first client program (a browser and editor), "WorldWideWeb," in October 1990. He wrote the first version of the "HyperText Markup Language" (HTML), the document formatting language with the capability for hypertext links that became the primary publishing format for the Web. His initial specifications for URLs, HTTP, and HTML were refined and discussed in larger circles as Web technology spread.

A graduate of Oxford University, England, Tim Berners-Lee has served as Director of the World Wide Web Consortium (W3C) since its inception. In October 1994, Tim Berners-Lee founded the World Wide Web Consortium (W3C) at the Massachusetts Institute of Technology, Laboratory for Computer Science [MIT/LCS] in collaboration with CERN, where the Web originated with support from DARPA and the European Commission.

In April 1995, INRIA (Institute National de Recherche en Informatique et Automatique) became the first European W3C host, followed by Keio University of Japan (Shonan Fujisawa Campus) in Asia in 1996. In 2003, ERCIM (European Research Consortium in Informatics and Mathematics) took over the role of European W3C Host from INRIA. In December 2004, in Boston, Massachusetts (USA), and in June 2005, in Sophia-Antipolis, France, W3C celebrated its tenth anniversary with symposia about the history and future of the Web and W3C.

W3C primarily pursues its mission through the creation of Web standards and guidelines. Since 1994, W3C has published more than ninety such standards, called W3C Recommendations. W3C also engages in education and outreach, develops software, and serves as an open forum for discussion about the Web. In order for the Web to reach its full potential, the most fundamental Web technologies must be compatible with one another and allow any hardware and software used to access the Web to work together. W3C refers to this goal as "Web interoperability." By publishing open (non-proprietary) standards for Web languages and protocols, W3C seeks to avoid market fragmentation and thus Web fragmentation.

W3C is an International Consortium. Organizations located all over the world and involved in many different fields join W3C to participate in a vendor-neutral forum for the creation of Web standards. W3C Members and a dedicated full-time staff of technical experts have earned W3C international recognition for its contributions to the Web. W3C Members, staff, and Invited Experts work together to design technologies to ensure that the Web will continue to thrive in the future, accommodating the growing diversity of people, hardware, and software.

W3C's global initiatives also include nurturing liaisons with national, regional and international organizations around the globe. These contacts help W3C maintain a culture of global participation in the development of the World Wide Web. W3C coordinates particularly closely with other organizations that are developing standards for the Web or Internet in order to enable clear progress. The document *Worldwide Participation in the World Wide Web Consortium* summarizes W3C efforts in broading our international impact.

W3C operations are supported by a combination of member dues, research grants, and other sources of public and private funding. W3C operations are jointly administered by the MIT Computer Science and Artificial Intelligence Laboratory (CSAIL) in the USA, the European Research Consortium for Informatics and Mathematics (ERCIM) headquartered in France and Keio University in Japan. W3C also has World Offices in fifteen regions around the world. The W3C Offices work with their regional Web communities to promote W3C technologies in local languages, broaden W3C's geographical base, and encourage international participation in W3C Activities.

Goals

In pursuit of its mission, W3C has these long-term goals for creating one World Wide Web. Important ones are :

(i) Web for Everyone : The social value of the Web is that it enables human communication, commerce, and opportunities to share knowledge. One of W3C's primary goals is to make these benefits available to all people, whatever their hardware, software, network infrastructure, native language, culture, geographical location, or physical or mental ability.

W3C continues to expand its real investment in initiatives that directly support the expansion of Web technologies and their benefits into the developing world. Work in areas like Web accessibility, internationalization, device independence, and mobile Web are particularly important as we work toward a Web for Everyone. In addition, through W3C Offices and other efforts to broaden participation, W3C pledges to make the Web available to more people around the world. The document *Worldwide Participation in the World Wide Web Consortium* summarizes efforts to increase global participation in W3C work and ensure that W3C results provide benefit to an even larger community.

(ii) Web on Everything : The number of different kinds of devices that can access the Web has grown immensely. Mobile phones, smart phones, personal digital assistants, interactive television systems, voice response systems, kiosks and even certain domestic appliances can all access the Web. The goal of W3C's Mobile Web Initiative, launched in 2005, is to make Web access from any kind of device as simple, easy and convenient as Web access from a desktop.

(iii) Knowledge Base : The Web is not merely an immense book where people can search, browse, and view information. It is also a vast database that, if designed carefully, can allow computers to do more useful work. By developing a Web that holds information for both human and machine processing, W3C aims to enable people to solve problems that would otherwise be too tedious or complex to solve.

(iv) Trust and Confidence : Ultimately, for the Web to be a useful medium for social transactions, people must be able to trust other parties who have earned their trust. While technology cannot guarantee trust, it should enable secure transactions with trusted parties, be they people, organizations, or services. One of the long-term goals of W3C is thus to promote technologies that enable a more collaborative environment, a Web where accountability, security, confidence, and confidentiality are all possible, and where people participate according to their individual privacy requirements and preferences.

Membership

W3C announced some important changes to its Membership fee structure in early 2005:

- W3C lowered fees for non-profit and small commercial organizations based in developing countries on 1 April 2005.
- W3C also lowered fees for commercial organizations with intermediate level revenues (for example, in the United States, between $50 million and $200 million per year, or in Europe between 51 million Euros and 204 million Euros).

More information about W3C fees may be downloaded from its site.

To Become a W3C Member,

- Your organization has to complete a Membership Application.
- W3C reviews the Membership Application. If W3C approves your Application, you begin to enjoy the benefits of W3C Membership as soon as you would like.
- Your organization and the three W3C Hosts (MIT, ERCIM, and Keio University) sign a customized version of the standard W3C Member Agreement. Note that (Interim) Membership Benefits only begin once W3C has received signed Member Agreements from your organization.

If you have any questions about W3C Membership or the process for becoming a W3C Member, please consult one of its Membership contacts.

Before you start the Member Application process, it is recommended that you:

- Review the standard W3C Member Agreement. This is the legal contract that your organization and W3C will sign and is the basis of your W3C Membership fees, rights, and benefits.
- Review the pages about W3C Membership, especially the Membership FAQ.

The W3C Membership Application consists of a series of three electronic forms. Each time you submit a form, your changes are saved at W3C. This means that you do not have to complete the entire Application in one sitting.

***Step 1* : Provide initial contact information :** In Step 1, you:

- Provide your name and email address. During the application process, W3C will send all correspondence to this email address.
- Identify the name of your organization and the country of your organization's headquarters. W3C Membership fees and the currencies used to express those fees depend on the country you select. More information on how W3C computes Membership fees is available.
- Choose the start date for your Membership benefits. This date will be used to determine some information shown in Step 2, such as the Membership fee.

When you submit this form, W3C will send you an email with information about advancing to Step 2. Please save the email as it contains information you will use for the duration of the application process, in particular, a unique Web address (URI) for your Application.

***Step 2* : Provide additional information about your organization :** In Step 2, you provide additional information about your organization that W3C will use to prepare a customized version of the standard W3C Member Agreement.

***Step 3* : Request W3C review of Application :** In Step 3, review the information you have provided and agree to certain conditions in order to receive interim Member benefits.

At the top of the form for Step 3, you will find a link to a customized Member Agreement. Before you complete Step 3, it is recommended that you circulate it among the appropriate people in your organization, especially the person who will sign the contract.

Once you have completed step three:

- W3C will acknowledge, by email, receipt of your Application and will begin to review it. If any information is incorrect or incomplete, W3C will contact you.
- Your Application will become "read-only" to you. Any further changes will be made by W3C. Important changes will only be made after discussion with you.

W3C Review and Approval of Membership Application

W3C will notify you by email when your Membership Application has been approved or whether there are problems with the application. The approval notification will include:

- the Web address (URI) of the customized Member Agreement that resulted from your Membership Application.
- instructions for signing the customized Membership Agreement and returning it to W3C.
- an invoice for your first Membership fee payment, which will include instructions for payment by check or electronic wire.

Please allow 5 days for W3C to review your completed Membership Application. If, for any reason, W3C expects any delays in processing your application, requires additional information, or cannot approve your Membership Application, Consortium will contact you.

W3C Management reserves the right to review the eligibility of the Applicant for the organization type and fee level chosen in the Membership Application.

Signing the Membership Agreement

Once you have received notification from W3C that your Member Application has been approved, please print four copies of the customized Membership Agreement. Have your Contract Agent (named in Step 2 of the Membership Application) sign all four of them and return them to the address provided in the email approval of your application. One copy will be returned to you when it is fully executed by all three W3C Hosts.

Once W3C has received your signed Member Agreements, your Interim Membership Benefits will either start immediately, or at the beginning of the next quarter, according to what you requested in the Application.

Your Membership formally begins once all parties have signed the customized Member Agreement and W3C has received payment of the Membership fee. Your Interim Membership will be suspended after W3C Team review, if W3C does not receive payment of the first invoice within 45 days of the start of your Interim Membership Benefits.

Benefits

As a W3C Member, the most important measure of value in joining the Consortium can be found in the adoption of W3C specifications worldwide, and the growing dependence of global commerce and information exchange upon these specifications. W3C Members help pioneer this growth process. Levels of involvement can range from simply associating your organization with W3C endeavours, receiving early access of Member-confidential information, assisting with driving work efforts, generating new ideas, and/or developing future Web technologies.

W3C Members enjoy a number of specific Membership benefits including:

- The opportunity to interact and work directly with the leading companies and organizations in the Web world;
- A seat on the W3C Advisory Committee (AC), including an invitation to semi-annual Advisory Committee meetings;
- Right to create Incubator Groups, part of a lightweight process for rapidly developing, on a time scale of a year or less, new Web-related concepts;
- Right to submit proposals ("Member Submissions") to be considered for future Consortium work;
- The ability to provide strategic direction to the consortium through review of W3C Activity proposals and operational policies;
- Participation in W3C Working Groups, where specifications and guidelines are developed, and in W3C Interest Groups, where discussions are conducted;

- Participation in W3C Workshops, frequently the catalyst for new technical work within the Consortium;
- Sponsorship and marketing opportunities such as those for W3C10;
- Access to the Member Web site (Member-only link) containing early information on emerging Web technologies, software, events, forums, news and announcements;
- Access to Member-only mailing lists, hosting discussions on work underway in the Consortium;
- Access to the W3C news service. Updates on W3C activities, announcements for meetings, workshops and conferences, the calendar of events, and team information are sent directly via email to AC Representatives and posted on the Member site;
- The right to use the W3C Member logo on your Web site and to participate in press releases, often through testimonials.
- Discounts for W3C Member employees at select conferences.

Major W3C Achievements

Below are given some of W3C's most important achievements. Obviously, this type of list is subjective and does not represent every aspect of W3C work. For a complete view of W3C work, you may consult the list of W3C Activities and the index of W3C's technical reports.

October 1996 : First W3C Recommendation published in Portable Network Graphics (PNG) 1.0. In the mid-'90s, more industrial and academic users were discovering the Web and its graphics capabilities. W3C developed Portable Network Graphics (PNG) to provide a cross-platform alternative to the graphics formats most prevalent at that time, some of which had raised some patent licensing concerns.

December 1996 : Separating content from structure, CSS Level 1 is published. Cascading Style Sheets (CSS) is a simple mechanism for adding style (e.g. fonts, colors, spacing) to Web documents. CSS Level 2 (1998) included further and more sophisticated features.

February 1997 : Web Accessibility Initiative launched. W3C's Web Accessibility Initiative (WAI) guidelines for Web content, user agents, and authoring tools would become very popular among the Web community. WAI, in coordination with organizations around the world, pursues accessibility of the Web through four primary areas of work: technology, tools, education and outreach, and research and development.

December 1997 : HTML 4.0 adds tables, scripting, style sheets, internationalization, and accessibility features to Web publishing. Whereas HTML 3.2 had been published to capture the then current state of support for HTML on the Web, HTML 4.0 added new features to enable authors to create significantly richer Web content. These features included the ability to specify style sheets, create tables, and make pages more dynamic through scripting. HTML 4.0 also included important features to promote more internationalized content and content more accessible to some users with disabilities.

February 1998 ; XML 1.0 promotes interoperability and domain-specific markup. Soon to become the lingua franca of the Web, XML would serve as the basis for dozens of standards ranging from digital signatures (XML-Sig) and Web forms (XForms), to privacy technologies (P3P).

August 2000 : Scalable Vector Graphics (SVG) 1.0 enriches Web graphics. A language to describe two-dimensional graphics and graphical applications in XML, SVG will serve as the foundation for new-generation mobile applications.

May 2001 : XML Schema provides an essential piece for XML to reach its full potential. This important specification delivers on the true promise of XML by providing a standard way to create XML vocabularies that permit mixing and a way to build more versatile and powerful commercial applications.

January 2002 : W3C launches Web Services Activity. Subsuming the XML Protocol Activity and extending its scope, Web services provide a standard means of interoperating between different software applications, running on a variety of platforms and/or frameworks.

May 2003 : W3C adopts royalty-free Patent Policy. The W3C Patent Policy governs the handling of patents in the process of producing Web standards, and explicitly encourages the development of open standards.

February 2004 : RDF and OWL make a strong foundation for Semantic Web applications. RDF and OWL are Semantic Web standards that provide a framework for asset management, enterprise integration and the sharing and reuse of data on the Web. Respectively, they deliver structured descriptions and Web-based ontologies.

March 2004 : W3C gives voice to the Web with VoiceXML 2.0. Voice Interaction can escape the physical limitations of keypads and displays as mobile devices become even smaller. The goal of VoiceXML 2.0 is to bring the advantages of Web-based development and content delivery to interactive voice response applications.

December 2004 : W3C describes principles of Web architecture. W3C's Technical Architecture Group (TAG) publishes "Architecture of the World Wide: Web," a description of the principles that make the Web we know work, and work well. This condensed assessment of fifteen years of observations about the Web authored by many of those who designed the core Web standards is a valuable foundation on which to design future Web standards.

February 2005 : Character Model brings unified approach to using characters on the Web. W3C's Internationalization Core Working Group publishes "Character Model for the World Wide Web 1.0: Fundamentals" with a goal of making it easier for all people to use the World Wide Web, regardless of their language, script, writing system, and cultural conventions, in accordance with the W3C mission of universal access. Building on the Universal Character Set defined jointly by the Unicode Standard and ISO/IEC 10646; the Character Model provides authors of specifications, software developers, and content developers with a common reference for interoperable text manipulation on the World Wide Web.

Recently in May 2005, Mobile Web Initiative launched to facilitate mobile Web access. W3C launched the Mobile Web Initiative (MWI) with the mission of making Web access from a mobile device as simple as Web access from a desktop device. MWI sponsors and participants develop authoring guidelines, checklists and best practices, as well as a database of descriptions that can be used by content authors to adapt their content to the strengths and capabilities of a particular device.

Appendix-2
Important Subject Gateways

1. Academic Info (http://www.academicinfo.com)

Academic Info, online since 1998, began as an independent Internet subject directory owned by Michael Madin and maintained with the assistance of a quality group of subject specialists. In the spring of 2000 Michael left the University of Washington Gallagher Law Library to focus solely on Academic Info. In 2002 Academic Info became a registered non-profit organization of the State of Washington. Academic Info is now ad-free and relies on donations to remain online. Academic Info aims to be the premier educational gateway to online high school, college and research level Internet resources. The primary focus of the site is academic, with its intended audience at the upper high school level or above. A priority is adding digital collections from libraries, museums, and academic organizations and sites offering unique online content. The current focus is on English language resources but selectively sites in other languages will be considered. Users can search by subjects like The Arts, Biological Sciences, Business, Digital Library, Education, Engineering, Health & Medicine, History, Humanities, Law & Government, Library & Info Science, Religion, Sciences, and Social Sciences.

2. Argus Clearing House (http://www.clearing house.net/)

The Argus Clearing House is a guide to the meta resources. It provides a central access point for value-added topical guides that identify, describe, and evaluate Internet-based information resources. The Argus Clearinghouse is a non-profit venture run by a small group of dedicated individuals. It is intended to be a resource that brings together finding aids for students, researchers, educators, and others interested in locating authoritative information on the Internet.

3. BIOME (http://biome.ac.uk/)

BIOME is a collection of gateways, which provide access to evaluated, quality Internet resources in the health and life sciences, aimed at students, researchers, academics and practitioners. A core team of information specialists and subject experts based at the University of Nottingham Greenfield Medical Library creates BIOME. The Internet resources are selected for their quality and relevance to a particular target audience. They are then reviewed and resource descriptions created, which are stored, generally with the associated metadata, and generally in a structured database. The consequence of this effort is to improve the recall and especially the precision, of Internet searches for a particular group of users. BIOME is a hub within the Resource Discovery Network (RDN) (http://wvvw.rdn.ac.uk), and is funded by the Joint Information Systems Committee (JISC) (http://www.jisc.ac.uk/). There are five dedicated subject services (gateways) within BIOME, each covering a specific area within the health and life sciences. These gateways are AgriFor, VetGate, OMNI, Natural Selection and Bio Research.

4. BioMedNet (http://www.bmn.com/)

BioMedNet owned by Elsevier Science, is a part of the Reed Elsevier group of companies. BioMedNet is the Web site for biological medical researchers. There are more than 800 000 members of BioMedNet with more than 20,000 people joining per month. Membership to BioMedNet is free and members can search all of BioMedNet without charge. However, viewing full-text articles from publishers often requires payment or a subscription. The site has links to more than 3500 reviewed information resources. The resource provides online access to more than 15,000 review articles. HMS Beagle, the BioMedNet Magazine is issued every fortnight. This magazine can be subscribed by e-mail or can be accessed online.

5. BUBL (http://bubl.ac.uk/):

BUBL LINK is the catalogue of selected Internet resources covering all academic subject areas and catalogued according to Dewey Decimal Classification or DDC. All items are selected, evaluated, catalogued and described. Links are checked and fixed each month. LINK stands for Libraries of Networked Knowledge. BUBL 5:15 provides an alternative interface to this catalogue, based on subject terms rather than DDC. The aim is to guarantee at least 5 relevant resources for every subject included, and a maximum of 15 resources for most subjects, hence the name 5:15. Big subject areas are broken down into smaller categories. However, the upper limit of 15 is not rigidly applied, so there may be up to 35 items for some subjects. The subject terms used in BUBL LINK / 5:15 were originally based on LCSH or Library of Congress Subject Headings, but have been heavily customized and expanded to suit the content of the service. The aim is to make it very easy to locate Internet information about a large number of subjects. The BUBL LINK catalogue currently holds over 11,000 resources. This is far smaller than the databases held by major search engines, but it can provide a more effective route to information for many subjects, across all disciplines.

6. Digital Librarian (http://www.digitallibrarian.com/)

It is maintained by Margaret Vail Anderson, a librarian in Cortland, New York. Internet information resources are catalogued according to subject categories and format-types. Digital Librarian does not have a search interface for the resources catalogued on the site. It has a browsing interface and see and see also references to related resources.

7. Direct Search (http://gwis2.circ.gwu.edu/~gprice/direct.htm)

Direct Search is a growing compilation of links to the Internet resources that contain data not easily or entirely searchable / accessible from general search tools like Alta Vista, Google, or Hotbot. Direct Search has its own search interface.

8. Edinburgh Engineering Virtual Library (EEVL) (http://www.eevl.ac.uk/)

Edinburgh Engineering Virtual Library (EEVL) is an award-winning free service, which provides quick and reliable access to the best engineering, mathematics, and computing information available on the Internet. It is created and run by a team of information specialists from a number of universities and institutions in the UK for students, staff and researchers in higher and further education, as well as anyone else working, studying or looking for information in Engineering, Mathematics and Computing. EEVL provides a central access point to networked engineering, mathematics and computing information. Resources being added to the catalogues are selected, catalogued, classified and subject-indexed by experts to ensure that only current, high-quality and useful resources are included. They include e-journals, databases, training materials, professional societies, university and college departments, research projects, bibliographic databases, software, information services and recruitment agencies. EEVL, in addition to Internet Resource Catalogues, provides targeted engineering search engines - to UK engineering sites, to engineering e-journals and to engineering newsgroups, and to specialized information services, such as the Recent Advances in Manufacturing (RAM) bibliographic database, and the Offshore Engineering information Service. MathGate at EEVL is involved in the Secondary Homepages Project for UK Mathematics Departments. EEVL's scope is limited to the three subjects, and is therefore more focused than the big search engines. Searching EEVL will retrieve high quality resources, but because EEVL's resources are handpicked, the numbers of sources covered in it are not comparable to the Internet search engines.

9. Galaxy (http://galaxy.einet.net/)

Galaxy, originally a prototype associated with the DARPA-funded Manufacturing Automation and Design Engineering (MADE) program, is the oldest browsable / searchable web directory. It is a searchable Internet directory with a mission to provide contextually relevant information by integrating state-of-the-art technology with the human touch. Galaxy employs the best of technology and human expertise to organize information in a way that makes it both understandable and highly relevant to users' needs. The information contents of the meta resource is compiled and organized by human Internet Librarians rather than by computer. The Galaxy hierarchy is built utilizing a vertical structure, i.e. the information on particular topics is very deep in content. While other search technologies may yield millions of pages per search, which are mostly extraneous, Galaxy provides concentrated and relevant results.

10. Ingenta

Since its launch in May 1998, Ingenta has developed and grown to become the leading Web infomediary empowering the exchange of academy and professional content online. Ingenta provides publishers of academic and professional content will technology-driven solutions for leveraging the Web as a profitable distribution and marketing channel. Ingenta provides libraries and researchers with access to the most comprehensive collection of academic and professional content available online. More than 8,000 academic, research and corporate libraries, institutions and consortia, from around the world, currently rely on Ingenta for managed access to academic and professional content.

The acquisition of Catchword helped Ingenta to give publishers access to the most comprehensive set of online publishing solutions available in the market.

11. Internet Public Library (http://www.ipl.org/)

Internet Public Library is a product of the University of Michigan's School of Information and Library Studies. It includes extensive directories of online texts, newspapers, magazines and reference materials; plus an exhibit hall and other special sections. At the moment, the home page features links to 4,699 critical and biographical sites dedicated to authors and their works, and an online history of the Harlem Renaissance in New York between 1900 and 1940.

12. Librarians' Index to the Internet (http://lii.org/)

The Librarians' Index to the Internet (LII) consists of more than 8,600 internet resources selected and evaluated by librarians for their usefulness to users of public libraries. Free e-mail subscription to the Lll. News This Week (http://www.lii.org/search/ntw) incorporates most recent resources added to the Lll. It has close to 12,000 subscribers in 85 countries. ILL also offers co-branding service to the libraries that are members of the Library of California. The site provides both browsing and searching interfaces.

13. LibrarySpot.com (http://www.libraryspot. com/)

LibrarySpot is a free virtual library resource centre for educators and students, librarians and their patrons, families, businesses and just about anyone exploring the Web for valuable research information. LibrarySpot.com aims at breaking through the information overload of the web and bring the best library and reference sites together. Sites featured on LibrarySpot.com are hand-selected and reviewed by an editorial team for their exceptional quality, content and utility, published by StartSpot Mediaworks, Inc. in the Northwestern University / Evanston Research Park. LibrarySpot is the first in a family of vertical information portals designed to make finding the best topical information on the Internet a quick, easy and enjoyable experience. The LibrarySpot.com has received more than 30 awards and honours. Recently, Forbes.com selected LibrarySpot.com as a "Forbes Favourite" site, the best in the reference category, and PC Magazine named it one of the Top 100 Web Sites. LibrarySpot.com has been featured on CNN, Good Morning America, CNBC and in many other media outlets.

14. LivingInternet.com (http://www.livinginternet.com/)

The mission of this web site is to make comprehensive, in-depth information about the Internet available around the world. The site was developed from 1996 through 1999, posted on January 7, 2000, and is , updated weekly. The site is equivalent to a book of more than 600 pages, with more than 2,000 intra-site links and 2,000 external links woven into the text, making it the first Internet publication of a reference work fully integrated with the web on this scale. Google ranks the site number one in the Internet courses category, and Yahoo lists it as one of the top three sites on Internet history.

15. QUEST.net (http://www.re-quest.net)

QUEST.net is a free online library offering substantive, fully annotated, links to valuable resources in both a unique frame version and a non-framed version. This web site serves to help students and professionals to locate day-to-day and much needed information and resources in a relatively quick and concise manner. It serves as a one-stop resource directory, providing the Internet community with thousands upon thousands of links, which it's committee of web surfers, have found to be the most useful, informative and productive. The meta resource provides fully annotated description of each link together with its URL allowing visitors to know what to expect from the Web site. Each link has been specially hand picked to provide with the best and most relevant links in each category. This web site is useful in an extraordinary way with it's devoted committee of web surfers work diligently, day-after-day, sorting through the vast galaxies of cyberspace to bring the best and most current resources available.

16. Social Science Information Gateway (SOSIG) (http://sosig.ac.uk/)

The Social Science Information Gateway (SOSIG) is a freely available Internet service which aims to provide a trusted source of selected, high quality Internet information for students, academics, researchers and practitioners in the social sciences, business and law. It is part of the UK Resource Discovery Network. The SOSIG Internet Catalogue is an online database of high quality Internet resources, which offers users the chance to read descriptions of resources available over the Internet and to access those resources directly. The Catalogue points to thousands of resources and each one has been selected and described by a librarian or academician. The catalogue is browsable or searchable by subject area. Social Science Search Engine is a database of over 50,000 Social Science Web pages. Whereas subject experts have selected the resources found in the SOSIG Internet Catalogue, those in the Social Science Search Engine have been collected by software called a 'harvester'.

17. The Scout Report (http://scout.cs.wisc.edu/report/sr/current/)

The Scout Report is the flagship publication of the Internet Scout Project. Published every Friday both on the web and by e-mail, it provides a fast, convenient way to stay informed of valuable resources on the Internet. A team of professional librarians and subject matter experts select, research, and annotate each resource. It is being published continuously since 1994, and it is one of the Internet's oldest and most respected publications. The Internet Scout Project is located in the Department of Computer Sciences at the University of Wisconsin-Madison, and is funded by a grant from the National Science Foundation.

18. The Virtual Library (http://www.vlib.org/)

The Virtual Library is the oldest catalogue of the web, started by Tim Berners-Lee, the creator of html and the Web itself. Unlike commercial catalogues, it is run by a loose confederation of volunteers, who compile pages of key links for particular areas in which they are expert; even though it is not the biggest index of the Web. The Virtual Library pages are widely recognized as being amongst the highest-quality guides to particular sections of the Web. Individual indexes live on hundreds of different servers around the world. A set of catalogue pages linking these pages is maintained at http://vlib.org. Mirrors of the catalogue are kept at East Anglia (UK), Geneva (Switzerland) and Argentina. Each maintainer is responsible for the content of their own pages, as long as they follow certain guidelines. The central affairs of the Virtual Library are now coordinated by a newly-elected Council.

Appendix-3
Model Interlibrary Loan Code for Regional, State, Local, or Other Special Groups of Libraries

(Endorsed by Reference and Adult Services Division Board of Directors, New York, June 1980)

Preface

The "Model Interlibrary Loan Code for Regional, State, Local or Other Special Groups of Libraries" is intended to provide guidelines for any group of libraries interested in developing an interlibrary loan code to meet special needs. The Model Code, while complementing the "National Interlibrary Loan Code, 1980," allows libraries more flexibility and creativity in satisfying interlibrary loan needs in a specific situation.

The Model Code is designed to provide a framework for cooperation. Since it is recognized that most networks and consortia can be more liberal in loaning materials, the Model Code has fewer restrictions than the National Code. All libraries in a network or consortium should participate in developing an interlibrary loan code. Each section of the code should be discussed and should be expanded or modified, if necessary, for local use. The bracketed sections of the Model Code indicate specific areas where local information may be

---

Source : Available from the American Library Association and printed in Boucher, Virginia Interlibrary Loan Practices Handbook, American Library Association, Chicago, IL, 1984, Appendix, pages 136-138

necessary. Libraries are encouraged to put as few restrictions as possible on the exchange of materials.

The use of interlibrary loan service is becoming increasingly important to libraries committed to providing a high level of service to their clientele. In *A Commitment to Information Services: Developmental Guidelines,* 1979, the Reference and Adult Services Division emphasizes the importance of considering "the needs and interests of all users, including children, young adults, adults ...". Interlibrary loan is a service that should be publicized and provided to all members of the library's clientele.

A strong interlibrary loan network within a local, state, or regional jurisdiction should be the primary source of interlibrary loan materials for all libraries. Only after all of these resources have been exhausted should a library request material outside of these arrangements. In making outside requests, the "National Interlibrary Loan Code, 1980" and the Interlibrary Loan Procedure Manual should be followed. This approach will distribute the burden of requests more equitably and provide better service for all libraries.

Model Interlibrary Loan Code for Regional, State, Local, or Other Special Groups of Libraries

This code is a voluntary agreement adopted by [system, consortium, network, etc.] on_____________________________ [date] to govern interlibrary lending among libraries _______ [metropolitan area, region, state, system, network, consortium, etc.].

Introduction

Interlibrary loan service is essential to the vitality of libraries of all types and sizes as a means of greatly expanding the range of materials available to users. Lending between libraries is in the public interest and should be encouraged. This code is intended to make interlibrary loan policies among those libraries adopting it as liberal and as easy to apply as possible. Interlibrary loan should serve as an adjunct to, not a substitute for collection development. When resources within the region have been exhausted, loan requests to more distant libraries would then conform to the provisions of the "National Interlibrary Loan Code, 1980."

I. Definition

An interlibrary loan is a transaction in which library material or a copy of the material, is made available by one library to another upon request.

II. Purpose

The purpose of interlibrary loan as defined in this code is to obtain library material not available in the local library.

III. Scope

Under the terms of this agreement, it is permissible to request on interlibrary loan any type of library material [except........].

IV. Responsibilities of Borrowing Libraries

A. Each library should provide the resources to meet the ordinary needs and interests of its primary clientele. Material requested from another library under this code should generally be limited to those items that do not conform to the library's collection development policy or for which there is no recurring demand.

B. Borrowing libraries should make every effort to exhaust their own resources before resorting to interlibrary loan.

C. The interlibrary loan staff of each library should be familiar with, and use, relevant interlibrary loan documents and aids including ________________________________. [List here pertinent interlibrary loan codes, interlibrary loan procedure manuals, and bibliographic tools and services].

D. Each library should inform its users of the purpose of interlibrary loan and of the library's interlibrary borrowing policy. Any member of the borrowing library's clientele should be eligible for interlibrary loan.

E. The borrowing library is responsible for compliance with the copyright law (Title 17, U.S. Code) and its accompanying guidelines, and should inform its users of the applicable portions of the law. An indication of compliance must be provided with all copy requests.

F. Requested material must be described as completely and accurately as possible following accepted bibliographic practice. If an item cannot be verified, the statement "cannot verify" should be included along with information about the original source of citation. [Variations in accepted bibliographic practice may be referred to here].

G. Requests should be routed through channels established by libraries participating in this agreement. These channels are outlined in ______________________. [List here specific documents outlining agreed-upon channels].

H. Standard interlibrary loan formats should be used for all requests, regardless of the means of transmissions. [Variations from standard interlibrary loan formats may be referred to here].

I. The safety of borrowed materials is the responsibility of the borrowing library from the time the material leaves the lending library until it is received by the lending library. The borrowing library is responsible for packaging the material so as to ensure its return in good condition. If damage or loss occurs, the borrowing library must meet all costs of repair or replacement, in accordance with the preferences of the lending library.

J. The borrowing library and its users must comply with the conditions of loan established by the lending library. Unless specifically forbidden by the lending library, copying by the borrowing library is permitted provided that it is in accordance with the copyright law and no damage to the original volume will result.

K. The borrowing library should encourage library users to travel to other libraries for onsite access to material when extensive use of a collection is required or the nature of the material requires special handling. The borrowing library should assist the user in making the necessary arrangements.

V. Responsibilities of Lending Libraries

A. The decision to loan material is at the discretion of the lending library. Each library is encouraged, however, to interpret as generously as possible its own lending policy with due consideration to the interests of its primary clientele.

B. A statement of interlibrary loan policy should be made available upon request and should be on file in the state library [or other appropriate agency].

C. The lending library should process requests promptly. [A specific number of days for processing may be inserted here].

D. A lending library is responsible for informing any borrowing library of its apparent failure to follow the provisions of this code.

VI. Expenses

A. The borrowing library should be prepared to assume any costs charged by the lending library and should attempt to anticipate charges and authorize them on the initial request. [List here any documents referring to charging policies]

B. If the charges are more than nominal and not authorized by the borrowing library, the lending library should inform the requesting library and ask for authorization to proceed.

VII. Duration of Loan

A. The duration of loan, unless otherwise specified by the lending library, is the period of time the item may remain with the borrowing library disregarding the time spent in transit.

B. Interlibrary loan material should be returned promptly.

C. A renewal request should be sent in time to reach the lending library not later than the due date. If the lending library does not respond, it will be assumed that renewal, for the same period as the original loan, is granted.

D. All material on loan is subject to immediate recall, and the borrowing library should comply promptly.

VIII. Violation of Code

Each library is responsible for maintaining the provisions of this code in good faith.

Appendix-4
Policy on Confidentiality of Library Records

The American Library Association strongly recommends that the responsible officers of each library, cooperative system, and consortium in the United States:

1. Formally adopt a policy which specifically recognizes its circulation records and other records identifying the names of library users with specific materials to be confidential.
2. Advise all librarians and library employees that such records shall not be made available to any agency of state, federal, or local government except pursuant to such process, order, or subpoena as may be authorized under the authority of, and pursuant to, federal, state, or local law relating to civil, criminal, or administrative discovery procedures or legislative investigatory power.
3. Resist the issuance or enforcement of any such process, order, or subpoena until such time as a proper showing of good cause has been made in a court of competent jurisdiction.

Source: *Handbook of Organization* 1990/91, American Library Association, Chicago, IL, 1990, page 256.

Appendix-5
Model Policy Concerning College and University Photocopying for Classroom, Research and Library Reserve Use

This model policy, another in a series of copyright advisory documents developed by the American Library Association (ALA), is intended for the guidance and use of academic librarians, faculty, administrators, and legal counsel in response to implementation of the rights and responsibilities provisions of Public Law 94-553, General Revision of the Copyright Law, which took effect on January 1, 1978.

Prepared by ALA Legal Counsel Mary Hutchings of the law firm Sidley & Austin, with advise and assistance from the Copyright Subcommittee (ad hoc) of ALA's Legislation Committee, Association of College and Research Libraries (ACRL) Copyright Committee, Association of Research Libraries (ARL) and other academic librarians and copyright attorneys, the model policy outlines "fair use" rights in the academic environment for classroom teaching, research activities and library services. Please note that it does not address other library photocopying which may be permitted under other sections of the Copyright Law, e.g., SS108 (Reproduction by Libraries and Archives).

Too often, members of the academic community have been reluctant or hesitant to exercise their rights of fair use under the law for fear of courting an infringement suit. It is important to understand that

---

Source: American Library Association, Washington Office, Washington, DC, March 1982. ISBN: 0-9389-5624.

in U.S. law, copyright is a limited statutory monopoly and the public's right to use materials must be protected. Safeguards have been written into the legislative history accompanying the new copyright law protecting librarians, teachers, researchers and scholars and guaranteeing their rights of access to information as they carry out their responsibilities for educating or conducting research. It is, therefore, important to heed the advice of a former U.S. Register of Copyrights: "If you don't use fair use, you will lose it!"

I. The Copyright Act and Photocopying

From time to time, the faculty and staff of this University [College] may use photocopied materials to supplement research and teaching. In many cases, photocopying can facilitate the University's [College's] mission; that is, the development and transmission of information. However, the photocopying of copyrighted materials is a right granted under the copyright law's doctrine of "fair use" which must not be abused. This report will explain the University's [College's) policy concerning the photocopying of copyrighted materials by faculty and library staff. Please note that this policy does not address other library photocopying which may be permitted under sections of the copyright law, e.g., 17 U.S.C. SS108.

Copyright is a constitutionally conceived property right which is designed to promote the progress of science and the useful arts by securing for an author the benefits of his or her original work of authorship for a limited time. U.S. Constitution, Art. I, Sec 8. The Copyright statute, 17 U.S.C. SS101 et seq., implements this policy by balancing the author's interest against the public interest in the dissemination of information affecting areas of universal concern, such as art, science, history and business. The grand design of this delicate balance is to foster the creation and dissemination of intellectual works for the general public.

The Copyright Act defines the rights of a copyright holder and how they may be enforced against an infringer. Included within the Copyright Act is the "fair use" doctrine which allows, under certain conditions, the copying of copyrighted material. While the Act lists general factors under the heading of "fair use" it provides little in the way of specific directions for what constitutes fair use. The law states:

17 U.S.C. SS107, Limitations on exclusive rights Fair use

notwithstanding the provisions of section 106, the fair use of a copyrighted work, including such use by reproduction in copies or phonorecords or by any other means specified by that section, for purposes such as criticism, comment, news reporting, teaching (including multiple copies for classroom use), scholarship, or research, is not an infringement of copyright. In determining whether the use made of a work in any particular case is a fair use the factors to be considered shall include —

(1) the purpose and character of the use, including whether such use is of a commercial nature or is for nonprofit educational purposes;

(2) the nature of copyrighted work;

(3) the amount and substantiality of the portion used in relation to the copyrighted work as a whole; and

(4) the effect of the use upon the potential market for or value of the copyrighted work.

The purpose of this report is to provide you, the faculty and staff of this University [College), with an explanation of when the photocopying of copyrighted material in our opinion is permitted under the fair use doctrine. Where possible, common examples of research, classroom, and library reserve photocopying have been included to illustrate what we believe to be the reach and limits of fair use.

Please note that the copyright law applies to all forms of photocopying, whether it is undertaken at a commercial copying center, at the University's [College's] central or departmental copying facilities or at a self-service machine. While you are free to use the services of a commercial establishment, you should be prepared to provide documentation of permission from the publisher (if such permission is necessary under this policy), since many commercial copiers will require such proof.

We hope this report will give you an appreciation of the factors which weigh in favor of fair use and those factors which weigh against fair use, but faculty members must determine for themselves which works will be photocopied. This University [College] does not condone a policy of photocopying instead of purchasing copyrighted works where such photocopying would constitute an infringement under the Copyright law, but it does encourage faculty members to exercise good judgment in serving the best interests of students in an efficient manner.

Instructions for securing permission to photocopy copyrighted works when such copying is beyond the limits of fair use appear at the end of this report. It is the policy of this University that the user (faculty, staff or librarian) secure such permission whenever it is legally necessary.

II. Unrestricted Photocopying

A. Uncopyrighted Published Works

Writing published before January 1, 1978 which have never been copyrighted may be photocopied without restriction. Copies of works protected by copyright must bear a copyright notice, which consists of the letter "c" in a circle, or the work "Copyright", or the abbreviation "Copr.", plus the year of first publication, plus the name of the copyright owner, 17 U.S.C. SS401. As to works published before January 1, 1978, in the case of a book, the notice must be placed on the title page or the reverse side of the title page. In the case of a periodical the notice must be placed either on the title page, the first page of text, or in the masthead. A pre-1978 failure to comply with the notice requirements results in the work being injected into the public domain, i.e., unprotected. Copyright notice requirements have been relaxed since 1978, so that the absence of notice on copies of a work published after January 1, 1978 does not necessarily mean the work in the public domain, 17 U.S.C. SS405 (a) and (c). However, you will not be liable for damages for copyright infringement of works published after that date, if, after normal inspection, you photocopy a work on which you cannot find a copyright symbol and you have not received actual notice of the- fact the work is copyrighted, 17 U.S.C. SS405(b). However, a copyright owner who found out about your photocopying would have the right to prevent further distribution of the copies if in fact the work were copyrighted and the copies are infringing. 17 U.S.C. SS405(b).

B. Published Works with Expired Copyrights

Writings with expired copyrights may be photocopied without restriction. All copyrights prior to 1906 have expired, 17 U.S.C. SS304(b). Copyrights granted after 1906 may have been renewed; however the writing will probably not contain notice of the renewal. Therefore, it should be assumed all writings dated 1906 or later are covered by a valid copyright, unless information to the contrary is obtained from the owner or the U.S. Copyright Office (see Copyright Office Circular 15t).

Copyright Office Circular R22 explains how to investigate the copyright status of a work. One way is to use the Catalog of Copyright Entries published by the Copyright Office and available in [the University Library] many libraries. Alternatively you may request the Copyright Office to conduct a search of its registration and/or assignment records. The Office charges an hourly fee for this service. You will need to submit as much information as you have concerning the work in which you are interested, such as the title, author, approximate date of publication, the type of work or any available copyright data. The Copyright Office does caution that its searches are not conclusive; for instance, if a work obtained copyright less than 28 years ago, it may be fully protected although there has been no registration or deposit.

C. Unpublished Works

Unpublished works, such as theses and dissertations, may be protected by copyright. If such a work was created before January I, 1978 and has not been copyrighted or published without copyright notice, the work is protected under the new Act for the life of the author plus fifty years, 17 U.S.C. SS303, but in no case earlier than December 31, 2002. If such a work is published on or before that date, the copyright will not expire before December 31, 2027. Works created after January 1, 1978 and not published enjoy copyright protection for the life of the author plus fifty years, 17 U.S.C. SS302.

D. U.S. Government Publications

All U.S. Government publications with the possible exception of some National Technical Information Service Publications less than five years old may be photocopied without restrictions, except to the extent they contain copyrighted materials from other sources, 17 U.S.C. SS105. U.S. Government publications are documents prepared by an official or employee of the government in an official capacity, 17 U.S.C. SS101. Government publications include the opinions of courts in legal cases, Congressional Reports on proposed bills, testimony offered at Congressional hearings and the works of government employees in their official capacities. Works prepared by outside authors on contract to the government may or may not be protected by copyright, depending on the specifics of the contract. In the absence of copyright notice on such works, it would be reasonable to assume they are government works in the public domain. It should be noted that state government works may be protected by copyright. See, 17 U.S.C. SS105. However, the opinions of state courts are not protected.

III. Permissible Photocopying of Copyrighted Works

The Copyright Act allows anyone to photocopy copyrighted works without securing permission from the copyright owner when the photocopying amounts to a "fair use" of the material, 17 U.S.C. SS107. The guidelines in this report discuss the boundaries for fair use of photocopied material used in research or the classroom or in a library reserve operation. Fair use cannot always be expressed in numbers — either the number of pages copied or the number of copies distributed. Therefore, you should weigh the various factors listed in the Act and judge whether the intended use of photocopied, copyrighted material is within the spirit of the fair use doctrine. Any serious questions concerning whether a particular photocopying constitutes fair use should be directed to University [College] counsel.

A. Research Uses

At the very least, instructors may make a single copy of any of the following for scholarly research or use in teaching or preparing to teach a class:

1. a chapter from a book;
2. an article from a periodical or newspaper;
3. a short story, short essay, or short poem, whether or not from a collective work;
4. a chart, diagram, graph, drawing, cartoon or picture from a book, periodical, or newspaper.

These examples reflect the most conservative guidelines for fair use. They do not represent inviolate ceilings for the amount of copyrighted material which can be photocopied within the boundaries of fair use. When exceeding these minimum levels, however, you again should consider the four factors listed in Section 107 of the Copyright Act to make sure that any additional photocopying is justified. The following demonstrate situations where increased levels of photocopying would continue to remain within the ambit of fair use:

1. the inability to obtain another copy of the work because it is not available from another library or source cannot be obtained within your time constraints;
2. the intention to photocopy the material only once and not to distribute the material to others;
3. the ability to keep the amount of material photocopied within a reasonable proportion to the entire work (the larger the work, the greater amount of material which may be photocopied).

Most single-copy photocopying for your personal use in research— even when it involves a substantial portion of a work— may well constitute fair use.

B. Classroom Uses

Primary and secondary school educators have, with publishers, developed the following guidelines, which allow a teacher to distribute photocopied material to students in a class without the publisher's prior permission, under the following conditions:

1. the distribution of the same photocopied material does not occur every semester;
2. only one copy is distributed for each student which copy must become the student's property;
3. the material includes a copyright notice on the first page of the portion of material photocopied;
4. the students are not assessed any fee beyond the actual cost of the photocopying.

In addition, the educators agreed that the amount of material distributed should not exceed certain brevity standards. Under those guidelines, a prose work may be reproduced in its entirety if it is less than 2500 words in length. If the work exceeds such length, the excerpt reproduced may not exceed 1000 words, or 10% of the work, whichever is less. In the case of poetry, 250 words is the maximum permitted. These minimum standards normally would not be realistic in the University setting. Faculty members needing to exceed these limits for college education should not feel hampered by these guidelines, although they should attempt a "selective and sparing" use of photocopied, copyrighted material.

The photocopying practices of an instructor should not have a significant detrimental impact on the market for the copyrighted work, 17 U.S.C. SS 107(4). To guard against this effect, you usually should restrict use of an item of photocopied material to one course and you should not repeatedly photocopy excerpts from one periodical or author without the permission of the copyright owner.

C. Library Reserve Uses

At the request of a faculty member, a library may photocopy and place on reserve excerpts from copyrighted works in its collection in accordance with guidelines similar to those governing formal classroom distribution for face-to-face teaching discussed above. This University [College] believes that these guidelines apply to the library reserve shelf to the extent it functions as an extension of classroom readings or reflects an individual student's right to photocopy for his personal scholastic use under the doctrine of fair use. In general, librarians may photocopy materials for reserve room use for the convenience of students both in preparing class assignments and in pursuing informal educational activities which higher education requires, such as advanced independent study and research.

If the request calls for only one copy to be placed on reserve, the library may photocopy an entire article, or an entire chapter from a book, or an entire poem. Requests for multiple copies on reserve should meet the following guidelines:

1. the amount of material should be reasonable in relation to the total amount of material assigned for one term of a course taking into account the nature of the course, its subject matter and level, 17 U.S.C. SS107(l) and (3);
2. the number of copies should be reasonable in light of the number of students enrolled, the difficulty and timing of assignments, and the number of other courses which may assign the same material, 17U.S.C.SS107(l) and (3);
3. the material should contain a notice of copyright, see 17 U.S.C. SS401;
4. the effect of photocopying the material should not be detrimental to the market for the work. (In general, the library should own at least one copy of the work), 17 U.S.C. SS107 (4).

For example, a professor may place on reserve as a supplement to the course textbook a reasonable number of copies of articles from academic journals or chapters from trade books. A reasonable number of copies will in most instances be less than six, but factors such as the length or difficulty of the assignment, the number of enrolled students and the length of time allowed for completion of the assignment may permit more in unusual circumstances.

In addition, a faculty member may also request that multiple copies of photocopied, copyrighted material be placed on the reserve shelf if there is insufficient time to obtain permission from the copyright owner. For example, a professor may place on reserve several photocopies of an entire article from a recent issue of *Time* magazine or the *The New York Times* in lieu of distributing a copy to each member of the class. If you are in doubt as to whether a particular instance of photocopying is fair use in the reserve reading room, you should waive any fee for such a use.

D. Uses of Photocopied Material Requiring Permission

1. *Repetitive copying* : The classroom or reserve use of photocopied materials in multiple courses or successive years will normally require advance permission from the owner of the copyright, 17 U.S.C. SS107(3).
2. *Copying for profit* : Faculty should not charge students more than the actual cost of photocopying the material, 17 U.S.C. SS107(1)
3. *Consumable works* : The duplication of works that are consumed in the classroom, such as standardized tests, exercises, and workbooks, normally requires permission from the copyright owner, 17 U.S.C. SS 107(4).
4. *Creation of anthologies as basic text material for a course*: Creation of a collective work or anthology by photocopying a number of copyrighted articles and excerpts to be purchased and used together as the basic text for a course will in most instances require the permission of the copyrighted owners. Such photocopying of a book and thus less likely to be deemed fair use, 17 U.S.C. SS 107(4).

E. How to Obtain Permission

When a use of photocopied material requires that you request permission, you should communicate complete and accurate information to the copyright owner. The American Association of Publishers suggests that the following information be included in a permission request letter in order to expedite the process:

1. Title, author and/or editor, and edition of materials to be duplicated.
2. Exact material to be used, giving amount, page numbers, chapters and, if possible, a photocopy of the material.
3. Number of copies to be made.
4. Use to be made of duplicated materials.
5. Form of distribution (classroom, newsletter, etc.).
6. Whether or not the material is to be sold.
7. Type of reprint (ditto, photography, offset, typeset).

The request should be sent, together with a self-addressed return envelope to the permissions department of the publisher in question. If the address of the publisher does not appear at the front of the material, it may be readily obtained in a publication entitled *The Literary Marketplace,* published by the R. R. Bowker Company and available in all libraries.

The process of granting permission requires time for the publisher to check the status of the copyright and to evaluate the nature of the request. It is advisable, therefore, to allow enough lead time to obtain permission before the materials are needed. In some instances, the publisher may assess a fee for the permission. It is not inappropriate to pass this fee on to the student who receives copies of the photocopied material.

The Copyright Clearance Center also has the right to grant permission and collect fees for photocopying rights for certain publications. Libraries may copy from any journal which is registered with the CCC and report the copying beyond fair use to CCC and pay the set fee. A list of publications for which the CCC handles fees and permissions is available from CCC, 310 Madison Avenue, New York, N.Y. 10017.

Sample Letter To Copyright Owner (Publisher)

Requesting Permission To Copy:

March 1, 1982

Material Permissions Department

Hypothetical Book Company

500 East Avenue Chicago, IL 60601

Dear Sir or Madam:

I would like permission to copy the following for continued use in my classes in future semesters:

Title	:	Learning is Good. Second Edition
Copyright	:	Hypothetical Book Co., 1965,1971
Author	:	Frank Jones
Material to be duplicated	:	Chapters 10, 11 and 14 (photocopy enclosed).
Number of copies	:	500
Distribution	:	The material will be distributed to students in my classes and they will pay only the cost of the photocopying.
Type of reprint	:	Photocopy
Use	:	The chapter will be used as supplementary teaching materials.

I have enclosed a self-addressed envelope for your convenience in replying to this request.

Sincerely,

Faculty Member

F. Infringement

Courts and legal scholars alike have commented that the fair use provisions in the Copyright Act are among the most vague and difficult that can be found anywhere in the law. In amending the Copyright Act in 1976, Congress anticipated the problem this would pose for users of copyrighted materials who wished to stay under the umbrella of protection offered by fair use. For this reason, the Copyright Act contains specific provisions which grant additional rights to libraries and insulate employees of a non-profit educational institution, library, or archives from statutory damages for infringement where the infringer believed or had reasonable ground to believe the photocopying was a fair use of the material, 17 U.S.C. SS504(c)(2).

Normally, an infringer is liable to the copyright owner for the actual losses sustained because of the photocopying and any additional profits of the infringer, 17 U.S.C. SS504 (a) (I) and (b). Where the monetary losses are nominal, the copyright owner usually will claim statutory damages instead of the actual losses, 17 U.S.C. SS504(a)(2) and (c). The statutory damages may reach as high as $ 10,000 (or up to $50,000 if the infringement is willful). In addition to suing for money damages, a copyright owner can usually prevent future infringement through a court injunction, 17 U.S.C. SS502.

The Copyright Act specifically exempts from statutory damages any employee of a non-profit educational institution, library, or archives, who "believed and had reasonable grounds for believing that his or her use of the copyrighted work was a fair use under Section 107," 17 U.S.C. SS504(c)(2). While the fair use provisions are admittedly ambiguous, any employee who attempts to stay within the guidelines contained in this report should have an adequate good faith defense in the case of an innocently committed infringement.

If the criteria contained in this report are followed, it is our view that no copyright infringement will occur and that there will be no adverse affect on the market for copyrighted works. (Many educational institutions will provide their employees legal counsel without charge if an infringement suit is brought against the employee for photocopying performed in the course of employment. If so, this should be noted here).

Appendix-6
IT Act 2000

Ministry of Law, Justice and Company Affairs (Legislative Department)
New Delhi, the 9th June, 2000/Jyaistha 19, 1922 (Saka)

The following Act of Parliament received the assent of the President on the 9th June, 2000, and is hereby published for general information:—

The Information Technology Act, 2000
(No. 21 of 2000)

[*9th June, 2000*]

An Act to provide legal recognition for transactions carried out by means of electronic data interchange and other means of electronic communication, commonly referred to as "electronic commerce", which involve the use of alternatives to paper-based methods of communication and storage of information, to facilitate electronic filing of documents with the Government agencies and further to amend the Indian Penal Code, the Indian Evidence Act, 1872, the Bankers' Books Evidence Act, 1891 and the Reserve Bank of India Act, 1934 and for matters connected therewith or incidental thereto.

WHEREAS the General Assembly of the United Nations by resolution A/RES/51/162, dated the 30th January, 1997 has adopted the Model Law on Electronic Commerce adopted by the United Nations Commission on International Trade Law;

AND WHEREAS the said resolution recommends *inter alia* that all States give favourable consideration to the said Model Law when they enact or revise their laws, in view of the need for uniformity of the law applicable to alternatives to paper-cased methods of communication and storage of information;

Source : www.naavi.org/importantlaws/itbill2000

AND WHEREAS it is considered necessary to give effect to the said resolution and to promote efficient delivery of Government services by means of reliable electronic records.

BE it enacted by Parliament in the Fifty-first Year of the Republic of India as follows:—

Section No. I. Preliminary

1. Short Title, Extent, Commencement and Application

(1) This Act may be called the Information Technology Act, 2000.

(2) It shall extend to the whole of India and, save as otherwise provided in this Act-it applies also to any offence or contravention thereunder committed outside India by any person.

(3) It shall come into force on such date as the Central Government may by-notification, appoint and different dates may be appointed for different provisions of this Act and any reference in any such provision to the commencement of this Act shall be construed as a reference to the commencement of that provision.

(4) Nothing in this Act shall apply to,

(a) a "Negotiable Instrument" (Other than a Cheque)* as defined in section 13 of the Negotiable Instruments Act, 1881; (* amended vide Negotiable Instruments Amendment Act 2002, Date of effect to be notified);

(b) a "Power-of-Attorney" as defined in section 1 A of the Powers-of-Attorney Act, 1882;

(c) a "Trust" as defined in section 3 of the Indian Trusts Act, 1882;

(d) a "Will" as defined in clause (h) of section 2 of the Indian Succession Act, 1925 including any other testamentary disposition by whatever name called;

(e) any "Contract for the Sale "or "Conveyance "of Immovable property or any interest in such property;

(f) any such class of documents or transactions as may be notified by the Central Government in the Official Gazette.

2. Definitions

(1) In this Act, unless the context otherwise requires,

(a) "Access" with its grammatical variations and cognate expressions means gaining entry into, instructing or communicating with the logical, arithmetical, or memory function resources of a computer, computer system or computer network;

(b) "Addressee" means a person who is intended by the originator to receive the electronic record but does not include any intermediary;

(c) "Adjudicating Officer" means adjudicating officer appointed under subsection (1) of section 46;

(d) "Affixing Digital Signature" with its grammatical variations and cognate expressions means adoption of any methodology or procedure by a person for the purpose of authenticating an electronic record by means of digital signature:

(e) "Appropriate Government" means as respects any matter.

(i) enumerated in List II of the Seventh Schedule to the Constitution;

(ii) relating to any State law enacted under List III of the Seventh Schedule to the Constitution, the State Government and in any other case, the Central Government;

(f) "Asymmetric Crypto System" means a system of a secure key pair consisting of a private key for creating a digital signature and a public key to verify the digital signature;

(g) "Certifying Authority" means a person who has been granted a licence to issue a Digital Signature Certificate under section 24;

(h) "Certification Practice Statement" means a statement issued by a Certifying Authority to specify the practices that the Certifying Authority employs in issuing Digital Signature Certificates;

(i) "Computer" means any electronic, magnetic, optical or other high-speed data processing device or system which performs logical, arithmetic, and memory functions by manipulations of electronic, magnetic or optical impulses, and includes all input, output, processing, storage, computer software, or communication facilities which are connected or related to the computer in a computer system or computer network;

(j) "Computer Network" means the interconnection of one or more computers through-

   (i) the use of satellite, microwave, terrestrial line or other communication media; and

   (ii) terminals or a complex consisting of two or more interconnected computers whether or not the interconnection is continuously maintained;

(k) "Computer Resource" means computer, computer system, computer network, data, computer database or software;

(l) "Computer System" means a device or collection of devices, including input and output support devices and excluding calculators which are not programmable and capable of being used in conjunction with external files, which contain computer programmes, electronic instructions, input data, and output data, that performs logic, arithmetic, data storage and retrieval, communication control and other functions;

(m) "Controller" means the Controller of Certifying Authorities appointed under subsection (7) of section 17;

(n) "Cyber Appellate Tribunal" means the Cyber Regulations Appellate Tribunal established under sub-section (1) of section 48;

(o) "Data" means a representation of information, knowledge, facts, concepts or instructions which are being prepared or have been prepared in a formalised manner, and is intended to be processed, is being processed or has been processed in a computer system or computer network and may be in any form (including computer printouts magnetic or optical storage media, punched cards, punched tapes) or stored internally in the memory of the computer;

(p) "Digital Signature" means authentication of any electronic record by a subscriber by means of an electronic method or procedure in accordance with the provisions of section 3;

(q) "Digital Signature Certificate" means a Digital Signature Certificate issued under sub-section (4) of section 35;

(r) "Electronic Form" with reference to information means any information generated, sent, received or stored in media, magnetic, optical, computer memory, micro film, computer generated micro fiche or similar device;

(s) "Electronic Gazette" means official Gazette published in the electronic form;

(t) "Electronic Record" means data, record or data generated, image or sound stored, received or sent in an electronic form or micro film or computer generated micro fiche;

(u) "Function", in relation to a computer, includes logic, control, arithmetical process, deletion, storage and retrieval and communication or telecommunication from or within a computer;

(v) "Information" includes data, text, images, sound, voice, codes, computer programmes, software and databases or micro film or computer generated micro fiche;

(w) "Intermediary" with respect to any particular electronic message means any person who on behalf of another person receives, stores or transmits that message or provides any service with respect to that message;

(x) "Key Pair", in an asymmetric crypto system, means a private key and its mathematically related public key, which are so related that the public key can verify a digital signature created by the private key;

(y) "Law" includes any Act of Parliament or of a State Legislature, Ordinances promulgated by the President or a Governor, as the case may be. Regulations made by the President under article 240, Bills enacted as President's Act under sub-clause (a) of clause (1) of article 357 of the Constitution and includes rules, regulations, bye-laws and orders issued or made thereunder;

(z) "Licence" means a licence granted to a Certifying Authority under section 24;

(za) "Originator" means a person who sends, generates, stores or transmits any electronic message or causes any electronic message to be sent, generated, stored or transmitted to any other person but does not include an intermediary;

(zb) "Prescribed" means prescribed by rules made under this Act;

(zc) "Private Key" means the key of a key pair used to create a digital signature;

(zd) "Public Key" means the key of a key pair used to verify a digital signature and listed in the Digital Signature Certificate;

(ze) "Secure System" means computer hardware, software, and procedure that -:

(a) are reasonably secure from unauthorised access and misuse;

(b) provide a reasonable level of reliability and correct operation;

(c) are reasonably suited to performing the intended functions: and

(d) adhere to generally accepted security procedures;

(zf) "Security Procedure" means the security procedure prescribed under section 16 by the Central Government;

(zg) "Subscriber" means a person in whose name the Digital Signature Certificate is issued;

(zh) "Verify" in relation to a digital signature, electronic record or public key, with its grammatical variations and cognate expressions means to determine whether:

(a) the initial electronic record was affixed with the digital signature by the use of private key corresponding to the public key of the subscriber;

(b) the initial electronic record is retained intact or has been altered since such electronic record was so affixed with the digital signature.

(2) Any reference in this Act to any enactment or any provision

thereof shall, in relation to an area in which such enactment or such provision is not in force, be construed as a reference to the corresponding law or the relevant provision of the corresponding law, if any, in force in that area.

Section No. II. DIGITAL SIGNATURE

II.3. Authentication of Electronic Records

(1) Subject to the provisions of this section any subscriber may authenticate an electronic record by affixing his digital signature.

(2) The authentication of the electronic record shall be effected by the use of asymmetric crypto system and hash function which envelop and transform the initial electronic record into another electronic record.

Explanation: For the purposes of this sub-section, "Hash function" means an algorithm mapping or translation of one sequence of bits into another, generally smaller, set known as "Hash Result" such that an electronic record yields the same hash result every time the algorithm is executed with the same electronic record as its input making it computationally infeasible:

(a) to derive or reconstruct the original electronic record from the hash result produced by the algorithm;

(b) that two electronic records can produce the same hash result using the algorithm.

(3) Any person by the use of a public key of the subscriber can verify the electronic record.

(4) The private key and the public key are unique to the subscriber and constitute a functioning key pair.

Section No. III : ELECTRONIC GOVERNANCE

III. 4. Legal Recognition of Electronic Records

Where any law provides that information or any other matter shall be in writing or in the typewritten or printed form, then, notwithstanding anything contained in such law, such requirement shall be deemed to have been satisfied if such information or matter is :

(a) rendered or made available in an electronic form; and

(b) accessible so as to be usable for a subsequent reference

5. Legal recognition of Electronic Signature

Where any law provides that information or any other matter shall be authenticated by affixing the signature or any document should be signed or bear the signature of any person then, notwithstanding anything contained in such law, such requirement shall be deemed to have been satisfied, if such information or matter is authenticated by means of digital signature affixed in such manner as may be prescribed by the Central Government.

Explanation : For the purposes of this section, "Signed", with its grammatical variations and cognate expressions, shall with reference to a person, mean affixing of his hand written signature or any mark on any document and the expression "Signature" shall be construed accordingly.

6. Use of Electronic Records and Digital Signatures in Government and its agencies

(1) Where any law provides for :

(a) the filing of any form, application or any other document with any office, authority, body or agency owned or controlled by the appropriate Government in a particular manner;

(b) the issue or grant of any licence, permit, sanction or approval by whatever name called in a particular manner;

(c) the receipt of payment or money in a particular manner, then notwithstanding anything contained in any other law for the time being in force, such requirement shall be deemed to have been satisfied if such filing, issue, grant, receipt or payment, as the case may be, is effected by means of such electronic form as may be prescribed by the appropriate Government.

(2) The appropriate Government may, for the purposes of sub-section (1) by rules, prescribe -

(a) the manner and format in which such electronic records shall be filed. created or issued:

(b) the manner or method of payment of any fee or charges

for filing, creation or issue any electronic record under clause (a).

7. Retention of Electronic Records

(1) Where any law provides that documents, records or information shall be retained for any specific period, then, that requirement shall be deemed to have been satisfied if such documents, records or information are retained in the electronic form, -

(a) the information contained therein remains accessible so as to be usable for a subsequent reference;

(b) the electronic record is retained in the format in which it was originally generated, sent or received or in a format which can be demonstrated to represent accurately the information originally generated, sent or received;

(c) the details which will facilitate the identification of the origin, destination, date and time of dispatch or receipt of such electronic record are available in the electronic record:

Provided that this clause does not apply to any information which is automatically generated solely for the purpose of enabling an electronic record to be dispatched or received.

(2) Nothing in this section shall apply to any law that expressly provides for the retention of documents, records or information in the form of electronic records. Publication of rules, regulation, etc. in Electronic Gazette.

8. Publication of rules, regulation, etc, in Electronic Gazette

Where any law provides that any rule, regulation, order, bye-law, notification or any other matter shall be published in the Official Gazette, then, such requirement shall be deemed to have been satisfied if such rule, regulation, order, bye-law, notification or any other matter is published in the Official Gazette or Electronic Gazette:

Provided that, where any rule, regulation, order, bye-law, notification or any other matters published in the Official Gazette or Electronic Gazette, the date of publication shall be deemed to be the date of the Gazette which was first published in any form.

9. Sections 6, 7 and 8 Not to Confer Right to insist document should be accepted in electronic form

Nothing contained in sections 6, 7 and 8 shall confer a right upon any person to insist that any Ministry or Department of the Central Government or the State Government or any authority or body established by or under any law or controlled or funded by the Central or State Government should accept, issue, create, retain and preserve any document in the form of electronic records or effect any monetary transaction in the electronic form.

10. Power to make Rules by Central Government in respect of Digital Signature

The Central Government may, for the purposes of this Act, by rules, prescribe :

(a) the type of digital signature;

(b) the manner and format in which the digital signature shall be affixed;

(c) the manner or procedure which facilitates identification of the person affixing the digital signature;

(d) control processes and procedures to ensure adequate integrity, security and confidentiality of electronic records or payments; and

(e) any other matter which is necessary to give legal effect to digital signatures.

Section No. IV : ATTRIBUTION, ACKNOWLEDGEMENT AND DISPATCH OF ELECTRONIC RECORDS

IV. 11. Attribution of Electronic Records

An electronic record shall be attributed to the originator :

(a) if it was sent by the originator himself;

(b) by a person who had the authority to act on behalf of the originator in respect of that electronic record; or

(c) by an information system programmed by or on behalf of the originator to operate automatically.

12. Acknowledgement of Receipt

(1) Where the originator has not agreed with the addressee that the acknowledgment of receipt of electronic record be given in a particular form or by a particular method, an acknowledgment may be given by -

(a) any communication by the addressee, automated or otherwise; or

(b) any conduct of the addressee, sufficient to indicate to the originator that the electronic record has been received.

(2) Where the originator has stipulated that the electronic record shall be binding only on receipt of an acknowledgment of such electronic record by him then unless acknowledgment has been so received, the electronic record shall be deemed to have been never sent by the originator.

(3) Where the originator has not stipulated that the electronic record shall be binding only on receipt of such acknowledgment, and the acknowledgment has not been received by the originator within the time specified or agreed or, if no time has been specified or agreed to within a reasonable time, then the originator may give notice to the addressee stating that no acknowledgment has been received by him and specifying a reasonable time by which the acknowledgment must be received by him and if no acknowledgment is received within the aforesaid time limit he may after giving notice to the addressee, treat the electronic record as though it has never been sent.

13. Time and place of despatch and receipt of Electronic Record

(1) Save as otherwise agreed to between the originator and the addressee, the dispatch of an electronic record occurs when it enters a computer resource outside the control of the originator.

(2) Save as otherwise agreed between the originator and the addressee, the time of receipt of an electronic record shall be determined as follows, namely -

(a) if the addressee has designated a computer resource for the purpose of receiving electronic records –

(i) receipt occurs at the time when the electronic record

enters the designated computer resource; or

(ii) if the electronic record is sent to a computer resource of the addressee that is not the designated computer resource, receipt occurs at the time when the electronic record is retrieved by the addressee;

(b) if the addressee has not designated a computer resource along with specified timings, if any, receipt occurs when the electronic record enters the computer resource of the addressee.

(3) Save as otherwise agreed between the originator and the addressee, an electronic record is deemed to "be dispatched" at the place where the originator has his place of business, and is deemed to be received at the place where the addressee has his place of business.

(4) The provisions of sub-section (2) shall apply notwithstanding that the place where the computer resource is located may be different from the place where the electronic record is deemed to have been received under sub-section (3).

(5) For the purposes of this section -

(a) if the originator or the addressee has more than one place of business, the principal place of business shall be the place of business;

(b) if the originator or the addressee does not have a place of business, his usual place of residence shall be deemed to be the place of business;

(c) "Usual Place of Residence", in relation to a body corporate, means the place where it is registered.

Section No. V : SECURE ELECTRONIC RECORDS AND SECURE DIGITAL SIGNATURES

V. 14. Secure Electronic Record

Where any security procedure has been applied to an electronic record at a specific point of time, then such record shall be deemed to be a secure electronic record from such point of time to the time of verification.

15. Secure Digital Signature

If, by application of a security procedure agreed to by the parties concerned, it can be verified that a digital signature, at the lime it was affixed, was -

(a) unique to the subscriber affixing it;

(b) capable of identifying such subscriber;

(c) created in a manner or using a means under the exclusive control of the subscriber and is linked to the electronic record to which it relates in such a manner that if the electronic record was altered the digital signature would be invalidated, then such digital signature shall be deemed to be a secure digital signature.

16. Security Procedure

The Central Government shall for the purposes of this Act prescribe the security procedure having regard to commercial circumstances prevailing at the time when the procedure was used, including –

(a) the nature of the transaction;

(b) the level of sophistication of the parties with reference to their technological capacity;

(c) the volume of similar transactions engaged in by other parties;

(d) the availability of alternatives offered to but rejected by any party;

(e) the cost of alternative procedures; and

(f) the procedures in general use for similar types of transactions or communications.

Section No. VI : REGULATION OF CERTIFYING AUTHORITIES

VI. 17. Appointment of Controller and other Officers

(1) The Central Government may, by notification in the Official Gazette, appoint a Controller of Certifying Authorities for the purposes of this Act and may also by the same or subsequent notification appoint such number of Deputy Controllers and Assistant Controllers as it deems fit.

(2) The Controller shall discharge his functions under this Act

subject to the general control and directions of the Central Government.

(3) The Deputy Controllers and Assistant Controllers shall perform the functions assigned to them by the Controller under the general superintendence and control of the Controller.

(4) The qualifications, experience and terms and conditions of service of Controller, Deputy Controllers and Assistant Controllers shall be such as may be prescribed by the Central Government.

(5) The Head Office and Branch Office of the Office of the Controller shall be at such places as the Central Government may specify, and these may be established at such places as the Central Government may think fit.

(6) There shall be a seal of the Office of the Controller.

18. The Controller may perform all or any of the following functions, namely

(a) exercising supervision over the activities of the Certifying Authorities;

(b) certifying public keys of the Certifying Authorities;

(c) laying down the standards to be maintained by the Certifying Authorities;

(d) specifying the qualifications and experience which employees of the Certifying Authorities should possess;

(e) specifying the conditions subject to which the Certifying Authorities shall conduct their business;

(f) specifying the content of written, printed or visual material and advertisements that may be distributed or used in respect of a Digital Signature Certificate and the Public Key;

(g) specifying the form and content of a Digital Signature Certificate and the key;

(h) specifying the form and manner in which accounts shall be maintained by the Certifying Authorities;

(i) specifying the terms and conditions subject to which auditors may be appointed and the remuneration to be paid to them;

(j) facilitating the establishment of any electronic system by a

Certifying Authority either solely or jointly with other Certifying Authorities and regulation of such systems;

(k) specifying the manner in which the Certifying Authorities shall conduct their dealings with the subscribers;

(l) resolving any conflict of interests between the Certifying Authorities and the subscribers;

(m) laying down the duties of the Certifying Authorities;

(n) maintaining a data-base containing the disclosure record of every Certifying Authority containing such particulars as may be specified by regulations, which shall be accessible to public.

19. Recognition of foreign Certifying Authorities

(1) Subject to such conditions and restrictions as may be specified by regulations, the Controller may with the previous approval of the Central Government, and by notification in the Official Gazette, recognise any foreign Certifying Authority as a Certifying Authority for the purposes of this Act.

(2) Where any Certifying Authority is recognised under sub-section (1), the Digital Signature Certificate issued by such Certifying Authority shall be valid for the purposes of this Act.

(3) The Controller may if he is satisfied that any Certifying Authority has contravened any of the conditions and restrictions subject to which it was granted recognition under sub-section (1) he may, for reasons to be recorded in writing, by notification in the Official Gazette, revoke such recognition.

20. Controller to act as Repository

(1) The Controller shall be the repository of all Digital Signature Certificates issued under this Act.

(2) The Controller shall -

(a) make use of hardware, software and procedures that are secure from intrusion and misuse;

(b) observe such other standards as may be prescribed by the Central Government, to ensure that the secrecy and security of the digital signatures are assured.

(3) The Controller shall maintain a computerised data-base of all public keys in such a manner that such database and the public

keys are available to any member of the public.

21. License to issue Digital Signature Certificates

(1) Subject to the provisions of sub-section (2), any person may make an application, to the Controller, for a licence to issue Digital Signature Certificates.

(2) No licence shall be issued under sub-section (1). unless the applicant fulfills such requirements with respect to qualification, expertise, manpower, financial resources and other infrastructure facilities, which are necessary to issue Digital Signature Certificates as may be prescribed by the Central Government.

(3) A licence granted under this section shall -

(a) be valid for such period as may be prescribed by the Central Government;

(b) not be transferable or heritable;

(c) be subject to such terms and conditions as may be specified by the regulations.

22. Application for Licence

(1) Every application for issue of a licence shall be in such form as may be prescribed by the Central Government.

(2) Every application for issue of a licence shall be accompanied by-

(a) a certification practice statement;

(b) a statement including the procedures with respect to identification of the applicant;

(c) payment of such fees, not exceeding twenty-five thousand rupees as may be prescribed by the Central Government;

(d) such other documents, as may be prescribed by the Central Government.

23. Renewal of Licence

An application for renewal of a licence shall be -

(a) in such form;

(b) accompanied by such fees, not exceeding five thousand rupees, as may be prescribed by the Central Government and shall be made not less than forty-five days before the date of expiry of the period of validity of the licence:

24. Procedure for grant or rejection of Licence

The Controller may, on receipt of an application under sub-section (1) of section 21, after considering the documents accompanying the application and such other factors, as he deems fit, grant the licence or reject the application:

Provided that, no application shall be rejected under this section unless the applicant has been given a reasonable opportunity of presenting his case.

25. Suspension of Licence

(1) The Controller may, if he is satisfied after making such inquiry, as he may think fit, that a Certifying Authority has -

(a) made a statement in, or in relation to, the application for the issue or renewal of the licence, which is incorrect or false in material particulars;

(b) failed to comply with the terms and conditions subject to which the licence was granted;

(c) failed to maintain the standards specified in Section 30 [Substituted for the words "under clause (b) of sub-section (2) of section 20;" vide amendment dated September 19, 2004].

(d) contravened any provisions of this Act, rule, regulation or order made thereunder, revoke the license:

Provided that, no licence shall be revoked unless the Certifying Authority has been given a reasonable opportunity of showing cause against the proposed revocation.

(2) The Controller may, if he has reasonable cause to believe that there is any ground for revoking a licence under sub-section (1), by order suspend such licence pending the completion of any enquiry ordered by him:

Provided that, no licence shall be suspended for a period exceeding ten days unless the Certifying Authority has been given a reasonable opportunity of showing cause against the proposed suspension.

(3) No Certifying Authority whose license has been suspended shall issue any Digital Signature Certificate during such suspension.

26. Notice of suspension or revocation of licence.

(1) Where the licence of the Certifying Authority is suspended or revoked, the Controller shall publish notice of such suspension or revocation, as the case may be, in the data-base maintained by him.

(2) Where one or more repositories are specified, the Controller shall publish notices of such suspension or revocation, as the case may be, in all such repositories.

Provided that, the data-base containing the notice of such suspension or revocation, as the case may be, shall be made available through a web site which shall be accessible round the clock

Provided further, that the Controller may, if he considers necessary, publicise the contents of the data-base in such electronic or other media, as he may consider appropriate.

27. Power to Delegate

The Controller may, in writing, authorise the Deputy Controller, Assistant Controller or any officer to exercise any of the powers of the Controller under this Chapter.

28. Power to investigate Contraventions

(1) The Controller or any officer authorised by him in this behalf shall take up for investigation any contravention of the provisions of this Act, rules or regulations made thereunder.

(2) The Controller or any officer authorised by him in this behalf shall exercise the like powers which are conferred on Income-tax authorities under Chapter XIII of the Income-tax Act, 1961 and shall exercise such powers, subject to such limitations laid down under that Act.

29. Access to Computers and Data

(1) Without prejudice to the provisions of sub-section (1) of section 69. the Controller or any person authorised by him shall, if he has reasonable cause to suspect that any contravention of the provisions of this Act, rules or regulations made thereunder has

been committed, have access to any computer system, any apparatus, data or any other material connected with such system, for the purpose of searching or causing a search to be made for obtaining any information or data contained in or available to such computer system.

(2) For the purposes of sub-section (1), the Controller or any person authorised by him may, by order, direct any person incharge of, or otherwise concerned with the operation of the computer system, data apparatus or material, to provide him with such reasonable technical and other assistant as he may consider necessary.

30. Certifying Authority to follow certain procedures

Every Certifying Authority shall-

(a) make use of hardware, software, and procedures that are secure from intrusion and misuse:

(b) provide a reasonable level of reliability in its services which are reasonably suited to the performance of intended functions;

(c) adhere to security procedures to ensure that the secrecy and privacy of the digital signatures are assured; and

(d) observe such other standards as may be specified by regulations.

31. Certifying Authority to ensure compliance of the Act, etc.

Every Certifying Authority shall ensure that every person employed or otherwise engaged by it complies, in the course of his employment or engagement, with the provisions of this Act, rules, regulations and orders made thereunder.

32. Display of Licence

Every Certifying Authority shall display its licence at a conspicuous place of the premises in which it carries on its business.

33. Surrender of Licence

(1) Every Certifying Authority whose license is suspended or revoked shall immediately after such suspension or revocation, surrender the licence to the Controller.

(2) Where any Certifying Authority fails to surrender a license under

sub-section (1), the person in whose favour a license is issued, shall be guilty of an offense and shall be punished with imprisonment which may extend up to six months or a fine which may extend up to ten thousand rupees or with both.

34. Disclosure

(1) Every Certifying Authority shall disclose in the manner specified by regulations –

(a) its Digital Signature Certificate which contains the public key corresponding to the private key used by that Certifying Authority to digitally sign another Digital Signature Certificate;

(b) any certification practice statement relevant thereto;

(c) notice of revocation or suspension of its Certifying Authority certificate, if any; and

(d) any other fact that materially and adversely affects either the reliability of a Digital Signature Certificate, which that Authority has issued, or the Authority's ability to perform its services.

(2) Where in the opinion of the Certifying Authority any event has occurred or any situation has arisen which may materially and adversely affect the integrity of its computer system or the conditions subject to which a Digital Signature Certificate was granted, then, the Certifying Authority shall-

(a) use reasonable efforts to notify any person who is likely to be affected by that occurrence; or

(b) act in accordance with the procedure specified in its certification practice statement to deal with such event or situation.

Section No. VII : DIGITAL SIGNATURE CERTIFICATES

VII. 35. Certifying Authority to issue Digital Signature Certificate

(1) Any person may make an application to the Certifying Authority for the issue of a Digital Signature Certificate in such form as may he prescribed by the Central Government.

(2) Every such application shall be accompanied by such fee not exceeding twenty-five thousand rupees as may be prescribed by the Central Government, to be paid to the Certifying Authority:

Provided that while prescribing fees under sub-section (2) different fees may be prescribed for different classes of applicants.

(3) Every such application shall be accompanied by a certification practice statement or where here is no such statement, a statement containing such particulars, as may be specified by regulations.

(4) On receipt of an application under sub-section (1) the Certifying Authority may, after consideration of the certification practice statement or the other statement under sub-section (3) and after making such enquiries as it may deem fit, grant the Digital Signature Certificate or for reasons to be recorded in writing, reject the application :

Provided that, no Digital Signature Certificate shall be granted unless the Certifying Authority is satisfied that -

(a) the applicant holds the private key corresponding to the public key to be listed in the Digital Signature Certificate;

(b) the applicant holds a private key, which is capable of creating a digital signature;

(c) the public key to be listed in the certificate can be used to verify a digital signature affixed by the private key held by the applicant :

Provided further that, no application shall be rejected unless the applicant has been given a reasonable opportunity of showing cause against the proposed rejection.

36. Representations upon issuance of Digital Signature Certificate

A Certifying Authority while issuing a Digital Signature Certificate shall certify that -

(a) it has complied with the provisions of this Act and the rules and regulations made thereunder;

(b) it has published the Digital Signature Certificate or otherwise made it available to such person relying on it and the subscriber has accepted it;

(c) the subscriber holds the private key corresponding to the public key, listed in the Digital Signature Certificate;

(d) the subscriber's public key and private key constitute a functioning key pair;

(e) the information contained in the Digital Signature Certificate is accurate; and

(f) it has no knowledge of any material fact, which if it had been included in the Digital Signature Certificate would adversely affect the reliability of the representations made in clauses (a) to (d).

37. Suspension of Digital Signature Certificate

(1) Subject to the provisions of sub-section (2), the Certifying Authority which has issued a Digital Signature Certificate may suspend such Digital Signature Certificate -

(a) on receipt of a request to that effect from -

(i) the subscriber listed in the Digital Signature Certificate; or

(ii) any person duly authorised to act on behalf of that subscriber;

(b) if it is of opinion that the Digital Signature Certificate should be suspended in public interest

(2) A Digital Signature Certificate shall not be suspended for a period exceeding fifteen days unless the subscriber has been given an opportunity of being heard in the matter.

(3) On suspension of a Digital Signature Certificate under this section, the Certifying Authority shall communicate the same to the subscriber.

38. Revocation of Digital Signature Certificate

(1) A Certifying Authority may revoke a Digital Signature Certificate issued by it

(a) where the subscriber or any other person authorised by him makes a request to that effect; or

(b) upon the death of the subscriber; or

(c) upon the dissolution of the firm or winding up of the company where the subscriber is a firm or a company.

(2) Subject to the provisions of sub-section (3) and without prejudice to the provisions of sub-section (1), a Certifying Authority may revoke a Digital Signature Certificate which has been issued by it at any time, if it is of opinion that -

(a) a material fact represented in the Digital Signature Certificate is false or has been concealed;

(b) a requirement for issuance of the Digital Signature Certificate was not satisfied;

(c) the Certifying Authority's private key or security system was compromised in a manner materially affecting the Digital Signature Certificate's reliability;

(d) the subscriber has been declared insolvent or dead or where a subscriber is a firm or a company, which has been dissolved, wound-up or otherwise ceased to exist.

(3) A Digital Signature Certificate shall not be revoked unless the subscriber has been given an opportunity of being heard in the matter.

(4) On revocation of a Digital Signature Certificate under this section, the Certifying Authority shall communicate the same to the subscriber.

39. Notice of Suspension or Revocation

(1) Where a Digital Signature Certificate is suspended or revoked under section 37 or section 38, the Certifying Authority shall publish a notice of such suspension or revocation, as the case may be in the repository specified in the Digital Signature Certificate for publication of such notice.

(2) Where one or more repositories are specified, the Certifying Authority shall publish notices of such suspension or revocation, as the case may be, in all such repositories.

Section No. VIII : DUTIES OF SUBSCRIBERS

VIII. 40. Generating Key Pair

Where any Digital Signature Certificate, the public key of which corresponds to the private key of that subscriber which is to be listed in the Digital Signature Certificate has been accepted by a subscriber, (*) the subscriber shall generate that [substituted for "the"vide amendment dated 19/09/2002] key pair by applying the security procedure. [* word *"then"-deleted vide amendment dated 19/9/2002].*

41. Acceptance of Digital Signature Certificate

(1) A subscriber shall be deemed to have accepted a Digital Signature Certificate if he publishes or authorizes the publication of a Digital Signature Certificate -

(a) to one or more persons;

(b) in a repository, or otherwise demonstrates his approval of the Digital Signature Certificate in any manner.

(2) By accepting a Digital Signature Certificate the subscriber certifies to all who reasonably rely on the information contained in the Digital Signature Certificate that -

(a) the subscriber holds the private key corresponding to the public key listed in the Digital Signature Certificate and is entitled to hold the same;

(b) all representations made by the subscriber to the Certifying Authority and all material relevant to the information contained in the Digital Signature Certificate are true;

(c) all information in the Digital Signature Certificate that is within the knowledge of the subscriber is true.

42. Control of Private key

(1) Every subscriber shall exercise reasonable care to retain control of the private key corresponding to the public key listed in his Digital Signature Certificate and take all steps to prevent its disclosure. ["to a person not authorised to affix the digital signature of the subscriber".-Omitted vide amendment dated 19/09/2002].

(2) If the private key corresponding to the public key listed in the Digital Signature Certificate has been compromised, then, the subscriber shall communicate the same without any delay to the Certifying Authority in such manner as may be specified by the regulations.

Explanation : For the removal of doubts, it is hereby declared that the subscriber shall be liable till he has informed the Certifying Authority that the private key has been compromised.

Section No. IX : PENALTIES AND ADJUDICATION

IX. 43. Penalty for damage to Computer, Computer System, etc.

If any person without permission of the owner or any other person who is incharge of a computer, computer system or computer network-

(a) accesses or secures access to such computer, computer system or computer network.

(b) downloads, copies or extracts any data, computer data base or information from such computer, computer system or computer network including information or data held or stored in any removable storage medium;

(c) introduces or 'causes to be introduced any computer contaminant or computer virus into any computer, computer system or computer network;

(d) damages or causes to be damaged any computer, computer system or computer network, data, computer data base or any other programmes residing in such computer, computer system or computer network;

(e) disrupts or causes disruption of any computer, computer system or computer network;

(f) denies or causes the denial of access to any person authorised to access any computer, computer system or computer network by any means;

(g) provides any assistance to any person to facilitate access to a computer, computer system or computer network in contravention of the provisions of this Act, rules or regulations made thereunder,

(h) charges the services availed of by a person to the account of another person by tampering with or manipulating any computer, computer system, or computer network, he shall be liable to pay damages by way of compensation not exceeding one crore rupees to the person so affected.

Explanation : for the purposes of this section -

(i) "Computer Contaminant" means any set of computer instructions that are designed -

(a) to modify, destroy, record, transmit data or programme residing withina computer, computer system or computer network; or

(b) by any means to usurp the normal operation of the computer, computer system, or computer network;

(ii) "Computer Database" means a representation of information, knowledge, facts, concepts or instructions in text, image, audio, video that are being prepared or have been prepared in a formalised manner or have been produced by a computer, computer system or computer network and are intended for use in a computer, computer system or computer network;

(iii) "Computer Virus" means any computer instruction, information, data or programme that destroys, damages, degrades or adversely affects the performance of a computer resource or attaches itself to another computer resource and operates when a programme, data or instruction is executed or some other event takes place in that computer resource;

(iv) "Damage" means to destroy, alter, delete, add, modify or re-arrange any computer resource by any means.

44. Penalty for failure to furnish Information, Return, etc.

If any person who is required under this Act or any rules or regulations made thereunder to -

(a) furnish any document, return or report to the Controller or the Certifying Authority, fails to furnish the same, he shall be liable to a penalty not exceeding one lakh and fifty thousand rupees for each such failure;

(b) file any return or furnish any information, books or other documents within the time specified therefor in the regulations, fails to file return or furnish the same within the time specified therefore in the regulations, he shall be liable to a penalty not exceeding five thousand rupees for every day during which such failure continues:

(c) maintain books of account or records, fails to maintain the same, he shall be liable to a penalty not exceeding ten thousand rupees for every day during which the failure continues.

45. Residuary Penalty

Whoever contravenes any rules or regulations made under this Act, for the contravention of which no penalty has been separately provided, shall be liable to pay a compensation not exceeding twenty-five thousand rupees to the person affected by such contravention or a penalty not exceeding twenty-five thousand rupees.

46. Power to Adjudicate

(1) For the purpose of adjudging under this Chapter whether any person has committed a contravention of any of the provisions of this Act or of any rule, regulation, direction or order made thereunder, the Central Government shall, subject to the provisions of sub-section(3), appoint any officer not below the rank of a Director to the Government of India or an equivalent officer of a State Government to be an adjudicating officer for holding an inquiry in the manner prescribed by the Central Government.

(2) The adjudicating officer shall, after giving the person referred to in sub-section (1) a reasonable opportunity for making representation in the matter and if, on such inquiry, he is satisfied that the person has committed the contravention, he may impose such penalty as he thinks fit in accordance with the provisions of that section.

(3) No person shall be appointed as an adjudicating officer unless he possesses such experience in the field of Information Technology and Legal or Judicial experience as may be prescribed by the Central Government.

(4) Where more than one adjudicating officers are appointed, the Central Government shall specify by order the matters and places with respect to which such officers shall exercise their jurisdiction.

(5). Every adjudicating officer shall have the powers of a civil court which are conferred on the Cyber Appellate Tribunal under sub-section (2) of section 58, and -

(a) all proceedings before it shall be deemed to be judicial proceedings within the meaning of sections 193 and 228 of the Indian Penal Code;

(b) shall be deemed to be a civil court for the purposes of sections 345 and 346 of the Code of Criminal Procedure, 1973.

47. Factors to be taken into account by the Adjudicating Officer

While adjudging the quantum of compensation under this Chapter the adjudicating officer shall have due regard to the following factors, namely -

(a) the amount of gain of unfair advantage, wherever quantifiable, made as a result of the default;

(b) the amount of loss caused to any person as a result of the default;

(c) the repetitive nature of the default.

Section No. X. THE CYBER REGULATIONS APPELLATE TRIBUNAL

X. 48. Establishment of Cyber Appellate Tribunal

(1) The Central Government shall, by notification, establish one or more appellate tribunals to be known as the Cyber Regulations Appellate Tribunal.

(2) The Central Government shall also specify, in the notification referred to in sub-section (1). the matters and places in relation to which the Cyber Appellate Tribunal may exercise jurisdiction.

49. Composition of Cyber Appellate Tribunal

A Cyber Appellate Tribunal skill consist of one person only (hereinafter referred to as the Presiding Officer of the Cyber Appellate Tribunal) to be appointed, by notification, by the Central Government.

50. Qualification for appointment as Presiding Officer of the Cyber Appellate Tribunal

A person shall not be qualified for appointment as the Presiding Officer of a Cyber Appellate Tribunal unless he -

(a) is or has been, or is qualified to be, a Judge of a High Court: or

(b) is or has been a member of the Indian Legal Service and is holding or has held a post in Grade I of that Service for at least three years.

51. Term of office

The Presiding Officer of a Cyber Appellate Tribunal shall hold office for a term of five years from the date on which he enters upon his office or until he attains the age of sixty-five years, whichever is earlier.

52. Salary, allowance and other terms and conditions of service of Presiding Officer

The salary and allowances payable to, and the other terms and conditions of service including pension, gratuity and other retirement benefits of, the Presiding Officer of a Cyber Appellate Tribunal shall be such as may be prescribed:

Provided that neither the salary and allowances nor the other terms and conditions of service of the Presiding Officer shall be varied to his disadvantage after appointment.

53. Filling up of Vacancies

If, for reason other than temporary absence, any vacancy occurs in the office of the Presiding Officer of a Cyber Appellate Tribunal, then the Central Government shall appoint another person in accordance with the provisions of this Act to fill the vacancy and the proceedings may be continued before the Cyber Appellate Tribunal from the stage at which the vacancy is filled.

54. Resignation and Removal

(1) The Presiding Officer of a Cyber Appellate Tribunal may, by notice in writing under his hand addressed to the Central Government, resign his office:

Provided that the said Presiding Officer shall, unless he is permitted by the Central Government to relinquish his office sooner, continue to hold office until the expiry of three months from the date of receipt of such notice or until a person duly appointed as his successor enters upon his office or until the expiry of his term of office, whichever is the earliest.

(2) The Presiding Officer of a Cyber Appellate Tribunal shall not be removed from his office except by an order by the Central Government on the ground of proved misbehaviour or incapacity after an inquiry made by a Judge of the Supreme Court in which

the Presiding Officer concerned has been informed of the charges against him and given a reasonable opportunity of being heard in respect of these charges.

(3) The Central Government may, by rules, regulate the procedure for the investigation of misbehaviour or incapacity of the aforesaid Presiding Officer.

55. Orders constituting Appellate Tribunal to be final and not to invalidate its Proceedings

No order of the Central Government appointing any person as the Presiding Officer of a Cyber Appellate Tribunal shall be called in question in any manner and no act or proceeding before a Cyber Appellate Tribunal shall be called in question in any manner on the ground merely of any defect in the constitution of a Cyber Appellate Tribunal.

56. Staff of the Cyber Appellate Tribunal

(1) The Central Government shall provide the Cyber Appellate Tribunal with such officers and employees as the Government may think fit.

(2) The officers and employees of the Cyber Appellate Tribunal shall discharge their functions under general superintendence of the Presiding Officer.

(3) The salaries and allowances and other conditions of service of the officers and employees of the Cyber Appellate Tribunal shall be such as may be prescribed by the Central Government.

57. Appeal to Cyber Regulations Appellate Tribunal

(1) Save as provided in sub-section (2), any person aggrieved by an order made by a Controller or an adjudicating officer under this Act may prefer an appeal to a Cyber Appellate Tribunal having jurisdiction in the matter

(2) No appeal shall lie to the Cyber Appellate Tribunal from an order made by an adjudicating officer with the consent of the parties.

(3) Every appeal under sub-section (1) shall be filed within a period of forty-five days from the date on which a copy of the order made by the Controller or adjudicating officer is received by the person aggrieved and it shall be in such form and be accompanied by such fee as may be prescribed:

Provided that the Cyber Appellate Tribunal may entertain an appeal after the expiry of the said period of forty-five days if it is satisfied that there was sufficient cause for not filing it within that period.

(4) On receipt of an appeal under sub-section (1), the Cyber Appellate Tribunal may, after giving the parties to the appeal, an opportunity of being heard, pass such orders thereon as it thinks fit, confirming, modifying or setting aside the order appealed against.

(5) The Cyber Appellate Tribunal shall send a copy of every order made by it to the parties to the appeal and to the concerned Controller or adjudicating officer.

(6) The appeal filed before the Cyber Appellate Tribunal under sub-section (1) shall be dealt with by it as expeditiously as possible and endeavour shall be made by it to dispose of the appeal finally within six months from the date of receipt of the appeal.

58. Procedure and Powers of the Cyber Appellate Tribunal

(1) The Cyber Appellate Tribunal shall not be bound by the procedure laid down by the Code of Civil Procedure, 1908 but shall be guided by the principles of natural justice and, subject to the other provisions of this Act and of any rules, the Cyber Appellate Tribunal shall have powers to regulate its own procedure including the place at which it shall have its sittings.

(2) The Cyber Appellate Tribunal shall have, for the purposes of discharging their functions under this Act, the same powers as are vested in a civil court under the Code of Civil Procedure, 1908, while trying a suit, in respect of the following matters, namely -

(a) summoning and enforcing the attendance of any person and examining him on oath;

(b) requiring the discovery and production of documents or other electronic records;

(c) receiving evidence on affidavits;

(d) issuing commissions for the examination of witnesses or documents;

(e) reviewing its decisions;

(f) dismissing an application for default or deciding it *ex parte*;

(g) any other matter which may be prescribed.

Every proceeding before the Cyber Appellate Tribunal shall be deemed to be a judicial proceeding within the meaning of sections 193 and 228, and for the purposes of section 196 of the Indian Penal Code and the Cyber Appellate Tribunal shall be deemed to be a civil court for the purposes of section 195 and Chapter XXVI of the Code of Criminal Procedure, 1973.

59. Right to Legal Representation

The appellant may either appear in person or authorise one or more legal practitioners or ' any of its officers to present his or its case before the Cyber Appellate Tribunal Limitation.

60. Limitation

The provisions of the Limitation Act, 1963, shall, as far as may be, apply to an appeal made to the Cyber Appellate Tribunal.

61. Civil court not to have Jurisdiction

No court shall have jurisdiction to entertain any suit or proceeding in respect of any matter which an adjudicating officer appointed under this Act or the Cyber Appellate Tribunal constituted under this Act is empowered by or under this Act to determine and no injunction shall be granted by any court or other authority in respect of any action taken or to be taken in pursuance of any power conferred by or under this Act.

62. Appeal to High Court

Any person aggrieved by any decision or order of the Cyber Appellate Tribunal may file an appeal to the High Court within sixty days from the date of communication of the decision or order of the Cyber Appellate Tribunal to him on any question of fact or law arising out of such order:

Provided that the High Court may, if it is satisfied that the appellant was prevented by sufficient cause from filing the appeal within the said period, allow it to be filed within a further period not exceeding sixty days.

63. Compounding of Contravention

(1) Any contravention under this Act [substituted for "Chapter" vide amendment dated 19/09/2002] may, either before or after the institution of adjudication proceedings, be compounded by the Controller or such other officer as may be specially authorised by him in this behalf or by the adjudicating officer, as the case may be, subject to such conditions as the Controller or such other officer or the adjudicating officer may specify :

Provided that such sum shall not, in any case, exceed the maximum amount of the penalty which may be imposed under this Act for the contravention so compounded.

(2) Nothing in sub-section (1) shall apply to a person who commits the same or similar contravention within a period of three years from the date on which the first contravention, committed by him. was compounded.

Explanation : For the purposes of this sub-section, any second or subsequent contravention committed after the expiry of a period of three years from the date on which the contravention was previously compounded shall be deemed to be a first contravention.

(3) Where any contravention has been compounded under sub-section (1), no proceeding or further proceeding, as the case may be, shall be taken against the person guilty of such contravention in respect of the contravention so compounded.

64. Recovery of Penalty

A penalty imposed under this Act, if it is not paid, shall be recovered as an arrear of land revenue and the licence or the Digital Signature Certificate, as the case may be, shall be suspended till the penalty is paid.

Secton No. XI. OFFENCES

XI. 65. Tampering with Computer Source Documents

Whoever knowingly or intentionally conceals, destroys or alters or intentionally or knowingly causes another to conceal, destroy or alter any computer source code used for a computer, computer programme, computer system or computer network, when the computer source code is required to be kept or maintained by law for the time being in force, shall be punishable with imprisonment up to three years, or with fine which may extend up to two lakh rupees, or with both.

Explanation : For the purposes of this section, "Computer Source Code" means the listing of programmes, Computer Commands, Design and layout and programme analysis of computer resource in any form.

66. Hacking with Computer System

(1) Whoever with the intent to cause or knowing that he is likely to cause wrongful loss or damage to the public or any person, destroys or deletes or alters any information residing in a computer resource or diminishes its value or utility or affects it injuriously by any means, commits hacking.

(2) Whoever commits hacking shall be punished with imprisonment up to three years, or with fine which may extend up to two lakh rupees, or with both.

67. Publishing of Information which is obscene in Electronic Form

Whoever publishes or transmits or causes to be published in the electronic form, any material which is lascivious or appeals to the prurient interest or if its effect is such as to tend to deprave and corrupt persons who are likely, having regard to all relevant circumstances, to read, see or hear the matter contained or embodied in it, shall be punished on first conviction with imprisonment of either description for a term which may extend to five years and with fine which may extend to one lakh rupees and in the event of a second or subsequent conviction with imprisonment of either description for a term which may extend to ten years and also with fine which may extend to two lakh rupees.

68. Power of Controller to give Directions

(1) The Controller may, by order, direct a Certifying Authority or any employee of such Authority to take such measures or cease carrying on such activities as specified in the order if those are necessary to ensure compliance with the provisions of this Act, rules or any regulations made thereunder.

(2) Any person who fails to comply with any order under sub-section (1) shall be guilty of an offence and shall be liable on conviction

to imprisonment for a term not exceeding three years or to a fine not exceeding two lakh rupees or to both.

69. Directions of Controller to a subscriber to extend facilities to decrypt information

(1) If the Controller is satisfied that it is necessary or expedient so to do in the interest of the sovereignty or integrity of India, the security of the State, friendly relations with foreign States or public order or for preventing incitement to the commission of any cognizable offence, for reasons to be recorded in writing, by order, direct any agency of the Government to intercept any information transmitted through any computer resource.

(2) The subscriber or any person incharge of the computer resource shall, when called upon by any agency which has been directed under sub-section (1), extend all facilities and technical assistance to decrypt the information.

(3) The subscriber or any person who fails to assist the agency referred to in sub-section (2) shall be punished with an imprisonment for a term which may extend to seven years.

70. Protected System

(1) The appropriate Government may, by notification in the Official Gazette, declare that any computer, computer system or computer network to be a protected system.

(2) The appropriate Government may, by order in writing, authorise the persons who are authorised to access protected systems notified under sub-section (1).

(3) Any person who secures access or attempts to secure access to a protected system in contravention of the provisions of this section shall be punished with imprisonment of either description for a term which may extend to ten years and shall also be liable to fine.

71. Penalty for Misrepresentation

Whoever makes any misrepresentation to, or suppresses any material fact from, the Controller or the Certifying Authority for obtaining any licence or Digital Signature Certificate, as the case may be, shall be punished with imprisonment for a term which may extend to two years, or with fine which may extend to one lakh rupees, or with both.

72. Breach of Confidentiality and Privacy

Save as otherwise provided in this Act or any other law for the time being in force, any person who, in pursuant of any of the powers conferred under this Act, rules or , regulations made thereunder, has secured access to any electronic record, book, register, correspondence, information, document or other material without the consent of the person concerned discloses such electronic record, book, register, correspondence, information, document or other material to any other person shall be punished with imprisonment for a term which may extend to two years, or with fine which may extend to one lakh rupees, or with both.

73. Penalty for publishing Digital Signature Certificate false in certain particulars

(1) No person shall publish a Digital Signature Certificate or otherwise make it available to any other person with the knowledge that –

(a) the Certifying Authority listed in the certificate has not issued it; or

(b) the subscriber listed in the certificate has not accepted it; or

(c) the certificate has been revoked or suspended, unless such publication is for the purpose of verifying a digital signature created prior to such suspension or revocation.

(2) Any person who contravenes the provisions of sub-section (1) shall be punished with imprisonment for a term which may extend to two years, or with fine which may extend to one lakh rupees, or with both.

74. Publication for Fraudulent purpose

Whoever knowingly creates, publishes or otherwise makes available a Digital Signature Certificate for any fraudulent or unlawful purpose shall be punished with imprisonment for a term which may extend to two years, or with fine which may extend to one lakh rupees, or with both.

75. Act to apply for Offence or Contraventions committed outside India

(1) Subject to the provisions of sub-section (2), the provisions of this Act shall apply also to any offence or contravention committed outside India by any person irrespective of his nationality.

(2) For the purposes of sub-section (1), this Act shall apply to an offence or contravention committed outside India by any person if the act or conduct constituting the offence or contravention involves a computer, computer system or computer network located in India.

76. Confiscation

Any computer, computer system, floppies, compact disks, tape drives or any other accessories related thereto, in respect of which any provision of this Act, rules, orders or regulations made thereunder has been or is being contravened, shall be liable to confiscation:

Provided that, where it is established to the satisfaction of the court adjudicating the confiscation that the person in whose possession, power or control of any such computer, computer system, floppies, compact disks, tape drives or any other accessories relating thereto is found is not responsible for the contravention of the provisions of this Act, rules, orders or regulations made thereunder, the court may, instead of making an order for confiscation of such computer, computer system, floppies, compact disks, tape drives or any other accessories related thereto, make such other order authorised by this Act against the person contravening of the provisions of this Act, rules, orders or regulations made thereunder as it may think fit.

77. Penalties and Confiscation not to interfere with other Punishments

No penalty imposed or confiscation made under this Act shall prevent the imposition of any other punishment to which the person affected thereby is liable under any other law for the time being in force.

78. Power to investigate Offences

Notwithstanding anything contained in the Code of Criminal Procedure, 1973, a police officer not below the rank of Deputy

Superintendent of Police shall investigate any offence under this Act.

Section No. XII : NETWORK SERVICE PROVIDERS NOT TO BE LIABLE IN CERTAIN CASES

XII. 79. Network Service Providers not to be liable in certain cases

For the removal of doubts, it is hereby declared that no person providing any service as a Network Service Provider shall be liable under this Act, rules or regulations made thereunder for any third party information or data made available by him if he proves that the offence or contravention was committed without his knowledge or that he had exercised all due diligence to prevent the commission of such offence or contravention.

Explanation : For the purposes of this section -

(a) "Network Service Provider" means an intermediary;

(b) "Third Party Information" means any information dealt with by a network service provider in his capacity as an intermediary.

Section No. XIII. MISCELLANEOUS

XIII. 80. Power of Police Officer and Other Officers to Enter, Search, etc

(1) Notwithstanding anything contained in the Code of Criminal Procedure, 1973, any police officer, not below the rank of a Deputy Superintendent of Police, or any other officer of the Central Government or a State Government authorised by the Central Government in this behalf may enter any public place and search and arrest without warrant any person found therein who is reasonably suspected of having committed or of committing or of being about to commit any offence under this Act.

Explanation : For the purposes of this sub-section, the expression "Public Place" includes any public conveyance, any hotel, any shop or any other place intended for use by, or accessible to the public.

(2) Where any person is arrested under sub-section (1) by an officer other than a police officer, such officer shall, without unnecessary delay, take or send the person arrested before a magistrate having

jurisdiction in the case or before the officer-in-charge of a police station.

(3) The provisions of the Code of Criminal Procedure, 1973 shall, subject to the provisions of this section, apply, so far as may be, in relation to any entry, search or arrest, made under this section.

81. Act to have Overriding Effect

The provisions of this Act shall have effect notwithstanding anything inconsistent therewith contained in any other law for the time being in force.

81A. Application of the Act to Electronic cheque and Truncated cheque

(Inserted vide Negotiable Instruments Amendment Act 2002, - Effective from 6th Day of February 2003)

(1) The provisions of this Act, for the time being in force, shall apply to, or in relation to, electronic cheques and the truncated cheques subject to such modifications and amendments as may be necessary for carrying out the purposes of the Negotiable Instruments Act, 1881 (26 of 1881) by the Central Government, in consultation with the Reserve Bank of India, by notification in the Official Gazette.

(2) Every notification made by the Central Government under subsection (1) shall be laid, as soon as may be after it is made, before each House of Parliament, while it is in session, for a total period of thirty days which may be comprised in one session or in two or more successive sessions, and if, before the expiry of the session immediately following the session or the successive sessions aforesaid, both houses agree in making any modification in the notification or both houses agree that the notification should not be made, the notification shall thereafter have effect only in such modified form or be of no effect, as the case may be; so, however, that any such modification or annulment shall be without prejudice to the validity of anything previously done under the notification.

Explanation : For the purpose of this Act, the expression "electronic cheque" and "truncated cheque" shall have the same meaning as assigned to them in section 6 of the Negotiable Instruments Act 1881 (26 of 1881).

82. Controllers, Deputy Controllers and Assistant Controllers to be Public Servants

The Presiding Officer and other officers and employees of a Cyber Appellate Tribunal, the Controller, the Deputy Controller and the Assistant Controllers shall be deemed to be Public Servants within the meaning of section 21 of the Indian Penal Code.

83. Power to Give Direction

The Central Government may give directions to any State Government as to the carrying into execution in the State of any of the provisions of this Act or of any rule, regulation or order made thereunder.

84. Protection of Action taken in Good Faith

No suit, prosecution or other legal proceeding shall lie against the Central Government, the State Government, the Controller or any person acting on behalf of him, the Presiding Officer, Adjudicating Officers and the staff of the Cyber Appellate Tribunal for anything which is in good faith done or intended to be done in pursuance of this Act or any rule, regulation or order made thereunder.

85. Offences by Companies

(1) Where a person committing a contravention of any of the provisions of this Act or of any rule, direction or order made thereunder is a Company, every person who, at the time the contravention was committed, was in charge of. and was responsible to, the company for the conduct of business of the company as well as the company, shall be guilty of the contravention and shall be liable to be proceeded against and punished accordingly:

Provided that, nothing contained in this sub-section shall render any such person liable to punishment if he proves that the contravention took place without his knowledge or that he exercised all due diligence to prevent such contravention.

(2) Notwithstanding anything contained in sub-section (1), where a contravention of any of the provisions of this Act or of any rule, direction or order made thereunder has been committed by a company and it is proved that the contravention has taken place with the consent or connivance of, or is attributable to any neglect

on the part of, any director, manager, secretary or other officer of the company, such director, manager, secretary or other officer shall also be deemed to be guilty of the contravention and shall be liable to be proceeded against and punished accordingly.

Explanation : For the purposes of this section –

(i) "Company" means any Body Corporate and includes a Firm or other Association of individuals; and

(ii) "Director", in relation to a firm, means a partner in the firm.

86. Removal of Difficulties

(1) If any difficulty arises in giving effect to the provisions of this Act, the Central Government may, by order published in the Official Gazette, make such provisions not inconsistent with the provisions of this Act as appear to it to be necessary or expedient for removing the difficulty:

Provided that, no order shall be made under this section after the expiry of a period of two years from the commencement of this Act. (2) Every order made under this section shall be laid, as soon as may be after it is made, before each House of Parliament.

87. Power of Central Government to make Rules

(1) The Central Government may, by notification in the Official Gazette, make rules to carry out the provisions of this Act.

(2) In particular, and without prejudice to the generality of the foregoing power, such rules may provide for all or any of the following matters, namely –

(a) the manner in which any information or matter may be authenticated by means of digital signature under section 5;

(b) the electronic form in which filing, issue, grant or payment shall be effected under sub-section (1) of section 6;

(c) the manner and format in which electronic records shall be filed or issued and the method of payment under sub-section (2) of section 6;

(d) the matters relating to the type of digital signature, manner

(e) the security procedure for the purpose of creating secure electronic record and secure digital signature under section 16;

(f) the qualifications, experience and terms and conditions of service of Controller, Deputy Controllers and Assistant Controllers under section 17;

(g) other standards to be observed by the Controller under Clause (b) of sub-section (2) of section 20;

(h) the requirements which an applicant must fulfil under sub-section (2) of section 21;

(i) the period of validity of licence granted under clause (a) of sub-section (3) of section 21;

(j) the form in which an application for licence may be made under subsection (1) of section 22;

(k) the amount of fees payable under clause (c) of sub-section (2) of section 22;

(l) such other documents which shall accompany an application for licence under clause (d) of sub-section (2) of section 22;

(m) the form and the fee for renewal of a licence and the fee payable thereof under section 23;

(n) the amount of late fee payable under the proviso to section 23;

(o) the form in which application for issue of a Digital Signature Certificate may be made under sub-section (1) of section 35;

(p) the fee to be paid to the Certifying Authority for issue of a Digital Signature Certificate under sub-section (2) of section 35;

(q) the manner in which the adjudicating officer shall hold inquiry under sub-section (1) of section 46;

(r) the qualification and experience which the adjudicating officer shall possess under sub-section (2) of section 46;

(s) the salary, allowances and the other terms and conditions of service of the Presiding Officer under section 52;

(t) the procedure for investigation of misbehaviour or incapacity of the Presiding Officer under sub-section (3) of section 54;

(u) the salary and allowances and other conditions, of service of other officers and employees under sub-section (3) of section 56;

(v) the form in which appeal may be filed and the fee thereof under subsection (3) of section 57;

(w) any other power of a civil court required to be prescribed under clause (g) of sub-section (2) of section 58; and

(x) any other matter which is required to be, or may be, prescribed.

(3) Every regulation made under this Act shal! be laid, as soon as may be after it is made, before each House of Parliament, while it is in session, for a total period of thirty days which may be comprised in one session or in two or more successive sessions, and if, before the expiry of the session immediately following the session or the successive sessions aforesaid, both Houses agree in making any modification in the regulation or both Houses agree mat the regulation should not be made, the regulation shall thereafter have effect only in such modified form or be of no effect, as the case may be; so, however, that any such modification or annulment shall be without prejudice to the validity of anything previously done under that regulation.

88. Constitution of Advisory Committee

(1) The Central Government shall, as soon as may be after the commencement of this Act, constitute a Committee called the Cyber Regulations Advisory Committee.

(2) The Cyber Regulations Advisory Committee shall consist of a Chairperson and such number of other official and non-official members representing the interests principally affected or having special knowledge of the subject-matter as the Central Government may deem fit.

(3) The Cyber Regulations Advisory Committee shall advise -

(a) the Central Government either generally as regards any rules or for any other purpose connected with this Act;

(b) the Controller in framing the regulations under this Act.

(4) There shall be paid to the non-official members of such Committee such travelling and other allowances as the Central Government may fix.

89. Power of Controller to make Regulations

(1) The Controller may, after consultation with the Cyber Regulations Advisory Committee and with the previous approval of the Central Government, by notification in the Official Gazette, make regulations consistent with this Act and the rules made thereunder to carry out the purposes of this Act.

(2) In particular, and without prejudice to the generality of the foregoing power, such regulations may provide for all or any of the following matters, namely –

(a) the particulars relating to maintenance of data-base containing the disclosure record of every Certifying Authority under clause (n) [Substituted for (m) vide amendment dated 19/09/2002] of section 18;

(b) the conditions and restrictions subject to which the Controller may recognise any foreign Certifying Authority under sub-section (1) of section 19;

(c) the terms and conditions subject to which a license may be granted under clause (c) of sub-section (3) of section 21;

(d) other standards to be observed by a Certifying. Authority under clause (d) of section 30;

(e) the manner in which the Certifying Authority shall disclose the matters specified in sub-section (1) of section 34;

(f) the particulars of statement which shall accompany an application under sub-section (3) of section 35;

(g) the manner by which a subscriber communicates the compromise of private key to the Certifying Authority under sub-section (2) of section 42.

(3) Every regulation made under this Act shall be laid, as soon as may be after it is made, before each House of Parliament, while it is in session, for a total period of thirty days which may be comprised in one session or in two or more successive-sessions, and if, before the expiry of the session immediately following

the session or the successive sessions aforesaid, both Houses agree in making any modification in the regulation or both Houses agree that the regulation should not be made, the regulation shall there after have effect only in such modified form or be of no effect, as the ease may be; so, however, that any such modification or annulment shall be without prejudice to the validity of anything previously done under that regulation.

90. Power of State Government to make rules

(1) The State Government may. by notification in the Official Gazette, make rules to carry out the provisions of this Act.

(2) In particular, and without prejudice to the generality of the foregoing power, such rules may provide for all or any of the following matters, namely -

(a) the electronic form in which filing, issue, grant receipt or payment shall be effected under sub-section (1) of section 6;

(b) for matters specified in sub-section (2) of section 6;

(c) any other matter which is required to be provided by rules by the State Government.

(3) Every rule made by the State Government under this section shall be laid, as soon as may be after it is made, before each House of the State Legislature where it consists of two Houses, or where such Legislature consists of one House, before that House.

91. Amendment of Indian Penal Code 1860

The Indian Penal Code shall be amended in the manner specified in the First Schedule to this Act.

92. Amendment of Indian Evidence Act, 1872

The Indian Evidence Act, 1872 shall be amended in the manner specified in the Second Schedule to this Act.

93. Amendment of The Bankers' Books Evidence Act, 1891

The Bankers' Books Evidence Act, 1891 shall be amended in the manner specified in the Third Schedule to this Act.

94. Amendment of Reserve Bank of India Act, 1934

The Reserve Bank of India Act, 1934 shall be amended in the manner specified in the Fourth Schedule to this Act.

The First Schedule
(Amendments to The Indian Penal Code)

1. After section 29, the following section shall be inserted, namely-
29A. The words "electronic record" shall have the meaning assigned to it in clause (s) of sub-section (7) of section 2 of the Information Technology Act, 1999.

2 In section 167, for the words "such public servant, charged with the preparation or translation of any document, frames or translates that document", the words "such public servant, charged with the preparation or translation of any document or electronic record, frames, prepares or translates that document or electronic record" shall be substituted.

3. In section 172, for the words "produce a document in a Court of Justice", the words "produce a document or an electronic record in a Court of Justice" shall be substituted.

4 In section 173, for the words "to produce a document in a Court of Justice", the words "to produce a document or electronic record in a Court of Justice" shall be substituted.

5. In section 175, for the word "document" at both the places where it occurs, the words "document or electronic record" shall be substituted.

6. In section 192, for the words "makes any false entry in any book or record, or makes any document containing a false statement", the words "makes any false entry in any book or record, or electronic record or makes any document or electronic record containing a false statement" shall be substituted.

7. In section 204, for the word "document" at both the places where it occurs, the words "document or electronic record" shall be substituted.

8. In section 463, for the words "Whoever makes any false documents or part of a document with intent to cause damage or injury", the words "Whoever makes any false; documents or false

electronic record or part of a document or electronic record, with intent to cause damage or injury" shall be substituted.

9. In section 464 –

(a) for the portion beginning with the words "A person is said to make a false document" and ending with the words "by reason of deception practised upon him. he does not know the contents of the document or the nature of me alteration", file following shall be substituted, namely: -

"A person is said to make a false document or false electronic record -First -

Who dishonestly or fraudulently -

(a) makes, signs, seals or executes a document or part of a document;

(b) makes or transmits any electronic record or part of any electronic record;

(c) affixes any digital signature on any electronic record;

(d) makes any mark denoting the execution of a document or the authenticity of the digital signature, with the intention of causing it to be believed that such document or a part of document, electronic record or digital signature was made, signed, sealed executed, transmitted or affixed by or by the authority of a person by whom or by whose authority he knows that it was not made, signed, sealed, executed or affixed; or

Secondly -

Who, without lawful authority, dishonestly of fraudulently, by cancellation or otherwise, alters a document or an electronic record in any material part thereof, after it has been made, executed or affixed with digital signature either by himself or by any other person, whether such person be living or dead at tile time of such alteration; or

Thirdly -

Who dishonestly or fraudulently causes any person to sign, seal, execute or alter a document or an electronic record or to affix his digital signature on any electronic record knowing that such person by reason of unsoundness of mind or intoxication cannot, or that by reason of deception practised upon him, he does not know the contents of the document or electronic record or the nature of the alteration."

(b) after Explanation 2, the following Explanation shall be inserted at the end, namely -

Explanation 3 - For the purposes of this section, the expression "affixing digital signature" shall have the meaning assigned to it in. clause (d) of sub- 50 section (1) of section 2 of the Information Technology Act, 1999.'

10. In section 466 -

(a) for the words "Whoever forges a document", the words "Whoever forges a document or an electronic record" shall be substituted;

(b) the following Explanation shall be inserted at the end, namely -

Explanation : For the purposes of this section, "register" includes any list, data or record of any entries maintained in the electronic form as defined in clause (r) of sub-section (1) of section 2 of the Information Technology Act, 1999.

11. In section 468, for the words "document forged", the words "document or electronic record forged" shall be substituted.

12. In section 469, for the words "intending that the document forged", the words "intending that the document or electronic record forged" shall be substituted.

13. In section 470, for the word "document" in both the places where it occurs, the words "document or electronic record" shall be substituted.

14. In section 471, for the word "document" wherever it occurs, the words "document or electronic record" shall be substituted.

15. In section 474, for the portion beginning with the words "Whoever has in his possession any document" and ending with the words "if the document is one of the description mentioned in section 466 of this Code", the following shall be substituted, namely: -

"Whoever has in his possession any document or electronic record, knowing the same to be forged and intending that the same shall fraudulently or dishonestly be used as a genuine, shall, if the document or electronic record is one of the description mentioned in section 466 of this Code."

16. In section 476, for the words "any document", the words "any document or electronic record" shall be substituted.

17. In section 477 A, for the words "book, paper, writing" at both the places where they occur, the words "book, electronic record, paper, writing" shall be substituted.

The Second Schedule (Amendments to the Indian Evidence Act, 1872)

1. In section 3,-

   (a) in the definition of "Evidence", for the words "all documents produced for the inspection of the Court", the words "all documents including electronic records produced for the inspection of the Court" shall be substituted;

   (b) after the definition of "India", the following shall be inserted, namely -

   the expressions "Certifying Authority", "Digital signature", "Digital Signature Certificate", "Electronic Form", "Electronic Records", "Information", "Secure Electronic Record", "Secure Digital Signature" and "Subscriber" shall have the meanings respectively assigned to them in the Information Technology Act, 1999;

2. In section 17, for the words "Oral or documentary,", the words "Oral or Documentary or contained in electronic format" shall be substituted.

3. After section 22, the following section shall be inserted, namely "22A. Oral admissions as to the contents of electronic records are not relevant, unless the genuineness of the electronic record produced is in question".

4. In section 34 for the words "Entries in the books of account", the words "Entries in the books of account, including those maintained in an electronic form" shall be substituted.
5. In section 35 for the word "Record", in both the places where it occur, the words "Record or an Electronic Record" be substituted.
6. For section 39 the following section shall be substituted, namely 39. When any statement of which evidence is given forms part of a longer statement, or of a conversation or part of an isolated document, or is contained in a document which forms part of a book, or is contained in part of electronic record or of a connected series of letters or papers, evidence shall be given of so much and no more of the statement, conversation, document, electronic record, book or series of letters or papers as the Court considers necessary in that particular case to the full understanding of the nature and effect of the statement, and of the circumstances under which it was made.
7. After section 47 the following section shall be inserted; namely When the Court has to form an opinion as to the digital signature of any person, the 47A opinion of the Certifying Authority which has issued the Digital Signature Certificate is a relevant fact.
8. In section 59 for the words "contents of documents" the words "contents of documents or electronic records" shall be substituted.

Special provisions as to evidence relating to electronic record

9. After section 65 the following sections shall be inserted, namely

   65A The contents of electronic records may be proved in. accordance with the provisions of section 65B.

   65B (1) Notwithstanding anything contained in this Act, any information contained in an electronic record which is printed on a paper, stored, recorded or copied in optical or magnetic media produced by a computer (hereinafter referred to as the computer output) shall be deemed to be also a document, if the conditions mentioned in this section are satisfied in relation to the information and computer in question and shall be admissible in any proceedings, without further proof or production of the original as evidence of any contents of the original or of any fact stated therein of which direct evidence would be admissible.

(2) The conditions referred to in sub-section (1) in respect of a computer output shall be the following, namely

(a) the computer output containing the information was produced to the computer during the period over which the computer was used regularly to store or process information for the purposes of any activities regularly carried on over that period by the person having lawful control over the use of the computer;

(b) during the said period, information of the kind contained in the electronic reform or of the kind from which the information so contained is derived was regularly fed into the computer in the ordinary course of the said activities;

(c) throughout the material part of the said period, the computer was operating properly or, if not, then in any respect of any period in which it was not operating properly of was out of operation during that part of the period, was not such as to affect the electronic record or the accuracy of its contents; and

(d) the information contained in the electronic record reproduces or is derived from such information fed into the computer in the ordinary' course of the said activities.

(3) Where over any period, the function of storing or processing information for the purposes of any activities regularly carried on over that period as mentioned in clause (a) of sub-section (2) was regularly performed by computers, whether -

(a) by a combination of computers operating over that period; or

(b) by different computers operating in succession over that period; or

(c) by different combinations of computers operating in succession over that period; or

(d) in any other manner involving the successive operation over that period, in whatever order, of one or more computers and one or more combinations of computers, all the computers used for that purpose during that period shall be treated for the purposes of this section as constituting a single computer; and references in this section to a computer shall be construed accordingly.

(4) In any proceedings where it is desired to give a statement in evidence by virtue of this section, a certificate doing any of the following things, that is to say -

(a) identifying the electronic record containing the statement and describing the manner in which it was produced;

(b) giving such particulars of any device involved in the production of that electronic record as may be appropriate for the purpose of showing that the electronic record was produced by a computer;

(c) dealing with any of the matters to which the conditions mentioned in subsection (2) relate, and purporting to be signed by a person occupying a responsible official position in relation to the operation of the relevant device or the management of the relevant activities (whichever is appropriate) shall be evidence of any matter stated in the certificate; and for the purposes of this sub-section it shall be sufficient for a matter to be stated to the best of the knowledge and belief of the person stating it.

(5) For the purposes of this section -

(a) information shall be taken to be supplied to a computer if it is supplied thereto in any appropriate form and whether it is so supplied directly or (with or without human intervention) by means of any appropriate equipment;

(b) whether in the course of activities carried on by any official, information is supplied with a view to us being stored or processed for the purposes of those activities by a computer operated otherwise than in the course of those activities, that information, if duly supplied to that computer, shall be taken to be supplied to it in the course of those activities:

(c) a computer output shall be taken to have been produced by a computer whether it was produced by it directly or (with or without human intervention) by means of any appropriate equipment.

Explanation : for the purposes of this section any reference to information being derived from other information shall be a reference to its being derived therefrom by calculation, comparison or any other process.

10. After section 67, the following section shall be inserted, namely–

67A Except in the case of a secure digital signature, if the digital signature of any subscriber is alleged o have been affixed to an electronic record the fact that such digital signature is the digital signature of the subscriber must be proved

11. After section 73, the following section shall be inserted, namely

73A In order to ascertain whether a digital signature is that of the person by whom it purports to have been affixed, the Court may direct -

(a) that person or the Controller or the Certifying Authority to produce the Digital Signature Certificate;

(b) any other person to apply the public key listed in the Digital Signature Certificate and verify the digital signature purported to have been affixed by that person

Explanation : For the purposes of this section, "Controller" means the Controller appointed under sub-section (1) of section 17 of the Information Technology Act, 1999.

12. After section 81, the following section shall be inserted, namely-

81A The Court shall presume the genuineness of every electronic record purporting to be the Official Gazette, or purporting to be electronic record directed by any law to be kept by any person, if such electronic record is kept substantially in the form required by law and is produced from proper custody.

13. After section 85, the following sections shall be inserted, namely-

85A The Court shall presume that every electronic record purporting to be an agreement containing the digital signatures of the parties was so concluded by affixing the digital signature of the parties.

85B *Presumption as to electronic records and digital signatures*

In any proceedings involving a secure electronic record, the Court shall presume

(1) unless contrary is proved, that the secure electronic record has not been altered since the specific point of time to which the secure status relates

(2) In any proceedings, involving secure digital signature, the Court shall presume unless the contrary is proved that -

(a) the secure digital signature is affixed by subscriber with the intention of signing or approving the electronic record; except in the case of a secure electronic record or a secure digital signature.

(b) nothing in this section shall create any presumption relating to authenticity and integrity of the electronic record or any digital signature.

85C *Presumption as to electronic messages*

The Court shall presume, unless contrary is proved, that the information listed in a Digital Signature Certificate is correct, except for information specified as subscriber information which has not been verified, if the certificate was accepted by the subscriber.

14. After section 88, the following section shall be inserted, namely

88A The Court may presume that an electronic message forwarded by the originator through an electronic mail server to the addressee to whom the message purports to be addressed corresponds with the message as fed into his computer for transmission; but the Court shall not make any presumption as to the person by whom such message was sent."

Explanation : For the purposes of this section, the expressions "Addressee" and "Originator" shall have the same meanings respectively assigned to them in clauses (b) and (z) of sub-section (1) of section 2 of the Information Technology Act, 1999.

15. After section 90, the following section shall be inserted, namely–

90A Where any electronic record, purporting or proved to be five years old, is produced from any custody which the

Court in the particular case considers proper, the Court may presume that the digital signature which purports to be the digital signature of any particular person was so affixed by him or any person authorised by him in this behalf.

Explanation : Electronic records are said to be in proper custody if they are in the place in which, and under the care of the person with whom, they naturally be; but no custody is improper if it is proved to have had a legitimate origin, or the circumstances of the particular case are such as to render such an origin probable.

This Explanation applies also to section 81A.

16. For section 131, the following section shall be substituted, namely -

131 No one shall be compelled to produce documents in his possession or electronic records under his control, which any other person would be entitled to refuse to produce if they were in his possession or control, unless such last mentioned person consents to their production.

The Third Schedule (Amendments to The Bankers' Books Evidence Act, 1891)

1. In section 2 -

(a) for clause (3), the following clause shall be substituted, namely -

(3) "Bankers' Books" include ledgers, day-books, cash-books, account-books and all other books used in the ordinary business of a bank whether kept in the written form or as printouts of data stored in a floppy, disc, tape or any other form of electro-magnetic storage device;

(b) for clause (8), the following clause shall be substituted, namely -

(8) Certified Copy" means when the books of a bank -

(a) are maintained in written form, a copy of any entry in such books together with a certificate written at the foot of such copy that it is a true copy of such entry, that such entry is contained in one of the ordinary books of the bank and was made in the usual and ordinary course of business and that such book is still in the custody of the bank, and where the copy was obtained by a mechanical or other process which in itself ensured the accuracy of the copy, a further certificate to that effect, but where the book from which such copy was prepared has been destroyed in the usual course of the bank's business after the dale on which the copy had been so prepared, a further certificate to that effect, each such certificate being dated and subscribed by the principal accountant or manager of the bank with his name and official title; and

(b) consist of printouts of data stored in an electro-magnetic data storage device, a printout of such entry or a copy of such printout together with such statements certified in accordance with the provisions of section 2A.

2. After section 2, the following section shall be inserted, namely -

2A A printout of entry or a copy of printout referred to in sub-section (8) of Conditions in section 2 shall be accompanied by the following, namely -

(a) a certificate to the effect that it is a printout of such entry or a copy of such printout by the principal accountant or branch manager; and

(b) a certificate by a person in-charge of computer system containing a brief description of the computer system and the particulars of -

(A) the safeguards adopted by the system to ensure that data is entered or any other operation performed only by authorised persons;

(B) the safeguards adopted to prevent and detect unauthorised change of data;

(C) the safeguards available to retrieve data that is lost due to systemic failure or any other reasons;

(D) the manner in which data is transferred from the

system to removable media like floppies, discs, tapes or other electro-magnetic data storage devices;

(E) the mode of verification in order ensure that data has been accurately transferred to such removable media;

(F) the mode of identification of such data storage devices;

(G) the arrangements for the storage and custody of such storage devices;

(H) the safeguards to prevent and detect any tampering with the system; and

(I) any other factor which Will vouch for the integrity and accuracy of the system.

(c) a further certificate from the person in-charge of the computer system to the effect that to the best of his knowledge and belief that the computer system operated properly at the material time, he was provided with all the relevant data and the printout in question represents correctly, or is appropriately derived from, the relevant data.

The Fourth Schedule (Amendment to the Reserve Bank of India Act, 1934)

In the Reserve Bank of India Act, 1934, in section 58, in sub-section (2), after clause(p), the following clause shall be inserted, namely-

(pp) the regulation of fund transfer through electronic means between the banks or between the banks and other financial institutions referred to in clause (c) of section 45-1, including the laying down of the conditions subject to which banks and other financial institutions shall participate in such fund transfers, the manner of such fund transfers and the rights and obligations of the participants in such fund transfers.

Index